THE SIXTH GREAT POWER

By the same author

THE DUCHESS OF DINO
ADDINGTON
THE BLACK DEATH
KING WILLIAM IV
MELBOURNE
DIANA COOPER
MOUNTBATTEN

The Sixth Great Power

BARINGS

1762–1929

PHILIP ZIEGLER

COLLINS
8 Grafton Street, London W1
1988

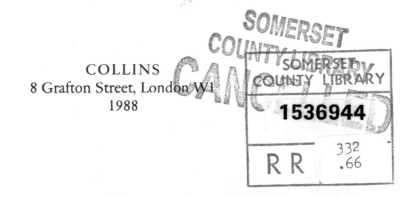

William Collins Sons & Co. Ltd
London · Glasgow · Sydney · Auckland
Toronto · Johannesburg

BRITISH LIBRARY CATALOGUING IN PUBLICATION DATA

Ziegler, Philip
The sixth great power: Barings, 1762–1929.
1. Barings (*Firm*)—History
I. Title
332.66'0941   HG2998.B/

ISBN 0-00-217508-8

First published 1988
Copyright © Baring Brothers & Co. Ltd
& P. S. & M. C. Ziegler & Co. 1988

Photoset in Digitek Janson by
Ace Filmsetting Ltd, Frome, Somerset
Printed and bound in Great Britain by
Butler & Tanner Ltd, Frome and London

CONTENTS

Contents

LIST OF ILLUSTRATIONS

ACKNOWLEDGEMENTS

My first acknowledgement must be to Nicholas Baring, who almost ten years ago suggested that I might write this book, and to those partners of Baring Brothers who have helped and encouraged me in my work. I have been given every facility and total freedom to express the truth as I saw it.

Mr T. L. Ingram, archivist of Barings between 1959 and 1978, was largely responsible for the formidable task of putting this enormous quantity of records into order. Without his efforts I would have found it impossible to write this book.

He was succeeded by Dr John Orbell. Dr Orbell not only possesses an encyclopaedic knowledge of the affairs of Barings and a wide understanding of economic and financial history, but also wisdom and – for me most important of all – endless patience. He and his staff have made my work not merely feasible, but enjoyable as well, and he has saved me from innumerable blunders and omissions.

Professor Christopher Platt of St Antony's College, Oxford, worked for several years on Barings' archives and related papers. I have been fortunate enough to see many of the fruits of his labours, both published and unpublished. They have been of inestimable value to me. His mastery of international finance and the history of Latin America give his work unique authority. I only wish I knew half as much on either subject.

I owe much to the assistance of Mr Christopher Cooper, Keeper of Manuscripts at Guildhall Library; Mr Henry Gillett of the Bank of England; Mrs Hodge and Miss Mace of the Rothschild Archive (London); Mr Thomas Dunnings, Curator of Manuscripts of the New York Historical Society; Ms Anne-Marie Schaaf of the Historical Society of Pennsylvania; Mr John Cushing of the Massachusetts Historical Society; Mr Albert Gordon of Kidder Peabody; Mr James Hutson of the Manuscript Division of the Library of Congress; Ms Anita Burdett and Miss Kennedy of the Public Archives of Canada;

Mr R. H. Harcourt Williams, Librarian and Archivist of the Marquess of Salisbury; Mme Brot, Conservateur aux Archives Nationales; Mlle Marie-Aimée Carli of the Européenne de Banque.

Anyone who ventures for the first time into a world as complex as that of the merchant bank must owe a great debt to all those who have gone before or who are currently working in the field. I am particularly grateful for help and advice to Dr Stanley Chapman, author of the invaluable *The Rise of Merchant Banking*; Professor H. S. Ferns, leading authority on the history of Britain and Argentina; Professor Vincent Carosso, historian of Kidder Peabody and of Morgans; Dr Samuel Amaral of the Instituto Torcuato di Tella in Buenos Aires; Dr Kathleen Burk and Dr Richard Roberts, respectively historians of Morgan Grenfell and Schroders.

Apart from those Barings and their colleagues who are active in the house I have been given much help and treated with great generosity by the Earl of Cromer, Lords Ashburton and Northbrook, Sir Mark Baring, The Hon. Mrs Mildmay-White, Miss Anne-Cecilia Baring and the late Mrs Daphne Pollen. The Marquess of Northampton kindly allowed me to see Baring papers in his possession. Among former members of the house or those closely associated with it, I have especially valued the opportunity of talking with Sir Andrew Carnwath, Mr John Phillimore and Mr Duncan Stirling.

So many people have helped me along the way that I hesitate to mention any for fear of the inevitable omissions, but I could not pass over Mr Ismael Benavides, Mr Leslie Bethell, The Hon. Raymond Bonham Carter, Mr Robert Cross, Mr Benjamin Davis, the late Mr Geoffrey and Mrs Gibson, Mrs Cecily Glazzard, Mr R. C. Haskell, Mr and Mrs Philip Jebb, Mr and Mrs David McCosh, Dr Miguel Mancera, Mr George Nissen, Mr Archie Norman, Mr Henry Roberts, Mr and Mrs John Shakespeare, Mr John Shepherd, Lord Sudeley, Dr Claudio Veliz, and Mrs S. D. Wyles.

My agent, Mrs Diana Baring, has managed with characteristic grace the difficult task of having a husband in one camp and a client in the other. Happily the two have never come to blows.

Finally my wife and children have once again endured with equanimity the inconveniences and irritations of having an author in the family. My wife's support has been, as always, the one element wholly indispensable to my work.

'There are six great powers in Europe: England, France, Prussia, Austria, Russia and Baring Brothers.'

Duc de Richelieu, 1818

PREFACE

Francis Baring established his house in London in 1762; 225 years later it is still managed and controlled by his direct descendants. It was the longevity of this dynasty which first intrigued me. What was there about the family which had enabled it to survive through so many vicissitudes and changing circumstances? The history of Baring Brothers must first and foremost be a history of the Barings themselves.

It is also to an extent a history of British merchant banking, for Barings blazed the trail along which so many have since followed. At first I thought that it would be the sociopolitical aspects of the story that would most interest me, but it did not take me long to discover the extraordinary fascination, and indeed excitement, inherent in this kind of banking. The expert will perhaps find my treatment of the financial issues too superficial for his taste, the general reader may wish that he was told less about issues and acceptances, but I hope that some at least will feel that I have hit a proper balance between the work of the banker and the personalities involved.

When to stop was an almost insoluble problem. No banker in his senses is going to tell inquisitive historians everything about the transactions in which he is currently engaged or in which living clients were involved. If I had continued the book beyond 1945, it would have taken on a different nature. By ending it at an earlier date I made it possible to claim that nothing had been concealed from me and nothing censored.

The possible points at which to cut off the history seemed to be 1918, 1929 and 1939. 1918 would have been too early, and involved the sacrifice of a lot of interesting material. At first glance 1939 was the obvious date. Yet 1929 was the year of the 2nd Lord Revelstoke's death. With his departure the bank took a fundamentally different course – or, perhaps more accurately, his existence had masked a change that was already happening. The process was exaggerated

11

and speeded up by the slump and the decline of sterling. International issuing withered, corporate financing throve. The decade between 1929 and the Second World War looks forward to the postwar world rather than back to 1918 and the years before it. Any cut-off date would have been arbitrary and unsatisfactory, but I felt that 1929 was less so than any other. I have added a short and non-critical epilogue, to give some indication of what has happened between then and the present day.

1

The Birth of Barings

1483–1776

The Barings were not Jews. So bald a statement may seem unduly negative as an introduction to the history of a dynasty. It may even inspire disquiet among those who consider that to betray an interest in whether or not an individual is Jewish is evidence, if not proof, of anti-Semitism. That the Barings were gentile, however, is by far the most important fact to emerge from a study of their eminently respectable but undramatic genealogy. It shaped the growth of their banking business throughout the nineteenth and into the twentieth century; dictated with which houses they should cooperate and with whom they should do battle; led them to involve themselves in certain countries and to eschew others. If the Barings *had* been Jews, the history of British merchant banking would have been different.

They were, in fact, low churchmen from North Germany. Some nineteenth-century historian, no doubt owing them money, once linked their name with that of the hero of the Bäring Saga, a Norse translation of an old German romance which featured a young knight who travelled from tournament to tournament, defeating all his adversaries with monotonous ease, and became first King of Saxony and then Emperor of Byzantium.[1] Another antiquarian claimed to have had access to the 'most indisputable documents' establishing the family's Saxon origins. Their ancestor, S. Beeringe, had been accepted as a proper attendant on a Norman baron because of his 'absolute Saxon worthiness and knightly birth'.[2] Reality was somewhat less romantic.

The first Baring about whom there is any accurate information is Peter, who was born in about 1483 in the free city of Groningen in West Friesland. His younger son, Franz, became a Carmelite friar

13

but fell under the influence of Martin Luther and ended his life as pastor of a parish near Hamburg. Franz's son was also Franz, and also a pastor.* His son Johann, a senior civil servant, married a pastor's daughter and settled in Bremen, and *his* son, Franz again, became a Professor of Theology. This tradition of diligent service to God or the state was now broken. The latest Franz married Rebecca Vogds, the daughter of one of Bremen's leading wool merchants. Franz died in 1697, aged only forty, and his son Johann was born a fortnight later. The Vogds found themselves charged with bringing up the fatherless boy.[3]

They elected to direct him towards their own rather than his father's interests. North Germany imported much wool and serge from Britain and exported large quantities of linen in return. A high proportion of the wool came from the West Country and this was almost all collected at Exeter for dyeing, finishing and shipment abroad. In the early eighteenth century Exeter was a boom town, with some 12,000 inhabitants and four out of five earners deriving their income in one form or another from the wool trade. The Vogds family firm imported most of its coloured serge from the largest Exeter merchant, Edmund Cock, and it was probably to this house that Johann, or John as he soon became, was apprenticed when he was sent to England in 1717.[4]

Though John Baring brought with him a handsome £500† as his share of his father's estate it seems unlikely that he expected when he first arrived to spend more than a year or two in Exeter learning about the trade from the English end and making contacts that would be useful to his mother's family. He liked the place, however, and soon felt thoroughly at home. His first task was to dispose of consignments of linen from the Vogds in Germany, which he sold on commission; doing so with such success that other merchants from Bremen invited him to handle their goods as well. From this he expanded into the wool trade, found it more profitable and gradu-

---

* The Barings were always parsimonious over Christian names. Among thirty Baring or near Baring partners in the house since 1762 there were five Thomases, four Johns, four Charleses and three Francises. This does not make life easy for the historian (or the reader).

† Attempts to translate the currency of the eighteenth and nineteenth centuries into a contemporary equivalent are wayward and inaccurate. A guide of a sort is contained in appendix VI.

ally let his interest in linen dwindle. By 1723 he had become so well established that he decided to become a British citizen. In this he set something of a fashion. He was the first foreign merchant to settle in Exeter, but John Duntze, also from Bremen, followed a few years later, with the Passavants from Frankfurt, the Mandrots from Amsterdam and other traders from the continent not long behind.[5]

He completed the process of assimilation by taking an English wife. He chose judiciously, marrying Elizabeth Vowler, daughter of a merchant who was then styled a 'grocer', but was in fact a substantial wholesaler of tea, coffee, sugar, dried fruits and other such commodities. John's father-in-law had already retired by the time his daughter married but was able to give her a handsome dowry which, at his death, was made up to some £20,000; in the first half of the eighteenth century a very considerable sum indeed. That Baring secured such a prize proves that he must have won a respected position in Exeter society, but also says something about his personality. Elizabeth Vowler was a most resolute young lady, who would not have allowed herself to be fobbed off with a German immigrant however well established, unless she had loved him. John was, wrote his son, 'a man of exceeding good parts, of a most pleasant, excellent disposition'. He had 'an admirable head and an excellent heart'.[6] Without the first he would not have made such a success of business; without the second he would never have won the esteem of his fellow citizens or the hand of Miss Vowler.

What he lacked was good health. He was never robust and he grew worse; the last part of his life, wrote his son, 'passed away very uncomfortably'. This did not prevent him having five children: the eldest, also John, was born in 1730, Thomas three years later, Francis in 1740, Charles in 1742 and a daughter, Elizabeth, in 1744. Nor did it stop him expanding his business and adding to his already considerable fortune. By the time Francis was born the family had moved from the centre of town and had settled in the substantial but unpretentious Larkbear House, standing in thirty-seven acres on the fringes of Exeter. When John died, probably of consumption, at the age of fifty-one, he was a landowner on a considerable scale and one of the richest merchants in the West Country. He, the bishop and the recorder were the only people in Exeter to keep their own carriages.[7]

Impressive though these achievements were, they did not suffice to bridge the gap between trade and the landed gentry. Referring to those who belonged to county society, Anthony Trollope wrote: 'It is very rarely indeed, that money alone will bestow this acknowledged rank; and in Exeter, which by the stringency and excellence of its well defined rules on such matters, may perhaps be said to take the lead of all English provincial towns, money alone has never availed.'[8] He was writing of Exeter a century later, but the pattern was unchanged. To move to a spacious house outside the town availed nothing. Trollope's Miss Stanbury, a stalwart of cathedral society, pronounced that 'there was doubtless a respectable neighbourhood on the Heavitree side of the town, but for the new streets, and especially for the suburban villas, she had no endurance'.[9] Larkbear House, one fears, would have been categorized by Miss Stanbury as a suburban villa. To break through the social barrier required measures more extreme than John had ever contemplated adopting; he had laid the foundation, however, and the next generation was to build on it most handsomely.

In 1748, with John dead and his eldest son only eighteen, prospects for such promotion must have seemed, at the best, uncertain. There was no shortage of money. John had left some £40,000; of which his widow received £17,000, his eldest son £15,000, and the other four children £2000 apiece. Mrs Baring could have lived comfortably on her inheritance and let the business go. She had, however, no intention of doing anything of the sort. While her husband had been dying she had already played an active part in managing the wool factory; now she took over the business altogether and did so to such good effect that the family property had grown to £70,000 by the time she died in 1766.

There were setbacks. In 1763 a fire destroyed the new press house and finishing room and at one time seemed likely to consume the rest of the factory buildings as well. Goods worth £8000 had to be carried into the grounds and exposed to the torrential rain, which helped put out the fire but did no good to the woollen products. Worst of all, the new buildings were uninsured. 'Tis a bad beginning for the two younger ones [Francis and Charles],' she told a friend, 'but otherwise the year must have proved a very advantageous one, this I hope will not carry off all the profit!'[10]

She had found it hard to surrender control and her easy-going elder son John did not press her unduly. Technically he and Thomas were in charge of the business after John's return from a period on the continent in 1755, but she continued to interfere and, in particular, to direct the lives of her younger sons. Charles, the youngest, complained ruefully that it had been his lot to grow up 'under the Eye of a Mother, excellent in many respects, but very severe'. Francis and Charles were sent off to London to be apprenticed to suitably distinguished merchants, but when their brother Thomas died suddenly in 1758 Charles, aged only fifteen, was recalled to Exeter to take his place. It was a misfortune both for him and for the family; in London he would have continued to learn the job in subordinate positions, in Exeter he was given too much responsibility too fast and made a lamentable mess of it.

Francis, the most talented of the children, indeed one of the most remarkable men of his generation, remained in London. He had already been educated there – at Mr Fargue's French school at Hoxton and at Mr Fuller's Academy in Lothbury[11] – and had shown an aptitude for algebra and mental arithmetic which was then and remained throughout his life phenomenal. More significantly, he proved capable of dedicated hard work and a degree of concentration on the matter in hand which raised him far above his fellow scholars. As a New Year's gift in 1743 his maternal grandfather, John Vowler, had given him an anthology of improving verses for children, recommended by the Rev. Dr Doddridge, a distinguished hymnologist.[12] The Rules for Youth included:

> Shun Idleness, the cursed Root of Vice
> Whence Shame, Disgrace and Poverty do rise;
> Yet worse than these, deplorable you'll find
> Is Ignorance, and Poverty of Mind.
>
> Save what you can. Contrive with prudent Care
> Costly superfluous Trifles to forbear.
> Imploy your Head and Hands, stick not at Pain,
> Plenteous Supplies by Industry you'll Gain!

Even Francis Baring would not have made much of these exemplary precepts when he was only two, yet he could hardly have taken them more to heart. He was never idle, never ostentatious, stuck not at Pain, and did indeed by his Industry gain Plenteous Supplies. He also abhorred Poverty of Mind; his range of interests was wide, his curiosity insatiable, he never had much time for reading but liked having books around him and possessed that precious knack of establishing what lay inside them without actually reading the contents. He was serious but not solemn, from a very early age he commanded respect and people listened to what he had to say confident that it would be worth hearing. His thoughts were clear and their exposition invariably lucid. Small, sharp-featured, even when young a little deaf, he was not immediately impressive to meet but soon asserted himself in any society. Though a tough businessman, he was tolerant and generous in private life. When two unknown and very distant cousins from Hanover wrote to say that they were imprisoned for debt in Lymington, Francis Baring sent them £60 without demur, 'and they need not trouble themselves about the reimbursement'.[13] Similar acts of benevolence abound; he could well afford them but not all rich men see this as a reason for helping others.

For seven years from 1755 Francis was apprenticed to Samuel Touchet, one of the leading Manchester and West Indian merchants. By the time his apprenticeship was over he considered that he had learned enough; what is more, he had considerable and, as it turned out, well-justified reservations about the way Touchet ran his business. He had no wish to return to Exeter, where Charles was firmly installed and opportunity limited. London was where he saw his future. Yet his capital was limited and he would have been hard put to start up in business on his own. A solution was offered by Nathaniel Paice, who for many years had been a close friend of the Baring family and their agent in London. He had for some time been contemplating retirement; now he proposed that Francis take over the business and develop it as a branch of the house in London. Barings would become, in effect, a partnership with two seats of business, in Exeter and London, and two sets of managers.[14] On a domestic scale, it was the same system as the Rothschilds were to practise internationally a quarter of a century later. For its success it depended on harmony between the different branches. It soon became clear that this would not be forthcoming.

John Baring, the eldest son, was the link between the two wings of the partnership, senior partner of John and Francis Baring and Co. in London, and of John and Charles Baring and Co. in Exeter, and in theory supervising the work of his younger brothers in both cities. In fact he rarely visited London and left Francis to his own devices. Nor did he occupy himself much more conscientiously with the business in Exeter. A gregarious, easy-going character, he found it more satisfying to cut a dash in West Country society and nurse political ambitions. In 1755, for 2000 guineas, he bought the Mount Radford estate with a fine, three-storeyed Georgian house fit for a country gentleman. This part he now proceeded to play with vigour and considerable success. it did not leave much time for matters of commerce.

Francis Baring's original and for some years main role was to be the agent for the Exeter business, buying the raw materials needed for its factory and seeking new markets for its products. He did the same for other Exeter manufacturers, but his brothers' company was much his most considerable customer. The financial services which he rendered these houses were equally important, collecting money due to them and arranging to honour their bills when presented to the new house.

But even if Francis Baring had been content to stick to this homespun fare, he would have found it difficult not to get drawn progressively into more ambitious enterprises. The eighteenth century witnessed a phenomenal growth in international trade, fuelled by increasing European penetration of the Indian subcontinent, South-East Asia and the Far East and by the expansion of the market in North America. The demand was there, the goods were there, the ships and entrepreneurs were there, but the financial machinery for making the process work evolved more slowly. Wools, dyes and cloths were the commodities with which Francis Baring felt most at home, but there were bigger profits to be made in other spheres. He began to take a financial interest in shipments of such things as cochineal, copper, diamonds, cream of tartar, sometimes merely handling the property of others on commission but increasingly buying cargoes on his own account, or more often joint account with other merchants, as a fully fledged merchant adventurer. Generally he kept his investment in any transaction to a level he could afford, but risks were high and one disastrous speculation in soda ash in 1774, in which his share of the loss was over £2000, must have come close to putting him out of business.[15]

The greatest need in international trade in the eighteenth century was for someone to fill the gap between buyer and seller. Smith had 2000 lbs of best tea lying in his warehouse in Calcutta, Jones knew that he could profitably dispose of it in Mincing Lane, there was no dispute over price or quantity, but Smith did not wish to dispatch his tea without being certain that he would be paid for it, and Jones did not wish to pay until the tea had arrived and was in his possession. The essential was a middleman who had confidence in and who had gained the confidence of both parties, who would accept the bills of exchange issued by one party and guarantee to pay that amount to the other. Francis Baring did not invent the business of acceptances, but he came into it when it was still relatively undeveloped and is associated as much as any other individual with its growing sophistication. Five years after John and Francis Baring and Co. was set up, its liabilities on acceptances stood at some £12,000. By 1776 they were more than three times as great.

Elizabeth Baring was somewhat alarmed at her son's growing independence and adventurousness. Business was booming in Exeter and there was no need to branch out. She wrote tartly to him in March 1766:

> As it was so long since I heard from you I imagined you had forgot you had a Mother. I am glad your business bears so promising an Aspect. I see you have begun in the Exchange way, as you say tis not a lucrative thing, advise you to be careful you do not run out of your depth. I am satisfied tis attended with risk and many houses called considerable abroad have often disappointed and sometimes absolutely ruined those who have placed Confidence in them, am sensible you may be drawn in to be answerable for large Sums before you are aware of it, and let Mr Touchet's example of grasping at too much and not being contented with a very handsome profit which he might have had without running

such enormous risks, be a warning to you. Consider the whole Family are embarked in one Bottom, our trade here is surprizingly great, in short we cannot get goods to supply the orders, nor money to pay for what we do buy, nor hands to finish them, a great deal we do, and more we might if we could procure the 3 very necessary ingredients, our people work from 5 in the morn to 9 at night and there is yet no prospect of coming to the end of it.[16]

She was right in believing that her son was embarking on dangerous and largely uncharted waters. The secret of successful merchant banking is above all good intelligence; to be well informed – and to be the first to be informed – about the resources, the policies and the capacities of all the companies with whom one deals, and about political and economic developments which will affect the course of their business. A merchant banker must not only be a mathematician but a historian and a geographer as well; he must know about church and state, not to mention the possibility of a revolution or a coup d'état; he must be agronomist, mineralogist and weather forecaster; a psychologist able to detect the hidden strengths and weaknesses of those with whom he works; a futurologist qualified to predict the vagaries of diet and fashion. Since he can hardly hope to unite so many parts in one mind, the essential is that he should have a great many informants and be skilled at collating and interpreting their information. Francis Baring was quick to see this, and to learn his trade, but networks of informants are not built up overnight and he made expensive misjudgements, both of people and of circumstances.

In the fourteen years in which the partnership with Exeter existed, Francis Baring lost money in eight of them. Profits were above £3000 in one of the remaining years but otherwise were far lower. When the joint partnership had been set up the personal property of the family, amounting to some £50,000, had been allocated £20,000 to London and £30,000 to Exeter, but in practice Francis had £4200 at his disposal when he opened his office off Cheapside in 1763. He inherited £5000 from his mother in 1766 and drew £2000 from his original inheritance in 1769. John Baring put in £7810 in 1766, £1500 in 1767 and £3000 in 1769. Yet by January 1777 Francis

Baring's personal capital in London was only £2,457.3.6d. He told Lord de Dunstanville that he had begun with a fortune of £10,000 and had spent all but a few hundred before 'he acquired anything but a knowledge of trade and commerce'.[17] It cannot be called a gloriously successful start to a career in business, and there can have been few who would have foreseen what immense rewards that 'knowledge of trade and commerce' were soon to earn.

Francis Baring himself admitted that inexperience and lack of caution were at the root of his problems, but he also blamed the association with the house in Exeter. His brother Charles, he claimed, was 'not calculated for the management of the house, an establishment which depended on steady order and attention, ill suited to his disposition of catching at every new project that offered'. Charles had travelled in Spain and Portugal; journeys which had proved expensive both in time and money and had involved John and Charles Baring and Co. in a number of unprofitable connections: 'This is not stated as a reflection on his intention, but solely to impeach the want of commercial knowledge and judgment, which he has manifested through life.' Nor was it merely in Spain and Portugal that Charles had blundered; not only had he 'interfered too much with the house in London, but by degrees he formed partnerships, connexions and speculations, of a wild, strange, incoherent description; and what is particularly unfortunate, not one of them has proved successfull'.[18]

John Baring was even stronger in his condemnation of his brother. 'The weakness, the capriciousness, the greediness, the shabbiness of Charles are so abominable it is hoped no occasion will arise again to mention him,' he wrote in his sketch of a family history.[19] In fairness to Charles one must wonder why, if his shortcomings were really so glaring, his elder brother and senior partner did so little to check them. Charles for his part complained that John had been guilty of undue severity and of never giving him a fair chance.[20] To this Francis retorted that the accusation reminded him of their mother, who had once been told that she sang out of tune. 'She said it was impossible for she could not sing out of tune if she would, and this may be correctly applied to my Brother, who could not be severe if he would.'[21]

It is possible to sympathize with Charles, who had been promoted too young and given authority which he was not fit to wield, but even with the most loving supervision it seems unlikely that he would ever have made a competent businessman; his judgement was too uncertain and his impetuosity too unbridled. Add to this vanity, and the arrogance of a weak man determined to prove himself strong, and all the ingredients were there for a disaster. It never quite came, but near enough; in June 1774 matters were so bad that the three brothers signed a memorandum agreeing that, if one of them died, £2000 should be deducted from his capital as his share of the likely total loss.[22]

For Francis Baring the most vexatious aspect of Charles's enterprises was that constant demands were made on the capital of the London house, thus preventing him using it for more profitable and enduring enterprises. 'Your unceasing projects, by absorbing so large a part of the family and of the Bank, hung as a dead weight and impeded my progress for many years.'[23] Whether, at that period, the money would have been used more gainfully by Francis is open to question, but he had no doubt himself that Charles was squandering the vital resources of the house. His brother compounded the offence by maintaining that it was *he* who was making a success of the business and Francis who was bungling, telling all and sundry that in his opinion Francis's family must in the end come to the parish.[24] Mrs Baring had said, 'the whole Family are embarked in one Bottom'; Francis regretted the truth of the statement and was more than ready to leave the ship and venture forth on his own.

The opportunity came in the autumn of 1776. Charles arrived in London accompanied, said Francis, by 'three low persons, projectors, who had offered a plan for spinning Wool by Machinery'.[25] Francis was ill at the time, and under considerable financial pressure, which he attributed entirely to Charles's thoughtlessness and mismanagement. He met Charles and his cronies with a notable lack of enthusiasm, an attitude which became more marked when he heard of his brother's plans to build woollen mills in Devonshire. The party departed for Lancashire with Francis still urging extreme caution; he was therefore not unnaturally disturbed when Charles returned triumphant announcing that 'he had found everything so satisfactory, that he had signed an agreement for a partnership with those persons, wherein he had stipulated to advance a Capital of £20,000'.[26]

Francis had no intention of being dragged into this morass, a view of the affair justified by the fact that two of Charles's three putative partners were shortly made bankrupt. He suggested that the partnership should continue on its present basis but that Charles should accept sole responsibility for and take all the benefit from this latest enterprise. Charles treated this proposal with contempt, and accepted with alacrity when Francis said that in that case the only thing to do was to dissolve the partnership. Without the support of the Exeter house, Charles believed, John and Francis Baring and Co. would quickly founder; and he advised John 'to consider well the hazard he ran by continuing the partnership'.[27] In the end John Baring decided to continue as a partner in both houses; perhaps still hoping that in time the family might be reunited. Bad debts were written off on each side and Charles Baring contributed £1000 towards a 'desperate debt of about £5500' which was outstanding in London. The ending of the partnership was deemed to take effect at the end of 1776 and the articles of dissolution were finally signed by the three brothers on 29 March 1777.

2

Laying the Foundations

1776–1793

Britain in 1776 was economically, and probably politically and socially as well, the most advanced country on earth. It was still dominated by a few hundred aristocratic families who monopolized a grotesque proportion of the nation's wealth, but though this caste jealously guarded its status and its privileges it was by no means immutable. The rule of primogeniture ensured that its poorer members were constantly dropping off to join the professional classes or landed gentry, while new blood could buy its way in if the price offered were high enough. Nor did its members disdain the delights of money-making; they usually ensured that their estates were run efficiently and that the coal, tin or other such resources found on their estates were mined to best advantage. They contributed to the nation's wealth.

If the aristocrats still largely ran the country, it was the 12,000–13,000 families of the country gentry that made it work. They ranged from baronets with a seat in parliament, whose large estates and grand houses made them the equal of most of the continental and some of the indigenous nobility, to impoverished squires who worked their own land and were barely to be distinguished from the yeoman farmers who were their neighbours.

The more they looked like farmers, however, the more they were aware of their gentility. They sometimes disliked but always respected the aristocracy; they always disliked and usually despised the industrialists and merchants who were bringing the country to undreamt-of prosperity. It was not until the nineteenth century that the phrase 'in trade' gained wide currency as a label for all that was mean and socially inferior, but the eighteenth-century squire knew well what the description signified.

Few of the country gentlemen realized that their importance in the social order was about to be overshadowed by this new breed of men. The *nouveaux riches* made their money in ways barely contemplated a century before. Wool was still Britain's leading export, employing one way or another some three quarters of a million people, but the metal trades were in violent upsurge and exports of iron and steel manufactures were doubled, redoubled and doubled again in a mere 75 years. The coal required to fuel these industries brought vast wealth to those lucky enough to own the mines, and also gave employment, brutish and ill-paid perhaps yet still acceptable, to many thousands more. The Industrial Revolution was rolling, towns such as Birmingham and Sheffield took on a new significance, and though London was still by far the largest city of the realm, its relative importance dwindled.

In one field, however, it remained not merely pre-eminent but unique. Birmingham and Sheffield might be generating the money, Liverpool and Bristol might be the entrepôts for a flourishing commerce, but London was the financial centre of Britain. Francis Baring could not have achieved, could not have attempted to achieve, what he did in any other city. London was also, of course, the seat of government; indeed, if it had not been the seat of government it could never have been the financial centre of the country, for, as Baring was soon to find out, the two were inextricably meshed together.

When the first Baring partnership began to operate in January 1763 George III had been a little over two years on the throne. It was to be another seven years before he was able to settle his pliant instrument, Lord North, in the office of prime minister. Increasing ill feeling between the Baring brothers in Exeter and London was matched on an international scale by the growing acrimony between North's government and the settlers in America. The United States' declaration of independence of 4 July 1776 preceded by six months Francis Baring's escape from the shackles of Exeter. It did not seem a wholly propitious prelude.

The American War of Independence not only tarnished Britain's military reputation but also gravely damaged her economy. Exports, which had grown steadily for a quarter of a century or more, fell by almost 20 per cent. To the North American market, much the most important to Britain outside Europe, they were halved. There was unemployment in the industrial towns and consternation in the City of London. It was hardly the ideal moment for Francis Baring to escape from the family bottom and paddle his own canoe.

He was not entirely alone. His brother John was still with him and could be counted on for encouragement at least, and probably a measure of financial assistance. Nor was he without other support. In 1767 he had married Harriet Herring, who being both an heiress and a cousin to a former Archbishop of Canterbury, neatly united God and mammon in the service of the new house. In the long run she was to bring a fortune of £12,000; not much of this was available on marriage but Baring immediately benefited by a share in the proceeds of the Prerogative Office (predecessor of the Court of Probate), which produced an average £156.11.4¾d per annum.[1] He needed this increment; the year after his marriage he spent £180 on his wine cellar, £160 on silver plate and £350 on furniture, but Harriet Baring proved a good and frugal manager, running a comfortable and well-conducted household at a cost of £800 a year. 'I can now assert,' wrote her husband after her death, 'that if those expenses had amounted to £1200 a year for the same period, it must have ruined me for ever.'[2]

Given a chance Harriet would have been convivial as well as capable. A description of her written in 1805 reported that she had a sociable nature and never missed a party if she could help it. Her own receptions were 'among the most brilliant in town' though her husband was seldom among those present, preferring 'the more tranquil enjoyment of a domestic circle to those gay but promiscuous assemblies'.[3] John Mallet, married to Francis Baring's niece, went further and described Harriet as a 'vain, worldly, fine woman, whose life was devoted to fashionable society'.[4] This may have been true of her in later life but certainly it was not the case in the years after her marriage, when she was not only short of money but had to bear twelve children and bring up ten, for the most part above the offices of Barings in Mincing Lane, in the City of London.

Francis Baring was a loving and conscientious father. Mallet, indeed, describes him as being 'the mamma of the family', ordering shoes and frocks for the children, fussing over the details of their nursery life and organizing schools for his sons.[5] The author was probably more intent on blackening Harriet's reputation than on giving an objective portrait of her husband. Francis Baring never seems to have felt that he was unreasonably put upon. If he did behave in a way so uncharacteristic of the late eighteenth century, it was because he wanted to. He never ceased to concern himself with his children's welfare and to applaud or rebuke them as seemed appropriate, always with patently sincere affection.

Mincing Lane was to be Francis Baring's office until 1793. At first he ran affairs with the help only of a handful of clerks, no doubt discouraged from taking on partners by the thought that he had a plethora of sons to support him in due course. He took the first £500 of any annual profit and split what was left with his brother John. By 1781, however, the burden had become impossible to bear alone. A young man called Charles Wall was admitted as a partner and the senior clerk, James Mesturas, promoted at the same time. They were given a generous salary of £900 a year (three times what Mesturas and more than ten times what Wall had been earning previously) and one seventh of the profit each. The fact that Francis Baring could afford to offer these lavish rewards showed how the business was prospering. In 1777, the year after the new partnership had been initiated, a profit of £3400 was recorded; in 1779 it was £4400. By 1781, when the new partners were appointed, it had risen to £10,300, and by 1788, admittedly an exceptional year, the profit reached a spectacular £12,000.

It was, in fact, a period of steady growth, with the occasional violent leap forward and less dramatic moments of recession. Most of the business, though not necessarily the most profitable element, was an extension of what the partnership had done in the past. There was a marked change in emphasis, however. Little by little the old connections with the West Country withered and were replaced by a network of international relationships. By 1780 the evolution was already clearly marked. Of the seven accounts that turned over more than £10,000 a year, only one was in Exeter and one in London. Two of the others were in Amsterdam, and one each in Cartagena, Leghorn and St Petersburg. This list excludes the substantial business done with John and Charles Baring and Co., still by far the largest single item on the books, but that too was in decline. By 1790 the West Country clients had almost disappeared, while business with the United States grew steadily more important. Trade across the Atlantic was back to the levels ruling before the revolution and Francis Baring was pre-eminent among British merchants who fostered this swelling commerce.[6]

Successful merchant banking depends on confidence, most of all in the world of acceptances where the banker is playing the honest broker between two other parties. It is essential that a house should be known to be rich, secure and well-informed, but its reputation, particularly in the eighteenth and nineteenth centuries, could be no better than that of its senior partners. John and Francis Baring and Co., in the 1780s, *was* Francis Baring, and it was in him that were first clearly marked those characteristics which subsequent generations have come to expect in members of the family. Lord D'Abernon summed it up as successfully as anyone in 1931 when he described the Barings as 'Strong, sensible, self-reliant men, with a profound belief in themselves, in their family and in their country – eminently just and fair; no trace of hypocrisy or cant; not only solid and square but giving the impression both of solidity and squareness . . . not subtle or mentally agile, but endowed with that curious combination of character which lends authority even to doubtful decisions, and makes those who possess it respected in counsel and obeyed as rulers.'[7] The Barings were above all reliable, on that everyone agreed, as also on the fact that their attitude towards the rest of humanity was detached and cool, at its best manifested in a balanced objectivity, at its worst disdainful and indifferent. Lord Welby in the mid-nineteenth century described Lord Northbrook's 'essentially Baring character' as being 'rather unsympathetic outwardly, certainly very undemonstrative, with a tendency to strong prepossessions, some would say prejudices', but always 'just and anxious to do justice'.[8] Barings were not expected to be warm, at any rate to the outside world. Fifty years later Christopher Sandeman found Maurice Baring 'tenuous and even ghostlike. Distinction *certainly*, in a high degree, but possibly the family coldness, which Strachey detested so in Evelyn Baring's replies to Gordon's frenzied telegrams.'[9] Nor were they supposed to be brilliant. 'We had a dull dinner at Lady

Ashburton's,' recorded Thackeray gloomily, 'A party of Barings chiefly.'[10] But they were sound.

Francis Baring was not in all ways typical of the dynasty which he founded. He would never have been so successful had he not possessed a strain of adventurousness, sometimes even of recklessness, which was not often to be found in those who built on his foundations. But in most respects he would have been instantly recognizable to Lord D'Abernon or Lord Welby.

'His manner was cold and his disposition reserved,' wrote Sir Denis le Marchant, 'so that he had few friends or even political followers, but no man was more respected and trusted by those who had to deal with him.'[11] By no means everyone would have agreed about the coldness of his manner – he seems often to have been positively jovial for a Baring – but on the respect and trust that he inspired there was no dispute.

It was this that contributed above all to the great growth of Barings' business in acceptances between 1776 and the French wars. The total of their liabilities rose from £42,000 at the end of 1777 to £121,000 in 1793, but the quality of the business they did was more important than the quantity. Like Othello, Francis Baring would have cried that he who stole his purse stole not trash perhaps, but certainly something of secondary importance, but 'he that filches from me my good name robs me of that which not enriches him, and makes me poor indeed'. At any time Baring would have sacrificed the whole of his house's profits to preserve his reputation, because he knew that without reputation his house would be worth nothing. His reward was that during this period Barings became one of the most respected houses in the City. The fact that their name was on a bill, that they had guaranteed it, gave it credibility and ensured that if it came to be sold or discounted before it fell due, it would be done at the most favourable rates.

Acceptances trebled in the seventeen years after Francis Baring broke with his brother Charles. In the same period commission income – the fees Barings levied on the issuing of acceptances, handling consignments of merchandise, and a wide variety of banking transactions – more than doubled, from £4000 or so per annum to £10,000. It was an important element in the house's affairs, but less so than previously. It was made the more profitable by the fact that

Baring was always ready to act, in effect, as an insurance broker; sometimes carrying the risk of a cargo himself, more often passing it on to others. In 1771 he had been appointed a director of the Royal Exchange Assurance, an association which must have helped considerably in building up this useful though never substantial line of business.

But the association which contributed more than any other to the growth of Barings' business and reputation was with the Amsterdam house of Hope and Co., probably at the time the richest and most powerful in Europe, and therefore in the world. Francis Baring always had a partiality for the Dutch. In 1787 he told Pitt's Treasurer of the Navy, Henry Dundas, that a commercial treaty with Holland would be 'preferable to one with any other nation as she can promote the sale of our Indian products and manufactures in a superior degree; and at the same time contribute very important political assistance. The two Countries have one great original object in view and which do not clash in the smallest degree. That of Great Britain is to maintain and preserve the Empire which she has acquired, in comparison of which, Trade is a subordinate, or collateral consideration. The great object of Holland is in the first instance to secure to herself the monopoly of the Spice Islands, and secondly to extend her general trade.'[12]

What was true for Britain was equally true for Barings. The Dutch mercantile houses had many interests in common with their British counterparts and were rarely in direct competition. But Hopes bulked far larger on the European scene. They were in origin a Scottish family, tenuously connected with the Earls of Hopetoun, who had settled in Holland in the sixteenth century and established themselves as the first bankers of the land. Henry Hope, head of the family and of the bank, lived in seigneurial style at Welgelen, near Haarlem, a palace modelled loosely on the Villa Borghese, but most of the day-to-day dealings with such houses as Barings were done by Robert – 'Little Bob' – Voûte, the son of a Huguenot emigré who had settled in Amsterdam.[13] To bring his house into intimate association with such a concern was one of Francis Baring's more remarkable achievements, and one which owed far more to his character and personal ability than to the resources at his disposal.

According to one report, the relationship between Hopes and

Barings began when the Dutch bankers decided to try out the fledgling house by passing them a few trifling bills for sale. Francis Baring
executed this task so promptly and secured so favourable a rate of
exchange that Hopes at once sent him £15,000 in bills with the same
instructions. Baring had never dealt with anything like so large an
order before, but undeterred he went to his bankers, Martin and
Stone, and possibly assisted by the fact that Richard Stone was about
to become his brother-in-law, had the bills discounted and immediately remitted the exchange to Amsterdam. The transaction demonstrated what Baring already suspected to be the case, that friends
or relations in the right place could be at least as useful as money in
the bank. 'The Hopes were exceedingly struck with the transaction
which bespoke not only great zeal and activity, but what was still
more important in the eyes of the mercantile men, either good credit
or great resources in their correspondent. From that day Baring
became one of their principal "friends".'[14]

They became friends, as well as 'friends' in the business sense.
By 1790 William Hope was apologizing that pressure of work had
prevented him writing before, but that he considered 'my communications with you, my dear Sir, as a family correspondence, and in fact
it is so on the footing you have been good enough to admit me'.[15]
When the Hopes visited London they stayed with the Barings and
were passed on to grand friends, like Lord Lansdowne at Bowood.[16]
'It was a notable characteristic of the Baring House,' wrote the Canadian historian, Adam Shortt, 'that, once an intimate connection was
established between it and the chief personages in any house, the
world around, that connection was maintained, not only for the lives
of the original heads, but for the lives of their successors to the second and even third generation.'[17] In the case of Hopes it was still
more long-lived, lasting from 1766 when the two houses first corresponded, to far into the twentieth century when Hopes ceased to
exist as an independent entity, or, indeed, until the present day, with
the successor firm of Bank Mees and Hope and its parent company,
the Algemene Bank Nederland.

The relationship was not always beneficial. In 1787 and 1788
Voûte involved Barings in an ill-judged scheme to corner the market
for cochineal. Secret purchase orders were sent out to correspondents all over Europe but stocks proved more substantial than had

been expected and extravagantly large prices had to be paid for the final deposits. Even when almost all the cochineal in Europe had been procured the price was obstinately slow in rising, and the discomfiture was complete when the new crop arrived from Mexico months earlier than expected. Barings only bore a quarter of the cost of this escapade but they still had to find some 500,000 guilders.[18] Such incidents were exceptional, however. On the whole Barings benefited immeasurably from their association with Hope and Co., both in directly financial terms, and from the prestige which their intimacy with so great a house earned them among competitors and potential clients.

In 1786 Francis Baring told Lord Lansdowne:

> My time and attention is chiefly employed by three great objects, my Commercial concerns, the public, and the East India Company. The first is the sole object to which I look for a pecuniary provision for my family; at present I am well supported, the business is in a very flourishing situation, totally divested of moonshine, and the attention which I bestow is fully sufficient, but if that support should fail, I should not hesitate a moment about renouncing every other consideration to my duty to my family. The public requires time and I am fully possessed with a hope of doing some good, but the time which is employed is not embarrassing to my mind. I have men of sense and conversant with business to work with and am under no apprehension about discharging my duty satisfactorily.[19]

The references to 'the public' – by which he meant above all the world of politics – showed how far Baring had advanced from being the mere agent of a West Country wool firm. The fact that the letter was written to the Marquis of Lansdowne, former Earl of Shelburne and one of the most notable grandees in the kingdom, marked the move still more clearly. It was a move which took him away from his occupation as a merchant and to that extent was detrimental to his financial wellbeing. Yet, eighteenth-century Britain being what it was, the move also opened up new possibilities that would never have existed for him if he had stuck to his counting house. The time that Francis Baring devoted to 'the public' was as valuable to John and Francis Baring and Co. as any spent poring over manifests or calculating the profit margin on consignments of cochineal.

Baring's introduction to politics came through John Dunning, nine years his senior, the son of a successful attorney from Devon who had made himself a fortune at the bar and was said by Burke to be 'the first of all his profession . . . there is not a man in any situation, of a more erect and independent spirit, of a more proud honour, or more manly mind, or more firm, determined integrity'.[20] Gainsborough credited him with sober sense and great acuteness; 'I begin to think that there is something in the air of Devon that grows clever fellows'.[21] Dunning became Solicitor General and later Chancellor of the Duchy of Lancaster, was created Lord Ashburton in 1782, and two years earlier married Elizabeth, the sister of that other clever fellow from Devon, Francis Baring. He was a close friend of Colonel Isaac Barré, who in 1782 was to become Pitt's Paymaster General and thus a man of almost limitless patronage. Dunning, Barré and Baring became a formidable triumvirate; so much so that in 1787 Baring commissioned Joshua Reynolds to paint a group portrait of the first two and Lord Lansdowne, their great patron. Lansdowne, while still Shelburne, had served briefly as Prime Minister with Pitt as his Chancellor of the Exchequer. While Prime Minister, and presumably on Dunning's recommendation, Shelburne wrote to Baring, to say he needed 'to have recourse from time to time to Mercantile advice', and that he hoped Baring would supply the need. The recipient proudly annotated the letter 'received and answered the same day, 31 July 1782. N.B. the first letter or message I ever received from His Lordship.'[22] It was far from being the last. In the Baring archives lie copies of a plethora of letters in which Baring proffered his advice on one subject or another. Shelburne asked how important Senegal was to the French slave trade. 'Senegal is not of the smallest importance to France with regard to negroes but solely with regard to gum,' Baring answered firmly. 'The Slave trade from Senegal is trifling as the Natives are a flimsy enervated race, unfit for labor.'[23]

In his dealings with Shelburne – or indeed any other politician – Baring never missed a chance to speak up for the mercantile interest.

In June 1783, for example, he argued that taxation fell more heavily on merchants and small shopkeepers than on country gentlemen. 'Commercial and personal property has very seldom been fairly represented in the House of Commons . . . When the tax on wheels was proposed there was a general clamor, and for which very few gentlemen can pay above £5 or £10 a year, whereas a tallow-chandler, grocer, or an obscure tradesman must under the stamps upon receipts pay £30, £40 or £50 per annum and some a good deal more.'[24] Shelburne for his part played Baring the compliment of being frank to the point of bluntness in his letters. When Baring complained that one of his greenhouses had burnt down, Lansdowne, as he had by then become, replied with some brutality that it was not much loss: 'It was not handsome of its kind or, I think, particularly well placed.'[25]

William Cobbett, in the splenetic vein which ran particularly rich when financiers of foreign origin were in question, referred to Francis Baring as being a merchant's clerk who owed his rise to 'having become a *handy city-man* to the father of the present Marquis of Lansdowne'.[26] In fact Baring seems to have done little in the way of promoting Lansdowne's personal finances, which presumably was what Cobbett had in mind. But he felt considerable loyalty to his patron, and since Lansdowne remained in opposition, he never grew close to the Prime Minister, William Pitt. This did not stop Pitt appealing to him for advice on a wide variety of subjects: on Turkey; on Gibraltar – only of value if Britain possessed a superior fleet; on Customs House reform – 'To obtain admission to the Commissioners is almost impossible; to obtain information from them is equally so.'[27] Baring was never slow to produce such replies, always decisive and to the point. But he was more hesitant when he was asked by Pitt to become one of the Commissioners enquiring into the fees and perquisites of certain public offices. He accepted in the end, but only on condition that he got no remuneration for his work and after first securing Lansdowne's blessing.[28]

In April 1786 Baring was accused in the press of having used his connection with the East India Company to make a profit out of sales of tea. The sales had in fact been made by Robert Voûte on behalf of Hopes and other companies. Hopes and the other houses involved signed a declaration stating that, though they would have been delighted to include Baring in their number if he had wished, no such request had been made. Voûte went further and said that he had repeatedly pressed Baring to take an interest in the transaction, but his friend 'constantly and firmly refused'.[29] In spite of this it took Baring nearly three years to clear his name. He felt particularly bitter, because he had only become involved in the business some two years earlier at the direct request of Pitt, when large stocks of tea were bought up in an attempt to defeat the widespread smuggling that was going on.[30] He had been impressed by Pitt at the time, telling Shelburne in some surprise that the Prime Minister was 'not only fully informed but appears equally well to comprehend the whole extent' of the Commutation Bill,[31] but approval turned to rancour when Pitt and Dundas not merely failed to come to his defence but seemed positively to egg on his accusers: 'The attack was rather encouraged than otherwise, my temper would not permit me to bring forward what would have justified me in a moment, namely, the papers and authorities under which I acted from Mr Pitt from whence it appeared that I had exceeded, and very considerably surpassed those expectations which I had held out and which Mr Pitt had entertained.'[32] Baring continued to work with and for Pitt, but he never wholly forgave him. After Pitt died he wrote to *The Times* to deny that he had contributed to the settlement of the Prime Minister's debts. 'With the highest respect for the talents, the integrity, and intentions of Mr Pitt,' he wrote, 'I have not been able to concur with him on any great political question for above 20 years, our political opinions and principles being different.'[33]

Lansdowne was constantly urging Baring to 'put his views before the Publick'. In terms that were presumably well intentioned but strike the contemporary reader as a little tactless, he told Baring that he should seek to 'lay the Foundation of solid Reputation and Character. It's the highest Injustice to consider every Merchant as a Jew, as if he was incapable of looking forward to anything but a Fraudulent Contract or a Line of Stockjobbing – the consequence of which is that their talents are left to prey upon the Publick instead of serving it . . . Dirtiness of character will occur in all Professions . . .'[34] When he urged Baring to 'put his views before the Publick', he meant that the banker should seek election to the House of Commons. By entering the House he would transcend the status of a mere merchant, enter as of right into the empyrean of the ruling classes, and not merely lay but build upon 'the Foundation of solid Reputation'. It was not a new idea to Baring, indeed it was one that had occurred already to both his brothers.

Charles, characteristically, was the first to chance his arm and, equally characteristically, failed. He stood for Tiverton, offering not merely to live in the town but, more extravagantly, to buy all their wool products into the bargain. In spite of this he was rejected, probably because he insisted that, if elected, he must also take over the lucrative post of Receiver of the Land Tax. The Tivertonians preferred another Exeter merchant, John Duntze, also a first-generation emigré, who was somewhat less exigent in his demands.[35]

John tried next, for Honiton in 1774. He too was defeated, in spite of the support of the Courtenays, and resolved never to stand again, but was provoked to change his mind when the son-in-law of John Duntze, John Cholwich (or sometimes Cholwych), contested Exeter in 1776. The Duntzes and Barings were the Montagus and Capulets of Exeter and a plank in Cholwich's platform was that the Baring influence in the city should be reduced. The challenge could not be refused. John stood against him, spent £6000 on the election and won the day.[36] Presumably he thought the money well spent, for he remained MP for Exeter until 1802. 'My supporters were fond of me as a candidate free with my money,' he wrote a little ruefully, and he calculated that the seat cost him in all more than £25,000.[37] By far the most expensive election was 1790, Baring spending some £10,000. His rival, Sir Charles Bampfylde, told the Prince of Wales that Baring was almost certain to be unseated as the result of a petition alleging bribery, corruption and undue influence: 'I have every reason to assure myself he would not venture a second contest.' Bampfylde might well have been right, but had no chance to find out, since the House of Commons decided Baring had been properly elected.[38]

Francis Baring prudently waited until his London business was well established before following his brothers into a pursuit that was certain to be both costly and time-consuming. He first came in for the rotten borough of Grampound in Devon at the cost of £3000, and then in 1790 decided to switch to Ilchester, agreeing to pay Samuel Smith £1500 for his interest in the borough. '. . . in case Mr Baring is not seated the sum of Two Hundred Fifty Pounds is to be returned to him by Mr Smith. This agreement to remain secret.'[39] Smith proved unable to supply what he had promised and Baring lost the election. Not long after Lansdowne offered him one of his boroughs, and from 1794 to 1806 he sat either for Calne or for Chipping Norton.

He was not a natural orator, nor did he ever feel at home in the House of Commons. He wrote to Lansdowne to deny having said something attributed to him by the press: 'My voice is so very unequal to the House of Commons, and I am consequently very much misrepresented in the papers.'[40] The *True Briton*, admittedly well-disposed to his politics, thought better of his efforts. In his speeches, it said, he was 'neat, flowing and perspicuous, aiming more by solidity of argument to arrest and convince his hearers, than by beautiful figures and impassioned eloquence to mislead the minds of men'.[41] He was, in short, a humdrum but competent performer who commanded the respect of the House not by fine words but by his command of his subject and obvious sincerity. The views that he expounded were much as might have been expected from a prominent merchant, and on the lines every Baring in Parliament was to follow for the next one hundred and fifty years. He advocated *laissez-faire*, in its most sweeping form. 'Every regulation', he said, 'is a restriction, and as such contrary to that freedom which I have held to be the first principle of the wellbeing of commerce.'[42] Trade must follow its own course, any interference with it could only stunt its growth and distort its proper pattern. He was consistent in his views, even when it was possible that their application would in the short term at least work to his disadvantage. In a memorandum that he prepared for Lansdowne he argued vigorously that there should be free trade with the United States and no limitations imposed on the use of American shipping.[43]

This condemnation of monopolies as much as any other artificial restraint on trade was qualified in the case of India. Baring had begun to invest in the East India Company in 1776, though never on a large scale, and in 1779 he became a Director. The Company more or less monopolized imports and exports from and to India; a breach of his principles which Baring tolerated with apparent equanimity. He fiercely opposed Charles James Fox's attempt to capture this rich fount of patronage for his section of the Whig party. 'It is such a system of influence and corruption as amazes me . . .' he told Shelburne of Fox's India bill. 'It will for ever remain as a monument of the boldest and most artful effort ever attempted by any subject since the restoration.'[44] But he did not deny that government had a right to influence the doings of the Company; on the contrary, he championed the right of ministers to make their opinions heard and, generally, heard with respect.

By 1783 Baring was accepted as the leader of the City interest on the Court of Directors of the East India Company, and he worked closely with a colleague and old friend, Robert Atkinson, in support of Pitt. Wraxall said of Atkinson that he 'possessed a long mathematical head, sustained by vast facility and rapidity in calculations of a pecuniary nature: qualities held in high esteem by Pitt',[45] and the same was *a fortiori* true of Baring. Atkinson, however, was dying of consumption, and when Laurence Sulivan also died in 1786, Baring was left as by far the most able and experienced member of the Court. He continued to work closely with Pitt and Dundas when he became Chairman in 1792–3, refusing to bring forward any nominations for senior posts without Dundas's previous agreement. But he was not a docile servant of ministers, opposing Dundas in 1791 when the minister wanted to abolish the Secret Committee, the inner Council of the Company, and to reduce the number of Directors.[46] When Dundas resolved to reform the structure of the Company, Baring was chief negotiator for the Directors. Dundas believed they could work together successfully and urged Pitt to take Baring fully into his confidence: 'If you do give him one of the papers, let him know it is done in concert with me, and that . . . we shall from time to time expect a return of unreserved communication from him.'[47] On the whole the partnership worked smoothly. It was in recognition of Baring's work as Chairman of the East India Company that in 1793 he was created a baronet.[48] 'I don't congratulate you on your Title,' wrote Lansdowne loftily, 'because I think in these times you do it more honour than it does you.'[49]

Though Baring dominated the Council, he never really enjoyed his time on it. 'The more I work,' he complained to Lansdowne, 'the greater degree of jealousy and difficulty I have to encounter amongst the Directors, who are in general composed of either Fools or Knaves.'[50] The main reason for staying on was that he wished to provide for two of his sons in the East; an end which he duly achieved in 1790 when Tom was packed off to Bengal, and Henry to China. Nor was this the only benefit gained from membership of the Council. The East India Company continued to buy woollen goods from the West Country for export to India long after it became clear that they would inevitably be sold at a loss. The records do not give reasons for the decision, but it is hard to believe that Baring's long association with Exeter was not in part responsible.[51]

Baring's close involvement with ministers and the confidence that they placed in him, won him important benefits when government contracts came to be placed. One such was for supplying British forces in the field at the tail end of the American War of Independence and related conflicts. Isaac Barré said of contractors as a class that they were 'animals of a greedy nature, always craving and never satisfied, their appetites for dishonest lucre and foul gain were as insatiable as their consciences were easily satisfied'.[52] Baring calculated that the profit made by his predecessors on government contracts in 1781–2 was 13.4 per cent, and that it had been even higher in previous years. He offered to do the same job for a commission of 1 per cent, and when Shelburne gave him responsibility for victualling the armed services in 1783, he did so at a total cost of 5d a head instead of the previous 5½d – thus saving the public some £70,000 and earning his own house over the same period a modest but satisfactory £11,000.[53] By March 1783 the end of hostilities meant that the operation had to be run down and much surplus disposed of. This too Baring handled successfully. About a third of the overstock had to be sold at a loss, but this was never more than 20 per cent; a result significantly better than that achieved by the Victualling Board when in a similar situation some twenty years before.[54]

In its minute recording the decision to award the contract, the Navy Board stated: 'Mr Francis Baring being represented to My Lords as a merchant of great character and responsibility, every way equal to the Trust, and the due execution of so important a Service; he is called in and asked at what rate he will execute the Business, which he offers to do for a Commission of £1 per cent.'[55] The fact that the recommendation came from Shelburne was all-important, yet no one doubted that Baring was indeed 'a merchant of great character and responsibility'. The same was true in another new field for the expansion of John and Francis Baring and Co. in the 1780s – that of public loans. Baring's connections with the mighty ensured him an inside track in the negotiations, but he would not have maintained himself there if he had not showed himself fully competent.

When in the early 1780s the Government wished to raise money to finance the American War it selected a banking house which would accept responsibility for the entire amount and raise it from its own resources, its clients or outside investors. Provided ministers got the money they needed, they were not too concerned about the amount the chosen banker charged the public. If he got his figures right, therefore, the banker had the chance to make a fat profit; if he got it wrong, however – put too high a price on the stock, misjudged the public mood, or was unlucky in his timing – then he could find himself with a lot of unsaleable paper on his hands and in a very difficult position. It was a high-profit, high-risk business. No one got it right all the time; the most successful banker was the one whose information and acumen enabled him to get it right more often than the others. Between 1780 and 1784 Baring made a profit of £19,000 out of raising money for the British Government; not a sensational figure but eminently satisfactory and a harbinger of the far bigger business to be done in the French wars.

Baring's forays into public life reaped rich dividends for his business house, but it would be wrong to deduce from this that financial profit was his only, or even primary, consideration. Baring did not court Pitt or Lansdowne because he foresaw pickings for John and Francis Baring in so doing. He did so because he was flattered to receive advances from such magnificos, because he relished the power and consequence earned by such associations, and because he sincerely wished to serve his country. But in the eighteenth century – as in the twentieth – those in power liked to deal with those they knew and trusted. Ministers knew and trusted Baring, they liked him and respected his ability, they felt they owed him something. What more likely then that they would push in his direction whatever plums were theirs for the giving?

With the ending of the war, the number of plums diminished. Merchant banking is often a matter of swings and roundabouts. The profit made from raising money to finance the American War compensated for the loss in trade that that war had involved; the revival of international trade after the war filled the gap left by the disappearance of public loans. The years between 1777 and 1793, despite occasional vicissitudes, were ones of almost uninterrupted growth for John and Francis Baring and Co. Capital grew from £20,071 to £66,177. Profits inevitably fluctuated, but reached £13,268 in 1792. Commission income and acceptances rose from year to year. By the outbreak of the French wars in 1793, Barings were among the best known and strongest houses in the City. The foundation had been well laid for the extraordinary expansion that was to come.

3

The French Wars

1793–1815

The always inconspicuous part that John Baring had played in the affairs of John and Francis Baring and Co. dwindled almost to nothing in the years after 1793. He remained a partner until the end of 1800 but his share of the profits was reduced to a quarter after 1796. 'Our ancient Firm will henceforward cease;' it was announced somewhat grandiloquently on 1 April 1800, 'but the remaining Partners will continue the Business under that of Francis Baring and Co.' The new partners were given as Francis, his elder son Thomas – twenty-eight years old* – and Charles Wall, the son of an attorney who had married Sir Francis's daughter Harriet in 1790.[1] Farington described Wall in 1806 as 'the principal manager of the business', and it was certainly he who did most of the day-to-day labour while Francis was relaxing his hold on affairs.[2]

John retired a prosperous and contented man but in old age things went wrong. Two daughters died and then his second son committed suicide. He retreated into melancholic solitude. He 'has the family characteristic', the Rev. Mr Patch told Farington. 'He never shows distress, but suppresses His feelings so far as not to make them apparent. He looked up to his brother [Francis] as being a very superior man.' When Patch complimented him on his firmness of mind John Baring replied: 'Look to my Brother. He is the firm man.'[3]

Francis's firmness, indeed hardness, was shown in his relationship with his brother Charles. In 1801 he was called in to unscramble the affairs of John and Charles Baring and with bad grace made Charles a loan to help him through his difficulties.[4] He never expected to get

---

* Most sources give 1804 as being the date Thomas became a full partner.

the money back and made his opinion contemptuously clear. 'You are exalted with every success, I am of late oppressed with many troubles,' wrote Charles pathetically. 'Your letter is a cruel one. I have never deserved from you such expressions.'[5] Francis's riposte was crueller still. 'You never did understand your own Character and your own situation,' he told his brother. 'We have had a very long test of your conduct in the almost monstrous management of the original and chief dependence of the Baring family and you are disposed to impute your want of success to the want of luck . . . In this I cannot agree with you as there is not a single instance which has come to my knowledge in which ultimate miscarriage was not to be discovered in the outset.'[6]

Though the performance of his brothers did not inspire him with great confidence, Francis Baring felt strongly that he was building for future generations and that his children and children's children should carry on where he had left off. Yet the problems that would beset any such dynasty were very obvious to him. Writing to his son Alexander's father-in-law in 1803 he admitted he was worried:

> Unremitting attention and exertion through a long life have placed objects within my reach, the value of which are acknowledged by all, but the difficulty to acquire them, and the facility with which they are lost, appear to me to be appreciated by none . . . Money or Fortune derive no security from the magnitude or amount, as it cannot be expected that the next in succession will possess equal prudence with the person who acquired . . . A man is considered as mean who does not spend his income; and although there are instances of young misers, they are very rare, and the imputation of meanness is so insupportable to a young man, that they *never* fail to plunge into the opposite extreme. It is for this reason that families founded on the acquirements of an individual do not last above sixty years one with another: families which are founded on the success of public Service continue longer, because the Children and Grandchildren of the founder are generally inclined to pursue the same line of Service: but the posterity of a Merchant, Banker etc., particularly when they are young, abandon the pursuit of their pre-

decessor as beneath them, or they follow it by agents without interfering themselves, which is only a more rapid road to ruin.[7]

That the Barings avoided this risk is attributable above all to the fact that they were philoprogenitive and tenacious in retaining family links. At any given moment, therefore, there was likely to be a plentiful supply of cousins acquainted with each other and eager for a job in the bank. Elder sons might drop out, deeming the work 'as beneath them', but there were plenty of hungry younger sons who needed to make their fortune. Those at the head of the bank were also ruthless when it came to disposing of the second rate; to carry the name of Baring was not enough, if one could not do the job successfully one was quickly banished to an outpost or consigned to some less exacting line of business. If the right Baring was not there, then somebody was brought in; in ten or twenty years a Baring would no doubt be available to take on the task, but in the meantime it was better that it should be well done by an outsider than bungled by a member of the family.

In 1803 Francis Baring doubted whether the right Barings were there. Thomas, the elder son and future baronet, had served the East India Company until 1801. He showed neither aptitude for nor interest in banking and made it clear that when his father died he expected to tend his estates, collect pictures, sit in the House of Commons, and generally behave in a gentlemanly way. He was technically a partner in the house but retired even before his father's death. The future seemed to lie with his younger brothers, Alexander and Henry; and Francis Baring did not look to them with great expectations. 'It would afford me some comfort if I could perceive anything that was rational or manly in their pursuits,' he wrote despairingly. 'I can make allowance for a considerable degree of frivolous dissipation on the outset of life, but when it carries the appearance of degenerating into system, I must withdraw that indulgence for it merits none.'[8]

So far as Alexander was concerned, these strictures are extravagant. He was an eminently, even depressingly, assiduous young man. He started his career at Hope and Co. in Amsterdam, where he showed himself 'very sensible for his age' but at the same time headstrong and impatient: 'His character was not yet modifyed in such a manner, as to act constantly with such an application as would be more agreeable to Mr Hope.'[9] When Hopes were chased from Holland by the invading French, Alexander was sent to the United States. He won good opinions there. General Cobb found him 'a Dutchman in negotiation' – by which he seems to have meant that Baring was tough, shrewd, but never unreasonable – yet with 'no art or cunning about him' and 'a good heart'.[10] Another American businessman described him as 'an extraordinary young man, of great mercantile talents and possessed of much information. Though a young man of about twenty-five [in fact he was twenty-three] he is respected by all the old characters who know him.'[11] The mistake over his age was typical; Alexander was born middle-aged and never failed to impress by the *gravitas* which throughout the generations has been the hallmark of his clan. In business this inspired confidence; in the more frivolous reaches of London society the enthusiasm was less marked. Miss Berry sat next to him at dinner and found him 'rather a heavy-looking young man, with a hesitating manner, but seems very clear in his ideas'.[12]

Francis Baring was unimpressed by reports from America of his son's good sense and maturity. The 'superior tone of mind' that Alexander had taken with him to America had been 'visibly impaired'; he had acquired 'enervating habits'; a trip to Paris that Alexander undertook with his new wife and American father-in-law was responsible for the rebuke that 'frivolous dissipation' was 'degenerating into system'.[13] The real cause of offence seems to have been that on his return from America he had refused to take up a partnership in Hopes, thus thwarting his father's dream of a grand Anglo-Dutch consortium that would rule the commercial world.[14] Not unreasonably Alexander felt that he should be allowed to spend some time at home again, but to Francis Baring it seemed that this wilful opposition to his views arose only because 'the pleasures of the present moment must not be sacrificed to the most brilliant prospects'.[15]

Alexander's brother Henry was more deserving of criticism. A shadowy figure, he seems to have been both more brilliant and more wayward than his brother. A passionate gambler, he was also a successful one, several times breaking the bank at the L'Entreprise

Générale des Jeux in Paris. Such a hobby was, however, deemed inappropriate to his role in the City.[16] For this, or for other reasons, he was never encouraged to play a prominent role in the house, though he remained technically a partner until 1823. He and Alexander married sisters, but Henry divorced his wife Marie in 1824. Alexander deplored this step; Marie had undoubtedly committed adultery, but to divorce her would be to 'throw her absolutely on the Dunghill'. Anyway, Henry's own 'anti-domestic life is of great notoriety and must tell heavily against him'. He might well fail to secure a divorce and 'both parties will come out of court covered with dirt'.[17] Henry paid no attention, got his divorce and in due course married a second time, to Cecilia Windham. Like Banquo, he got kings though he was none; inconsiderable in the bank himself, his son and grandson were to dominate it for well over fifty years. The mud of the divorce court did not stick to Henry; he became a popular figure, prominent in the London clubs and asked to all the best shoots – 'Mr H. Baring's shooting quite wonderful,' recorded an awe-struck Henry Fox.[18]

The two youngest brothers, William and George, were both dispatched to the East. William showed promise – 'he will at no distant period be fully capable of conducting his own private Business without Assistance,' a Baring correspondent reported from Canton[19] – but he frequently fell ill. 'My hopes of enjoying very robust health are frail and I must be contented in being free from violent irritability,'[20] he wrote wistfully in 1806, and it was judged by the doctors that banking and irritability too often went hand in hand. He died in 1820. George was a raffish figure. He married against his family's will, lost a lot of money speculating in opium, then left the East India Company to join the Church. However, wailed his brother Henry, 'the quiet and useful life of a respectable Country Clergyman was much too tame and unobtrusive for him' and he became 'the ranting preacher of a wild Sect'.[21] He combined this activity with an extravagant style of living that drove him to bankruptcy in 1827. Thomas Baring was for letting him stew in his own juice but Alexander insisted that 'we must extricate him. I say *we* because it is quite clear that his family must come to the aid of this unfortunate member of it and that you as our head must proceed to make the necessary arrangements.'[22] George was packed off to live in a villa in Florence where Henry Fox found him in 1828 puffing cigar smoke at Lady Dudley and decidedly the worse for drink, surrounded by his daughters, 'tall, raw-boned, vulgar misses, very underbred and unladylike in their conversation and manners'.[23] William and George both had sons, but though one of William's descendants found his way back into the bank, it was the progeny of Thomas, Alexander and Henry who were to ensure the future of the house of Baring.

It was these three brothers who took formal control of the house when Francis Baring retired. He gave up his share in the profit and loss of the house from mid-1803, leaving as much of his capital behind as his sons cared to use and charging only a generous 4 per cent interest. Unlike most people who have built up their own businesses, he was delighted to pass over power to his successors, would indeed have done so earlier if he had felt his sons were ready. By early 1803 his doubts about their capacity had long been put at rest. He told John William Hope that his sons were anxious to show that they could stand alone and he quite as anxious to give them the chance, 'for the Success of which I do not entertain the slightest apprehension . . . They all possess abilities and although differing from each other in qualifications yet each has something which the other wants and . . . there can be no doubt that they will act with the most perfect cordiality in support of a common Cause.'[24] By October 1807 he was able, no doubt with some satisfaction, to refuse a loan to the Duke of Kent on the grounds that he was retired and his property 'disposed of and dispersed'. 'Although I have appeared as Contractor for loans', he wrote, 'yet I have not for three years had the least concern, nor gained or lost myself a single penny; but I have appeared because it was thought my name would be useful in the opinion of the publick, and at the desire of my successors.'[25] His retirement was shortly followed in 1805 or 1806 by the move of the business from Devonshire Square, where it had been since 1793, to a much larger building at 8 Bishopsgate. This solid Georgian house, with garden at the back, was approached from the street through an archway and open courtyard with stables on one side. Its site was to accommodate Barings' headquarters until the present day.[26]

Francis Baring had begun the transition from banker to gentleman of leisure in 1796 when at an auction at Garraway's Coffee House he had acquired a reversionary interest in 623 acres and the manor house of Lee, near Lewisham. Lee had a distinguished pedigree; a continuous line of lords of the manor descending from Aluuin, the last recorded Saxon thane, by way of Lord Montifichet, one of the barons at Runnymede, and the Marquis of Dorset whose daughter married Edward IV, to Baring's friend Joseph Plaice.[27] Baring bought the reversion for £20,000 with a Mrs Angerstein in residence who had a life interest. When she died unexpectedly four years later, putting Baring into possession far earlier than he had expected, he insisted on paying his friend an additional £7000, saying it was 'absolutely necessary for my peace of mind' and that the money should not be returned, even in Plaice's will.[28] By then he had already acquired a further 583 acres from Lord Sondes, and he settled contentedly into the 'Capital Uniform Modern Brick and Stone Mansion House', which had probably been built by Richard Jupp, architect of the East India Company's building in Leadenhall Street.[29] To run his establishment, a modest staff for a medium-sized country house, he had a butler, under-butler, two footmen, housekeeper, cook, laundry maid, two housemaids, two kitchen-maids, a coachman, and a second coachman.

But this was only a sighting shot for finer things. In 1801 Francis Baring laid out £150,000 on the purchase of an estate from the Duke of Bedford near Micheldever in Hampshire. George Dance was commissioned to refashion the house, which he adorned with a massive portico of Doric columns. This was much admired in the neighbourhood and inspired the banker Henry Drummond to add a still mightier portico to his neighbouring house, the Grange. Dance's work cost £25,000 or so, extravagant enough but trifling compared with the £400,000 Beckford squandered on Fonthill.[30] Baring spent another £40,000 planting the grounds and never missed a chance to snap up an adjoining property. 'Sir Francis Baring is extending his purchases so largely in Hampshire that he soon expects to be able to inclose the county within his own park paling,' wrote some contemporary satirist.[31]

By mid-1801 Farington was describing the alterations as 'nearly finished', but it does not seem that the house was fully habitable till a couple of years later.[32] It was about that time that Count Stahremberg, the Austrian minister, wrote to thank Baring for 'your kind reception in your Kingdom of Stratton'.[33] Lawrence went there in September 1806 'to paint three portraits in one picture, viz: Sir Francis Baring, His Brother John and Mr Wall, his Partner'.[34] In the picture Wall and John Baring are posed over an open volume while Sir Francis looks away from them with his hand raised to his ear. This caused some ribaldry. 'Sir George [Beaumont] remarked on Sir Francis turning his head from those He was listening to as if to hear Thunder; Beechey sd He turned his head from Mr Wall as if the latter on looking on the Book before him announced a deficit of £100,000.'[35] James Ward engraved the portrait for three hundred guineas, but when it was proposed to publish the print the project was vetoed by Sir Francis's sons – 'because they do not like to have their Father exhibited with a Ledger before him,' surmised Farington.[36]

Stratton was furnished with a fine collection of paintings, notably Dutch. Like many collectors, Baring repented in old age the enthusiasms of his youth and by 1804 was telling his son-in-law that he had 'done with all except the very superior' and of those it was only 'Rembrandt, Rubens or Van Dyck that tempt me, and the first must not be too dark, nor the second indecent'.[37] He had a good opinion of his purchases, noting, on the catalogue of an exhibition in Paris in 1802, of Cuyp, '229 and 230 the best but none equal to mine'; of Ostade, 'some fine specimens but not equal to mine'; of Adrian Van der Velde 'not equal to mine'; of Rembrandt 'none fine or equal to mine'; of Wouvermans 'many pretty, none v. fine. I prefer my own'.[38] His farm was probably as close to his heart as any of his pictures. He kept a farm of 600 acres in hand, tended it lovingly, and took particular pride in his 'famous flock of sheep'.[39]

That he bought pictures because he liked them and reared sheep because he enjoyed doing so, is incontestable, but equally the acquisition of estates and a stately home was an essential step in the process of social consolidation. It was commonly believed that Baring was angling for a seat in the House of Lords. When in May 1806 he was one of only four Directors to support Lauderdale's nomination as Governor General, Colonel Toone told Hastings that this was because he wanted a peerage.[40] When the Duke of York's alleged corruption was debated by the House of Commons in 1809, it was whispered that Baring and Sir Robert Peel had both paid Mrs Clarke £5000 for a peerage.[41] That he would have been delighted to receive one is undoubtedly true, that he would have bribed Mrs Clarke to that end would have been wholly out of character. Nor can he seriously have expected such an honour. As F. M. L. Thompson has convincingly shown, Disraeli's claim that Pitt 'created a plebeian aristocracy and blended it with the patrician oligarchy . . . He caught them in the alleys of Lombard Street and clutched them from the counting-houses of Cornhill' is picturesque nonsense.[42] The only peer created by Pitt from a similar background to Baring was Robert Smith, Lord Carrington, and Smith had severed his connection with banking long before his elevation. The best that Baring could realistically hope for was that he might procure aristocratic marriages for his children and that his descendants might one day achieve nobility.

By 1810, when Francis Baring died, there was no house in which a Baring would have been socially unacceptable. But this did not mean that they were wholly integrated with the aristocracy. If one of his daughters married a lord, it was taken for granted that a fat dowry would garnish the *mésalliance*. When Alexander Baring was admitted to that elite Whig dining club, the King of Clubs, Sydney Smith told Lady Holland that this was 'upon the express promise that he lends £50 to any member of the Club when applied to'.[43] Smith was joking, of course, but there was a half truth concealed in the jest. The Barings had gone astonishingly far in a short time, but there was still some way to go.

When he died Francis Baring left £625,000. Four hundred thousand pounds was in land, £27,000 in pictures, furniture and jewels. His capital in Barings, Baring Brothers as the house had been called since 1807, was £68,507; an enormous sum, but not as large as that of Charles Wall, who was credited with £86,126, and only a little more than his eldest son, Thomas, with £67,448. It is a testimony to the skill with which the house had been built up that his death caused it hardly a tremor. 'At his death,' wrote Lord Erskine, 'he was unquestionably the first merchant in Europe; first in knowledge and talents, and first in character and opulence.'[44] To him, almost alone, Baring Brothers owed the stability of its foundations; it was largely his doing that it had so far sailed successfully through the perilous waters of the war with France.

*　　*　　*

Bankers do not like war. There are already too many imponderables in their lives without the extra financial, military and political hazards that accompany hostilities. What they hope for is steadily expanding trade in a predictable economic climate and with a minimum of political interference. But though war carries alarming risks, it can also yield amazing profits. Traditional fields of business may wither, but there are always opportunities for something new, and the banker who is resourceful, bold and resolute; who possesses a cool head and a long purse; above all, perhaps, who knows the right people, and who enjoys the priceless gift of being in the right place at the right time, will make a great deal of money. Barings had all these advantages and they made the money.

Francis Baring approached the war in a spirit of detached pragmatism. He disliked the Bourbons but found the revolutionaries even more alarming. He thought the émigrés and their pretensions absurd and believed that what France needed was a constitutional king, but since Britain was committed to the unconditional restoration of the Bourbons he accepted resignedly that the war was likely to continue for many years.[45] In the meantime, he sagely observed: 'People will eat, drink and be cloathed in defiance of their rulers.'[46] He agreed with his son Alexander that it was certainly futile and probably mischievous for a government to attempt to interfere with the course of trade. In a memorandum of 1805 Alexander argued that the blockade of the continent had done more harm to the British than the French. 'The most desirable system for the trade of this country is to abstain from all restrictions, to leave it as free and uncircumscribed as possible, and to desist from, or mitigate all Naval blockades as much as other more important considerations will permit.'[47] To this view he remained consistent.

The question of whether there was a conflict of interest between the mercantile community and the nation as a whole, or whether official policy corresponded with the real national interest, did not cause the Barings many sleepless nights. They went on trading wherever it was possible, avoiding the overtly illegal but not too preoccupied with the spirit of the law. In 1802 Cobbett wrote to William Windham to complain: 'The French fleet and army in St Domingo continue to be supplied with provisions and other necessaries by Willings and Co. of Philadelphia who draw on Barings and Co. for payment.'⁴⁸ At that moment the war was in temporary abeyance but Cobbett would probably have had as much and as little justification for his accusation two years before or two years later. Certainly he could not have proved his case. Through Willing and Francis, who were Barings' closest correspondents in the United States, and many other American merchants, Barings were involved in much trade with continental Europe conducted under the cloak of 'neutrality'. Barings' money in part at least must have financed many cargoes that were smuggled illicitly under the noses of the Royal Navy and the French authorities. Barings themselves were not and did not need to be involved in smuggling. They cannot possibly have been ignorant of what was going on, but did not wish to have any formal knowledge of it. In this they differed little from those in authority. Though the official policy of the British government was that the trade should be stopped, it is doubtful whether the breaches of that policy caused much greater real concern in Whitehall than in Bishopsgate.

Of course there was much international trade that was in no way questionable. A typical adventure in July 1801 concerned the *Canton*, a vessel valued at $50,000 with a cargo worth four times as much: nankeens and silks, porcelain, sugar and Bohem, Souchong and Hyson tea. The ship arrived in mid-September and Barings wrote to reassure the American merchants who shared the profit or loss on joint account: 'The cargo is very valuable and will find a ready sale at good prices, as our Market is again bare of Indian goods.'⁴⁹ The voyage was made during the short-lived peace after the Treaty of Amiens, but even if it had not been, it would have been entirely legal. Yet the markets of Europe were still more bare of Indian goods than those of London and in wartime the prices paid there might be twice as high. It would be surprising if none of that silk and tea ended up across the Channel.

There were periods during which trade was severely curtailed. In the autumn of 1805 Francis Baring described his business as having 'sunk to nothing'.⁵⁰ Yet this was the exception. In the first five years of the war commission income grew by more than 150 per cent, and it only dropped below £20,000 once between then and 1815. Liabilities on acceptance rose even more dramatically from £89,458 in 1793 to £454,807 in 1797, and remained over £200,000 for the rest of the war, again with the exception of one year. The United States was responsible for the greater part of the growth; in the last five years of the war nearly 80 per cent of commisssion income was attributable to 'American and Colonial' trade. British exports remained remarkably stable throughout the wars, and the proportion of the world's trade carried in British ships and financed by British money grew considerably as the merchant fleets of the continent were driven from the seas. But Barings prospered more greatly than the national norm. There were not many houses that could match their resources, expertise and worldwide connections.

Their resources had been greatly strengthened in 1795 by an inrush of funds from Hope and Co. 'I am so completely in the habit of considering Holland and England as the same Country that I can very easily find myself as much at home in the one as in the other,' Henry Hope wrote to Francis Baring in January 1794.[51] Within a year he was forced to put his words to the test. As the French revolutionary troops advanced into Holland, the Hopes fled to London. The Royal Navy sent a frigate to escort their ship – not so much to protect the Hopes themselves as the gold and other forms of wealth they brought with them. Alexander Baring and the youngest and most capable of Hopes' partners, Peter César Labouchère, stayed at their posts until the last minute and then escaped across the ice-packed estuaries just as the French troops entered Amsterdam.[52]

Labouchère was one of the most talented bankers of his generation. It is said that, aged only twenty-two, he asked Hopes if he might be made a partner. He was refused. 'Would it be different if I were Sir Francis Baring's son-in-law?' he asked. 'Yes,' he was told. 'Well, I am going to be.' He then rushed to Francis Baring and asked for the hand of his daughter, Dorothy. Baring refused. 'Would it be different if I were a partner in Hope and Co.?' he asked. 'Yes,' he was told. 'Well, I am going to be.' He brought off a left and right, winning both partnership and wife.[53] In fact, he does not seem to have become a partner of Hopes for several years, but the spirit of the story at least is true. Dorothy may have felt that she was the only loser by the transaction. Labouchère was an ungainly figure; short on wit and education; generous, honourable and exceedingly astute but with a touching determination to ape the manners of a pre-war French aristocrat.

He spoke his native French with an English accent and English with a French.[54]

When the Treaty of Amiens brought fleeting peace to Europe in 1801, Hopes planned to return to Amsterdam, but it was November 1802 before they finally reopened in Holland and even then much of their capital remained effectively at the disposal of Barings. It was at this point that Alexander caused such offence to his father by refusing to take up a partnership in the Dutch house.[55] He was proved right when the French returned and Hopes' fortunes waned. Labouchère was briefly prominent in 1810 when he acted as mouthpiece for a group of French dissidents – Fouché and Ouvrard among them – who were trying to negotiate peace with England. Francis Baring put him in touch with Wellesley, the Foreign Secretary, but Napoleon discovered what was going on and quickly put a stop to it.[56] By 1813 Hopes was an empty shell. Alexander Baring took it over at a cost of £250,521 and at first intended to strip its assets and close it down. On second thoughts, however, he decided it was worth preserving, if only to provide a berth for his brother Thomas's sons.[57] Hope and Co. resumed life and was to be an active trading partner of Baring Brothers for more than another century.

Their virtual integration with Hopes was as much as anything responsible for Barings' increasing involvement in a new field; they had long financed international trade; now they began to concern themselves with the affairs of foreign governments. The negotiations with Portugal illustrate well the hazards and tribulations of such work. In March 1797 the Prince of Brazil sought to raise £1.2 million in London. He was prepared to pledge diamonds and the revenue from the snuff contract as security, or if these were unsatisfactory, 'the rich Kingdom and Islands of Mozambique'. Francis Baring was tempted but referred the matter to Pitt,[58] who expressed extreme distaste for the proposed colonial *quid pro quo*, and said that, in the 'particular distressed situation of this country', he was unenthusiastic about the loan in principle. If Barings wanted to make it privately, then he would not oppose it, but there would be no official backing. In view of his attitude Baring concluded that negotiations should be continued but 'the terms must be onerous and the conditions rendered very flattering to the publick'.[59] The terms were too onerous and the matter was allowed to drop.

In 1801, when the Portuguese had to raise a large sum to pay off their war debts, the question of a loan was revived. This time, with Pitt out of office, Francis Baring decided to go it alone: 'Just at the crucial period,' he told Labouchère, 'it may be desirable not to have the subject to discuss with our own Ministers, as you know very well how ignorant they are of foreign finance.'[60] Labouchère and George Baring were sent on a taxing midwinter journey by mule across the Pyrénées to Lisbon. The negotiations proved almost as exhausting as the journey, Labouchère complaining that the Portuguese 'constantly alter the text, and I have to puzzle my brain to find out in a language which I do not understand the right from the wrong'.[6] Urgency was lent to the affair when, in March 1802, Baring reported 'a competition in the persons of some Jews, which is formidable from the powers they possess as they have money, but there is nothing more to fear as they cannot afford to pay so high a price as ourselves. A competitor however is always dangerous and must be attended to.'[62] It was attended to, and the Portuguese Diamond Loan of 1802 ensued, initially for 6.5 million guilders but eventually for 13 million. The loan was not a total success; Hopes took the larger part but Barings were responsible for 5 million guilders, and by the end of 1802 had placed only a little over 1.5 million on the British market.

The conclusion drawn from this début was that international loans were potentially profitable but needed to be handled with caution. In 1800 Francis Baring was urging the claims of his house to handle the Austrian account in London,[63] but when it was a question of a small loan of £150,000 to be transmitted immediately to Vienna he was more reticent. It was not the amount, which was guaranteed by the British government, but the impossibility of ensuring that it would reach its destination; 'they could as soon undertake, that the Enemy shall not cross the Danube'.[64] Canning, the Foreign Secretary, gloomily accepted that Barings must do their best nevertheless. If they failed, then future subsidies to Austria would have to be suspended, 'For I think you will agree with me that there could be no great use in sending money to the Continent to subsidize Buonaparte'.[65]

Sometimes an immense profit seemed possible but had to be rejected on grounds of principle. In 1799 Barings had the opportunity to collect silver in Spanish America and pay dollars to the Spanish government, making a profit of some 80 per cent on the transaction. The risks would be high, wrote Francis Baring, 'But the second objection decided us – namely that it was conveying the treasure from America to Spain for the use of the Government and of course the King's enemies. It is possible we might have obtained a licence as nothing can exceed the ignorance of our Ministers . . . But to have obtained that licence we must have presented a memorial so equivocal and in truth so unfounded that it would not suit us and therefore was abandoned.'[66] The distinction between financing trade of which the British government officially disapproved and giving direct aid to the enemies of Britain might sometimes appear a fine one, but it was very clear to Baring.

In business like the loan to Austria, Barings were in effect acting as the agent of the British government. This was not the first time that they had been approached this way by ministers. In 1803 Vansittart, the Chancellor of the Exchequer, asked Barings whether they could hire ships, clothing and provisions for an expeditionary force under Home Popham of 2000 infantry with supporting cavalry and artillery to capture Buenos Aires. Barings expressed their willingness, but the matter was never followed up. Francis Baring wrote the minister a slightly injured letter· 'I never solicited, nor ever invited, to be employed by Government for the sake of emolument. I can therefore assure you very sincerely that it is a disappointment to me that the service should be performed by another.'[67] In fact the service was not performed by another until Home Popham's expedition to the River Plate finally took place three years later under another government. To add insult to injury, ministers used Baring's supposed reluctance to cooperate as a reason for inaction – 'New evidence of what little, miserable Schemes these people avail themselves, to delay doing what all the world says they ought to do,' wrote the American chargé d'affaires.[68] Ten years later, when the question arose of supplying money for the use of Allied troops in Holland, Vansittart made amends. 'Many houses have already offered their services to me,' he reported, 'but Barings . . . appears to me on every score the most proper channel for our many transactions.'[69]

It was in loans raised by the British government itself that Barings made the greatest profits and benefited most from the confidence

reposed in them by ministers. Between 1793 and 1815 the government borrowed some £770 million at varying rates of interest. Until
1799 the market was dominated by William Boyd, but after he ran
into difficulties early that year Barings took the lead. In twelve out of
the next fifteen years they headed the list of successful contractors
for public loans.[70] Even before his father retired, Alexander Baring
made this line of business his particular responsibility. Profits on the
loans were usually high: £21,000 in 1799 and a spectacular £77,000
from two loans in 1813 yielding a total net profit of £190,000 over
the next seventeen years. But it was not easy money. The public had
to be persuaded to subscribe and this meant that their confidence
both in the government and in Barings must remain unshaken.
When confidence failed, an expensive catastrophe could follow. In
1810 a combination of the death of Sir Francis Baring and the
activities of the Bullion Committee of the House of Commons – a
Whig-dominated body, on which Alexander Baring was prominent,
which urged a substantial reduction of paper money and the
resumption of payments in gold by the Bank of England – caused a
panic in financial circles. The £22.3 million loan, for which Barings
and Abraham Goldsmid were jointly responsible, fell to an 8 per cent
discount.[71] Goldsmid committed suicide and the year ended with a
heavy loss – in the short term at least costing Barings more than
£43,000. When Goldsmid and Baring were described in *The Times* as
'the pillars of the city',[72] Cobbett exploded with indignation. 'A
couple of dealers in funds and paper,' he described them. 'I look
upon the life of Sir Francis Baring or that of Goldsmid as being of no
more, if so much, value to England, as that of any one of your
apprentices or plough boys.'[73]

Francis Baring's association with the East India Company had dwindled as he grew older. In 1792 he was vigorously defending the new
Governor of Bengal, Sir John Shore, against Burke, who claimed that
Shore was too closely involved with Warren Hastings. However that
might be, said Baring, he was 'one of the ablest and most upright Servants of the Company in India'.[74] In 1798 he got the credit for finding the indigent Charles Lamb a place as clerk in the India Office, but
his contribution seems in fact to have been small.[75] When the Court

of the East India Company debated what reward Nelson should receive for destroying Napoleon's fleet at Aboukir Bay, and thus frustrating his designs on India, Baring pointed to the statues of Clive, Lawrence and other worthies and proposed they should 'place the Hero of the Nile by the side of the Heroes of the Ganges'. The Court instead voted Nelson £10,000; a reward which the Hero of the Nile would have felt decidedly more appropriate.[76]

But Baring never supported the expansion of Britain's role in India. When Dundas, speaking of private trade with India, wrote that the Company's monopoly did not 'rest on principles of colonial exclusion', Baring noted in the margin: 'India is not a Colony and God forbid that it ever should be one.'[77] He opposed the majority of the Directors when they wanted to impose severe curbs on American trade with India, arguing that American prosperity would increase the market for British products and that, anyway, India needed the trade.[78] Progressively, he grew more disenchanted with his fellow Directors, and more spasmodic in his attendance. In 1808 he argued that the Christian missions were responsible for the recent mutiny. He was voted down. His colleague Sweny Tone commented: 'Sir Francis has lost much of that consequence with the Court which his superior knowledge, experience and abilities entitle him to, by rarely appearing among them.'[79]

In the House of Commons, too, increasing deafness and disinclination to put himself out led to his playing an ever smaller role. He was still canvassing support with some enthusiasm in 1802 'I must devote the remainder of this week to expressing my gratitude to my constituents through the solid medium of roast beef, plumb pudding and suet,' he told his American friend Rufus King[80] – but it did not go much further than that. His sons Thomas and Alexander were left to carry the family fortunes in the House. Alexander sat for Taunton from 1806. He was always listened to with respect on financial questions but his painstaking fairness of mind did not equip him to be an ideal party politician. Daniel Webster described him as 'a good man to deal with, who could see that there were two sides to a question'.[81] The trouble was that he expounded one side as vigorously as the other: 'He always gave his speech one way and his vote another.'[82] His brother Henry wrote of his 'hesitating Spirit' and told Peel that when he was a boy a phrenologist had said that one side of his head was at war with the other; 'his eyes go one road and his legs another'.[83] It was fortunate for Baring Brothers that Alexander's diffidence was more marked in the House of Commons than in the counting house; in business he was shrewd, and though generally prudent he was capable of striking boldness.

By the end of the Napoleonic wars Barings had by far outdistanced their rivals. The merchant bankers had established themselves as an indispensable instrument by which government could finance its operations and manage them overseas.[84] A crop of new houses had sprung up: N. M. Rothschild and Sons and J. Henry Schroder in 1804; Wm Brandt and Sons in 1805; Antony Gibbs in 1808; Brown, Shipley and Co. in 1810.[85] Of these, Rothschilds at least were providing formidable opposition. Barings were still supreme. Yet the future was uncertain. With the end of the war it was reasonable to suppose that government borrowing would dwindle if not cease and that the merchant banks would be thrust back upon their traditional means of making money. For Barings there could be no doubt that such means were to be found above all in the United States.

4

'The Highest Fame for Respectability'

The United States, 1783–1828

Barings' involvement with America was older than the United States. One of the best markets for the British cloth industry was North America. American exports had to be fostered if they were to be able to pay for what they bought, and in both these traffics Barings were busily engaged. The War of Independence put an end to that and it was not until 1783 that Robert Morris of Philadelphia, one of the new republic's most prominent and successful financiers, wrote on behalf of a group of Philadelphia's leading merchants to urge Barings to enter into correspondence with them.[1] A few months later, Senator William Bingham, a millionaire from Philadelphia whose family as well as financial future were to become entwined with those of Francis Baring, extolled the excellent prospects for commerce with England and offered to settle there as resident Minister. He wrote from London and was already a regular visitor at Baring's house.[2]

Barings welcomed such overtures with enthusiasm. But they were not content with a profitable trading role. The next step in their march to pre-eminence among the 'American' houses – a phrase loosely used to describe houses either American in origin or specializing in American trade – came in 1795. The American Minister in Lisbon, David Humphreys, was negotiating with the Barbary powers of North Africa over the free movement of shipping in the Mediterranean and needed funds with which to satisfy their demands. Francis Baring was sent $800,000 of 6 per cent stock from the United States and told to remit the proceeds to Humphreys in Lisbon: in a

61

way characteristic of treasury officials, the American authorities both stressed the extreme urgency of the transaction and enjoined Baring to sell the stock 'without causing a depression in the prices and thus injuring the credit of American funds'.[3] Various things went wrong – there were difficulties in procuring the necessary silver bullion and still more in delivering it in the right place – and Barings in several cases ran a considerable risk by taking what they believed to be essential action without waiting for authority from Washington. The Treaty could not have been carried into effect, Francis Baring told the American Minister in London, 'if I had not acted with a degree of zeal, perhaps imprudence, in going beyond the letters of my orders'.[4] The stocks sold slowly, and Barings mildly complained: 'Our respect for the United States and zeal for their interest will not permit us to proceed to an instant sale if you shall think it desirable to wait for a reasonable time,' but they were still making considerable sacrifices 'in being deprived of a beneficial arrangement of our funds for many months'.[5] Yet only a month later they put up a further $200,000 to meet Humphreys's urgent needs.[6] Francis Baring could reasonably feel he had served the Americans well, and King wrote to congratulate him on 'the liberal and skilfull manner in which you have assisted Col. Humphreys in a very critical operation. I have written to the Secretary of the Treasury on this Subject and shall communicate to him the assurance that I have given to you of my conviction that the United States will entertain a proper sense of your Services in this Business.'[7]

At much the same time Barings were scouring the market for muskets and cannon to equip the United States for what seemed an imminent war with France. It proved a frustrating commission. One thousand five hundred muskets were shipped on the *Woodrop Sims* and captured by the French; another 2000 were put aboard the *Washington*, which also fell in with a French privateer and had to put back into Lisbon for repairs.[8] In the end some £45,000 was spent and nearly 10,000 muskets and 330 cannon reached America.[9] By the end of the eighteenth century Barings, though not yet appointed agents of the US Government, were established as the British bank to whom the Americans turned when they wanted something done in Europe.

*　　　*　　　*

In 1793 William Bingham headed a syndicate which bought three million acres of Maine lands at a little over 10 cents an acre. The area – about the size of Yorkshire – was a remote and rugged wasteland. Bingham was pledged to establish 2500 settlers on the land by 1803, and would be fined $30 per settler if he failed. It did not take him long to realize that a large part of this bleak empire would have to be disposed of at a profit if financial disaster were to be avoided. A Virginian gentleman, Major William Jackson, was sent to Europe to try to find a market.[10]

Jackson was the very pattern of an estate agent; plausible, enthusiastic and not over-preoccupied with the need for rigorous accuracy. When he compared description with reality, Alexander Baring wrote from New York: 'All Americans that go to Europe to sell lands make up their speeches and character with hypocritical art, and from a general deficiency which certainly exists throughout this country of that nice honour which is not merely contented with being exactly within the pale of the law.'[11] Francis Baring was not wholly taken in by Jackson but he was interested in principle in investment in undeveloped lands in America. It was a curious choice for one who, like every merchant banker, hated to lock up his precious capital in long-term enterprises that would prevent him using it more profitably elsewhere. He must certainly have been strongly encouraged by Hopes, who were anxious to invest as rapidly as possible some part of the money they had brought with them from Holland. Hopes were partners in the enterprise from the start, agreeing to put up three-quarters of whatever was invested.

By April 1795 Jackson had concluded that Barings were the best, if not the only serious prospect among possible purchasers in Britain. He reduced the asking price to 44 cents an acre and urged instant acceptance of the unrepeatable offer, 'the most certain and the most profitable that ever was offered to the public'.[12] Alexander Baring was under-employed, having recently returned from Amsterdam, and his father decided that it would be to everyone's benefit if he now visited America, to look at the Maine lands and to assess the market generally. Nolte – a close associate of Barings over many years – in his memoirs claims that Alexander was given two bits of advice by his father: not to invest in uncultivated lands which 'can be more readily bought than sold again'; and not to bring home an

American wife, 'a wife is best suited to the home in which she was raised, and cannot be formed or trained a second time'.[13] The first piece of advice was obviously never given; and the second, if given, was to be ignored.

By the time Alexander arrived Bingham was growing desperate. If Barings did not buy, he told his partner General Knox, he would be 'in a most cruel and embarrassed situation'.[14] Another partner, General Cobb, was sent to meet Baring 'accidentally' at Boston, and other local worthies were briefed to speak warmly to him of the prospects for Maine. Baring was sufficiently deluded to report that he found the Maine lands 'well thought of, collectively considered', but he was in no hurry to commit himself. He made a point of speaking, and being seen speaking, to people with land to sell in other parts of the United States. In fact he had already made up his mind that the Maine lands would be an excellent investment, that the population would inevitably increase, that the demand for cultivated lands would grow proportionately, and that these factors would put 'the real solid value of the article beyond the reach of almost any events'.[15] Bingham, however, was thoroughly alarmed and reduced his price still further. In the end Baring settled to buy a million acres at 33 cents an acre – he later proudly claimed that he had been ready to pay considerably more.[16] The total cost to Hopes and Barings was £106,875. 'It is, Gentlemen,' he wrote on 26 February 1796, 'with the greatest pleasure I inform you that every circumstance weighed and every object worth attention in this Country considered I have after much discussion and treating closed this important bargain with the most *perfect* confidence of its being a most *lucrative* and *secure* investment.'[17] In fact it proved to be reasonably secure but far from lucrative; when the partners finally extricated themselves from the property fifty years later they got little more than they had originally paid for it.[18]

Alexander liked America. 'This is not a country to afford great Luxuries as enjoyments for a young man,' he wrote with some pomposity to Henry Hope, 'but I am sure he will very shortly perceive that though the curiosities of Rome are not to be found in it, nor the refinements of London and Paris, it offers a curiosity of a larger and more gratifying import, of a rising country, a spectacle the most grateful to a liberal mind and the most instructive, whether considered with the eye of the Philosopher, the Politician or the Merchant.'[19] In June 1797 he proposed to his father that he should stay in America to manage the Maine lands. Later Francis Baring endorsed the letter: 'His object must then have been a marriage with Miss Bingham.'[20]

During the negotiations Alexander had been a regular visitor to William Bingham's home and duly fell in love with the Senator's seventeen-year-old daughter Anne. *The Times* was uncivilly to suggest that this was little more than a business arrangement,[21] but there is no reason to believe the charge. Anne, though by 1844 she was severe and solid,[22] was pretty enough as a girl. Some people in later life found her cold and snobbish, but Alexander's nephew H. B. Mildmay voiced the general opinion when he described her as 'a kind and good woman, thoroughly subordinate to her husband'.[23] However, though the match may not have been made for money, it was financially advantageous. Bingham gave his daughter a marriage settlement of £500 a year and the elegant Powel House on Third Street in Philadelphia.[24] At his death it was said – though probably with some picturesque exaggeration – that his daughter inherited $900,000.[25]

Alexander was not given the management of the Maine lands – a task for which he would have been singularly ill-equipped – but he did remain for a while in America. The purchase of the land was only part of his brief, and from the moment of his arrival he had been on the lookout for new business. His impressions were not entirely favourable. He found the Boston merchants well established and respectable, but unfortunately 'people in general have all some peculiar tye to some house in England'.[26] Connections could be built up, but it would take time. Outside Boston things were still less hopeful:

> The Merchants in this Country are generally speaking a low Class of Man, having all raised themselves from Nothing, the best at this place [Philadelphia] and New York are travelling Clerks to English manufacturing houses . . . The Northern States are always some degrees above their Neighbours in everything and the scale sinks lower as you go South . . . to the south of Baltimore I understand there is nobody worth

trusting. The proper mode of doing business with this Country to most advantage is certainly to give a large Credit to *very*
few, selecting only one or two houses you can depend on in
each place, and then to give the others liberal assistance in
their houses on proper Security which will attract as much as
any one Establishment can wish. The Rage for Speculation is
so great and the ups and downs in fortunes so sudden that it
is necessary to keep up a constant Communication with your
confidential Correspondent.[27]

Despite the hauteur with which he spoke of American merchants,
Baring in fact soon built up excellent relationships with several of the
most important. The Codmans in Boston; Willing and Francis in
Philadelphia; Robert Gilmor and Co. and Robert Oliver and Brothers in Baltimore were all felt worthy of large uncovered credits.
Credit of a year or more was by no means unusual, but the money
was usually safe and the return substantial. Alexander told Charles
Wall that one of Barings' correspondents in Philadelphia was 'the
most barefaced liar and dirty equivocator' he had met in his life,[28]
but he eventually concluded that such scoundrels were few and far
between. By 1798 Alexander Baring's business in America was bringing in a profit of £10,000 a year.

He visited Canada in 1797. Upper Canada, he reported, was
'beyond the reach of any export market and must like Switzerland
subsist from its own resources'. Both it and Lower Canada were 'a
perfect deadweight to Great Britain'. The settlers were without any
kind of patriotism and as soon as self-interest dictated a change of
policy, 'the same scene will be played which we witnessed in these
States [he wrote from Philadelphia] with the only difference that the
Contest will be much shorter'. The only reason for occupying the
Canadas had been to secure the northern frontier of what was now
the United States, 'but since the loss of the latter they are of no service but to the empty vanity of large territorial possessions and to
increase Ministerial patronage at the expense of the Nation'.[29]

He had no such doubts about the future of the United States. 'The
accession of Mr Jefferson may have excited apprehensions,' he wrote
early in 1801, 'but you may depend on it that they are unfounded.'
Jefferson might be personally disposed to favour France if the Euro-

pean war was renewed but the country as a whole did not share this predilection. 'The consequences of a war with England would be fatal to every description of people throughout America. . . . You may rely on it that there is no danger from this side at present unless goaded by increasing aggression of the British ministers.'[30]

One of the reasons for his journey had been to investigate the merits of American stocks. Alexander soon concluded that these were eminently suitable for investment, giving a high yield and offering as much security as anything in Europe. The problem would be to convince the British capitalist that this was the case. The French Revolution, Alexander believed, had persuaded the monied classes that republicanism was synonymous with Jacobinism; to express any sympathy for the United States was to lay oneself open to a charge of condoning violent revolution if not regicide. In fact the British were by no means so hostile to their former colonists as Alexander imagined, but it was not until he saw the names of the Duke of Northumberland and some European princelings on a list of those who held large quantities of American stock that he accepted this might be so.[31]

Cause and effect is as difficult to establish in banking as in any other branch of history. American stocks would undoubtedly have become acceptable in London even though Barings had never supported them. The fact, however, that so powerful and generally respected a house was known to be investing in the United States, both for its friends and on its own account, must have been an important factor in shaping the opinion of the public. Once the first steps had been taken there was no looking back. At the very end of the eighteenth and in the early nineteenth century British investment in US stocks rose rapidly; by 1803 almost half the total $32 million of stock held by foreigners was domiciled in Britain. And Barings were at the heart of the business; from 1799 indeed they acted in conjunction with London merchants, Cazenove and Co., on behalf of the Bank of the United States in paying dividends on all American stock in Britain.

In 1799, too, Alexander Baring was closely associated with a new $5 million loan. He was dismayed by what seemed to him the naïvety of the Treasury in Washington. 'Our Financiers of America as well as our Politicians are quite Novices,' he wrote to his father, 'they know nothing of what Mr Burke called the small ware of either Diplomaticks or finance.' The Secretary of the Treasury borrowed his wants by 'fixing his interest and opening a Great Book for subscriptions without ascertaining by receiving offers the *Minimum* of interest it could be obtained for'.[32] Francis Baring agreed with his son's strictures, quoting with approval Talleyrand's dictum that Americans *'sont des ostrogothes qui ne se connaissent pas en affaires'*.[33] The Secretary, Oliver Wolcott, compounded his folly in Alexander's eyes by his reluctance to entrust the London end of the loan entirely to Barings. 'I positively declined taking any share in such a scramble unless I could be put on higher ground than my competitors,'[34] wrote Baring, with an arrogance that would have been only too easily recognizable by anyone who had dealings with successive generations of the family. His father was wise enough to realize that Wolcott would have to take endless pains to avoid giving the impression of favouring anyone, least of all a foreign banker.

Thomas Willing of the Bank of the United States had been one of Francis Baring's staunchest allies since the early 1790s. Cazenoves had previously been the closest associate of the Bank and were not at all pleased to see their cosy relationship disturbed. In July 1793 Baring wrote to thank Willing for trying to steer all the Bank's business in his direction. 'I flattered myself, however, that our rivals would have been contented with a fair participation to which they solicited us strongly, and as we conceived that their interest would have induced them to conciliate on all occasions with us, we so far yielded as to write to the bank that we should readily concur with them in a joint operation, whenever circumstances would permit.' Cazenoves' response had been to pocket the entire commission on a loan that had been raised in Holland. 'Although we think ourselves equal to any degree of fair competition, yet we know from experience that we have no chance against Men of an intriguing disposition, that I beg to mention to you in perfect confidence the determination of my house not to act in concert with them on any occasion whatsoever.'[35]

Such dire threats are usually soon forgotten, and Barings were associated with Cazenoves only two years later in a new $600,000 issue of certificates.[36] In February 1803, however, Willing, with some help from Rufus King in London, secured Barings the prize they had long coveted – the agency of the government of the United States in

London. When Barings took over the payment of dividends on US government stock, Alexander had argued that in this way they would 'secure a species of monopoly in the direction of American Stocks in Europe and become more obvious for individual operations of Commerce'.[37] The government agency was the logical next step. After the failure of the previous agents Bird, Savage and Bird, Rufus King told Barings, the American government had decided to employ 'an English house of the first Reputation and Solidity' to make the 'large Remittances to the Continent' which were periodically necessary and to keep in funds various US diplomatic missions.[38] The work was often troublesome and the recompense in commission income insignificant, but the prestige was all important. From 1803 no one could doubt that Barings were the leading 'American' house in London.

'I have been so often disappointed about Alex's return,' Francis Baring wrote to Bingham in November 1800. 'His presence is so indispensable to a Man of my Age, infirmities and numerous family, that I must request of you to bind him hand and foot, and put him on board some Ship bound to England.'[39] Baring could only regain his son at the price of Bingham losing his daughter, so it is perhaps not surprising that Alexander was not pressed too vigorously to move. At one time it seems that he contemplated settling permanently in Philadelphia but 'it is by no means a desirable country to live in and will never be so in my days,' he concluded.[40] By mid-1802 it seemed that he was at last on the move, Willing reporting that he was in Philadelphia 'perhaps for the last time',[41] but it was not until February 1804 that he wrote from New York to Albert Gallatin at the Treasury in Washington to thank him for his kindness and assistance. 'Like an itinerant peddler,' he told Gallatin, 'I have been opening my shop.' He had left Washington charged with the placing of the latest loan, had sold $200,000 worth in Baltimore at about par, the same amount in Philadelphia and $100,000 in New York, 'and I find in many instances the first purchasers have resold with a profit'. If he had stayed longer he might have sold more, but there was not much point in doing so if the stock would be at once put back on the market, perhaps in Europe where he hoped to place the rest of the loan himself.[42] Besides, his father-in-law and wife were already in Europe, and the thought of a holiday in Paris was most appealing.

Some time before, Bingham had written from London: 'None of my friends have as yet informed me, what Impression the Cession of Louisiana to France had made on the United States.'[43] The omission is surprising, because little else was being talked of in America at the time. Louisiana had been a French colony until 1763, then was ceded to Spain, only to be restored to its original owner in 1800 by the treaty of Saint-Ildefonse. The Americans disliked having the Spaniards there, but at least could rely on them to remain inert. The thought of a French army installed to their south appalled them. The British obligingly offered to conquer the area and hand it over to the United States after the war. This alarmed the Americans even more. Instead Jefferson sent an emissary to Paris to see if Napoleon might be prepared to sell part of the area. To his surprise he found that the Emperor was happy to dispose of the entire territory. Napoleon needed the money and had no real interest in Louisiana, indeed his main reason for demanding it back from Spain had been to frustrate any similar move from Britain: '*Pour affranchir les peoples de la tyrannie commerciale de l'Angleterre, il faut la contrepoiser par une puissance maritime qui devienne un jour sa rivale: ce sont les Etats-Unis.*'[44]

The United States in 1803 were thus offered the chance of doubling their land space and acquiring the entire Mississippi valley at a single throw. It was an opportunity that could not be missed. 'A little more or less money cannot be an object with a Country circumstanced like ours,' wrote Rufus King, 'especially when it is applied to secure advantages so important.'[45] In fact the price was a bargain – $15 million from which $3.75 million were to be deducted for American claims against France – but the negotiators were still stupefied by the immensity of their undertaking. Someone announced that a pile of 15 million dollar pieces would be three miles high, a calculation of dubious relevance but symptomatic of the disquiet felt in many circles.[46] Where was the money to be found?

The answer was to hand. Alexander Baring had been in Paris throughout the negotiations in an unobtrusive role and, according to his father, was largely responsible for reducing the French demands to so low a figure.[47] Barings and Hopes, it was understood, would underwrite the purchase. Francis Baring, normally imperturbable, was almost overwhelmed by the responsibility his son was incurring. 'I must request that no calculation may be made,' he wrote to Labouchère, 'those sent to Alexander Baring should be burnt, and even this letter after extracting such notes as you may think useful. My nerves are equal to the operation, but not to the imprudences which I see committed to paper. We *all* tremble about the magnitude of the American account.' At the very most Barings might contract for 60 per cent of the whole.[48] But though the risks were great, the potential rewards were still greater. 'I am satisfied if we can manage this business well,' he told his son, 'we shall have frequent occurrence to us in circumstances or events that *must arise* and keep the Ball at our feet for many years to come.'[49] The final agreement was that Barings and Hopes would acquire $11.25 million of 6 per cent American bonds against payment to the French of 52 million francs. The bonds would be handed over in three tranches, and similarly payments to the French would be spread over two years; 6 million francs payable in the first month and 2 million a month thereafter. What in fact happened was that the two banks bought Louisiana from France and resold it to America.

A curious feature of this operation was that, while Britain was still at peace with France, it seemed certain that war would soon be resumed. The money Napoleon obtained through the sale of Louisiana could be used to launch an attack on Britain. Rather belatedly, Francis Baring in June 1803 told the Prime Minister, Henry Addington, what had been done. 'I asked distinctly if he approved the treaty and our conduct. He said that he thought it would have been wise for this country to pay a million sterling for the transfer of Louisiana from France to America, that he saw nothing in our conduct but to approve.'[50] With this ministerial blessing Alexander Baring set off for Washington to settle the last details with the Americans.[51]

By June 1803 the war with France had already been renewed. It was not long before Addington began to wonder whether he could really justify a situation in which a British bank was remitting 2 million francs a month to a country with which Britain was at war. In December he formally requested Barings to cease paying remittances to France. If there were sums of money on the continent which were due to France on this account, 'and you should have the

Means of withdrawing them, or of diverting them into other Channels, I fully rely on your doing so'.[52] Barings dutifully passed this on to Hopes, in a letter that was cautiously phrased, 'from a persuasion that our correspondence is watched'.[53] Hopes' reply was blunt: 'We have no objection to the discontinuance of your Remittances as we shall not want them. But we cannot comply with the rest of your request.'[54] It is hard to believe that this somewhat formal exchange is all that passed between the two houses. Barings must have known that Hopes would continue to pay remittances to the French, and Hopes must have known that Barings would make only a token protest: if the British government expected anything else then they were deluding themselves.

Albert Gallatin estimated the profit which Hopes and Barings made from this business at $3 million.[55] No precise figures exist, but though Gallatin's figure must be too high, there were undoubtedly rich pickings. There was some rancour between the two partners over the division of the spoils. Labouchère claimed that he had originated the operation and that a sixth of the profit was due to Henry Hope in London. Barings denied the claim. 'To put an end to such discussions, which can answer no good purpose,' Francis Baring wrote finally, 'we are compelled to state to you that we claim as "*a Right*" one moiety of the profits as proposed to you by Alexander Baring. We do not ask this as a favor, for we should think meanly of ourselves if we received a single penny as a concession or favor, but we claim it as a strict indisputable right.' He dismissed the argument that Hopes deserved more because of the political risks to which they had been exposed. His own political situation had been far worse; 'what I suffered can never be described and it completely overpowered my nerves for the first and I hope the last time'.[56]

The fact that Barings were the foreign bankers most trusted by the American government did not mean that they were treated as sacrosanct or given the benefit of every doubt. In 1806 the former Vice-President, Aaron Burr, was accused of plotting to dismember the Union and was widely believed to have British backing. Vincent Nolte found himself looked on with suspicion by the commanding general in New Orleans, 'since he had ascertained that the house of Baring, at London, had placed itself in readiness to furnish the funds necessary to secure the success of Burr's conspiracy; and I was well known to be the agent for that firm'.[57] Such rumours were fantastical and easily disproved – nothing would have suited Barings less than the disintegration of the United States – but they illustrated the alarm with which Americans viewed British intentions and also the mounting hostility between the two nations.

Barings were constantly preoccupied by the bad relations between Britain and the United States. The problem was personal – with both Alexander and Henry married to daughters of Senator Bingham, they could hardly contemplate the threat of war without distress – but it was also, and more immediately, a business one. 'American stocks have fallen here in consequence of the alarm generally prevalent of War with this Country,' wrote Alexander to a friend in Philadelphia in October 1807.[58] For a house that dealt so largely in American stocks, that was bad news. In 1807 the risk receded. The following year Alexander argued cogently that the Orders in Council, which sought to curb American trade, should be rescinded. He inveighed against the 'injustice as well as impolicy of ruining one trade to support another', and urged the need to increase trade with the United States by every means. What Britain most needed, he claimed, was an American nation 'politically independent, but commercially as dependent on us as habits and interest can make them'. France had largely succeeded in excluding British trade from Europe, 'but with prudence and skill we might move our island, commercially speaking, out of Europe'.[59]

Baring indignantly denied that he was actuated by anything except the most disinterested and patriotic motives: 'It can hardly be supposed that merchants, naturally more interested in preserving than in acquiring, should be occupied with collecting a few paltry profits from their trade, at the expense of their dearest interest.'[60] His protestations did not convince everyone. In the House of Commons J. Marryat complained that he too had commercial interests and family connections in America but 'these should not induce *him* to forget his great and paramount duty to his country'.[61] Writing of Francis Baring later in the same year *The Times* alleged that he was an American merchant 'whose heart and affections are fixed on that country where the fountainhead of his treasure is'.[62] The jibe was largely unjustified; in the last resort the Barings had no doubt where both their loyalties and their interests lay, but they would do everything they could to prevent that last resort being reached. They were not optimistic. Francis Baring wrote to Rufus King in May 1809 to thank him for the assurance that the Americans did not want war: 'You may entertain the same confidence on our side with regard to the sober-sided part of the nation, and even those of the high ranks in ostensible situation, but the *farceurs* and *intrigants* have always too much to say, and in truth generally rule.'[63]

War came in 1812. Barings took the line that, as British citizens, they would do nothing of which their government would disapprove; but that the war was a temporary aberration and they would never cease to plan beyond its ending. Alexander Baring said frankly that it was his object to help maintain the credit of the United States, and it is an interesting comment on the attitude towards war in the early nineteenth century that ministers felt this to be not merely reasonable but actually desirable. Barings continued to pay interest to holders of American bonds, even though the funds were not available from the United States, and to perform other routine transactions like the liquidation of outstanding converted 6 per cent bonds, but they refused to sell new Federal issues.[64] Their main preoccupation was to support any initiative that might lead to peace. 'A senseless war,' Alexander described it to Gallatin. 'That we wish for a restoration of peace with you need not be argued. Our situation . . . makes it impossible that we should be otherwise than heartily desirous of putting an end to a contest from which we suffer considerably . . . and from which no good can result.'[65]

In July 1813 Gallatin came to Europe as one of a commission nominated to negotiate for peace. The commission went first to St Petersburg, in the mistaken belief that the British would welcome, or at least accept, Russian mediation. Alexander Baring found himself acting as middleman between Gallatin and the Foreign Secretary, Castlereagh. He had to tell his American friend that the British would never accept a Russian role in 'a sort of family quarrel, where foreign interference can only do harm'.[66] Gallatin finally reached London in March 1814. 'I find London very dull in comparison to Paris and St Petersburg,' complained his son James. 'Our position is not a very pleasant one; we have many invitations, and I think all mean to be civil and kind, but there is always a feeling of constraint. . . . The only house where we seem to be really welcome is Mr Baring's.'[67] A year later, when Gallatin finally left, James had evidently had a change of heart. 'All the Barings were so kind. The dinner was delightful and we parted with them with deep regret. I will be glad to get home; after all it is my home and I love it. But I want to come back.'[68] Alexander Baring, said James Gallatin, 'had done more than any other man in England, or perhaps, with one exception, even in America, to hasten the peace, and had, with the knowledge and consent of his own government, rendered very important financial assistance even while the war was going on'.[69]

With so much goodwill working in their favour, immense financial resources and unrivalled connections, Barings should have continued to dominate Anglo-American trade in the decades after the Napoleonic wars. Certainly no one house can be said to have displaced them, but their prominence was not so absolute as at first seemed probable. This was due more to a lack of interest and energy on the part of Barings than to any machinations of their rivals. Things began well. In 1817 John Sergeant came to London on behalf of the Bank of the United States to select as agent for the Bank the house that would 'be of the greatest solidity and integrity and possess, in the highest degree, the confidence of the public'.[70] To no one's surprise, the choice fell on Barings. The distinction may have seemed of questionable value when mismanagement in the Bank led to its being $1.76 million in debt to Barings and other European houses by the middle of 1818 but the problems proved transitory.[71] By the time its greatest, if most erratic President, Nicholas Biddle, took over in 1823, affairs seemed soundly based. The Montagu Norman of his days, he believed that his task was to fuel the growth of the American economy. He scorned the cautious attitude of his predecessor and embarked on a bold, and at times alarmingly expansionist course. Some dismissed him as a playboy but he was in fact supremely professional. He was not belying himself when he wrote:

> I prefer my last letter from Barings or Hope
> To the finest epistles of Pliny and Pope.[72]

Ambitious, autocratic and impetuous, he left his mark strongly upon American banking and, indeed, upon America itself.

His recklessness must have been one factor in Barings' noticeable caution in American affairs. It was anyway a period of transition so far as loans were concerned. Capital was no longer so hard to come by across the Atlantic and the Bank of the United States tended more and more to take responsibility for Federal indebtedness. The amount of British capital invested in American funds, according to S. C. Holland, fell from some £5.7 million in 1805 to £1.3 million in 1818.[73] It was only slowly that the individual states began to emerge as serious borrowers in their own right. When they did so Barings regarded them with marked caution.

New York, whether for banks or State loans, was held to be in a class of its own. In 1823 Barings placed £200,000 Bank of New York stock and found little trouble in doing so. The 'old States north of the Chesapeake' were felt to be almost as sound. But more far-flung regions were a different matter. 'The credit of Virginia is not good, we hardly know why,' Barings wrote in 1825 to Le Roy Bayard of New York, 'and we find with difficulty buyers for some of it which we hold.' They saw no reason for believing that the Stock of Ohio, 'a State the name of which is hardly known in Europe', would appeal any more to the British investor.[74] They were not wholly consistent in their position. Their interest in the cotton trade made them more sympathetic to Louisiana than they would otherwise have been, and in 1829, to finance the Planters' Bank, Barings made a public issue of Louisiana securities, the first to be made payable in London at a fixed rate of exchange.[75] But their attitude was more often that which was shown to one of the most eminent of Philadelphians, General Cadwalader, when in 1824 he tried to involve them in an operation in bank shares: 'In other times,' Barings apologized, 'it might have suited us . . . to have entered into your views, but at the moment, being engaged in large financial operations in France, we do not feel disposed to divest ourselves of our own Capital, by placing it at a distance from us. Indeed, our object always is to have our Capital within reach that we may command it as necessary.'[76]

In the event they relented far enough to buy 4000 US Bank shares on joint account with the General at £25. Their initial caution seemed justified when the economic crisis of 1825–6 sent prices tumbling. By the end of 1825 the theoretical price of the shares was £22. 10s., 'but we doubt whether any buyer would now be found even at a considerable reduction'.[77] Three months later £21 was quoted, again with no takers.[78] It was not until the middle of 1827 that Barings finally extricated themselves, and even then at a loss of 8 shillings a share.[79]

In ordinary trading transactions also, Barings did not expand as vigorously as in 1815 had seemed likely. It was not that the opportunities were not there. Between 1820 and 1830, 36 per cent of American exports went to and 43 per cent of their imports came from Britain; 80 per cent of Lancashire cotton came from the Southern States.[80] Yet Barings did not maintain their market share. In part this reflected increased competition, from the United States as well as Europe; in part it reflected the personalities of the partners. Alexander Baring was bored by the bread-and-butter business of American trade; he concerned himself mainly with the more glamorous European loans or was often absent from his house. Swinton Holland, who was charged mainly with the routine side of the business, knew a lot about American trade but was ultra-conservative, cautious, restrictive in granting credit and singularly graceless in refusing it. He made many enemies in the United States and lost the house much business.

An example was John Jacob Astor. Astor had regularly used Barings to draw on and treated them with considerable confidence, in 1814 sending them $200,000 of government stock to sell or hold as security for bills drawn on them, as they should prefer.[81] It was often convenient to him to leave a large debit in his current account at the end of the year, and since his credit was undoubted, no one had objected. Holland, however, who was by nature inflexible and saw no reason to treat one American house differently from another, wrote to Astor to protest, in terms 'couched in very sharp language'.[82] Astor was not surprisingly displeased, and though his name continued to appear in Barings' American and Colonial Ledgers until 1829, the account dwindled markedly in the last decade.

By 1828, a particularly shrewd observer commented, Barings still enjoyed the 'highest fame for respectability and wealth' in the United States but 'for business it did not stand very high'.[83] The potential for renewed growth was there, but someone was urgently needed to take the task in hand.

5

'Accidental Chances' and 'Lucky Hits'

1815–1828

In the eighteenth century France was the richest country in Europe. The Revolution and twenty-five years or so of almost unbroken war had left its wealth essentially unscathed. Francis Baring had told Voûte in 1801 that France was 'the pivot on which the Commerce of Europe depends',[1] and his son would have seen no reason to revise that opinion in 1815. But there has always been a striking distinction between the prosperity of the French people and their government. The French investor was dubious about lending money to his leaders, never more so than when he surveyed the uncertain future of the restored Bourbons in a country garrisoned by allied troops. When the Duc de Richelieu, Louis XVIII's Prime Minister, found it necessary to raise money to pay the indemnities owing to the victorious allies, he realized that he would have to look abroad. It was not impossible for a French government to obtain money from its own people. The Parisian *haute banque* – the private banks of important standing who operated in rivalry with each other and yet with a common purpose – had raised a substantial sum early in 1816.[2] But something vastly greater was now in question. Few believed that Richelieu would be notably more successful in London or Amsterdam than he would have been in Paris. The country's most eminent financier, Jacques Laffitte, predicted boldly, '*La France ne trouverait pas un petit écu à emprunter sur aucune place de l'Europe.*'[3]

It seems to have been Gabriel-Julien Ouvrard who first approached Barings. Ouvrard had been Napoleon's financial adviser. 'A clever good-for-nothing man,' the future Lord Northbrook

78

described him in 1826, who nevertheless would make 'a very decent figure in history.'[4] In this he underestimated that ingenious Artful Dodger, who enjoyed the resourcefulness and the indestructibility of a Talleyrand or a Fouché. Ouvrard's original idea had been to float a vast issue, large enough to pay off the allies for once and for all, and persuade the allied powers themselves to take over the issue in settlement of their debts. This failed to inspire enthusiasm in London, Berlin or St Petersburg.[5] When the Duke of Wellington, then British Ambassador to France, was staying with him in Paris towards the end of 1816, Ouvrard raised the possibility of persuading Hopes and Barings to find the money. Wellington cautiously approved and Richelieu agreed that it was worth a try.[6] Hastening to London, Ouvrard persuaded Alexander Baring and Labouchère to say that they might be prepared to undertake the operation if the British government approved it. With the French Ambassador he then tackled Castlereagh, who said that he would not merely approve but would strongly support the proposal – *'en se chargeant de cette transaction, qu'ils rendraient un service éminente à l'Europe entière'.*[7] The report of the conversation comes from the French Ambassador; it suggests a change of heart on the part of Castlereagh, who the previous year had been disposed to veto any attempt by France to borrow her way out of her difficulties with British money.[8]

Ouvrard almost over-reached himself. He told Baring that Richelieu and the Minister of Finance, Corvetto, had specifically instructed him to negotiate with the Anglo-Dutch consortium for a loan,[9] and told the French minister that Baring and Labouchère were committed to the deal. Neither statement was wholly true, as quickly transpired when Baring called on Richelieu, but Ouvrard cheerfully admitted that he had strained the truth in the interests of getting negotiations started. Fortunately for him all the principal parties were sufficiently keen on doing business to treat his misrepresentations as established fact. Baring, as it turned out, was keener than Labouchère. At the Tuileries the two were cornered by men who wished to see the negotiations fail and regaled with accounts of France's economic weakness. Labouchère stayed and listened; Baring shrugged his shoulders and moved on. Next day, when negotiations resumed, Labouchère began to go back on what had previously been agreed but *'la franche loyauté de Baring s'y opposa, et il combattait lui-même les arguments de son associé*.[10] Talleyrand, who had his own private fish to fry, was one of those who would have liked to see the talks break down. Louis XVIII told Baring that France was happy to have him in Paris. *'Placer la bonheur de France chez un banquier anglais n'est pas bien noble de la part du souverain du pays,'* wrote Talleyrand bitterly. *'Mais on fait comme cela à present.'*[11]

In December 1816 things had advanced far enough for Wellington in Paris to write formally to Castlereagh. The sum initially in question, he said, was 300 million francs (about £12 million). Of this, £2 million would probably have to be found in London. Baring had originally hoped to get a guarantee from the allied governments, but had quickly been convinced that this was out of the question. There was no law to prevent him going ahead nevertheless, but he had made it clear he would not proceed without at least the tacit blessing of the British government. Wellington felt strongly that this should be forthcoming: 'It is my opinion that unless some arrangement of the description proposed is adopted, France will be aground this year, and our settlement of last year will be entirely destroyed.'[12] Back in London, Baring was confronted by Liverpool, the Prime Minister, as well as Castlereagh and the Chancellor, Vansittart. 'He distinctly intimated that his share and Mr Hope's in the business was to be that of an agency to realise the scrip . . . upon a moderate commission; but they were not to be contractors, or to take the profit or loss of the French stock upon themselves.'[13] He was told that the British government had no objection to his proposals.

In fact Barings were very definitely acting as contractors, and the size of their profit would depend on the price they paid for the stock and the price they got for it. This was shown in February when they tried to force the price of the loan down from the proposed 55 to 52½. Richelieu consulted Wellington and said he would agree if advised by the Ambassador that it was necessary. This Wellington refused to do, 'first, because it is not true; secondly, it would have brought on me and the British government all the odium of this bad financial bargain'.[14] He urged Richelieu to stick out for 55, and it was at this price that the deal was done.

In all Barings raised 315 million francs for the French government in 1817, in three tranches of 100 million, 100 million and 115 million. The issues were an unqualified success; so much so that the

John Baring (1697-1748) by
William Hoare.

Elizabeth Baring (1702-1766) by
Thomas Gainsborough.

Sir Francis Baring (1740-1810) by Benjamin West.

Sir Francis Baring, John Baring (1730-1816) and Charles Wall, the three partners at the end of the eighteenth century, by Thomas Lawrence. The ledger is open at the account of Hope and Co. of Amsterdam.

Alexander Baring (1774-1848), first Lord Ashburton of the second creation, by Thomas Lawrence.

third tranche was brought out at the higher price of 61½ and the French bankers took half the amount instead of the quarter which they had put up for the first two tranches. If there is one thing for which Barings deserved the gratitude of the French government and people, it is that they re-established public credit and restored the morale of the French bankers. Even the stock which was offered for sale in London and Amsterdam largely ended up in Paris; it was French money that paid off the indemnities, but without the catalyst provided by Hopes and Barings it would not have been forthcoming.[15]

Despite his success, Alexander Baring at the end of 1817 was in a cautious mood. 'Too much stock has been emitted and credit thereby overstretched,' he complained to Wellington. The last 115 million had been too much. 'Our sales move very heavily, or rather for a long time we have sold nothing, and I should calculate that there must be in our hands, or in those of other speculators, at least 80 million unliquidated.' British demand seemed to have been satiated. What the French government now called for was one last massive operation to pay off all the foreign claims, but he had no wish to handle the business himself: 'I should much wish to withdraw if I could do so decently . . . but at the same time, after the liberal manner in which I have been treated, and the very profitable operation I have made, I cannot with propriety withdraw as long as I can really be of service.'[16] His disenchantment may have been fanned by the hostility that his operations aroused in some quarters in England: the *Commercial Chronicle* attacked 'the base and wretched avidity of the Monied Interest, which at the prospect of gain, is ready to forget all the claims of patriotism', while *The Times* complained that a moment when industry and agriculture were so depressed was not appropriate for transferring funds to Britain's most dangerous rival.[17]

Wellington did not take Baring's protestations too seriously. 'The fact is,' he told Liverpool a few weeks later, 'that Baring having the French finances in his hands, and French loans being in fashion in England, has to a certain degree the command of the money market of the world. He feels his power, and it is not a very easy task to succeed in counteracting him.'[18] The Rothschilds were at least going to try. With powerful branches in Vienna and Paris as well as London, they considered it monstrous that they had not been involved in the business from the outset. 'You are writing that I should not worry, because these people [Hopes and Barings] cannot take all the world,' James from Paris had written to his cousin Salomon in London at the beginning of March 1817. 'However, you don't know how clever they are.'[19]* A few days later James met Labouchère: 'A nice and intelligent man. I never saw like him. And I assure you they are expert merchants, clever ones, and they do merit the business they get. Unfortunately, they are getting so big that others therefore are dwarfed.' James offered, somewhat optimistically, to take over the whole Barings–Hopes interest, on the grounds that if Barings tried to handle it alone, 'the business world would become frightened and the quotations would fall'. Labouchère replied that some £600,000 was the maximum needed; of this Rothschilds could have £50,000. So far as the 1817 loans were concerned, that was that.[20]

Relations became more embittered when negotiations began for the 1818 loan. In October 1817 rumours began to circulate about a new loan to pay off all the remaining reparations so that the foreign occupation forces could be withdrawn. Baring was alleged to have told Lord Liverpool that the money would be raised exclusively by French bankers. If he made any such statement it was inaccurate. Salomon Rothschild told Nathan from Paris that Barings and Hopes in fact had a 50 per cent interest. 'He is quite a crook, this Baring. . . . We must certainly watch our step as far as he is concerned. The Baring lot is and was well versed in the way of using influence, as we are. There is not a single man of importance among the authorities here who would not work with Baring hand-in-glove . . . Baring and the French Minister of Finance are sharing the profit. The Minister is reported to be one of the most corrupt of all.'[21] Barings' leading ally in Paris was Jacques Laffitte of the bank Perregaux-Laffitte. In a postscript to Salomon's letter, James Rothschild reported that he had just called on Laffitte. 'He gave me his word of honour that we are not going to be left out in the next loan. . . . However, I don't believe a single word of what the Frenchman says.' The following

* Quotations from Rothschild correspondence at this period are usually translations from the Jüdendeutsch made by immigrants whose command of English was less than perfect. Hence the fact that, though the sense is clear, the phraseology is often clumsy.

month Alexander Baring called on Rothschilds and tentatively suggested a deal by which Rothschilds would take a share equal in size
to that of Hopes and Barings.[22] This offer was still supposedly the
basis for negotiations at the end of the year, but Baring was now
expressing doubts about Labouchère's attitude. 'Baring again and
again uses the expression "If my partner agrees . . ." However,
Labouchère, who thinks himself greater than the Messiah himself,
wants to rule alone.'[23]

It may have been a case of Dickens's celebrated couple, Spenlow
and Jorkins, with Labouchère playing the role of the invisible but
allegedly intractable partner, but if conflict really existed, it was
Jorkins/Labouchère who won. As late as 9 February the Duke of
Wellington was giving 'his word of honour that Baring had not yet
got any further in this matter',[24] yet within a few days came a scream
of rage from Paris. 'In Frankfurt one got used to confront anti-
semitism, so one is not astonished,' wrote James Rothschild, 'but
here the case is the contrary, and if something of the kind happens
here one is more amazed.' Baring had assured Laffitte that he had no
objection to working with Rothschilds; now he had changed his
position and said that his associates would not allow him to do business with any Jew. 'It all originates in Labouchère's pride and in
Sillem's envy and greed; as these two *are* Hopes, they think that their
honour would suffer if they would have to get in line with a Frankfurt Jew.' Rothschild poured out his woes to David Parish, the
Anglo-German banker from Hamburg, who told him that it was not
Hopes alone who were recalcitrant. Baring had told him: 'Those gentlemen are working like Jews. How could we co-operate if their principles are different? They are working on 20 transactions at the same
time . . . with the only aim to do business. It is like stock-jobbers.'[25]

The Rothschilds meditated organizing a party in opposition to the
Barings–Hope coalition, but thought better of it. 'Opposition groups
are an abomination,' wrote Salomon. They did not want to make
themselves too unpopular in London. 'This Government gives us
our bread and butter, further, our accounts with this Government
are still open.' There could be unpleasant repercussions if it was said:
'The Rothschilds organized a diversion, the loan fell through, the
troops can't be withdrawn.' Besides, he did not want to make too
pronounced an enemy of Baring, who was a Member of Parliament

and as such could make trouble when the accounts came to be debated.[26]

No papers survive to give the Baring point of view on this imbroglio. Where the letters are to be found in both archives it is usually the case that Rothschild complaints about the duplicity and arrogance of the Barings are matched by equally vehement Baring denunciations of the skulduggery and malevolence of the Rothschilds. Both points of view were sincerely held and no doubt had some justice in them. Whatever the rights and wrongs in 1818, however, the Rothschilds were bitterly aggrieved and the Barings had made dangerous enemies. The Rothschilds did not wreak revenge on this occasion, but they almost had the last laugh.

On 30 May 1818 Barings and Hopes contracted for a loan of 265 million francs. They offered 20 million to Laffitte and only 10 million to Rothschild, to share with David Parish. Laffitte wrote later, '*M. de Rothschild, qui n'était pas encore un si grand personnage, trouva le procédé abominable.*'[27] But he had to accept or get nothing. He was soon to rejoice at his ill-treatment. In view of the success of the previous loans, and no doubt also in consideration of being given exclusive control of this one, Barings, who had originally agreed to take it at 66, with payments in twelve instalments,[28] under pressure raised the price to an optimistic 76. They thus set themselves a formidable task of salesmanship. Simultaneously Lord Liverpool removed any possibility that they might escape from the consequences of their rashness by insisting that the contractors would have to take full responsibility for the payments, if the allied troops were withdrawn before the full amount had been received: 'We could not look with such an object to mere French contractors; . . . the intervention of Baring, Hope etc. is absolutely necessary to give credit to the transaction.'[29] This was no doubt very flattering to Baring, Hope etc., but it was a compliment they could well have done without.

All would have gone well if the public response to the loan had been the same as in 1817. Instead purchases were sluggish and by 8 September the stock was at a discount. The English investors panicked and threw their holdings on to the market. Soon the quoted price was 71 with few takers. Baring appealed to Wellington. To continue to make the scheduled payments to the allies would be ruinous: 'As far as we are concerned we are amply prepared and could . . .

make all our payments without a single further sale, but in collecting our own funds we should produce the same distress as if we were to sell stock.'[30] The Foreign Secretaries of the allied powers were at that moment in Congress at Aix and fortunately for Baring the principals among them – Metternich, Nesselrode and Hardenberg – had all participated personally in the loan and would have lost heavily if the terms had not been amended. It was agreed that the second half of the loan should be cancelled and payment of the rest deferred to 1819.

The Duke of Wellington, who had been instrumental in bringing about this – for Hopes and Barings anyway – happy result, was widely accused of having taken a bribe. The charge caused him little unease. He told Lord Colchester ten years later that he and Castlereagh had saved Barings from absolute ruin, but, he maintained, 'neither Castlereagh or I ever thought that we had done more upon that occasion than our Duty towards our own Country and the World at large'.[31] Certainly the consequences would have been dire for France and Europe if Barings had been forced to default at this crucial moment.

All was well that ended well. The allies got their money, France was relieved of the burden of the occupation, and Barings had no cause to feel themselves inadequately rewarded. 'Mr Baring returned from Paris a few days before me and we shortly afterwards settled the affairs relating to the French loan,' wrote one of the partners in Barings, 'which produced to the House the enormous and unheard of profit of about £720,000 . . . forming as I conceive the most profitable undertaking in which any mercantile House ever engaged.'[32] Nor was their reward only financial. Their reputation stood higher than that of any other banking house. 'There are six great powers in Europe,' said the Duc de Richelieu: 'England, France, Prussia, Austria, Russia and Baring Brothers.'* They could be forgiven for feeling pride; but pride went, if not in this case before a fall, then at least before a slow decline.

---

* This aphorism is frequently quoted but never with a very convincing attribution. The earliest printed citation I have found is in Lady Dorothy Nevill's *My Own Times* (London, 1912, p. 24). But even if it was not said, it should have been.

The problem lay with the men in charge of the house, particularly with the main partner. Alexander Baring had never taken any very keen interest in the bread-and-butter business of commissions and acceptances, and the negotiations for the French loan – during which he had hobnobbed daily with men like Wellington and Richelieu and savoured the delights of being at the centre of the stage – had not disposed him to buckle down to it in future. From 1818 onwards he largely withdrew from the day-to-day management of the bank, devoting his time to travels on the continent, political activities and the demanding grind of establishing himself as a country gentleman on the largest scale.

In 1816 or 1817 Baring bought for £136,620 from his fellow-banker Henry Drummond an estate adjoining his brother's property at Stratton. The house, the Grange, had been entirely remodelled by William Wilkins, architect of the National Gallery, and completed only seven years before. A passable sighting shot for the Parthenon, its relevance to the Hampshire countryside was not immediately apparent: the sun never filtered through its vast Doric portico; the damp and cold, on the other hand, were omnipresent. It had cost Drummond some £30,000 to build and Baring spent as much again trying to make it habitable. The result was never comfortable, still less cosy, but it was indubitably imposing. 'The place is like, not *one*, but a conglomeration of Greek temples,' wrote Jane Carlyle some years later, 'set down in a magnificent wooded park some five miles in length. The inside is magnificent to death – the ceilings all painted in fresco – some dozen public rooms on the ground floor all hung with magnificent paintings and fitted up like rooms in an Arabian night's entertainment – but the finest part of it is the entrance hall and staircases, which presents a view of columns, frescoes and carved wood and Turkey carpet that one might guess a quarter of a mile long!' Alexander Baring himself stated it more modestly. 'Our air is healthy,' he told Rufus King in 1825, 'and you may rely on a warm and comfortable room.'[33]

The 'magnificent paintings' admired by Mrs Carlyle followed the fashion of the time in being predominantly Dutch. Baring seems to have had a sound if not particularly sensitive taste; his collection included good examples of work by Rembrandt, Hals and Cuyp. In 1826 he bought Lord Radstock's pictures, including an undoubted

Titian of Herod's daughter for 1800 guineas and a somewhat less certainly attributed Giorgione – 'the latter a charming picture' – for 700.[34] He was well known as being ready to pay high prices for what he wanted. Sheridan, short of money as usual, planned to sell his pictures, which contained two Gainsboroughs and two by the then much-sought-after Morland. 'The Good you can do me,' he told Samuel Whitbread, 'is to speak to some fair men like Baring or Angerstein etc. etc. who will deal liberally that I may not be forced to take half their value for them.'[35]

It was not until the next generation that the Grange became a centre for the *haut ton* of the intelligentsia, but Alexander Baring entertained lavishly. The results were not always applauded. Emily Eden confessed that she found 'the Barings rather failures – I mean as to agreeableness. It will be some time before Mr Baring fails in the moneyed sense of the word: but I see you, in fact, think of the Grange just as I do – charming place and family, but a dull visit.'[36] But others were less censorious or perhaps less sophisticated: the Gallatins 'had a delightful Christmas with the Barings, who are hospitality itself. There are Barings of all shapes and colours, all sizes – tall ones, short ones, lean ones, fat ones, but all are so nice and cheerful; they seem indeed a united family. We played all sorts of silly games and became children again.'[37]

Nothing was spared to make the estate the non-pareil of stately residences. Colonel Peter Hawker, who devoted his life almost exclusively to the destruction of miscellaneous fauna, grumbled in 1826: 'The whole county was, and is now for ever likely to be, ruined by the presence of Mr Alexander Baring, of the Grange Park, who feeds and monopolizes, merely to ornament his water and tickle his fancy, half the fowl in Hampshire. I drove there expressly to see his collection, and I am confident I saw not less than 8000 fowl on the water before his house.'[38] But it was in the acquisition of land that Baring's presence was most felt. He was resolved to match if not surpass the territorial conquests of his brother. In 1818 he bought Abbotstone and Itchen Stoke from Lord Bolton for £64,200 to swell the Grange estate. This would be, he wrote, 'the last of my follies in the way of land purchases. . . . I pay very fully, but the property is very essential to me, and I am therefore a very willing purchaser.'[39] Far from being the last, it was a mere apéritif. In 1824 he acquired the

Brown and Chilton Candover estates from Sir Thomas Freeman
Heathcote for £85,000; in 1835 the Itchen Abbas estate was added.
And these were just the more conspicuous transactions. 'The Barings
are now the great men in Hampshire,' wrote Cobbett in 1822. 'The
small gentry are all gone, nearly to a man, and the small farmers along
with them. The Barings alone have, I should think, swallowed up
thirty or forty of these small gentry without perceiving it. They,
indeed, swallow up the biggest race of all, but innumerable small fry
slip down unperceived, like caplins down the throats of the sharks,
while these latter *feel* only the codfish.'[40] Mallet noted in 1825: 'Alexander Baring has invested nearly a million sterling in land; probably
the largest purchase ever made by any one individual.'[41] Mallet exaggerated, but Baring paid high prices for the land he bought and at his
death his estates were estimated to be worth about £800,000. Even as
late as 1843 he was acquiring a property of 160 acres belonging to a
Mr Brittingham on the grounds that 'it is the only speck of alien
property in five adjoining parishes'.[42]

   Cobbett accused him of being a notably inefficient landlord, far
worse than his brother Thomas. His trees were covered with moss
and dying at the top. 'Everything that has been done here is to the
injury of the estate, and discovers a most shocking want of taste in
the proprietor.'[43] Certainly he did not devote as much attention to
his estates as did Sir Thomas Baring. When in England he was more
often to be found in London. In 1821 he rebuilt the Pulteneys' old
Bath House at 82 Piccadilly in the most sumptuous style: 'the
Palazzo di Piccadilly', Swinton Holland called it, and Cobbett more
unkindly 'Scrip Castle'. Even before that his parties were among the
best in London. 'Think of the pineapples and strawberries and ices
and temporary rooms and magnificent hangings and beautiful flowers at Mrs Baring's,' wrote Emily Eden enviously. 'I wish I was a rich
old banker, but then I would not have, or *own*, so many fellow creatures as the Barings do.'[44] He loved to do everything in the grandest
possible style, with generosity as well as flamboyance. He could
sometimes be impulsive, but there was usually calculation somewhere behind it. He was apt to say that there were two things he particularly disliked, 'an abolitionist and a saint', yet he did not allow
these prejudices to deter him when young Henry Thornton, who
was both, appealed for a loan so that he could start a business.

Instead 'he very carelessly offered him £200,000 to begin with'.[45] It was a splendid gesture – but he knew that Thornton had plenty of money behind him and a shrewd business head as well.

Of the 31 millionaire merchant bankers who died between 1809 and 1939, 24 were Jewish and only 4 were Anglicans.[46] As a gentile and a member of the Church of England, Baring was therefore in a minority, a fact which could generally be turned to his advantage but sometimes led to his being excluded from business in which he could profitably have taken a share. As a gentile, too, a range of distractions was open to him from which his Jewish rivals were excluded. In the eyes of the Rothschilds the fact that several Barings were members of the House of Commons was an unfair advantage which gave them the chance to pull strings, secure confidential information and pervert policy to their own ends. To some extent – though less than the Rothschilds supposed – it was all those things, but it was also an unconscionable distraction. If Alexander Baring had passed in the counting house the time he spent in the House of Commons, or gossiping about politics in the clubs, then Baring Brothers would have benefited greatly by his increased attention. Whether they would have gained more than they lost is an open question; given Baring's personality, probably not, but the balance was by no means so heavily tipped in his favour as the Rothschilds imagined.

For most of his political career Baring remained a Whig, sufficiently prominent to be numbered among the grandees of the party who met at Brooks's in February 1821 to discuss the possibility of making some financial provision for the beleaguered Queen.[47] Though not an orator, his obvious honesty, independence of mind and determination to seek the truth won the respect of the House. In 1826 a Mr Alexander Robertson claimed to find something sinister in the fact that the grant by the President of the Board of Trade of a licence to incorporate a silk company in which Baring had invested £200 was shortly followed by Baring proposing an increase in the President's salary. Robert Peel replied that if Robertson was suggesting that Baring 'on account of the miserable profits which he might realize from a venture of £200 was induced deliberately to propose an increase of the salary of his right hon. friend, he would only look for the answer to so unfounded an imputation, in the smile which sat upon every face from the moment it was uttered'.[48] Even if the sum had been £20,000 the feeling of the House would have been the same.

On his chosen subjects he could be an effective debater, specializing in a line of bloodcurdling gloom. 'You have no conception with what attention Baring was heard in a full house last night,' Fremantle told Buckingham, 'when for an hour or so he described the commercial state of England in the most lamentable terms.'[49] In partnership with Brougham he was instrumental in organizing the unexpected defeat of the Government over the income tax. He was particularly disturbed by the 'inquisitorial' nature of the tax: 'He would much rather be summoned before the bench of bishops to be questioned about his belief in the doctrinal points of religion than appear before the commissioners under the property tax.'[50] His belief in the right of a businessman to do what he wanted with his own money made him an impenitent opponent of any legislative interference with the slave trade. In a debate in 1828 he argued that the misfortunes of the slaves were much exaggerated by ill-informed meddlers; they were in reality well fed and housed and generally treated with justice and kindness, living in conditions 'in many respects superior to that of most of the peasantry of Europe'. He appealed for moderation, causing the abolitionist Fowell Buxton to protest that his speech was 'the most immoderate, intemperate, violent and exasperating that ever I heard in my life'.[51] Though a Whig, Baring could never have been called liberal. 'He pretends to be a great Whig, but he is just as bad as any of the Tories,' wrote Cobbett indignantly.[52]

Alexander Baring's eldest son, William Bingham, did not follow his father into the House of Commons. Shy and maladroit, he did not do justice to his in fact considerable intellectual powers and interests, 'Giving an impression of mental weakness and even moral inferiority,' wrote Lord Houghton.[53] There was never any question of his going into the bank; not for want of aptitude, but because it was considered no place for an elder son. The same was true in most banking houses. 'It will not be necessary that my Grandson, who is likely to be Heir to the Estate, should be brought up to the Banking Concern,' wrote Sir Richard Glyn to his son. 'His Fortune will I trust be ample and sufficient to give him consequence in life and in the Country.' Possible professions for such a favourite of fortune were deemed to be 'the Guards or the Law and Parliament'.[54] No Baring was ashamed of his association with the counting house, but equally it was not something of which he talked too much in polite society. When William married Lady Harriet Montagu, daughter of the Earl of Sandwich, he was left in no doubt that he was being done a singular honour. His father made a settlement of £25,000 and a jointure for the bride of £3000 a year, while his mother – an American as well as a banker's wife – was treated with much disdain: 'I am told that at her son's marriage she was not invited to the déjeuner,' wrote one generally reliable observer. 'Certainly Lady Harriet, who was the most perfect example of insolent ill-breeding I ever saw, treated the poor old lady in her own home with great coolness if not impertinence.'[55] Lady Holland described Mrs Baring dining with the Sandwiches and looking 'quite mortified and wretched' while Lady Harriet brushed aside her future husband's views on travel: 'He is but a boy just out of College. What can he know or what can he like?' Lady Harriet was just seventeen.[56]

It was Alexander's second son, Francis, who was destined in his father's eyes to take over Baring Brothers. He seemed eminently well equipped for the role. 'Bountiful nature,' wrote Nolte, 'had endowed this man . . . with so lavish a hand, that it might almost be termed spendthrift profusion.' He was intelligent, quick, perceptive, with a phenomenal memory and 'iron strength of will'.[57] It was not until he took off on his own and involved the House in some disastrous speculations in Spanish America that his volatility and lack of judgement became evident. He was an attractive figure, and always his father's favourite, but he never played an important role in the Bank again.

Only after Francis's career foundered was Alexander forced to consider the possibility of taking his brother's sons into the business. Like Alexander, Sir Thomas felt no wish to involve his eldest son in commerce, but his second and third sons, Thomas and John, were a different matter. Whether from doubts about their capacity or a wish to keep the plums for his own children, Alexander was at first reluctant to fall in with his brother's plans. John was dispatched to Hope and Co., where Labouchère described him as being 'steady, assiduous and of an obliging disposition'. He would continue to encourage him, 'and the docility with which he follows our advice will render it an easy and grateful task'.[58] He sounds a dull dog. 'As sensible and as sedate a young man as I have ever known at his age,' Alexander

Baring described his nephew when he visited the United States in 1825. Francis had been there a short while before. 'The last visitor of our name was perhaps rather more shewy, but I think this one will please better in your country where the steady and sedate is more praised than the volatile.'[59]

In 1817 Sir Thomas suggested that Thomas should join Baring Brothers. Alexander was still cautious. He would like to help 'if it can be done in a manner consistent with the interests and safety of the establishment'. Tom too had better learn the job at Hopes. After he had been there for some years, the time might be ripe for considering his future in Barings. 'When the time for decision arrives it will be made with a strict reference to merits. If I had a boy of my own to hand his case would be exactly the same and so far I can assure you that my anxiety for yours will be quite as great.' The essential thing was that the partnership should work as a team: 'Ill-assorted partnerships can produce no good results, and not only all the essential qualities of character and temper are requisite, but every partner must be able to contribute to the general stock of execution and usefulness.'[60]

Alexander seems to have been playing for time, hoping that if the matter was postponed for long enough his nephew would become inextricably involved elsewhere. He was disappointed. In 1825 Sir Thomas returned to the attack. Tom was now a partner in Hopes but the future for that House looked gloomy, while John had no immediate prospects. Sir Thomas proposed that John at least should now join Baring Brothers. He was rebuffed. He wrote to his sons in dismay about 'the unexpected determination of your Uncle to exclude him [John] from the London House, of which I shall say no more than that it was a great disappointment to my expectations'. Partly, one suspects, to induce his brother to change his mind, he now proposed advancing £40,000 with which his sons could start a 'House of Trade' in London. 'It might be in some respects objectionable to your Uncle that another House of the same name should be formed in England, yet I am well persuaded that his opinion of you and his affection for me will induce him to take an interest in your welfare and probably to assist you.'[61] If he really entertained so sanguine a hope, he was soon disillusioned; Alexander made it clear he would neither help this new enterprise nor take his nephews into the Bank.

Sir Thomas told his sons 'it was the wish at the Grange to fix Tom permanently at Amsterdam and to find an opening for John at Hamburg or some other place upon the continent, and thus to exile you both from your Country and family'.[62] Tom soldiered on at Hopes, John went to the United States where in 1826 he set up in business with a Boston merchant called Joshua Bates. But for the blighting of Francis's rosy prospects, they might well have stayed there all their lives.

Pending Alexander's change of heart, Baring Brothers drifted on with the somewhat shoddy personnel that was left to man it. In 1824 Alexander had given a partnership to Humphrey Mildmay, husband of his eldest daughter Anne. Mildmay had been a Captain in the Coldstream Guards. He was prudent, diligent, and considered fit to be a Director of the Bank of England, but he had no experience of mercantile matters and never overcame his extreme timidity in making decisions involving large sums of money. He was quite unfit to run the Bank. Most of the work was done by Swinton Holland. Holland was a Liverpool merchant who had done business in many parts of the world and established a reputation for diligence and rocklike probity. In December 1814 he noted in his diary, a document rich in sanctimonious prosing: 'This day is a remarkable event in my life as promising an increased degree of prosperity . . . Mr Baring of the house of Baring Brothers and Co. of London, perhaps at this day the first mercantile house in the world, made me a proposition to become a general partner in their concern: giving me one sixth share of the whole business after the next 30 June . . . Omnipotent Ruler of the Universe, may I be grateful to thee, for this mark of thy goodness in elevating my situation in Life.'[63]

Holland brought £30,000 with him, and on the whole served Barings well. If Alexander had been there to temper his pettifogging inflexibility and inject a little imagination and vision, his undoubted skills might have been properly used. 'Industry, application and commonplace talents I can promise . . . but I do not feel I have any extraordinary talents,' Holland wrote on taking up his new work. He was right. He was no leader and the house suffered because he was forced to act as one. In June 1823 Henry Baring retired and a new partnership was formed, with Alexander holding a half share and Holland and Francis Baring a quarter each. The introduction of

Mildmay did something to relieve the pressure on Holland, but by 1826, with Alexander out of touch and Francis in disgrace, it was clear reinforcements were urgently needed.

It was not only the personnel of Barings which was weak; the house was starved of capital as well. Holland, like Alexander Baring, fancied himself as a landowner, acquiring an estate from Lord Somers for £80,000[64] and another eighteen months later for £66,000. Both Alexander and he could afford the purchases, but they still needed to withdraw large sums of money from the business, which otherwise would have been available for profitable investment. The capital of the house, which amounted to £622,000 in 1821, fell to little more than a third of that in 1823, and though it recovered, it was never at this period at the proper level to support the international loans on which Alexander Baring wished to concentrate. Rothschilds, with their greater resources and branches all over Europe, were better placed to secure new business abroad, while the British government largely stopped borrowing once the war was over.

It was a sign of the times that it was James de Rothschild who in 1824 called together his London cousins, Barings and Laffitte, when the French Prime Minister, Villèle, put forward a scheme for converting the French debt. Public response was unpredictable and the preliminary negotiations were conducted in great secrecy. Old animosities were forgotten, or at least temporarily buried. James de Rothschild urged Alexander Baring to come to stay in his house on the outskirts of Paris for discussions with the minister,[65] while Baring assured Villèle: *'J'ai la conviction que je pourrai toujours agir avec M. de Rothschild de Londres dans une parfaite intelligence.'*[66] Rothschild and Laffitte had perhaps something less than perfect confidence in Barings' intentions, in that they put a clause in the contract stipulating that they would manage the affair themselves if Barings dropped out. In the event the project foundered when it was not ratified by the Senate, but it was an alarming affair while it lasted. At one moment Barings found themselves in advance to Rothschilds by some £625,000. 'I must candidly confess that I have not nerve for his operations,' Holland told Baring. 'They are generally well planned, great cleverness and adroitness in execution – but he is in money and funds what Bonaparte was in war, and if any sudden shake comes, he will fall to the ground like the other. I really wish we were out of his clutches.'[67]

Collaboration, even abortive, was the exception rather than the rule. In 1818 Barings, in collaboration with Hopes and Bethmanns, raised some £3 million for the Austrian government. Rothschilds were offered financial participation but no share in the management of the loan. 'These people behave with incredible pride,' complained James de Rothschild. 'I was yesterday speaking to Bethmann at the Minister of Police's when Labouchère came and took him from my side without even a "good evening". Baring is giving a big ball tomorrow and Laffitte asked me whether we could talk over the French loan on this occasion. Well, Baring didn't even invite me.'[68] From Berlin, Carl was more philosophic. 'Pro primo, we are Jews; pro secundo, we are not born millionaires; pro tertio, we are fighting Baring. Why should he be so great a friend?'[69]

Russia was another battleground. Traditionally Hopes and Barings had enjoyed a monopoly of Russian bonds, with the Dutch house taking the larger share. The loans of 1817 and 1818 were organized on this basis, with less than a quarter of the bonds sold in London. Yet in 1822 a loan for £6.5 million was brought out by Rothschilds – only, believed Sillem of Hopes, because they had suborned the Russian Ambassador in London, Prince Lieven.[70] To Barings' gratification, the issue was a failure with much stock left unsold.

Foreign loans were risky work, and though the rewards could be great, they were at the best erratic. Swinton Holland stated his view of the problem when reviewing the excellent results for 1820/21:

> These profits do not arise from any merit of mine, but rather from accidental chances, lucky hits in Stocks foreign as well as domestic. The Stocks for Public securities of all countries . . . are a dangerous commodity to deal in, by those who do not understand them, and the wisest . . . are often deceived with regard to them: probably in ordinary times they depend more on the scarcity or abundance of money in the market, than on any other circumstance. . . . Looking around London in the present day we find that the most prosperous are

those who had to do with Loans and Stocks of different
Countries. This is the advantage of dealing in Stocks, to all
other *commodities*, if you purchase what you have money to
pay for and they afterwards fall, by holding on, if the security
is good, you are always receiving some capital, in lieu of your
invested capital.[71]

Francis Baring for one would not have found much consolation in
this last consideration. He believed that nothing was more unfortunate for a merchant banker than to see his capital indefinitely locked
up, and few lock-ups were so intractable as an unsaleable foreign
stock. Nor was Holland's certainty that at least there would always
be a regular income coming in borne out by events; it was to be only a
few years before the apparition of countries defaulting on their
foreign debts arose to haunt the sleep of the less wary merchant
banker.

By 1825 Rothschilds, when it came to international loans, were
unequivocally the most powerful house in Europe. At this period the
capital of the London house alone was £1.14 million, against
£490,000 for Barings;[72] the capital of all the branches of the
Rothschild empire put together was probably over £5 million. In
part at least because of the default of Alexander Baring, Nathan
Rothschild had become the leading figure – '*maintenant sans conteste
le commerçant le plus entreprenant d'ici*,' the Prussian Ambassador,
Humboldt, described him. '*C'est aussi un homme sûr, avec qui le
gouvernement anglais traite beaucoup d'affaires.*'[73] It was indeed to
Rothschild that the British government was becoming accustomed
to turn in need; '*L'intérêt du ministère anglais pour M. Rothschild est
bien vif,*' reported the French Ambassador.

Nor was Barings even wholly secure in second place. In 1818
Byron asked:

> Who holds the balance of the world? Who reign
>   O'er congress, whether royalist or liberal?
> Who rouse the shirtless patriots of Spain
>   (That make old Europe's journals squeak and gibber all)?
> Who keep the world both old and new, in pain
>   Or pleasure? Who make politics run glibber all?

The shade of Buonaparte's double daring?
Jew Rothschild and his fellow, Christian Baring.[74] *

If Byron had written *Don Juan* a few years later and had known his facts, he would have had to consider substituting Brown, Shipley for Barings (though for reasons of rhyme and scansion if no other he would certainly not have done so). Barings were still ahead on most counts but Brown, Shipley, blood brothers to the Baltimore, New York and Boston firm of Brown Brothers, were uncomfortably close behind. Their capital was already £350,000 and growing at a faster rate than Barings'.[75]

In fact an unadventurous approach to foreign lending was no bad thing in the 1820s. In 1819 Alexander Baring had declared that never before had so much money been withdrawn from enterprise at home to invest in foreign funds: 'There was a general *sauve qui peut* among monied men.'[76] The speculation mania of the next few years was by no means confined to foreign funds. Over 200 new joint-stock companies were approved by parliament, ranging from highly respectable railways to a Cemetery Company which promised 'to combine the beauties of the celebrated Cimetière du Père Lachaise with perfect security for the dead'.[77] But it was the foreign loans that the investor found most alluring; Latin America in particular, with loans to among others Chile, Colombia, Brazil, Buenos Aires, Mexico and, especially bizarre, a little loan of £200,000 to the republic of Poyais, which was supposed to exist somewhere in Honduras but appeared in the works of no cartographer.[78] Peacock's Sir Flimsy Kite extolled the beauties of his bank's holdings:

> Good bills a monstrous lot, sir;
> And Spanish bonds a store, sir;
> And Mining Shares still more, sir;
> Columbian scrip and Chilian;
> And Poyais half a million:
> And what will make you sleek, sir,
> Fine pickings from the Greek, sir.[79]

* The usual reading is 'fellow-Christian Baring'. This would only make sense if one assumed that Byron thought (1) the Barings were Jews and (2) the Rothschilds tried to pass themselves off as Christians. The first is unlikely, the second absurd. Surely Byron meant that, Jew or Christian, bankers were equally powerful (and, no doubt, equally odious)?

The cautious Barings eschewed such exotic delights and had cause to congratulate themselves when the financial crisis of 1825 crippled international trade and caused almost every borrower in Latin America to default on his payments of interest. To quote Peacock again, the British people belatedly discovered 'That paper is not metal, and promises of payment are neither food nor raiment'.[80] In December 1825 it was even feared that the Bank of England might fail. One Saturday night it closed with only a few thousand pounds of gold left in its vaults and applied to the Government for an Order in Council to suspend cash payments. An emergency meeting of Liverpool, the Chancellor Huskisson, the Governor of the Bank and Alexander Baring agreed to postpone this disastrous measure and the Bank was saved; chiefly, Baring told Greville, 'by the accidental discovery of a box of one-pound Bank of England notes, to the amount of a million and a half, which had never been issued, and which the public were content to receive'.[81]

Barings did not emerge unscathed. In October 1825 Alexander reported to Francis: 'There is considerable distress and difficulty about money. . . . An extensive Cotton Speculation failing has upset Liverpool, Manchester, and by a contre coup the United States. The bubble has also burst of all joint stock companies and loans. . . . All houses lose because all houses have their joint capital in something and everything has fallen in value. We are caught with Consols and French 3 per cents and must lose considerably. Nolte is completely wrecked, fortunately we are likely to be paid and lose nothing by him. This however is the only piece of good luck and this year cannot fail to be largely a losing one.'[82]

It was. In July 1825 Barings had divided profit of £120,000; a year later it was a loss of £56,000. In fact things were less disastrous; substantial sums were transferred from Profit and Loss to meet estimated losses on French stock which turned out to be smaller than expected. It was a bad business, though, and exposed brutally how dependent Barings had become on their profit from foreign loans. The economic stagnation that followed the Napoleonic wars had been gradually relieved, but Barings had not taken their proportionate share of the reviving trade. In 1824 Holland surveyed the scale of their business with some satisfaction but observed 'its profits are derived more from loans to foreign Governments [and] the rise in

English Stock, than from mercantile operations'.[83] Between 1813 and 1817 accepting and commission income had averaged a little over £50,000 a year, between 1818 and 1822 it fell to £35,000 and between 1823 and 1827 to £26,000. In 1827/28 the figure was a pitiful £20,672 and capital was only £310,000, of which much was locked up in more-or-less worthless stock. Barings' reputation in the world still stood high: the Comte de Bertrand, secluded in Elba with the Emperor Napoleon, gave them *carte blanche* to do whatever they thought best with his property;[84] they found themselves responsible for procuring four small enamelled gold watches from Mr Pybus of Old Compton Street at a price of £220 for the Emperor of China.[85] But serious business was in short supply. Something needed to be done, and when, on 17 December 1827, Swinton Holland died at his desk, it was clear that it would have to be done immediately. Before describing what came next, however, it is necessary to go back in time and consider what was going on in a part of the world which was to bulk large in the history of Barings – Latin America and, in particular, Argentina

6

'Magnificent in Promise'

Latin America to 1848

Barings had been interested in a small way in Latin America since almost the time that they involved themselves in international trading, but any idea that they should play a more prominent role in this remote and alien continent was far from their minds before the end of the Napoleonic wars. In 1807 the *Southern Star*, first English-language paper on the River Plate, announced that there would shortly arrive 'an accredited Agent from the House of Baring and Co. . . . It will be a great accommodation to the inhabitants of this country, through the medium of this house, to place their money in safety in Spain, Portugal, China, the East Indies, or indeed in any part of the world, without any possible risk.'[1] The news was premature, the inhabitants would have to wait some time yet for such a facility.

The recession that afflicted Europe after 1815 and the end of the Spanish and Portuguese empires kindled a new interest in Latin America. By 1817 Brougham was declaring in the House of Commons: 'There can be no field of enterprise so magnificent in promise, so well calculated to raise sanguine hopes, so congenial to the most generous sympathies, so consistent with the best and the highest interests of England, as the vast continent of South America.'[2] Professor Platt has ably demonstrated how very limited that magnificent promise in fact was.[3] Barings were intrigued enough to commission a report on the trade of the River Plate from the British firm of John Parish Robertson,[4] but they remained cautious about the prospects of the area as a whole. For this they earned the abuse of Disraeli, who had himself put money he could ill afford into Mexican mining shares and was most upset when Alexander Baring decried the investment, supporting his criticism of the security

100

offered, said Disraeli, 'by statements which are so utterly unfounded that they might make mendacity blush and so awfully ridiculous that they might make folly grave'.[5]

But Barings were not averse in principle to investment in Latin America. In 1820 they offered to subscribe £10,000 to a Chilean loan, only to see the project disavowed by the Senate in Santiago.[6] The following year they almost contracted for a small loan to Colombia, but backed out when their agent was discovered to be both a gunrunner and dead. The Colombian government negotiated a second loan elsewhere.[7] They saw no reason to lament the loss of these two pieces of business, yet they had an uneasy suspicion that they were missing the bus. They felt this particularly about the River Plate, to which area the British exported more than £1 million worth of goods in 1824 alone.[8] If the right opportunity offered, Barings would grasp it.

An opportunity soon offered. In 1822 Congress authorized the raising of a loan of £1 million to build a port at Buenos Aires, provide running water for the capital and finance frontier settlements. The loan was to pay interest of 6 per cent and the minimum price was 70 – that is to say £100 worth of stock would be offered to the public for £70, plus whatever commission was taken by the middleman. The government would receive £700,000 against a debt of £1 million and would in effect be paying 8.7 per cent interest on the money. The authorities in Buenos Aires might not seem to have made a particularly good bargain, and even at the time there was criticism of the terms, but if they had tried to raise the money at home they would have had to pay considerably more, perhaps even twice as much.

By the time William Parish Robertson and various Argentine associates finally contracted to take the loan early in 1824 the purposes to which the money was to be applied had been modified but the terms remained the same. The Minister of Finance in Buenos Aires had urged them to involve Barings in the transaction if they possibly could, since nothing would help more to establish the country's credit. Robertson spared no pains to bring this about. He assured Barings that the business was absolutely safe: 'In resources, in Government stability, in every regard Buenos Ayres holds a different rank from the other Independent States.' For him it was potentially a most lucrative deal. The consortium took the loan at 70, they believed they could sell it to the British public at 90; the £200,000 difference less expenses and whatever they had to allow to Barings would be theirs to pocket. Barings for their part could hope to do well, though not so well, taking a fee of £30,000 to cover expenses, and a 1 per cent commission on the stock they sold.[9]

Hopes were disappointed. Barings dismissed the idea of floating the loan at 90 as absurd, but against their better judgement offered the bonds at 85. This would have given the investor a 7.05 per cent return on a stock emanating from a country about which he knew little or nothing. Speculators briefly kept the price at a premium but they soon cut their losses and threw their stock on the market. Barings bought much of it back in an effort to keep up the price, but their exertions meant that they had an uncomfortably large amount of capital locked up in virtually unsaleable bonds. By October Robertson was regretting 'that you are under the necessity of considering the Buenos Ayres Loan as a failure'. The government and the contractors, he assured Holland, 'feel themselves under peculiar obligation to your House for the decided and most liberal support of the Loan'.[10] On the whole Argentine historians have supported his view. 'The name of Alexander Baring,' concluded the first serious study of the loan from the Argentine point of view, '. . . is worthy to figure among the loyal servants of our country.'[11]

Not everyone has been so kind. Revisionist historians have presented Barings as unscrupulous adventurers who took an unfair advantage of the inexperienced Argentines and made monstrous profits at their expense. The 1824 loan, according to this thesis, was just the first of a long series of misfeasances, by which Argentine industry was crippled to serve the needs of British exporters, and its workers exploited to enrich British capitalists.[12] A second line of attack, somewhat more moderate, while not acquitting Barings altogether of sharp practice, suggested that the main blame must be borne by Argentine politicians who were certainly inept and probably corrupt as well.[13] The assumptions common to both sets of historians are that Barings made a fat profit out of the loan and that the Argentine government received only a small part of what it was entitled to expect.

Neither contention is correct. The decision to buy in the bonds when they went to a discount may be attributed to self-interest or chivalry according to taste, but it certainly ensured that Barings lost money on the deal. If anyone made money it was the original contractors. As for the amount received by the Argentine government, they contracted for £700,000 and that is what was paid to them. The Argentine dictator Juan Manuel Rosas contended that the money had not been needed and had been squandered shamefully, but he never denied that it had been received.[14] Seven hundred thousand pounds was perhaps not an over-generous amount to receive against a debt of £1 million, but the reception the loan received in the British market showed that it was a realistic approximation to what people were prepared to pay.

The investors' scepticism was soon proved justified. Things went merrily for two or three years, Robertson reporting from Buenos Aires in 1825: 'Nothing can be more satisfying than to observe the rapid strides which the Country makes in every branch of public and domestic economy.'[15] But war with Brazil changed all that, draining the National Bank and making the currency almost worthless. Buenos Aires 'has been gradually sinking into a state of Poverty and Disorganization, from which it will require many years for her to emerge,' Robertson wrote gloomily at the end of 1827.[16] The hero of the Liberation, San Martín himself, provided an ironic commentary on the prospects for his continent. He came to London with money to invest and called at Bishopsgate to seek advice. Barings offered him a tempting range of Latin American stocks, including the 1824 Argentine loan, which was now at so much of a discount as to be yielding a return of nearly 9 per cent. He rejected them all in favour of British 3 per cent Consols.[17] He was proved right in January 1828 when the Argentine government defaulted on its interest payments. For Barings this was the most painful of the many shocks they had suffered in the previous two years.

They had already had a nasty fright in Mexico. Apart from Brazil, Mexico, with its long-established and profitable export of silver, was economically the strongest country in Latin America. Barings were interested in the possibilities of increased trade and perhaps even some investment. In 1825 Francis Baring, Alexander's second son, was sent out on a fact-finding mission.

His first reactions were of dismay. 'This country is a desert,' he told

Humphrey Mildmay. He urgently requested six boxes of Seidlitz powders and 'a stoutish hunting crop with bronze handle, the dogs are wolves, and one's legs are always in danger'. The country could be prosperous if properly run, but 'I do not see any material in this country out of which they could form a good set of ministers, and even were such treasures to be found, there is not public spirit or intelligence sufficient to support them in their measures'. Mexico would go on borrowing so long as England would lend, 'and they will end up by a complete break up or bankruptcy'.[18]

What happened next is hard to establish with any exactness, but it effectively ended his career in banking. He found the climate oppressive, took to drink, and was still further borne down by a shooting accident, in which he contrived to kill an English friend, Augustus Waldegrave.[19] Then he fell among thieves, in particular one Robert Staples who had previously been British Consul in Mexico City. Egged on by these new acquaintances, he concluded that Mexico was the country of the future – 'When I was in Mexico,' he wrote long afterwards, 'I believed – God help me! in Mexican stability.'[20] He began to invest largely in mining shares and miscellaneous bonds. His crowning folly came when he bought for 800,000 pesos (about £160,000) 9 million acres of the Parral estate in northern Mexico from the creditors of the Marqués de San Miguel de Aguallo.[21] 'I mention for the information of the gentlemen of your house,' he wrote proudly to Le Roy Bayard in New York, '. . . that I have lately made an extensive purchase of land here in conjunction with Mr Staples's house, and that I have great confidence in the soundness of the operation.'[22]

His confidence was not shared by his partners in London. He had committed Baring Brothers to pay 25 per cent of the purchase price immediately and this obligation was duly honoured, but enough was enough. Alexander Baring wrote in outrage to his errant son:

> Our position with respect to your operation is the most perplexing possible. After repeated readings of your letter I cannot make out what you have been doing. . . . If you have been buying a large tract of land, with herds of oxen, sheep and all the appendages of farming, I have only to say that however the world may consider your bargain, I have no

doubt that it would prove ruinous to you if for your own account, and that for *us* it is totally unsuited. We are a house of *trade*, and have no business with any adventure of the kind, to say nothing of one out of all proportion to the extent of our capital. . . . You may conceive the surprise and uneasiness which your letters and projects have created, and being quite unable to reconcile them to my opinion of your conduct and judgment, I live in hope that I have not properly understood you, and that on further reflection you will have been able to back out, and remit your money home in safe bills *before you leave Mexico*. . . .

Mr Holland and I have work'd hard for our fortunes and do not wish to risk them. Humphrey, just beginning to get on his legs, cannot afford such risk, and I know pretty well what your position requires. . . . One of your bad qualities, my dear Francis, and I do not attribute many to you, is that you are a bad taker of advice, but if, on this occasion, I administer mine rather harshly, it is because I have no time for circumlocution and because you are entitled to have from me my unequivocal sentiments. At all events, what I must insist on is, that if you have made any landed or mining adventure for us to the extent of £40 or 50,000, you do not leave the country until you have placed it in good hands and that you in any case come straight to me.[23]

There was no escape for Barings from the portfolio of dubious investments with which Francis had endowed them, but from the contract to buy the Parral estate at least they were able to extricate themselves with no more than the loss of their original £40,000. Nationalist sentiment in Mexico had always been hostile to the ownership of land by foreigners, and it did not take more than lobbying and a few small but judiciously apportioned bribes to contrive that the Chamber of Deputies passed a bill retrospectively forbidding foreigners to buy country property. How far Baring Brothers in London were aware of the activities of their agents and friends in Mexico City in bringing about this happy conclusion is an open question. Formally they were acquitted. In 1844 Staples and Co. brought an action against them, claiming that Barings' agents had been acting on the instructions of their principals in London and that Staples and others of Barings' partners in Mexico had been grievously injured as a result of these machinations. Lord Denman summed up in favour of Barings and the jury acquitted them.[24]

Not everyone was convinced, however. 'Did you see that cause of Lord Ashburton's [as Alexander Baring had by then become] where he was indicted for a conspiracy to bribe the Mexican Government?' asked Sydney Smith. 'The letters directing his agents to do so, and mentioning what each man was worth were read in open Court, and the fact was not denied. The Jury found him not guilty, but it was a narrow escape, for the Jury were out of court for an hour and a half.'[25] Baring's partner, Joshua Bates, not surprisingly saw things a little differently. The only reason the verdict took so long to reach was because 'one ignorant man' was put in to fill the place of one of the Special Jury. 'It was the most abominable suit that ever was undertaken, and that by a man whose bills the old House held for £160,000 for which they never could get sixpence. It sickens one of human nature.'[26] On the whole the evidence suggests that the partners in London were ignorant of the skulduggery being practised by their associates in Mexico; that they would tacitly have condoned it seems probable at least; that tactics quite as questionable were practised by the other parties to the dispute is likeliest of all.

This was an unhappy start to Barings' relationship with Mexico, but it did not alter their opinion that the country had much to offer. In 1826 the agents of the Mexican government in London, Barclay, Herring Richardson and Co., were one of the many firms that foundered in the crisis. Barings took on the agency, servicing the country's external debt and accepting responsibility for payments to the Mexican legations in Europe. It proved an expensive and time-consuming business. Time and again Barings found themselves having to make payments before they had received funds from Mexico City, and sometimes the delays were embarrassingly protracted. The sums involved were not enormous, but the uncertainty, with the consequent need to tie up funds unprofitably, was a constant irritant. 'We are sorry that your caution not to trust the Government came rather too late,' they wrote in 1832 to their correspondents in Mexico City, 'for we had unfortunately by advancing the deficiency for the Dividends and the monthly payments to the Legation,

already allowed it to become our debtor to a very large amount.'
They would make no further payments to the legations until matters
had been put in order.[27]

A few years later they had had enough. The Mexican economy was
in total disarray and it was clear that the government would only
with the greatest difficulty be able to maintain the interest payments
on its external debt. When Lizardi and Co., a Mexican house which
had recently opened up in London, offered to take on the agency,
Barings did nothing to defend their position. They had by this time
disposed of part of the government stock which Francis had so
improvidently secured but quite enough remained to provide an
unappealing souvenir of their involvement with Mexico. Even without the long-drawn-out unpleasantness over the Parral estate,
Barings had little reason to view their association with Argentina and
Mexico with satisfaction. Not until they took on the agency for the
Chilean government in 1844 did they again play an important part in
the part of the world with which they were thenceforward to be so
intimately concerned.

By then some progress was at last being made in Argentina. From the
time of the Argentine default in 1828 Barings had been preoccupied
by the need to secure a settlement which would give partial satisfaction at least to the people who had invested on their recommendation. Though Barings had originally retained part of the 1824 loan
for its own account, and had bought back more to protect the price,
the bulk was still owned by private investors in Britain and on the
continent. So far, so good, but no merchant banker who wished to
survive as a leading house could afford to ignore the woes of the
bondholders who had bought stock from them. If a loan backed by
Barings ended in such abject failure, who would trust their judgement in the future? Self-interest as well as a sense of honour dictated
that they should do all they could to ensure a speedy resumption of
payments and compensation for the loss of interest during the
period of default.

Not much help was to be expected from the British government.
Canning had defined the official position towards investment overseas when the Colombian government had defaulted in 1823. He

refused to make a resumption of payments a precondition for diplomatic recognition. Not only would he not send a gunboat to manifest British displeasure, he declined to allow British diplomats and consular agents to bring pressure on the defaulters. If British investors chose to risk their money overseas, then it was their own funeral if they lost it.[28] Lord Aberdeen was somewhat less austere in his approach, but though he would allow his diplomats to give such help as they could and to make sympathetic noises, there was still no question of official intervention. Not until 1847 did Palmerston suggest in the House of Commons that in certain circumstances it would be permissible for Britain to take action in defence of its holders of foreign bonds.[29]

Barings were on their own. Their strongest card was that the Argentine government wanted a settlement, since until one was reached there would be no hope of returning to the European money markets. But good intentions alone availed little, and Argentine politics were in such turmoil that successive Ministers of Finance were quite unable to do anything in practice. It was not until the end of 1829, when Juan Manuel Rosas was elected Governor and Captain General of the Province of Buenos Aires, that some hope of stability returned. Woodbine Parish, the British chargé d'affaires, praised Rosas's 'modesty and moderation', and predicted that his regime would last.[30] On the second point he was right – Rosas's rule continued for 21 years; but neither modesty nor moderation was ever a conspicuous attribute of the dictator.

Rosas was more concerned with paying his army and domestic creditors than with satisfying foreign investors, but he was enough of a realist to stress in his first message to the Assembly that it was 'necessary to recover our credit jeopardized abroad'. It was some time, however, before he could do much about it, since virtual civil war continued in parts of the country and drought aggravated his already crippling problems.[31] In 1828 the Minister of Finance had tentatively suggested that an easy way to settle the debt would be for them to hand over a couple of unwanted frigates in final settlement.[32] Barings had dismissed the idea out of hand, but when Rosas took power he cast around for something else which might satisfy the British investor without involving a drain on Argentina's currency. It took him eighteen months to concentrate on the matter but at the end of 1831 his Finance Minister, Manuel García, approached Parish with the proposal that repayment should be made in the form of land in Patagonia. 'The fine and healthy Climate of these Countries is known in Europe to everyone of ordinary information,' he told Parish.[33] The notorious fact that no Argentine citizen was prepared to brave the rigours of that bleak, southern outpost did not dispose Barings to look kindly at what would anyway have been a far-fetched expedient. 'The holders of Buenos Ayres securities,' wrote Francis Baring coldly, 'are principally among a class of persons little inclined by habits or experience to adventures of this kind.'[34] Barings continued to deplore the duplicity and incompetence of the Argentine government: 'We are unable to meet the charge against the good faith of Buenos Ayres with any defence which would appear to justify it in the eyes of its creditors,' they complained to their new representatives, Zimmerman, Frazier and Co. 'If the Buenos Ayres government wishes to be put by the sides of those other civilized countries, she must lose no time in removing the blot which has for so long tarnished her credit.'[35]

For a decade or so little was heard except the grumbling of the British bondholders. Not everyone despaired. In 1832 a Miss E. Caton wrote eagerly: 'I have an *inspiration* about Buenos Ayres bonds and must have some, even though I have to part with some of my Spanish bonds.' Barings do not seem to have tried to dissuade her, but the inspiration soon faded. Some three years later she was writing: 'If I can get out of the Buenos Ayres bonds without loss I should like to do it.'[36] She at least had bought at a considerable discount; for those who had taken up the original offer, the chances of getting their money back seemed slim indeed. Their indignation did not diminish with time. At the end of 1842 the bondholders were planning a protest meeting: 'They naturally think it very hard that, while Chile and Mexico have provided for their public debt and several other South American states are making efforts to do so, Buenos Ayres should do nothing.'[37]

The increasing turbulence of the bondholders and modestly encouraging signals from Buenos Aires convinced Barings that they must at least appear to be taking action. In April 1842 an intelligent, young Spanish speaker, Francis Falconnet, was dispatched to reopen negotiations. No miracles were expected. It was too much to hope that the government would at once resume full payment of interest. 'The first thing you must do is to make up your mind by all the information you can get, how much they can pay annually and then make your arrangements accordingly.'[38]

Falconnet's initial report was gloomy and his second gloomier still. There was a war in progress over Uruguay and the condition of the country's economy was as chaotic as ever: 'It is almost impossible to give you an idea of the wretched state in which matters stand here, both in a moral and physical point of view.'[39] He was modestly encouraged by an interview with Rosas. The dictator said bluntly that he thought the loan had been useless and expensive but that he was nevertheless anxious to satisfy the bondholders as soon as possible.[40] But the method that he proposed early in 1843 was quite as unpromising as any that had been advanced before. The Argentine Minister in London, Rosas told Falconnet, had 'been authorized to propose the absolute cession of the Malvina Islands to the English Government on condition it should take charge of the Loan'. Falconnet expressed 'surprise and disappointment' but asked that the proposal should be put into writing, and this was duly done a few days later.[41]

Barings were no less surprised and disappointed than their representative. The Falkland Islands seemed no more appropriate in settlement of the debt than two frigates or part of Patagonia. Besides, as the British government was quick to point out, there was nothing to cede; Argentina had no claim to the Falkland Islands, which were British territory. This contention Rosas, not surprisingly, did not accept; he 'expected a just compensation from the English Government for the entire cession of their rights of Sovereignty, upon which they partly relied to enable them to settle the claims of the Bondholders'.[42] It is interesting to speculate how different the history of the last few years might have been if the British government had taken over the loan as Rosas asked and thereby gained title to the Falkland Islands unquestioned even by the Argentines.

This was not Rosas's last word, however. Under a Convention of 1840 the Argentine government was bound to set aside 5000 silver dollars a month in settlement of certain French claims. These claims would be met in full by April 1844. Falconnet suggested that the payments should then be transferred to the bondholders. Rather to his surprise, Rosas agreed. Falconnet was jubilant. The payments would only amount to some £12,000 a year, as opposed to the £60,000 which was properly owing, but they were still a start and they reaffirmed the existence of the debt and the acceptance of responsibility by the Argentine government. 'However limited is this first step towards a final arrangement,' wrote Falconnet, 'I have the conscience that nothing else could be obtained for the present . . . and great credit must be given to the Governor for what he has done.'[43]

Even this first step proved precarious. After the payments had been continuing for little over a year, an Anglo-French fleet, for reasons which were presumably clear to Lord Aberdeen at the time but now seem singularly obscure, blockaded Buenos Aires.[44] One immediate result was that the bondholders once more lost any interest on the loan. Like most British businessmen, Joshua Bates of Barings was outraged by this intervention. 'The Buenos Aires affair is one of the most infamous interference and the most stupid in my opinion,' he wrote to T. W. Ward, the house's agent in Boston. 'It is much the same as if the United States had sent a fleet to Vera Cruz and had seized all the Mexican ships and said, "You shall make peace with Texas. Commerce suffers by your contest . . . therefore we will stop all Commerce." '[45] Barings protested to the Foreign Office and in the end the British element in the fleet was withdrawn and the blockade broke up, having achieved little. It was not until January 1859 that payments were resumed. This time it was for good, however. It was the beginning of a new and vastly important chapter in the history of Barings' involvement with Argentina and the rest of Latin America.

7

Baring and Bates

1827–1847

With Holland dead at the end of 1827, Alexander Baring taking ever less interest in the bank and Francis discredited, it was clear that Baring Brothers needed reinforcement, not only at the top but in the middle echelons as well.

Alexander was still in charge, but he was disenchanted with routine and resentful of the fact that Holland's death forced him to spend more time than he liked in the partners' room. He was rich enough to live in style on his estates without bothering about his income from the bank and his main interest was now in the world of public affairs. In 1830 he retired. T. W. Ward wrote in alarm: 'I do not think it would be advisable for Mr Baring to leave at a time when the eyes of the World are on the House as the sheet anchor of mercantile safety and confidence.' In the United States everyone would be asking how much money had been withdrawn and whether the house could now meet its commitments.[1] Joshua Bates, one of the two new men brought in to take over Baring Brothers, scoffed at such fears: 'For my part, I cannot say I regret it,' he said of his senior partner's retirement. There was plenty of talent left, and capital too. 'Besides, it is ridiculous to have a partner who has long since given up all connexions with mercantile men. The Americans who come over – some of them – expect that Mr Alexander Baring will shew them some attention, and they go back dissatisfied if he does not. . . . If in losing Mr Baring we lose the advantage of his individual respectability and great wealth as a security for the funds placed in our hands, we are called on to use double diligence and endeavour to acquire that fame for ourselves that he has so justly attained.'[2] Six months later Bates concluded that time had proved him right: 'As the wheel moves round this seems to be now forgotten; and as your House is not a common House, it is not to be measured by common rules – and I have no doubt that the judgment, character and talent which conducts its operations will give it a standing even higher than it has yet attained.'[3]

It was freely surmised that Baring's retirement from banking was the step on the road to the peerage he sought so earnestly. 'He has money and lands and Parliamentary influence enough to procure anything he may desire,' Bates told Ward.[4] Only his everyday association with commerce seemed a bar.

> Bob Smith lives here,
> Billy Pitt made him a peer,
> And he took the pen from behind his ear,

ran the jingle when Pitt ennobled Robert Smith as Lord Carrington in 1797.[5] Now Baring's pen had been taken from behind his ear as well. For him to become a peer would still have been something freakish. He would only have been the second banking creation, and no industrialist or heir to an industrial fortune was to become a lord for twenty years.[6] But the possibility, even the probability, existed.

That Baring wanted a peerage seems evident. He had already married his son into the aristocracy, and in 1830 engineered a match for his daughter Harriet with Lord Henry Thynne, future Marquess of Bath. It cost him £50,000, as against the £10,000 his son-in-law put into the marriage pool, but he felt the money well spent.[7] 'As the Barings want connection and he wants money, it was a natural marriage for all the world to insist upon,' commented Emily Eden.[8] Yet if a title was indeed his primary objective, he behaved with remarkable independence of mind. All his political life he had been a Whig; then when the Whigs were at last in office, and he might hope to reap the rewards of loyalty, he defected to the Tories.

His waning enthusiasm for the Whig cause had long been apparent. His conservatism was notorious. In July 1830 he had done his best to restrain his colleagues from an all-out onslaught on the wilting Tories[9] and he inveighed publicly against the perils of mob rule.[10] 'Such a finished blockhead as the great Baring is, I never witnessed,' complained O'Connell.[11] He was somewhat offended when offered no job by Grey in the Whig administration and still more put out when he asked that his son should be made a Lord of the Treasury and instead saw the job given to his nephew Francis, Sir Thomas Baring's eldest son. 'I suspect he would have lost no time acting like Lord Carnarvon,' wrote Brougham's secretary, Denis le Marchant, referring to a recent Whig renegade, 'had not the hopes of a coronet kept him with his party.'[12]

But not even the certainty of a coronet could have stifled his growing doubts about the Whig Reform Bill. The measure, he told the House of Commons, amounted 'as much to a new Constitution as if it had been drawn from the pigeon holes of Abbé Sieyès'. He objected to the Bill's 'democratic tendency'. The Commons were made all-powerful, the influence of the aristocracy swept away. 'He should be as sorry as any man to see the lower classes, even the lowest classes, of this country, without considerable influence in that House,' but enough was enough. What he wanted was 'liberty for all'.[13]

The Duke of Wellington believed that Alexander's change of heart – 'See-saw Baring' he was nicknamed henceforth – would herald the move of the rest of the clan to the Tory ranks. In this he was over-optimistic. The new minister, Francis Baring; his father, Sir Thomas; Henry Labouchère; Charles Baring-Wall (the only son of Charles Wall by Sir Francis's daughter, Harriet); and even Alexander's elder son, William Bingham Baring: all voted for the Reform Bill – 'as I believe will in truth my uncle,' wrote Francis Baring, 'and consequently Francis [Alexander's second son, and the villain of Mexico]'.[14] He was mistaken; Alexander remained loyal in his disloyalty, but for the moment at least the other Barings stayed in the Whig ranks. Alexander was said to have been indignant with his two sons for not following his example and to have tried to turn them out of their seats, but if displeasure there was it can only have been fleeting. Alexander's relationship with his sons remained amicable and William, anyway, soon rallied to Peel. There can be no doubt that Alexander's defection was made on principle and against his personal interests. Nevertheless, there were to be times in the next decades when it was advantageous to the Barings to have a foot in both political camps.

It was anyway far from certain that Alexander would have gained his longed-for peerage even though he had stayed with the Whigs.

Grey was notoriously fastidious about opening the delights of the House of Lords to those who had sprung from outside the ranks of the aristocracy, or, at the worst, the country gentry. According to Creevey he at one time seriously considered offering a peerage to Sir Thomas Baring as a reward for his loyalty and 'as an additional mortification' to his brother.[15] The rumour was heard by Disraeli, who had high hopes of inheriting Sir Thomas's seat at Wycombe.[16] When it came to the point, however, Grey was deterred by the fact that Thomas had sons. To turn a banker into a lord might – just – be acceptable if the title died with him, but to create a dynasty was another matter. As it turned out, Alexander's change of loyalty was in the long run to serve him well. For the moment, however, his only reward was to have his windows smashed by the mob, which at least put him in the distinguished company of the Duke of Wellington.

The association was not confined to broken windows. In May 1832 Baring was a key figure in the Duke's misguided effort to form a Tory administration which would pass a measure of reform. He at first refused to serve as Chancellor of the Exchequer, 'on account of the state of his health', according to Bates,[17] but in fact because he felt the Duke was opposed in principle to even the modest measure of reform which he himself felt desirable.[18] Soon he changed his mind, agreeing to serve if the Speaker, Manners-Sutton, would take the lead. His decision was felt by some to be of crucial importance – 'The Whigs say we are landed if we get Baring,' wrote Lord Ellenborough hopefully[19] – but in fact this belated effort by the Tories to take over and themselves pass a Reform Bill was greeted with fury by a rampant House of Commons. Baring spoke four times in the debate and in the end was personally responsible for proposing that the Whig ministers should resume office.[20] 'I would face a thousand devils rather than such a House of Commons,' he told the Duke.[21]

He remained on reasonable terms with his former colleagues, if only because so many of them were his relations. 'I have a favour to ask,' Sydney Smith wrote to Alexander's wife in July 1834 when the death of Lord Althorp's father meant that a new Chancellor had to be found from the House of Commons. 'Could you lend our side such a thing as a Chancellor of the Exchequer? . . . We will take great care of him, and return him so improved you will hardly know him.'[22] In fact Althorp's resignation led to the downfall of the Whigs and Robert Peel's brief Tory administration. Baring agreed to serve as President of the Board of Trade and was alarmed when he found that he was also being referred to as Treasurer of the Navy – 'This Treasurership is of all inflictions that which I should most lament.'[23] Disraeli states Baring took the job on the promise that he would be given a peerage:[24] it is unlikely that the bargain was struck in so many words, but when Peel resigned after only a few months Baring got his reward in the dissolution honours. He called himself Lord Ashburton, reviving the now defunct title of his uncle by marriage, John Dunning. He got his title, commented *The Times* unkindly, 'since no human being can assign a valid reason why he should not have been made a lord'.[25]

In the House of Lords, Ashburton discarded the last shackles of his former liberalism and spoke invariably as champion of capitalism incarnate. When Lord Ashley tried to introduce a bill limiting working hours, Ashburton commented that he had no idea whether a ten-, eleven- or twelve-hour working day was most desirable, 'but I should be sorry to incur the responsibility of any restrictions at all. . . . The most mischievous men of our day are our conceited political economists and our ultra-humanitarians, good men some of them, but theirs is a description of cant just suited to the capacities of the majority of our electoral body.'[26] One of his speeches stung Lord Clarendon to almost hysterical rage: 'There was no exploded fallacy, no stupid prejudice, no reference to selfish interests, which this faithful representative of his own breeches pocket did not hash up together in language mainly characterized by spite against those whom he supposed to be meddling with his interests.' He compounded his offence in Clarendon's eyes when he referred to 'the bloated mass of commercial prosperity' which existed in Britain. 'He! Lord Ashburton! whose £40,000 a year was made by commerce – whose connexions are all in trade.'[27]

In 1839, and again in 1841, Ashburton forestalled any plan Peel might have had for offering him another place in government by insisting in advance that he did not want one. 'The truth is that my work is done and my lease of life too near its natural close to undertake efficient occupation.'[28] He did, however, hold out for a job for his son William Bingham; 'The Vice Presidency of the Board of

Trade would suit and satisfy him.' This vacancy was booked for Gladstone, wrote Peel apologetically, but the Board of Control (of Indian affairs) was 'of equal importance'.[29] The Board of Control it was.

At the end of 1841 Lord Aberdeen persuaded Ashburton that his work was not done and despatched him on a special mission to solve the boundary disputes still outstanding between Britain and the United States. He was, Aberdeen told Queen Victoria, one of the few eminent Englishmen who would be acceptable to the Americans.[30] Some thought he was too acceptable. 'There is much of popular objection to him from his American connections and his supposed strong American interests,' wrote Lord Melbourne. 'He is supposed to possess much funded property in that country, and to have almost as strong an interest in its welfare as in that of Great Britain.'[31] The settlement he brought back certainly gave away more than ardent British patriots thought proper, but Melbourne spoke for the more moderate opposition when he concluded that nothing of real importance was lost and 'any settlement is better than none'.[32] Ashburton himself felt the government did not do enough to show that they approved the terms he had secured. He told Peel he should be made an earl. Peel countered with the offer of a viscountcy and the Order of the Bath. 'Probably many would prefer the more flashy distinction of a Star and Ribbon,' wrote Ashburton, 'but I feel so strongly that this does not suit me, and that the decoration would attach a certain degree of ridicule to me, that I hope I shall lose nothing of your good opinion of me if I adhere to my first impression of the case.'[33] Peel maintained that an earldom for Ashburton would suggest 'undue exultation on the part of this country,' and lead the Americans to question the justice of the settlement.[34] It was an ingenious argument, but it did not convince his correspondent; the exchange ended with Ashburton embittered and still a baron.

The men were reconciled at the end of 1844 when Ashburton played with the idea of rejoining the Cabinet, but fell out in 1846 over Peel's commitment to Free Trade. Ashburton agreed, he told Peel, with all previous relaxation of protection, 'but to the entire removal of all protection from domestic industry I have an insuperable objection'.[35] His son, William Bingham, did not agree – 'he is a devoted disciple of the School of Doctrinaires, and everything called

Free Trade has with him irresistible attraction' – but he felt he should nevertheless resign in solidarity with his father.[36] Peel replied that Bingham's resignation would be absurd; as to the point at issue Ashburton was 'the practical founder of the School of Free Trade. The Doctrinaires could have done nothing without your help and the help of men in your position. It was your hand that shook the fabric of Prohibition and of Protection.'[37] There was no shortage of unkind critics who saw a link between Ashburton's conversion to protection and his acquisition of vast agricultural estates.

Bingham did not resign but his political career never prospered. He retired with some relief after his father's death and devoted himself to more congenial pursuits, such as being a Trustee of the National Gallery and President of the Royal Asiatic Society. His nearest approach to fame came in 1830 when he confronted a group of riotous rustics, who were apparently bent on burning down the Grange. One of them, a ploughboy aged nineteen called Henry Cook, hit him on the head with a hammer and was later hanged for his pains. 'It was worse than treason to knock off the hat of a Baring,' commented Cobbett bitterly,[38] but in fairness to British justice an eyewitness recorded that Cook had knocked his victim down and was on the point of finishing him off when bystanders intervened.[39] There was much agricultural disorder in 1830 and the Baring lands were in the thick of it. At neighbouring Stratton, Francis Baring found his father Sir Thomas policing the neighbourhood 'at the head of tag, rag and bobtail, looking all very gallant with laurel leaves in their hats – many of them the very fellows who had broken his machinery – so laid hold of one to my father's utter astonishment'.[40]

After his uncle Alexander's defection, Francis Baring became the family's most prominent representative among the Whigs. 'A morose and rigid millionaire,' Greville described him;[41] 'very rigid and severe in his principles' was Sir James Graham's verdict,[42] and though many disliked him, no one questioned his total reliability. 'A thoroughly honest man, and an able public servant,' Melbourne called him to Queen Victoria.[43] His cautious attitude towards reform – 'I consider all organic change an evil,' he told a constituent[44] – would certainly have commended him to Lord Melbourne, and in 1839 he was offered the Exchequer. 'I told him that I did not wish it,' Francis Baring told his father, but Sir Thomas persuaded him to take a more robust view, and in the end he accepted.[45]

He did not have an easy time. 'We have everything excepting a revenue and a majority,' he wrote gloomily in his journal.[46] There is nothing in his papers, or in those of Baring Brothers, to suggest that while he was Chancellor he had any close dealings with his uncle, brothers or cousins at the bank. Equally, they must often have been in each other's company, both in London and in the country. They had no need to put anything on paper. Matters must from time to time have been discussed which bore on the affairs of the house, and it would be surprising if Baring Brothers never gleaned information of interest and value from such conversations. So, no doubt, did the Exchequer. What does seem supremely unlikely, given the awesome rectitude of Francis Baring, was that any disclosures were improperly made or any unfair advantage given to his kinsmen. The Rothschilds would never have believed it, and their scepticism is wholly pardonable, but though Francis and Thomas Baring were affectionate brothers, the Chancellor and the banker treated each other with cautious restraint.

Francis Baring never considered that his own son Thomas, heir to a great fortune and a baronetcy at least, should go into the bank. 'Your position is fixed,' he told him, 'that of an English country gentleman, and it will be your business "to do your duty in that station of life to which it has pleased God to call you".' Ideally, he felt, that duty should take his son into public life, but 'a quieter life' could also be useful. Banking might be good enough for his cousins, or his uncles Thomas and John, but not for an elder son.[47]

Of the older generation, Alexander's son Francis remained as a partner after 1830; technically, indeed, the senior partner. The distinction meant little; his record hardly induced his associates to trust him very far. His career in politics was as undistinguished as in banking; once, when he introduced a bill about New Zealand in the House of Commons, he lost his audience so rapidly that soon not even a quorum was left.[48] In 1833 he married Hortense, daughter of the Duke of Bassano, and henceforth spent the winters and springs at his house in the Place Vendôme in Paris. He treated his position in the bank with some levity, once replying to an urgent letter: 'The senior partner in the first house in the first city was at Chantilly races when your letter arrived . . . it will be clear to you that I can assume no responsibility in the matter.'[49] But he took offence if he thought he was being slighted. In 1845 he discovered that Barings had given their closest associates in Paris, Hottinguers, power to sign for them. 'I do not understand upon what principle this is done when I am on the spot,' he wrote indignantly, 'and I cannot for one moment allow any business to be carried on in a manner which I consider as a reflection upon myself.'[50] His cousin John Baring good-naturedly apologized – 'If there has been any error or irregularity . . . it is I who must cry *peccavi*'[51] – but they had done the same thing in the past and were to do so again.

Thomas Nixson, clerk promoted partner, had retired in mid-1828, so that Humphrey Mildmay was the only other partner surviving after Holland's death. His new partners treated him with affectionate contempt. 'He is a most estimable man and his punctuality and attention to business deserve great praise,' wrote Joshua Bates, but he 'suffers from weak nerves, and having had but little experience his natural timidity is thereby heightened.'[52] On one occasion he panicked, decided the house would need at least £400,000 within the next few weeks and wrote letters appealing for help to Hope and Co., Hottinguers and other close friends. Bates went into the matter and found Barings had funds perfectly adequate to meet any conceivable need – 'Some arrangement must be made by which I can avoid this annoyance of Mr Mildmay's weak nerves.'[53]

Sir Thomas's third son, John, was one of the new partners who began work in July 1828. A curiously elusive figure, his main significance to the house was that he had gone into business with Joshua Bates and now brought his partner back to join Barings in London. 'Able but indolent,' was how Ward described him, and all the – not very plentiful – traces of his tenure in London suggest a man who was affable, easy-going and somewhat diffident. 'The truth was I was very tired of the thing,' he told Bates, when he retired in 1837. If he had been senior partner it might have been different, 'but being junior I could not give myself airs, particularly as my seniors are workers, and as really it requires pretty close working and watching to keep the house at its present pitch'.[54] After ten years in the business he retired with £180,000; 'probably the largest fortune gained by any one individual in business in which there is very little speculation,' commented Bates.[55] He flourished in retirement for fifty years, living alone and modestly and giving the surplus of his income to the poor. 'He is one of the best and most pure-minded of men,' wrote Bates.[56]

His brother Thomas was altogether more formidable. Tactful, witty, affable, yet with the Baring aptitude for ensuring that he was taken seriously, he was as ready as his brother to relax when the occasion offered, but far more ready to work when the need was there. 'I feel a want of the desk, and a yearning after the dear Bankers' book and the insinuating book of acceptances,' he wrote when on holiday in Paris.[57] But in fact the book of acceptances was far from being his favourite reading. He hankered after the more glamorous side of banking and like Alexander before him preferred the world of high finance and international loans to the more humdrum business of the counting house. He not merely enjoyed such work, but he was outstandingly good at it. 'Tom Baring writes you about stocks,' Bates told Ward. 'He does that sort of correspondence to admiration – so much better than I can that I have made him take charge of that department.'[58]

In 1835 he joined the family contingent in the House of Commons; a conservative like his uncle, and thus at odds with his father and brother. In 1843 he fought a particularly spirited by-election in the City of London. 'You must read Tom's speeches,' Bates told Ward. 'He has astounded everybody by his readiness and even eloquence, his manner and fluency are quite remarkable.'[59] Unfortunately he was opposed by the Anti-corn Law League, who had been stirred up by the great financier, Lord Overstone. Overstone, a passionate free-trader, denounced Baring as being at the best lukewarm on the theme. 'I see by the papers that you have given me a very hard hit, which falls the heavier on me as it had not been expected,' Thomas Baring wrote to his fellow banker. 'I hope you do not approve of the coarse manner in which Mr Pattison speaks of Lord Ashburton and my family' – a reference to the claim of his opponent that Baring was standing only to satisfy the ambitions of his uncle and had quarrelled with his own family in consequence.[60]

Baring spent £5485.6.3d. on the City of London election but lost by 6367 votes to 6532. The following year, however, he enjoyed a walkover at Huntingdon. 'Our business is in good order now and we can spare one or two partners a portion of the time,' wrote Bates.

'Tom will do us credit. He should be Chancellor of the Exchr.'[61] Peel did in fact seek to push him forward, asked him to second the address in February 1845 and proposed that he become President of the Board of Trade a few months later. Baring refused – 'the Bishopsgate House has too many temptations yet,' wrote Bates, but it was felt by most people that he would become a minister within a few years.[62]

He never did. The following year he joined his uncle in opposing Peel's policy on Free Trade. Disraeli much admired his performance: 'The member for Huntingdon brought the great name of Baring, and all the authority of his pre-eminent position in the commercial world, to support the principle of regulated competition. His mastery of the subject would under any circumstances have commanded attention. The house liked to receive the latest and most authentic information as to the state of the markets from the greatest merchant in the country.'[63] Nor was this praise exceptional; in 1848 Disraeli was extolling Baring for 'one of the best speeches ever made in the House of Commons. Few more combine mastery of the case with parliamentary point than this gentleman.'[64]

In time Disraeli was to press him to join his government, but for the moment Baring was more than satisfied with the back benches. Not that his freedom from ministerial office meant that he was under-employed. 'The fact is,' said Bates, 'he is the best worker I ever saw. This, combined with his ability, makes him sought after as Chairman and on Committees, Irish relief, etc.'[65] He tried to do too much, and as a result was often in bad health. His frequent absences also imposed an additional burden on the third of the new partners introduced by Alexander Baring in 1828. Fortunately it was a burden Joshua Bates was well able to bear.

Bates was the most imaginative of Alexander Baring's appointments: not a member of the family, not an Englishman, not even with a particularly brilliant career behind him. Massachusetts born and bred, he had spent much of his career in the counting house of a Boston merchant specializing in trade with Russia and Calcutta. He had worked in Europe and had an unrivalled knowledge of American business and businessmen. His association with John Baring had been soundly if not sensationally prosperous, and it must have been the fact that both his partner and Peter Labouchère confidently recommended him that led Alexander to make the experiment. Clearly he had the experience and skills to be a useful partner; whether he had the temperament took longer to establish.

Bates was pawky, dour, charmless; with little imagination and less humour. 'His tone was dry, his words few,' wrote Samuel Ward, whose father T. W. Ward was an ardent admirer and protégé of his fellow countryman.[66] He could be touchingly naïve. He noted in his diary that he was charmed by Boswell's *Johnson*: 'perhaps this partly owing to the fact that I find Johnson's opinion on many subjects coincide with my own, and as I have never derived any great advantage from Books, never having read much, this is greatly in favour of my intellect'.[67] A man of grinding conscientiousness, his joy was work; 'You are the most uniformly laborious man I know,' wrote T. W. Ward.[68] Bates sometimes tried to persuade himself that there were other pleasures in life than those of the counting house. 'I would rather make a quarter of the money I do and free myself from the necessity of that day and night attention to business which becomes irksome to me,' he told Ward.[69] No doubt he believed it at the time, but if ever he tried to put it into practice he quickly found himself pining for the delights of trading. 'The man was illiterate and ignorant but possessed a strong mind and much business ability,' was the verdict of one of the many Americans who visited him in London, and it does not seem unfair.[70]

Bates displayed in his private life the same rectitude and meticulousness as in the office. 'From this date Mrs Bates to be allowed £150 per year for her dress, thread, tapes, needles, pins and for charitable purposes; Tolls, expenses in carriage, ices at Gunter's,' he noted in his diary.[71] It was not ungenerous, but woe betide Mrs Bates if she exceeded her allowance. Bates was a hard man. 'My gardener seems to be much in debt,' he noted. 'He has too many children, which is the great difficulty with all labouring men. I must discharge him.'[72] Another time two of his house servants fell in love and conceived a child. They were ready to marry but Bates dismissed them. It was 'more important to set a good example to the other servants than redeem these servants'. But he could be as coolly realistic about himself as about others. In 1833 the *Edinburgh Review* described him as 'the first Merchant of the country' and 'unquestionably the ablest'. 'The Quarterly will probably style me the most insignificant,' commented Bates. 'These periodicals cut one up or praise one just to suit their own purpose.'[73]

He 'has a trial in his wife as great as almost any person living', wrote Ward.[74] Another American described her as an 'audaciously vulgar old woman'. She had been complaining that her daughter had nowhere fit to live, in spite of the fact that she had huge houses in both London and the country: 'This kind of whining comes from a woman who was born in a four roomed log house in Massachusetts and never saw a carpet until she was a woman grown.'[75] Mrs Bates must have been one of the factors that made it hard for Bates to win the place he felt he deserved in British society.In theory he despised the fripperies of fashion, in fact he hankered after them. One of his few weaknesses, Ward felt, was undue deference to wealth and rank.[76] Bates believed he got the balance just right. He told Ward that a certain new American arrival in London was too voluble and noisy, 'but that will wear off. A residence of one year in London would make a perfect gentleman of him . . . In London no extravagance of word or gesture is allowed in good society and since I have got a little into it I am charmed with that which I at first thought objectionable.'[77]

He wrote thus confidently as early as 1831, but his progress into high society was in fact slow and arduous. It was from the Barings themselves that he received the most painful rebuffs. Lord Ashburton's return from the United States in 1844 'renewed the mortification and pain I have always felt in consequence of my social position. On joining the house of Baring Brothers and Co. when Lord Ashburton was a partner, I found that he and Mr Mildmay did not consider that by forming a co-partnership with me they had incurred the so-called necessity for any intercourse with me and my family.'[78] He was almost never invited to the Grange and only to dinner in London when there were American visitors – and even then Mrs Bates was not included. 'This must not continue,' wrote Bates angrily, but it did.[79] When Bates asked if Lady Ashburton would present his wife and daughter at Court, Ashburton found some polite excuse. 'This is the first favor I have asked of this family and it will be the last.'[80]

Fortunately Thomas Baring, more easy going and good-natured than his uncle, and with a far clearer appreciation of Bates's qualities, showed no such arrogance in his attitude to his partner. Indeed, he treated Bates to all intents and purposes as the senior partner. Though Baring made the running where international loans were in question, Bates ruled supreme over all the routine trading business and the administration of the office. In particular, he took responsibility for the rapidly increasing American business. He was a first port of call for all important American visitors to London and regarded by most of them as the ultimate fount of wisdom on British and international affairs. 'Have you letters for Mr Bates?' Charles Summer asked his brother. 'You will find him a person of sterling honesty and sense.'[81] Louis McLane advised his successor at the American Legation to use Schultz as his tailor and Adams as his hostler. 'Lady Wellesley . . . will instruct you in the mysteries of fashion and Mr Bates, your Banker – whom you will find the kindest man in the world – will instruct and aid you essentially in all matters of business and housekeeping.'[82]

Thomas Baring and Joshua Bates liked and respected each other, and admirably complemented each other's abilities. On them depended the future of Baring Brothers. When Alexander Baring retired in 1830 he left five partners: his brother Francis, his son-in-law Humphrey Mildmay, his nephews Thomas and John, and Joshua Bates. In theory three partners had to endorse any decision of importance, but with Francis often in Paris and generally ignored and John withdrawing in 1837 and anyway disposed to follow his brother's lead, the practice became that the three managing partners did all the business and only invoked the other two in case of disagreement.[83] At the end of 1835 there had been something of a confrontation, when Mildmay had tried to limit the house's free capital at any one time to £100,000 and had recruited Lord Ashburton to support him. Bates argued that £500,000 was the minimum essential for a reserve sufficient to embrace any profitable business that might come along, established that John and Thomas agreed with him, and convinced Ashburton that Mildmay's course 'would reduce the profits of the House in a short time so much so as not to make it worth anyone's attention to the business'.[84] He won the day, but remained dissatisfied. 'Too much falls on me,' he complained in his diary. 'To talk to everybody, sell the goods, draw the plans for operations which require a vast deal of thought and hard thinking too;

then I have all the disadvantage of not being supported by my partners. No one lends a helping hand to render myself or my family
more respectable, and they never take the least notice of my countrymen unless I request it. Then the timidity of Mildmay will spoil any
business.'[85]

The timidity of Mildmay was a constant cause for complaint. In
1837 he unusually succeeded in winning the support of John and
Francis and blocking some new business which Bates and Thomas
Baring – the two activists – wished to introduce. 'Someone else
should therefore take the lead,' complained Bates, but he had no
intention of letting anyone do so,[86] and as Mildmay became more
preoccupied with his parliamentary life, his power to irritate vanished. By 1844, with Thomas Baring also active in parliament, Bates
was taking $7/24$ of the profits, against $6/24$ to Thomas, $5/24$ to Mildmay
and $4/24$ to Francis. The remaining $2/24$ went to Charles Baring Young,
a grandson of Charles Baring of Exeter, who had come to
Bishopsgate in 1843 to take some of the load off Bates. Young was
assiduous and able but had only one leg and was in poor health;
there was never any possibility that he would play a more responsible role.[87]

Mildmay considered retirement as early as 1841 but stayed on to
build up a larger fortune for his sons. By 1847, however, it was evident even to Francis Baring that he was increasingly a liability to the
house: 'The man is to be pitied for his mind is in a morbid state. . . .'[88]
Finally he agreed to retire at the end of the year. The retirement of a
partner who owned as large a proportion of the capital as did
Mildmay was bound in some measure to reduce the resources of the
house, but this was greatly mitigated by the fact that the partnership
contract stipulated that capital should only be withdrawn in stages
over a period of years. 'If we have our ordinary luck,' Bates assured
Ward, 'his retirement will produce no diminution of the Capital of
the House.'[89] In every other way it was an unmixed blessing. Thomas
Baring and Joshua Bates were now in undisputed control.

8

The Trade in Bishopsgate

1830–1848

The house as reorganized by Joshua Bates was altogether more orderly than it had been under his predecessors. Alexander Baring understood the need for system. 'You should well impress on your mind the importance in a counting house of many clerks is the necessity of *minute* punctuality,' he told his nephew Thomas. 'It is not generally a Baring virtue and therefore requires some self-command. This is more important in the management of business than genius or higher talent, and you may rely upon it that your business will move unsatisfactorily and in some degree unsafely unless you attach importance to the apparent trifling circumstance of minute discipline.'[1] But he himself had rarely found time or inclination to practise what he preached, and though Holland kept the clerks to their office hours, he had little idea of more sophisticated measures to improve the running of the office.

With Bates's arrival a new system is apparent in the records of Baring Brothers. Correspondence was properly entered and copies of the replies retained; reporting on economic and commercial matters from all corners of the earth was vastly increased and rationalized; annual trial balances were henceforth struck. Barings in 1830 were one of the largest houses, employing some 30 clerks in their Bishopsgate office against 40 to 50 at Rothschilds and 10 to 15 at most of the other important houses.[2] They were well paid, earning between £250 and £500 a year for an experienced clerk down to £40 for a beginner. Bates started with the view that their number could be reduced, but by early 1831 found that business grew so fast that even more were called for. 'It is extremely difficult to arrange a counting house so as to have so much business go on as it should go,' he complained to Ward. 'As soon as I get proper clerks and the business goes easy, it is found that the increase of work requires additional hands.'[3] Four years later, with the total now over 40, he was looking for yet more staff.[4]

But though he did not succeed in reducing numbers, and actually raised the basic salaries, he cut down on the commissions, unofficial but tacitly condoned, which the clerks had grown used to taking. He made himself exceedingly unpopular as a result.[5] His advice to himself in his diary on how to run the office is typical both of the man and his regime. 'Having been generally successful in business we have become too free and open in our conduct and have incurred risks that it will not be wise to repeat. A system of secrecy should be encouraged and . . . none but clever persons admitted into the office. A rigid economy should also be enforced as much as in less prosperous times. Avoid all pride, ostentation and unnecessary show.'[6]

The regulations laid down for the clerks suggest that their life was austere but not over-taxing. Juniors arrived at 9.30 a.m., seniors at 10 a.m., there was an hour for lunch, and all left at 5 p.m. except when the international mail was departing. Anyone under the age of sixty had to sign a book on arrival; after one's sixtieth birthday it was presumably hoped the habit of punctuality would have been finally inculcated. 'Unnecessary conversation in the Office, one with another,' was deplored, as were visits by friends or disappearances from the office on personal affairs. 'When it is considered that these Regulations, on ordinary days, only require attendance for the Superior Clerks about Six Hours per day, and the Junior Six and a half Hours, and Two Hours additional on Post and Packet Days, it cannot be thought severe,' concluded the notice somewhat defensively. 'It is therefore insisted on that the short time be devoted earnestly to the duties of the office.'[7]

William Rathbone, who joined Barings in 1840, would not have felt this unreasonable. He found his life 'full of very hard and varied work, but of perfect health and freedom from anxiety or disturbance or worry of any kind'. Bates was an exacting but not unreasonable taskmaster, he 'had the knack of seeing everything without appearing to take any trouble to do so'.[8] Humphrey Mildmay's son Henry Bingham was taken on in 1845, initially to copy letters. His handwriting was not considered to come up to the required commercial standards and he was sent to take lessons from an expert in the Gray's Inn Road. His only complaint was that he had to work on Saturday afternoons.[9]

In 1828 Labouchère took a young American, Russell Sturgis, to Bishopsgate. Sturgis was amazed by the volume of business transacted. The postage on the letters each day amounted to £25. Sturgis remarked that the partners must have an easy time of it since all they had to do was sign their names, and was told that on that one day they would have 3000 cheques to sign for French dividends and 500 for American.[10] (The same was still true in 1912, when Patrick Shaw-Stewart, confronted by 500 dividend warrants, cursed the day he had opted to sign with his full name rather than as P. Stewart.)[11] The ritual was that all the letters, often 200 a day, were looked at by Bates, inspected more meticulously by Mildmay and then distributed around the office. An immense part of the burden was borne by Bates, who personally handled almost all the correspondence with the United States as well as making regular visits to Exchange to buy and sell bills, draw and remit. 'This requires promptness and decision, and a degree of experience,' wrote T. W. Ward, who visited Bishopsgate when the new partnership was forming. He noticed how conscientious Bates was in his attendance compared to his colleagues or those from other houses: 'This is an advantage Bates has – he is devoted to business and willing to labor.'[12]

It was almost certainly Bates who propounded the golden rule on which Baring Brothers based its operations: '. . . by being too liberal we lose our money and not being sufficiently liberal we lose our business. Therefore the middle course is the one it should be our aim to follow.'[13] Admirably rational though it was, the precept still comes into the category of 'easier said than done'. Barings operated under certain self-imposed restrictions, which safeguarded them from much loss but at the price of missing many opportunities. They would rarely enter into business with a house abroad unless it had been introduced by one of their own trusted correspondents. They never parted with bills of exchange endorsed by themselves until the bills fell due: 'It is a source of pride and satisfaction to me,' wrote Bates of the 1837 financial crisis, 'that by foresight on the part of myself and partners our House has never discounted a bill and never had aid from the Bank in any way'.[14] They disliked granting credits unless assured that the correspondent kept his account solely with Barings.

In applying such rules they were deemed ultra-conservative by many of their most successful rivals. Rothschilds habitually borrowed large sums from the Bank of England and discounted many bills with Overend, Gurney, the leading discount house. Brown, Shipley were more adventurous over accepting clients who took credit elsewhere, and won much good business from Barings by their policy. Their record hardly proves them wrong. Yet as Barings successfully rode out the successive economic crises of the 1830s and 1840s, their prudence did not seem misplaced. They missed opportunities for profit but they slept more securely in their beds, and in the circumstances of the time that was a comforting reflection for their correspondents as well as for themselves.

Sometimes profit was not a consideration. In November 1845 the failure of the Irish potato crop led to the government ordering £100,000 to be spent on buying maize in the United States. The problem was that as soon as the buyer was known prices would soar. Sir Randolph Routh, head of the Commissariat Department of the British Army, suggested his brother-in-law in Quebec should do the job, but the Chancellor of the Exchequer politely replied that, while this gentleman was 'doubtless respectable', he was 'hardly likely to be a first-class merchant'. He preferred Baring Brothers.[15] Thomas Baring offered to put their agent, T. W. Ward, at the disposal of the government and in December they undertook to procure £100,000 worth of 'Indian Corn and Meal' to ship to Cork.[16] The business was done with extreme discretion; no one in the United States had any idea what was going on and the maize was bought at rock-bottom prices. C. E. Trevelyan was so impressed by Barings' performance that he tried to use them on a similar job in Britain a year later.[17] This Barings declined, but they did not take a penny in commission for their trouble in the Irish business.

The Liverpool office was the brainchild of Joshua Bates, set up to foster the American trade which was his special pride and which demands attention in a separate chapter. He had envisaged a Liverpool house as early as 1830, but hesitated to establish it in case 'we may be thought too grasping and people will be set against us'.[18] Mildmay was characteristically reluctant to endorse so bold a step and it was not until 1832 that the office was opened, under Charles

Baring Young and S. S. Gair. 'It is a grand move,' wrote Thomas Baring from Paris, 'which has been wanting for the last three years but not, I hope, too late.' It was not. By 1833 twenty clerks were employed and Bates could report proudly that 'We are No. 5 in the list of receivers of cotton, and may be no. 2 before the year is out. . . . I foresee that this Liverpool House will one day rival ours in London, and I am quite enamoured of it.'[19]

The business in Liverpool, with its concentration on cotton, admirably exemplified the sort of general trade in which Barings excelled. Thomas Baring relished the major deal which might take years to set up but could yield a fortune if it came off; Bates favoured a multiplicity of minor bargains, each one producing a small but sure return. Unlike Rothschilds, who specialized in bullion, mercury or diamonds, Barings were interested in any commodity that was widely in demand, which could be bought and sold or on which advances could be made or shipping and insurance organized: tea, sugar, coffee, indigo, copper, grain, rice, tobacco. . . . But Bates was a prudent man and he was always quick to retreat from a field if he felt that the future was uncertain. He withdrew almost entirely from advances to the European wool growers, and cut off credit to Calcutta in 1832 and 1833 when the tea planters failed to produce enough to cover their bills. He was criticized at the time, but saved Barings a great deal of money.[20]

Very occasionally Bates could be adventurous, however, as in 1830 and 1831 when political disturbances on the continent meant that the amount of capital deposited with them had become almost embarrassingly large. The knowledge that many cattle in Russia had died of distemper made him think that the price of tallow was bound to rise, and Barings bought large amounts for their own account. Then he decided that they would do well to control the market, so in collaboration with the St Petersburg banker, Baron Alexander Stieglitz, he set out to corner all the existing stocks. By mid-December Barings had bought 44,000 casks and the price was beginning to rise, and a month later they had invested more than £120,000 and could claim 'to have under our control all the yellow Candle Tallow in the market . . . but for distant delivery in order not to affect the market. Now the chance is that we shall gain £70,000 by it and Stieglitz as much more.'[21]

But a storm arose. Furious protests from importers and manufac-

turers led to questions being asked in the House of Commons, and
the radical member 'Orator' Hunt inveighed against monopolies.[22]
Nor did Barings have it all their own way in the market. Stieglitz was
told about 'the violent opposition of the Jews, who have made use of
every stratagem in their power to depress prices and deter buyers
from coming forward'.[23] There were rumours that the duty on can-
dles was about to be taken off. Barings sold most of their holdings at
a respectable price but were left with an uncomfortably large quantity which they had to dispose of at a loss. At the end of the year Bates
claimed that none of the operations he had championed had been
misguided; 'the tallow spec is proved to have been right, we wanted
courage to hold'.[24] Overall Barings probably lost money on the operation, but it was not a disaster and, as Thomas Baring told his partner: 'You needed some such contest to put you fairly on your legs in
London!' Bates drew a different moral from the affair. 'I never wish
to grapple with a whole community again.'[25]

There is nothing to indicate what havoc the tallow speculation
wreaked on the frail nerves of Humphrey Mildmay. He had, however, little reason to be disturbed by any other feature of Bates's trading activities. He may have felt that some advances to tea planters in
Ceylon were made injudiciously, so that after the crisis of 1847
Barings found themselves unwilling proprietors of three planta-
tions, but though this locked up capital that could have been better
employed, in the short and middle term it did not prove a bad investment. Bates's most important contribution was to build up Barings'
representation abroad, by picking the right men and offering them
financial backing. T. W. Ward, with the American agency in Boston,
was immeasurably the most important but by no means unique. In
1833, for instance, Bates was considering strengthening the house of
Gisborne and Co. by putting in a partner and 'furnishing him with
capital sufficient to enable them to assume an importance in Calcutta worthy of our patronage'. Shortly afterwards John Richards
joined Gisbornes with a £20,000 advance from Barings by way of a
dowry. After the disasters that had afflicted Calcutta in the previous
years, felt Bates, 'we cannot fail to become receivers of a large proportion of the goods from that country'.[26]

It was only a short step from financing international trade and
organizing transport and insurance, to taking an interest in the

vessels themselves. In October 1833 the newspapers reported that Barings were building a ship that would be manned exclusively by seamen who had taken the pledge not to drink alcohol or to indulge in blasphemy; the reports were true, wrote Bates, 'and may do some good by calling public attention to the subject, which is one of deep interest'.[27] The ship was the *Alexander Baring* of 550 tons, built mainly for the East India and China trades. In February 1835, carrying freight worth £150,000, she reached Canton after a rapid 103 days' transit. By that time Barings also owned the *Antoinette* of 350 tons, *General Palmer* of 531 tons and *Diana* of 487 tons.

Usually, however, they chartered ships for each operation. A typical venture of 1839 involved sending an American ship, the *Washington*, to Canton. It was anticipated that the Bocca Tigris would shortly be blockaded by British naval units, so the captain, Francis Booth Wells, was told, 'you will do well to avoid speaking to any British ship, particularly ships of war. . . . Of course you will be ignorant of any Blockade and are justified in proceeding until you are notified of it and warned off by competent authority.' In Canton the *Washington* was to discharge her cargo of woollen and cotton goods and iron and stock up with tea and raw silk. 'Be as quick as practicable as it is probable a Blockade will be declared.' The ship should then continue to Singapore and Macao to 'transfer your cargo to a good English boat, ideally the *Alexander Baring* if it can be found'. The *Washington* itself should try to get a freighting job between Singapore and Manila; at Manila or Batavia it should load up with sugar and continue to Cowes. Various alternative instructions covered the action the captain should take if Canton was blockaded before the *Washington* arrived.

> In conducting your business you will always find a great advantage in keeping it all to yourself. Communicate nothing beyond what is absolutely necessary to anyone. To the young man who is a passenger, who by the by is a talented youth, we would advise you to communicate nothing of your own business as he is going to join a House that you are not likely to deal with.
>
> When you get out or before you arrive on the coast of China you will do well to have all the letters and newspapers

in the ship collected in a bag. Have it sealed and take it into your own possession for you cannot tell until you reach Canton what advantage it may be to your operation that other people be kept in ignorance.

You must never think that these advices comprise everything you have to think of and decide about. Various changes may take place in the position of things before you leave Canton or afterwards, which may render a different course preferable and you should always be prepared for any emergency and act promptly, having always in view the perfect safety of your investment.

Wishing you a prosperous voyage we are
            Dear Sir
                    Very truly yours,
                        Baring Brothers[28]

Bates's success can be measured by the acceptances outstanding at the end of each twelve-month period. In 1828 these were a mere £295,000; after one year of Bates's stewardship the figure had risen to £604,000. By 1831 it was £1.4 million and in 1833 £2.3 million. In 1837, in line with world trade, it dropped back to just under a million, but it quickly rose again and averaged £1.26 million throughout the 1840s. Commission income rose similarly. It had been allowed to fall away to £25,000 or so a year in the 1820s, now it doubled in five years, doubled again, and remained at about £80,000 a year during the 1840s.

There were plenty of fanciful speculations in which Bates could have risked these solid profits. In 1835 'Sir Anthony Carlisle writes me that his machine for flying is nearly bro't to perfection and he only wants a clever person to bring it out. It seems impossible but he says it is quite an affair of science, floatage being all that is required.'[29] In 1846 the failure of some merchants in Smyrna made Barings the surprised owners of 1000 chests of opium.[30] In 1832 an invention for making wrought iron nails was under consideration. Since iron cost £7 a ton, producing the nails including the inventor's royalty would cost £5 a ton, nails were selling at £24 a ton and it was expected that 70,000 tons a year would be sold, the annual profit should be £480,000 a year – 'enormous and must be fallacious,' commented Bates pessimistically.[31]

But it was iron that introduced Bates to one of his few ventures into British industry. Since the early fifteenth century when the Bishop of Durham began to produce at his own forge, Weardale had been a cradle of the English iron industry.[32] In 1844 Mr Chas. Attwood, who had secured leases of mineral deposits in the Wear Valley, tried to interest Barings in a new process for manufacturing pig iron. The present price was £5.10/– and Attwood calculated he could produce it at 16/–, giving a potential annual profit of £350,000. 'This may well seem incredible,' wrote Bates. 'In about one month we shall know about it and decide.'[33] It was nails all over again, but this time the outcome was different. By May 1845 the only question was whether Weardale ironstone and coal would together make good iron: 'I entertain no doubt.'[34] He took his partners along with him. Thomas Baring found it hard to believe so good a thing had been so long undiscovered, but was prepared to let Bates have his head; Francis Baring and Charles Baring Young had no objections. Even Mildmay was ready to support the enterprise on the grounds that he had some friends who had done well out of iron. Usually he would have opposed it, he said, as not being the right sort of employment 'for the capital of a House of business', but he was prepared to make an exception because of the 'unusually tempting circumstances'.[35]

Thomas Baring remained mildly sceptical. He had been in Paris pursuing a loan. 'Now that our French much ado about nothing is all over and ended in smoke,' he wrote, 'you can only look to your Weardale project for a fortune. I hope that will end in smoke and something else.'[36] By late 1846 Barings had paid Attwood £14,000 for half his leases of ironstone and coal and had advanced £100,000 to the Weardale Iron Co. 'Secret,' Bates told Ward. 'We are making Iron very fast and at a very cheap rate, but don't mention it in reply, for it so happens that no one appears to suspect us of being concerned in Iron making.'[37] A triumph seemed at hand, but every time that production began to build up, some technical hitch occurred. 'There are more difficulties in Iron making than I ever dreamed of,' Bates wrote in his diary.[38] The dream was to teeter on the edge of nightmare before the saga of Weardale had run its course.

No house doing business of the kind undertaken by Barings, however astutely run, could flourish irrespective of the vagaries of world trade. In 1831 all seemed set fair. Alexander Baring's retirement had done good, declared Bates. 'Each man in the House now sees the necessity of taking a stand for himself; the consequence is an aggregate mass of influence which will in a short time carry the House above what it ever was as a commercial establishment.'[39] Rothschilds had been caught with huge holdings of French stocks after the 1830 revolution and their credit had suffered. 'It is really unpleasant,' wrote Bates with transparent insincerity, 'to see Mr R. drawing at 25 12½ on Paris while we find eager takers at 25 2½. I cannot understand it, for altho' he has lost by the turn of events he must be a man of great wealth; to be sure, he draws on his Brothers, while we draw on Hottinguers, Baguenault and Hope.'[40]

The euphoria did not abate in the following years. Profit for 1832 was £98,000 and the following year £119,000 'Between ourselves,' Bates boasted to Ward, 'BB and Co. are as much beyond what they ever were as a Commercial House as Prime is beyond Shipman or any other small concern.' The problem was how to escape being overwhelmed by the flood of business.[41] The economic crisis in the United States in 1837 involved them in severe losses at the time but in the end strengthened their position by removing some of their more dangerous rivals from the field.*

In 1839 it was a British crisis, brought about by an outflow of sterling to pay for wheat imports from the continent and the unrestricted growth of joint stock banks, all merrily issuing notes in spite of their inadequate capital.[42] The Bank of England, drained of its gold reserves, was close to having to stop payments. The Comte d'Argout, Governor of the Bank of France, was in London and offered to help. The Bank of France could not lend itself, but would advance £2 million on bills payable in Paris. Barings were asked to help in the operation and at once put together a syndicate of Paris bankers, led by Hottinguers; 'the operation of which this forms part is intended to set at rest the agitations of our money market and prevent any further export of gold,' they explained to J. B. Gossler and Co. of Hamburg.[43] Barings, who took a 1 per cent commission on the transaction, sent Thomas Baring to Paris to supervise it. Rothschilds refused to join the syndicate, though they belatedly tried to get in on

---

* See pp. 148–9 below.

the act. Why not approach the Bank of England and offer to sell them franc bills at a cheap rate? suggested Baron James to his London nephews. 'I am sure that the Bank encounters difficulties when buying through Barings, because as soon as Baring shows up everybody knows that it is for the Bank and people start to speculate. Transactions through the House of Rothschild would be a relief to all concerned.'[44]

The 1840s were at first marked by the recovery of the world economy and proved extravagantly fat years for Barings. 'Our business is too good and too extensive for us to keep it many years. . . . As we now stand the permanent means of the House would enable us to buy all our competitors out and have half a million to spare,' wrote Bates vaingloriously in 1846.[45] But at the same time Barings were battening down the hatches against the storm they believed Robert Peel's free trade legislation of 1845 was certain to conjure up. Huge imports of corn from the continent and the outflow of sterling to finance the new European railways once again put the Bank of England under pressure. 'There seems to be a dreadful crumbling to pieces around you,' wrote Thomas Baring to Bates from Aix, 'and it shows your good management that we are not as yet hit harder than we are and that according to prospects we seem tolerably safe.'[46] Once again Bates could legitimately congratulate himself on having saved his house from great loss: 'We do not hold on our own account £20,000 worth of goods, and our consignments, which are also moderate, will sell for enough to cover our advances.'[47]

Bates put the blame for the crisis on the folly of the British government and British merchants – 'The developments that are daily taking place surpass anything American.'[48] Inevitably the crisis spread to the continent and was fomented by the wave of revolutions that swept Europe in 1848. Bates's answer was to keep credits to a minimum and treat commodities as if he was playing a mercantile variant of pass-the-parcel, shifting them on with the utmost rapidity, even though the profit was minimal or non- existent. Thomas Baring disliked the policy but generously accepted that his partner probably knew best: 'I have no doubt that you are right – indeed my confidence in your judgment is so implicit that if you were to shut up shop I should be sure that you had the best reasons for doing so, and if I thought that one or two of your moves showed too rapid and short a tack for that character of steadiness which gives us a superiority over the Jews and makes people prefer doing business with us, it was because I was not on the spot and could not understand all the circumstances of the case.'[49] At the height of the crisis Ashburton told John Baring that the house was 'very snug and comfortable'.[50] Not many houses could have said the same.

In 1831, when Ward had urged Bates in future to concentrate exclusively on commission and acceptance business, Bates replied: 'Whatever may have been the character of our House formerly, it is no longer a House concerned in foreign loans. At the same time, with a constantly accumulating capital [in 1831, £326,424], it is not worth while to say that it will not suit us to enter into any monied operations that we deem safe. Indeed, our capital is too large unless we were to take an interest sometimes in operations that require money in large sums.'[51]

Though the first part of Bates's statement may have been true at the time it was made, it did not remain so for long. What is certainly the case, however, is that it was not a house concerned in domestic loans. If the British government was in the market Barings were prepared to participate, but even then not very enthusiastically. When the Chancellor raised £8 million in 3 per cent Consols in 1847 Barings did a deal with Rothschilds. Each made a tender for the whole loan at the same price and then divided it. Since they were the only competitors, they not surprisingly secured the loan: 'Our bid was, we have reason to believe, close to the minister's minimum, if indeed it was not exactly the same.'[52] The views of the Chancellor on what he might reasonably have felt to be a somewhat unsporting cartel, are not recorded. So far as British industry was concerned, with the freakish exception of Weardale, where they set up their own company, Barings felt they had nothing to contribute. Nor, indeed, were they asked to; the merchant banks were not seen as a source of funds for industrialists in Britain in the mid-nineteenth century. The exception for some banks, but not for Barings, was railways.

In the 1840s the railway boom in Britain absorbed the best part of £60 million a year.[53] In *Endymion* Disraeli marvelled at the reluctance of British bankers to take part in this orgy: 'The mighty loan-mongers, on whose fiat the fate of kings and empires sometimes depended, seemed like men who, witnessing some eccentricity of nature, watch it with mixed feelings of curiosity and alarm . . . it was only by the irresistible pressure of circumstances that a banking firm . . . was ultimately forced to take the leading part that was required.'[54] The reluctant leader was Glyn, Hallifax, Mills; though few if any loan-mongers were mightier than Barings they viewed such operations with distaste. 'There seems to be an increasing mania for railroads,' Bates wrote in his diary in 1836, '. . . which must lead to confusion and embarrassment before a year.' He comforted himself with the thought that, since the money would be spent at home, it would at least 'have been scattered to do good in the country'.[55]

The same could not be said of the European loans in which they were engaged. When Bates said that Barings was no longer a house concerned in foreign loans, he tacitly conceded that the pre-eminence Rothschilds had established in this field was theirs to keep. Thomas Baring was less ready to yield the day. He did not find it easy to reassert himself. In Vienna, indeed, Barings suffered a further reverse when Hopes were replaced as agent of the Austrian government – 'It is probably that the Jews have been paying for the agency . . . as they usually do,' commented Barings darkly.[56] In Portugal Barings provided a small short-term loan of £140,000 in 1846, but against the better judgement of several of the partners. 'Portuguese credit has been so tainted by the mismanagement of the Jews and Jobbers,' wrote Mildmay, that '. . . it would not be a very desirable connexion for any House wishing to stand well with the Public.'[57] The Mildmay view prevailed when in 1847 they were invited to take on the financial agency of the Portuguese government; Barings refused the poisoned chalice with unflattering alacrity and left the field to their competitors.

Spain was another Rothschild preserve but here Barings put up a stouter fight. They steered clear of a loan in 1834 and had reason to congratulate themselves when the Stock Exchange panicked and the price fell heavily: 'I hope they will take a lesson from experience and never carry their operations so far again,' wrote Bates smugly.[58] But there was money to be made in Spain. Mercury was an essential element in the refining of silver, and Spain controlled the source of the best and cheapest mercury. Every so often the Spanish government would contract for the disposal of the mercury production over the next few years. In 1835, 1838 and 1843 Rothschilds secured the contract and Barings held off; then in 1847 Francis Falconnet was dispatched to Madrid, among other things to look into the possibilities of intervention in the mercury market. Through the first half of 1848 desultory negotiations dragged on. 'Thank God that Barings do not intend interfering in the quicksilver business,' wrote Anthony de Rothschild in June, but his relief was premature.[59] Barings were far from having withdrawn, yet were ready to accept that Rothschilds could not be wholly driven from the field. The possibility of some sort of joint operation was taking shape by the time the 1848 revolutions put a brake on the pace of business all over Europe.

In Paris the ascendancy of Rothschilds was still more evident; they were indeed so strongly entrenched there that at any time they were ready to pay above the odds to keep rivals at bay. From time to time Hottinguer tried to put together a gentile syndicate to disturb their hegemony but rarely with success. In 1841, when a huge loan was in prospect, Hottinguer had to accept a quarter share from Rothschilds and Barings ended up with only 54,000 francs of rentes. In 1844 Hottinguers insisted on taking half and, when this was refused, went into opposition. Thomas Baring visited Paris to join the battle. 'Hottinguer is decidedly of opinion that my arrival had better not be known,' he told Bates, '. . . because if it did not bring Rothschild to terms it would induce him to raise his bid. . . . I am to be shut up till after Monday, which seems rather absurd but I obey orders.'[60] Whether or not he knew of Baring's presence, Rothschild outbid Hottinguer handsomely: Baring comforted himself with the reflection that it was of the greatest importance for 'our rival to be successful, while . . . it is of little consequence to us'.[61] By the time another loan came up in 1847 Rothschild was alone in the field. It was a costly victory, for the growing economic and political problems of 1847 and 1848 made it almost impossible to dispose of the stock. 'The Jew took the loan out of vanity,' wrote Francis Baring, who regularly showed himself the most vigorously anti-Semitic of the partners, 'not chusing that any great arrangement should be made without him.'[62]

It was a different matter when it came to the French railways, in which some £40 million was invested in the 1840s.[63] In 1843 Barings joined a consortium to oppose Rothschilds in their bid for the railway concession from Paris to the Belgian frontier. 'Barings have joined the rival company,' reported Anselm de Rothschild; and two days later, 'The rival company intrigues like the devil against us.'[64] In the end neither group obtained the concession. But there were plentiful pickings for everyone and a formula was generally worked out by which the profits were spread around the interested parties. Barings never took the lead in the negotiations but did quite nicely all the same. When the shares in the Northern Railroad were distributed in August 1845, Bates reported that they had taken them at £12 and sold at £20: 'I hope it is not wicked to make money so fast. I settle the account with my conscience in the belief that a share is really worth £40.'[65]

Though Francis and Thomas Baring were both made directors of the Northern Railroad, the part played by Barings in the financing of the French railways was not considerable. Except for a brief flurry around 1845 the British investor's interest was cautious and limited. The significance of Barings and other British banks, as Professor Platt has put it, was that they 'stimulated the *haute banque* and opened the floodgates for domestic speculation and investment'.[66] By 1846 they were decidedly disenchanted with even this secondary role. 'There is now a very general gloom and depression . . .,' they told Hottinguers. 'All foreign rail are a deadletter. . . .'[67]

If in France Barings played second fiddle to Hottinguers or Rothschilds, in Russia it was Hopes who took the lead. Traditionally Amsterdam was the main centre for Russian stocks. The few relatively small loans that were brought out in the 1830s and 1840s met with a poor response in London, where the public was repelled by the Tsar's autocratic rule and harsh treatment of his neighbour, Poland. 'If the Emperor continues the system of moderation which he is following in Poland . . . then the prejudice against a new Russian loan here will entirely subside,' Barings told Hopes in 1831,[68] but though on this occasion they successfully placed 500,000 roubles of stock in London, sustained moderation seemed incompatible with the nature of the Russian state. There were other hazards too. In November 1832 Barings reported: 'It has been observed that

Rothschild paid yesterday a long visit at the Russian Embassy where he has not been seen for the last 3 years.'[69] Ten years later the threat became reality when Rothschilds in Berlin and Frankfurt handled the larger part of a new 4 per cent loan raised to finance a railroad from St Petersburg to Moscow.[70]

In spite of this setback Barings still hoped to secure the agency for the Russian government in London; not that it was likely to prove lucrative but because, as Mildmay modestly admitted, 'there is a certain credit even to such a House as Baring Brothers and Co. in being appointed to such an Agency'.[71] From retirement Lord Ashburton urged his nephew on, but he was sceptical about the chances. 'I am afraid your competitor will prove too strong for you,' he wrote. 'He has winning ways which you cannot imitate. . . . You will gain nothing by stooping too low and though the Agency is very desirable it would not even be worth having with engagements which would leave the Court masters of your Capital at all time.'[72] When the negotiations went sour, Barings consoled themselves with the thought that they were well rid of what could have been an embarrassing encumbrance. The grapes were, perhaps, genuinely sour, but in Russia as in almost every country in Europe the power of Rothschilds had proved superior.

Looking at Europe alone, Bates's contention that Barings were no longer a house interested in foreign loans, though not the whole truth, was at least a large part of it. Such loans contributed only a small element to the total turnover and were generally more trouble than they were worth. But Europe was not the whole story. There was a world elsewhere; and it was across the Atlantic that Barings' business, in loans as well as in the more traditional trading, prospered most mightily.

'American Resources and Wealth'

North America, 1828–1848

Given the experience and predilections of Joshua Bates it would have been amazing if North America had not witnessed Barings' most dramatic growth in the 1830s and 1840s. But it was not Bates alone who was responsible. When the firm of Bates and Baring had been taken into Baring Brothers in 1828 it brought with it business worth some £14,000 a year, and though no one doubted that Bates had been the most active partner, the name of John Baring was remembered and well liked in business circles throughout New England. Thomas Baring was also well known in the United States. He was introduced to the former President, James Madison, as being one of those 'whose interests, as well as their feelings, are interwoven with the prosperity of this country'[1]. The house of Baring had been less conspicuous over the last decade than directly after the Napoleonic wars, but there was still a solid basis of reputation and good will on which to build.

In London it was Bates who made himself responsible for the American visitors to London, a stream which became a torrent after the steamboat service was established in 1838. Even in 1833 some 100 or 150 Americans might be in town at the same time with introductions to Barings. 'I doubt if anyone goes away under the idea that his business is neglected but he may have an idea that personally he has received but little attention,' wrote Bates. What was to be done? Even if he were able to ask them all to his house it would be at the risk of 'offending the higher by mixing them with the lower, and the Americans display none of that equality or want of aristocratic feeling, which they are so famed for at home'[2].

It was, however, Thomas Baring who went to the United States in

1829 to consider how best Barings' business should be built up. The obvious course was to appoint an agent, but Bates had doubts about this. '. . . an Agent, unless he is a very clever man and stands high, does an injury to any House,' he had written while he was still working in Boston. 'People are perfectly sick of the name of Agent, both here and in New York.'[3] Baring was quite ready to echo this opinion – 'In general agents don't succeed here,' he concluded while in New York[4] – but by the time he reached Boston he found Bates had changed his mind. 'This relieves me from the decision of a question of which I can be in no way a competent judge,' he wrote with some relief.[5] The favoured candidate was T. W. Ward, who had unfortunately just blown off his left hand in a gun accident and was in peril from lockjaw; but once this hazard was overcome, Baring thought well of him.

Thomas Ward was an old colleague of Bates; slow, somewhat unprepossessing, brusque and graceless in manner: 'What would you think of a man,' asked Bates, 'so forgetful of himself and everyone else as to come into your room while your family was at breakfast, put his hat, gloves and spectacles down on the breakfast tray, take a sausage with his fingers out of the dish and, holding it by its two ends, bite off the middle and put the two ends back into the dish without a word being said?'[6] But Ward was honest, meticulous, and with an encyclopaedic knowledge of American business and businessmen. Trading on his own account he would never have made a fortune, as Barings' agent his value was immense. On 1 January 1830 he took up his duties at a basic salary of £2000 a year. Bates told him later that he had the entire confidence of the house and that they had permitted him to enjoy power which no one partner would have been allowed to exercise in London.[7] In fact he was constantly being enjoined to do this and eschew the other, but he was still given wide discretion. He took his duties with becoming seriousness. His new role, he wrote in his diary, 'makes it important I should rise early and do up my business in the morning, that I should keep a memorandum or diary of occurrences . . . If I am to succeed as an agent I must be more attentive to the minor modes of pleasing others, and mix more with the busy world. The great object, however, is to do what I think right on all occasions, and to be deliberate in my decisions.'[8]

His main task was to select the individuals and houses with which

Barings should do business, to assess their credit-worthiness, probe their weaknesses, gauge their honesty, secure information on their bank balances. His instinct was to expect the worst: 'My own confidence in our mercantile community as a whole was never great, and is now lessened by what I see. We have bad habits, and not easily cured.'[9] His assessments of the people concerned were brisk and to the point: in a typical list, one was 'poor and miserable'; one 'doing nothing, safe'; one 'snug, has some property'; one 'capable, an only son and his father is rich'.[10] Barings meanwhile responded with information about their clients in England: one was 'very safe and very respectable'; another was a '3rd or 4th rate cotton broker. Habits not the best.' But it was not just people about whom Ward kept Barings informed: political trends, projected railroads, prospects for crops, all were relevant; even the level of the Mobile River was of interest, since this affected the shipping of cotton and might give Barings a chance to dispose of stocks in Liverpool.[11]

The branch of Barings at Liverpool was one of the most important factors in the development of their American business, putting them into direct competition with one of their most formidable rivals, W. and J. Brown and Co. in the United States, Brown, Shipley in Britain. It did a healthy export and import trade in many commodities, but cotton was its speciality and the huge resources Barings could deploy quickly made it one of the largest importers. The business was conducted on the lines Bates had laid down in London – dispose of a consignment quickly and accept a smaller profit rather than hold and risk a loss. For this they were criticized, sometimes with reason, but it stood them in good stead in times of crisis.[12]

'I feel quite satisfied with the position of the House in the United States,' wrote Ward in 1831. 'The foundation is good, the business increasing. . . . You can hardly do justice to the great increase of trade in this country. There is much competition, but you cannot fail to take the lead and the best business . . . We lose none, and gain from others and take the best of the new ones.' Traditionally the fiercest opposition came from 'the three Ws', the long-established 'American houses' of George Wildes and Co., Thomas Wilson and Co. and Timothy Wiggin and Co., but W. and J. Brown and Co. was growing fast – 'This house,' admitted Barings in June 1831, 'or rather this family of houses, commands an immense business in the US.'[13]

Rothschilds were inconsiderable in the commercial field, but after their setbacks in 1830 in France they began to look with interest at the United States. In 1834 this brought them into direct conflict with Barings. The new administration under President Andrew Jackson was known to be violently opposed to Nicholas Biddle's Bank of the United States, with which Barings were closely allied, and Barings had also been somewhat less than sympathetic when the Secretary of the Treasury carelessly drew a bill without first appropriating the necessary funds. It seemed possible the United States government might wish to change its agent. Rothschilds evidently volunteered for the role, for in July 1834 the Treasury Department wrote to thank them: 'The high standing and character of your house is well understood in the United States, and I take pleasure in saying that the Government of this country will probably avail itself of yr offer.'[14]

The first Barings heard of it was a brusque note from the Secretary of the Treasury telling them that the account would be transferred in just over two months.[15] The news was received, wrote the historian of Rothschilds, with *'un mélange d'orgueil froissé et d'amertume'*.[16] Certainly the identity of their replacement caused them more distress than the loss of the account, which in financial terms was more trouble than it was worth. 'They might have written us a more civil letter,' was their temperate comment.[17] They comforted themselves with the reflection that they had kept the far more profitable US Navy account, and that since the change had been a political one, 'and as parties are rapidly changing, it is probable that we shall have it back in two or three years'.[18]

In this they were proved right. In 1843 Tyler became President, with Barings' staunch friend, Daniel Webster, as Secretary of State. At once the account was restored to Barings. Webster then resigned. Rothschilds' man in America, August Belmont, saw a chance to regain the prize. 'It would be an easy matter to get the account back,' he wrote, 'provided, however, the place is not filled by a creature of Webster's, who for *weighty* reasons is very attached to Barings.'[19] Some months later, he was pointing out to all and sundry the merits of transferring the account to Rothschilds in Paris, arguing 'how impolitic it is on the part of the United States Government to keep her accounts for the disbursement of her diplomatic agents and a great portion of her foreign fleet not only in England, the only country with which ever a collision is likely to occur, but moreover in the hands of a banking house whose close connection with a member of the House of Lords puts the accounts of this Government almost under the immediate eye of the British Cabinet'.[20] Ingenious though his arguments were they availed him nothing, and the Rothschilds in London did little to urge him on. It was more than twenty years before Barings finally lost the agency, and then only to an American bank.

Ward felt that Barings did not use their pre-eminence in Anglo-American trade to full advantage, and that they underestimated the potential of the New World: 'You have altogether too low ideas of American resources and wealth, intelligence, efficiency of labour, extent of production, ease of subsistence.'[21] Bates had said scoffingly that there were 3000 houses in England as powerful as the largest in the United States and that the capital of Barings was almost equal to that of Boston. 'We have 15 millions of people active, intelligent, industrious, full of eager competition and free of taxes,' retorted Ward. 'We have a fertility of soil unexampled . . . So far as wealth consists in commodities, good land, houses, people, power, roads, canals, it would seem that we have both wealth and the means of increasing it.'[22] When things were going badly Barings were too quick to apply restrictions: 'By acting with freedom I have done you great good . . . Is it not desirable that your commercial correspondents should feel that in times of security . . . they can have some advantage from the resources of so great a House in delay or accommodation? Is it not very important to keep up the impression that there is nothing like Barings, and is there no danger that the charm may be broken?'[23] When things went better they were too slow to relax: 'Two years ago,' Ward wrote in 1835, 'we seemed to be monopolizing the business of this country, but . . . various causes have combined to lessen the proportion you have of the American business. Your prudence has been a leading cause.'[24]

He scored the occasional debating point. When, in 1832, the Hamburg firm of Sillem and Co. closed with considerable loss to Barings among others Ward wrote with barely concealed satisfaction: 'I must say I am surprised at such an event so near you, and that you should not have kept clear – not that the amount is anything of importance, but I have valued your watchfulness and sagacity.' How much better things were ordered in the United States.[25] But Barings changed their policy not one whit. Constantly they were calling Ward to order and reminding him of the rules of the house: 'It is a bad way to get into to allow people to postpone remittances *and we wish your particular attention to this point now*'; 'As it is probable business will become unprofitable it will be absolutely necessary to limit the issue of credit . . .'[26] By the end of 1836, when the economic storm had already broken over the United States, what had been previously pettifogging conservatism suddenly seemed the acme of wisdom. 'It is now easy to perceive how wise Messrs Barings have been in that restricted course which they have lately pursued, in consequence of which they are now so snug and easy,' wrote a friend in London to Thomas Ward. 'The other American acceptors, tho' they will get safely through, will have an anxious and painful time of it.'[27] The writer thought the storm was almost over, in fact the worst was still to come.

The long period of American expansion, with an inflow of foreign goods and capital paid for by the issue of more and yet more stocks, was halted abruptly when the European investor lost interest and confidence in these securities. In the crisis that followed, American merchants found themselves unable to remit the huge sums owing to their European creditors, and brought down not only their own houses but the houses of their creditors as well. Barings, who had been systematically running down their American commitments for a year or more, and anyway had far larger capital reserves than their rivals, were seriously inconvenienced, recording a loss of £168,000 in 1837 and writing off bad debts of some £118,000 the following year. For the other 'American' houses it was disaster. The Bank of England gave help to tide the weaker houses over the worst of their difficulties and give time for remittances to resume. The Committee of Treasury concerned itself in the matter. 'Barings stood up to the Committee as equals,' recorded the historian of the Bank of England, 'gave them much and rather patronizing advice through their American specialist, Mr Joshua Bates, and were never in danger', but by mid-1837 Wiggins had £384,000 acceptances with the Bank and Wilson and Wildes some £250,000.[28] The 'three Ws' were effectively driven out of business; W. and J. Brown survived, but only with much and prolonged aid from the Bank and a rescue operation by other houses.

Rumours abounded that Barings too were heavily over-committed, that they had outstanding acceptances of £1.5 million. 'Even the House of Baring are in a frightful dilemma,' reported a letter to Thomas Raikes in April 1837. 'Lord Ashburton has been obliged to support them with £800,000 and the Bank is called upon by them for fresh advances.'[29] When the dust settled and they were seen to be hardly impaired, their stature was immeasurably increased. 'There is very great reliance on your House,' wrote Ward in May 1837, 'and it will be the sheet anchor of the commercial world, and command the deposits of the shipping interest of the United States and any other business which may be desirable to you.'[30] This for a time was literally the case; at the end of 1837 there was no rival in sight.

It could not last long, of course. As the American economy slowly recovered, other houses returned to the scene. To the chagrin of Ward, Barings had no inclination to relax the prudence that they had showed before the crisis or to go out hungrily for new business. Lizardi and Co. and Huth and Co. began to reassert themselves. W. and J. Brown and Co. were particularly active in taking on small accounts and had none of Barings' reticence when it came to offering credit to houses which did not deal exclusively with them. Barings' power remained massive, but as the 1840s wore on their attention was more and more focused upon the public borrowing on which the future of the United States seemed so much to depend.

By and large the American investor looked after the needs of the Federal government; it was the individual States that turned to Europe for development capital. With high interest rates and security believed to be complete at least in the richer and longer established States, it seemed a promising field for investment. In 1828 Alexander Baring urged his partners to take up a loan for Massachusetts: 'I should think the engagements of this old sober state the very best security in which any man could invest his property.' New York was another favourite. But caution was always necessary: 'You may find the public not so discriminating as a good judge

would be between the credit of Massachusetts and Louisiana.'[31]
Barings saw their role as being, if not to educate the public, then at
least to protect it by offering only stocks in which they had confidence and which they would be happy to hold on their own account.

Curiously, Louisiana was one of the first States in which Barings
became deeply involved. Before the first Massachusetts loan had
been floated, Thomas Baring's friend Edmond Forstall had talked
him into taking 1250 of the $1000 bonds raised to finance the bank
which the Planters of Louisiana were intent on establishing. Two
years later he again involved Barings in the setting up of the Union
Bank in New Orleans.[32] In 1832 a Louisiana Loan was introduced
and Barings secured it. 'We shall all make money, and pretty easily
too,' Bates wrote with satisfaction. 'At one time . . . Rothschild gave
out that he should take the loan. When he found out we had got it he
said he hoped we would give him a part of it. We told him we would
gladly do so at the same price that we gave it to the public, which he
declined.'[33] Rothschild had the last laugh, however. In July 1833
Bates was ruefully admitting: 'It was probably a mistake bringing the
Louisiana Loan out in the market, altho' at the time it was thought it
would go off . . . the takers bring it to market for a ½% or 1% profit
and if you do not support the market by buying at 1% premium one
gets the reputation of not supporting one's loan.'[34]

Barings were far from being the only house dealing in American
securities, and Rothschilds became more interested as the scale
expanded. Their motives seem to have been as much to spite Barings
as to make money. Urging his nephews in London to buy American
State bonds, James de Rothschild wrote, 'I do this, so that Barings
should not be in the position to say: "I forced Rothschild out of the
way." Therefore, even if there is not a penny profit, so long as there is
no loss – I shall carry on with the business.'[35] When Barings' closest
New York associates, Prime, Ward and King, made a joint offer with
Rothschilds for a Maryland loan and offered Barings a share, Barings
remonstrated with their friend in tones more of injury than anger:
'Such an interest as you contemplated giving would not have been as
satisfactory to us as what you do for us usually is.'[36] But though the
opposition was real, it was erratic, and there were not many contracts
which Barings could not obtain if they set their heart on it. They
remained as clearly the leading house in American loans as
Rothschilds were in Spain or Austria.

Barings continued to be discriminating about the States whose loans they would handle. Mississippi they espoused with caution, and were confirmed in their doubts when they failed to persuade Hopes to join them. In general 'old' States were felt desirable, 'new' were to be eschewed. 'The Public here do not like the Securities of the new States,' wrote Bates. 'I do not think they offer the same security as the old States, for the population of all the new States is necessarily rude and not much used to the possession of Money.' Barings would not touch Indiana but Ohio was very popular 'owing to its being an old State, the oldest of the Western States, and was peopled from New England'.[37]

As directly relevant as any State loan to the development of North America was the close relationship that grew up between Barings and the Bank of the United States under its ambitious, headstrong and sometimes maverick President, Nicholas Biddle. Biddle was an economic nationalist, who felt that the Bank should be used to free the United States from the shackles of European capitalism.[38] Up to a point Barings supported him in the enterprise, and even the cautious Mildmay was in 1829 prepared to increase the Bank's credit from £100,000 to £250,000: 'We will not deny that the mortification would be great were we to see the Institution in correspondence with any other House in London as their Agents.'[39] With Biddle at the helm, things rarely ran altogether smoothly – in 1831 Barings seriously considered giving up the agency[40] – but a more or less amicable relationship was maintained until the crisis of 1836 and 1837.

In April 1836 Samuel Jaudon arrived in London on behalf of the Bank, demanding an extended credit of £1 million. It was a moment at which Barings were cutting back on their American commitments and though the credit was not refused outright it was granted only in part and grudgingly. When it was discovered Jaudon had also been in touch with the Governor of the Bank of England, Bates lectured him on the impropriety of opening negotiations with anyone else while Barings were still in the field.[41] Biddle was affronted. The following year Jaudon returned to London, with orders to replace Barings as agent and thus provide a representative 'devoted exclusively to American concerns'.[42] But though Jaudon did as well as could have been hoped for in London, Biddle, the Bank of the United States and the American economy generally were drifting into ever stormier waters. Crop failures in North America and a recession in Europe combined to make it almost impossible to sell American stocks in London. With a million pounds of notes maturing in the autumn of 1839, Jaudon's position became impossible.[43]

Biddle saw no recourse but to swallow his pride and ask Barings to resume the agency. Nor surprisingly, Barings did not make it pleasant for him. 'We do not consider ourselves in any way pledged to resume the agency of the Bank,' they wrote loftily in August 1839, 'which if hereafter desirable must be open to fresh negotiations.'[44] They insisted that the Bank should forthwith cease borrowing on its bonds, a condition Jaudon had to accept. That done, they contributed £100,000 to a subscription of £740,000 designed to assist the Bank through its worst problems, and in November helped raise another £300,000 – 'Jaudon was with me on Saturday,' wrote the great financier, Lord Overstone. 'He wants another lift . . . Bates also came up on the same errand. I gave a positive refusal to have anything to do with the business – stating distinctly that I was disgusted with the whole concern.'[45]

Ward, who loathed Biddle, regretted that Barings had come to the rescue. 'I think the Bank should never be allowed to rise again into power,' he wrote, '. . . and were I not in your service I should consider it a high public duty to use my influence to put it down for ever.'[46] He was particularly incensed when the New York *Courier and Enquirer* accused Barings of double-crossing Jaudon and working to destroy the Bank.[47] Jaudon was enlisted to deny the story in the *Morning Chronicle*[48] and an injured rebuttal of the charges was sent to all Barings' favoured correspondents.[49]

By the middle of 1840 it was clear that Barings had done no more than buy a breathing space for the Bank, and they did all they could to dissociate themselves from its death throes. It was finally suspended in February 1841. 'What a set of swindlers the Directors must be,' wrote Bates to Ward. 'I think you will stand very high in the opinion of the people for your judgement in this matter.'[50] He thought that this was the last act in a protracted tragedy; he soon found that it was only a curtain raiser. In February 1841 Ward warned Barings that it was unlikely that several of the Western States would be able to pay the next dividends on their loans, and that even Pennsylvania was in trouble.[51] 'I feel ashamed of my country,' wrote Bates. Maryland caused him the greatest concern. Barings had recently sold £700,000 worth of this State's securities and were the agents for paying the dividends. 'If we can keep Maryland right I shall be very happy,' he wrote. 'It is the only one which our fame would suffer by in case of default, therefore pray look to it without delay.'[52] Ward was not surprisingly baffled by this somewhat exigent instruction. 'I cannot comprehend your thinking I should be able to do anything with Maryland,' he protested. The State government continued to claim that it intended to pay but his guess was that both it and Pennsylvania would soon default, joining Florida, Mississippi, Indiana, Illinois, Arkansas and Michigan.[53]

European bankers and investors were outraged. American residents in London encountered a hostility they had never experienced when the two countries were at war – cut in the streets and black-balled in the clubs. 'The State of Pennsylvania cheats me this year out of £50,' complained Sydney Smith. 'There is nothing in the Crime of Kings worse than this Villainy of Democracy. The mob positively refuse all taxation for the payment of State debts.'[54] Bates bemoaned the fact that his homeland was disgraced; finding a little comfort in the fact that Massachusetts at least was sound but still concluding, 'the damning proofs against the moral honesty of the States and individuals are so numerous . . . that all efforts are useless and Americans abroad are doomed to that sort of sorrow that I can conceive a brother to feel for a loved sister who had deviated from the paths of virtue'.[55]

Though the federal government was in no way legally responsible for the plight of the States, its credit was inevitably tarnished by what had happened. In 1842 agents of the US Treasury came to London to try to raise a new loan. 'The United States are wealthy, thrifty, and rapidly increasing in wealth, and as a government out of debt,' pleaded Ward.[56] Such arguments made no impression on the European investor. 'You may tell your government,' said James de Rothschild grandiloquently, 'that you have seen the man who is at the head of the finances of Europe, and that he has told you that they cannot borrow a dollar, not a dollar.'[57] Barings would have enjoyed proving him wrong, but they knew that he spoke for the British investor as much as the French. They tentatively tried to interest Hopes in a loan to the fledgling Republic of Texas but found the Dutchmen disinclined to anything so adventurous: 'It strikes us that the fate of the new South American Republics is as yet so uncertain, that notwithstanding the great differences in the Origin, habits and pursuits of the Texan population, there is no saying what will ultimately grow out of the sort of anarchy which prevails in Mexico.'[58]

Even if they had not been agents for the American government, Barings could not possibly have washed their hands of the defaulting States. They had too much at stake. Thomas Baring, perhaps because he felt less personally involved than Bates, was the more optimistic of the two. 'It seems that all goes on *le mieux du monde dans ce meilleur des mondes* except that dark spot America,' he wrote to Bates in August 1842, 'but I cannot help believing that we shall see a clear up there.'[59] Though several of the States seemed particularly loath to resume payments, even if the money could somehow be raised, only Mississippi had gone so far as formally to repudiate its debts. There was still hope. The most practical step that Barings could take to restore American credit was to persuade the more respectable of the defaulting States to resume payment; with luck the rest would then come into line. Pennsylvania, Maryland and Louisiana were the three States with whom they felt a particular involvement, and it was on these that they instructed their agent, Ward, to concentrate.

Ward's campaign in Pennsylvania was a model of lobbying and media-manipulation. Politicians were persuaded that self-interest demanded a rapid resumption of payments; the press was fed with letters and articles arguing that the economic development of the State would be crippled unless access to foreign funds was restored; appeals were made to pride and a sense of propriety; the clergy was enlisted to preach that credit-worthiness was next to godliness, 'every Christian man and woman . . . will feel this obligation when it is presented to their attention'.[60] He laid out about £1500 on the operation and thought that every penny had been well spent when Pennsylvania resumed payments early in 1845. He did not hesitate to use occasional small but well-placed bribes or promises of favours to come. His activities filled Bates with fastidious horror. 'What you say and what I see of many people in the United States makes me think that you and I on the whole are very respectable Gentlemen. I have a sort of instinctive horror of doing one thing to effect another, or using any sort of subterfuge or reserve. It never was practised . . .

by any of the Barings. My whole life has been a stranger to any such doings.'[61]

Bates's chief preoccupation was that Barings should not expose themselves to any charge that they were interfering in American politics. 'Your payment to Mr Webster would not appear well if it should get out,' he wrote anxiously to Ward. 'It is very important that we should not in any way interfere in the Elections . . . The claims of the creditors of the States rest on a firmer basis than that which is influenced by party politics and we must not damage our case by doing that which we are bound not to do.'[62] Daniel Webster was one of the most talented and influential figures in American public life, a man whose oratorical powers and lucid, powerful mind were matched by his greed and unscrupulous pursuit of self-interest. Ward had given him $500 in 1839 to subsidize a visit to London and Barings had looked after him while he was there.[63] It had proved a good investment, but Webster was an instrument that had to be used with care. 'I do not give him my confidence,' wrote Ward in 1843. 'That he is desirous of sustaining his reputation as a great statesman . . . I do not doubt; but he wants and must have money, and will in what he does or omits look very much to its results to himself.'[64] On the issue of State debts he proved a redoubtable champion, and did as much as anyone to ensure that one by one the sinners returned to the fold.

By the mid-1840s Barings were beginning tentatively to reintroduce the better American securities to the European market. There were obstacles beyond those caused by the defaulting States. For one thing, railroad fever was consuming most of the capital Europe had to offer.[65] For another, the possibility of war over the north-west frontier between the United States and Canada was real if remote. 'Go to war about the snow peaks and desolate regions of Oregon!' protested a friend from Illinois to Thomas Baring. 'A country thought of as a residence only by restless pioneers who like the buffalo fly before civilization, or perhaps by Canadian French who find a copper-coloured wife in every wigwam! I should as soon think of getting into contest about the navigation of the Arctic Sea.'[66] But wars had begun for odder reasons, and it was one more factor to disquiet the market.

It was nevertheless the rancour inspired by the defaults that caused the greatest problem. There was genuine distrust of American securities on the part of the British investor, and plenty of bystanders who for one reason or another wanted to keep these doubts alive. *The Times* was one of the more conspicuous of these. Joshua Bates professed to dismiss its operations as insignificant. 'The *Times* has always had a spite against B.B. and Co. on account of political differences,' he told Ward in 1845. 'They have usually attacked every American loan or anything else that they could trump up a story about, but the result of these attacks has, I believe, almost always operated in favour of the project or operation attacked. Public attention was drawn to them and the attacks only served as an advertisement. Newspapers in this country do not represent public opinion.'[67] But in this case at least *The Times* was articulating the fears of its readers rather than creating them. It was not until Europe slipped into political chaos in 1848 that the British investor began to think that there might be something to be said for the New World after all.

One part of North America was not directly affected by the problems of the defaulting States; but Canada had more than enough of its own problems. Alexander Baring had visited the colony in 1797 and reported that it was economically beyond hope: barren, bleak, cut off from access to any seaport, it was 'a perfect deadweight to Great Britain, serving only to feed the empty vanity of large territorial possessions and to increase Ministerial patronage at the expense of the nation'.[68] Early approaches for loans from the government of Upper Canada were dismissed by Barings as offering flimsy security and inadequate interest. To geographical remoteness and inhospitable terrain, the region now added extreme political instability; the French population had been by no means successfully assimilated and the growing power of the United States posed a constant threat from the south.

It was not until 1835, when money was particularly plentiful, that Barings could be prevailed on to tender for a small £400,000 loan to Upper Canada, and even then they did so without marked enthusiasm. They were glad to split the loan with the rival bidders, Thomas Wilson and Co. Even this they had cause to regret, the financial crisis of 1836 and 1837 soon spread to Canada and by 1838 Wilsons were bankrupt and Barings still had £60,000 worth of stock on their hands. It was an unpromising start to what was to be a long and close association.

Why Barings did not cut their losses and have done with Canada is hard to see. Probably it was that combination of obstinacy and honour which so often led them to continue to fight for causes which, if not losing, at least promised to be unprofitable in the short and medium term. Having backed Canada once, they would continue to do so. In 1837, in place of the tottering Wilsons, they took over as financial agents in partnership with Glyn, Hallifax, Mills.[69] Ward strongly approved of this new interest. 'They appear to be thriving in Canada,' he told Bates in 1841, 'and to be a prudent, frugal and good sort of people. . .'[70] The following year, fortified by a guarantee from the British government, Barings and Glyns raised £1.5 million for public works in Lower and Upper Canada.

They were still, however, something less than whole-hearted in their support. At the end of 1848, the Canadian government suggested that Barings should now take over the sole agency. Barings refused; out of friendship to Glyns, they declared. If the Canadians insisted on a sole agency, then Glyns were 'fully as able and willing as ourselves to promote the interests of the Colony'.[71] No doubt they were sincere in their protestations of affection for Glyns, but it is not over-cynical to detect also some uncertainty about the future for Canada's economic development. It is also fair to say that, at the end of 1848, the partners in Baring Brothers had other, more pressing considerations on their mind.

10

'A House Which We Intend to be Perpetual'

1848–1873

The year 1848 saw the end of the second generation of the Barings of London: Sir Thomas; Alexander, Lord Ashburton; and Henry Baring all dying within a few months of each other. The head of the family was now Sir Thomas's eldest son Francis, who served in Lord John Russell's Whig administration from 1849 to 1852 as a modestly innovative First Lord of the Admiralty. According to Francis Baring's journal he took a day to consider John Russell's offer: 'In the evening more talk and I accepted. Alas!'[1] Greville, however, suggests he grasped the offer with almost unbecoming alacrity.[2] He never took office again but soldiered on as a reliable and influential member of parliament, representing Portsmouth until he was created Lord Northbrook in January 1865. The honour bore heavily upon him; he died eight months later.

That other Baring peer, the 2nd Lord Ashburton, was equally remote from the bank. Thomas Carlyle thought he found little pleasure in his new glory. 'He is immensely rich, but having no children, and for himself no silly vanity, I believe does not in the least rejoice at such a lot. Poor fellow! He looked miserably ill the day I called on him . . . One could not but ask oneself, thinking of £60,000 a year, "Alas, what is the use of it?" '[3] His gloom was possibly induced by his wife Harriet, who knew only too well what was the use of £60,000 a year. Greville called her 'perhaps the most conspicuous woman in the society of the present day';[4] she was intelligent, quick-witted, with just enough education to pass for a bluestocking and enough vivacity to pass for a wit. She was anxious to shine in the high aesthetic line, and turned the Grange into a menagerie where literary lions like Carlyle and Thackeray grazed among politicians and assorted grandees. Her main defects were arrogance and a propensity for conversational bullying so marked as to verge on sadism. 'I don't mind being knocked down,' complained one victim, 'but I can't stand being danced upon afterwards.'[5] Anything to do with the bank seemed to her tedious and common: when the wife of a new Baring partner, Mrs Russell Sturgis, asked to be introduced to her at a party, she replied 'in a dawdling tone that she must decline as she had already been introduced to two ladies of that firm'.[6] But she made sure that her guests enjoyed the best: what impressed an American visitor, Mrs Laurence, when she visited the Grange was not so much the resident physician; the groom of the chambers, butler and under-butler; the spectacular silver and the turkey stuffed with truffles; but the fact that at breakfast the boiled eggs were marked with the day of the month on which they were laid.[7]

When the 2nd Lord Ashburton died without a son in 1864, the title went to his brother Francis. Until then Francis had gone on living mainly in Paris, paying little attention to the bank of which he was technically senior partner, but complaining querulously if neglected: 'I have not had a line from Mildmay or anyone since I left,' he wrote to Thomas Baring, 'but I suppose I am not thought of sufficient consequence to be written to.'[8] He retired from even nominal partnership when he inherited the title.

Joshua Bates and Thomas Baring were thus very much in charge, at first in that order, then, as Bates aged and the bank became more involved in international loans, with the balance of power shifting to the younger man. Bates by 1848 was an extremely rich man, living in great grandeur. He bought a mansion standing in 24,000 square feet on the site of what is now the Ritz on Piccadilly and Green Park. T. W. Ward was overawed by its splendour: 'Most magnificent, adequate for Royalty itself; the ceilings some 20 or 25 feet high in the drawing rooms; the walls of the rooms all lined with satin damask, and the painting white and gold.'[9] The guests were as imposing as the drawing rooms; at dinner on 24 March 1858 were the Duchess of Cambridge and Princess Mary, the Duke and Duchess of Manchester, the Duchess of Inverness, Earl and Countess Grey and, among many others, the Bishop of Oxford.

Bates owed his breakthrough into high society largely to his daughter, who married Jean Sylvain Van de Weyer, the Belgian minister in London. The Van de Weyers were befriended by Queen Victoria and their children invited to play in the royal nurseries. 'I started at Weymouth with $5 in my pocket and have increased it to $4 million,' wrote Bates in wonder. 'I am on friendly terms with King Leopold and the French Emperor, my Grand Children play with Princes and Princesses. The world, as old Rothschild used to say, has been very kind to me.'[10] Perhaps the most notable victory was that he and Mrs Bates were now received at the Grange. 'Had a very pleasant time,' he noted with satisfaction in 1850.[11] What Harriet Ashburton said of him once his back was turned is another matter.

Bates still ate, drank and breathed his work but a suggestion of mellowing was apparent. He paid several visits to the Great Exhibition, for which he had put up £500 and offered a further £10,000.[12] 'Great curiosity to see the Nepalese Ambassador and the Hippopotamus,' he wrote in June 1850, demonstrating a finely eclectic approach to sightseeing.[13] But he remained touchy and preoccupied with his dignity. In 1855, when Louis Napoleon visited Windsor, Bates was only belatedly invited to join a party of City dignitaries who presented an address to the Emperor. 'I declined to go – not knowing what position I might be placed in . . . I feel that I should not expose myself to the chance of mortification. This is always the case with the British merchants, as they are called, they are so pushing for notoriety that a Modest Man is always neglected.'[14]

Bates's invitation to go to Windsor on this occasion arose because Thomas Baring, who had been asked to read the address, had better things to do. When Ward dined with him he noted, 'Mr Baring's house is very simple compared with Mr Bates's.'[15] But though Baring may have been more unassuming than his partner, he possessed in full the gravitas which marked his family through the generations. He was a perfect choice for all those semi-public posts that call for men of patent integrity, stature and sound judgement: chairman of Lloyds, deputy-chairman of the Royal West India Mail Steam Packet Co., chairman of the Savings Bank, trustee of Merton College. 'He will damage his health if he is not careful,' wrote Bates, 'but he is a most generous, talented and agreeable man and well calculated to lead in anything.'[16]

Joshua Bates, by an unknown artist.

Thomas Baring (1799-1873) by George Richmond.

With more enthusiasm on his part Baring could certainly have played a leading part in politics. Disraeli's admiration for his ability was undiminished; he possessed, wrote the Tory leader, 'a talent for the exercise of which he is responsible to his sovereign and his country'.[17] Baring did not accept the responsibility. In June 1851, discouraged by some minor setbacks, Disraeli urged him to take over as leader of the party in the House of Commons. Baring professed to find the suggestion a joke, but Disraeli renewed it.[18] Baring was unmoved; he had too many other commitments, he said, even if he was up to the task. Derby spoke bitterly about the reluctance of certain Tories to take office; 'the one whose private affairs prevented him,' wrote Greville, 'was Tom Baring.'[19] Derby had no more luck the following year. 'It is supposed Lord Derby may be sent for to form a ministry,' wrote Bates. 'If so they will want my partner Tho. Baring for the Exchequer but I doubt if they will get him.'[20] The invitation duly came, and Bates was right.[21]

But though he eschewed office, Thomas Baring could not avoid being one of the most influential of the Tories – 'the most sensible and respectable of the Derbyites,' Greville described him.[22] His instincts were conservative: 'In dealing with great commercial questions and with great interests,' he declared in the House of Commons, 'sudden revolutions are the worst and most dangerous experiments.'[23] But unlike some members of his family, he was in social terms never illiberal. He was the only leading Conservative of the main stream to give Disraeli full and effective backing in his battle for Jewish emancipation, aligning himself on this and similar issues with Peel and Gladstone rather than his usual allies.[24]

He had many interests to distract him from both politics and business. He was already a very rich man when, in 1853, his cousin, Charles Baring-Wall, left him his house and fortune, estimated at between £350 and £150,000. Norman Court was a pleasant if undistinguished house set in 7000 acres near Stockbridge in Hampshire. The house was not large for the park, noted Mrs Reeve, 'but pictures and china are renowned; so is the cooking; and with such wealth as is at our host's command, all the details are in perfection'.[25] It was the pictures that Baring particularly cherished. In 1838 his younger brother John gave him a drawing of Rome by Samuel Palmer; a replica, but one which the artist thought better than the original: 'I offered to make him a duplicate for twenty or thirty guineas according to the time spent upon it and if I did my very best for forty. He at once commissioned me to make a duplicate for forty guineas.'[26] From then on Baring collected avidly. In 1846 he combined with Humphrey Mildmay and Lord Overstone to buy the celebrated Dutch pictures of Baron Verstolk van Soelen. They acquired the collection *en bloc* and then held a private auction, splitting the profit or loss between them.[27] By the time he died his collection of Dutch and Flemish pictures was spectacular, including works by Lucas Cranach the Elder, Jan Gossaert, Jan Van Eyck, Mabuse, Bol, Dou, Peter de Hooch, Metsu, a doubtful Rembrandt and a splendid Hals. He paid more money for Murillo's portrait of Don Andres de Andrade – £1020 – than for any other single picture; his Mantegna from Cardinal Fesch's collection cost him £420, his Titian portrait of Charles V £204.15/– and his small Zurbaran of St Francis in Meditation a mere £12.[28] The total value of his collection was put at about £100,000.[29]

An American railway tycoon in London in 1853 remarked how curious it was that in the greatest city in the world, 'there should be only one man to look to and consult, and to guide action in important financial matters . . . Ask about anything and the reply is, "What does Mr Thomas Baring say, or think?" '[30] With all these extra-curricular activities, it is amazing that he managed to devote as much time as he did to the affairs of Baring Brothers. These remained his prime concern, however, and he was painfully aware that he and Bates were a two-man band, with no one clearly destined to succeed them. This was not at all what he wanted: 'Half my pleasure,' he declared in 1849, 'is to work for a house which we intend to be perpetual; *le Roi est mort, vive le Roi.*[31]

Where to look for the next king was the problem that exercised Bates and Baring. Young, wrote Bates dismissively, 'is a useful partner, discreet and gentlemanly but he has no head for business'. The only member of the family who seemed likely ever to come into the house was the child of Henry Baring's second marriage, Edward, and he was only twenty. He had stayed with Bates in 1845 and had been found to be 'evidently fond of business and only wants good advice and opportunity to make himself master of it,' but it would be a long time before he would be ready to be made a partner, let alone to run the house. 'I can't wait for him . . . What is to become of the House after a few years I know not, but I am quite sure that it will never be organized as efficiently as now.'[32]

Bates was now sixty and very conscious of it. It was to take death to release his tenacious grip on the affairs of the counting house, but business from 1848 onwards was increasingly conducted against a background rumble of threats to resign and complaints at the unfair burden put upon him. In 1849 a step was taken to relieve the strain by the appointment of a new partner, an American, Russell Sturgis. Sturgis was a lawyer by training who had then worked in the family mercantile house, mainly in the East. 'Query: is he the man for us?' Bates asked himself.[33] He was taken on for an initial three years at a salary of £2000 a year and within a month had won golden opinions. 'I judge he is just the man for us,' concluded Bates. 'Good manners, agreeable temper, industrious and attentive to his business, knows how to receive Strangers and will by and by relieve me very much.'[34] A note of caution crept in towards the end of 1850 – 'Mr Sturgis is a little too vain and jumps to a conclusion without sufficient thought' – but the faults were felt to be trivial and easily corrected.[35] He was admitted into partnership in 1851, taking 1/24 of the profits.

Then the snags began to appear. He was industrious enough when in the office, but left his work behind him when he went outside, conduct unaccountable to the dedicated Bates. He was extravagant, too; spending his income on good living instead of ploughing it back to build up the house's capital. He was ostentatious and inclined to frivolity; when his father died, 'he puts on no mourning and has gay company at his Country House which looks very odd. It is something more than eccentricity.'[36] His vanity was not so easily cured as Bates had hoped and he began to put on airs, professing himself the equal of Bates in matters of American trade and his superior in other fields. Crowning offence to the staunch Bostonian Bates, he took the side of the South in the American Civil War and treated Barings' trading partners from the North with scant courtesy – 'He is now anti-American in everything,' commented Bates sadly.[37]

But he was there; and Baring had a better opinion of him than Bates. In 1853, indeed, when Baring was becoming increasingly concerned about the amount of time he was devoting to other matters, including long stints on his doctor's orders taking the waters in

Germany, Sturgis's share of the profits was doubled to $\frac{1}{12}$. At the same time two young men were brought into the counting house at a salary of £1000 a year: Humphrey Mildmay's son Henry Bingham and the young Edward Baring who had so impressed Bates a few years before. Mildmay was brought in as a sop to his father, who was still offended at having been eased out of the house in 1847 – 'a very good young man, but can never become a manager of the House,' judged Bates.[38] Ned Baring was a different matter. 'His morals are bad, but he is clever,' felt Bates. The extent of his immorality, to judge from other entries in Bates's diary, was that he was fond of society, slovenly in his accounts, expensive in his habits, apt to hurry his business and not stay late in the office, and 'desirous of playing the first fiddle' – hardly the pinnacle of viciousness but black enough in the eyes of Bates.[39] 'I doubt his judgement' was Bates's summing up – which was in time to be proved perceptive indeed.[40] 'My impression is that neither of them will make a good merchant,' he concluded gloomily. If he and Thomas Baring were to retire, with more than £1 million of capital between them, there would be little left in the way of capital or talent. 'I suppose I must continue two years longer during which T. Baring will do very little.'[41]

In spite of these misgivings, Mildmay and Ned Baring were admitted partners at the beginning of 1856: of the 24 shares, Francis Baring, still the senior partner, retained 3; Joshua Bates 6; Thomas Baring 5; Charles Baring Young and Russell Sturgis 3 each and Mildmay and Ned Baring 1 each. The remaining 2 were kept in reserve against possible needs. The business they had joined could hardly have seemed more prosperous. In 1858, Bates noted proudly, Baring Brothers were agents for the governments of Russia, Norway, Austria, the United States, Chile, Buenos Aires, New Grenada, Canada, Nova Scotia, New Brunswick and Australia; they had 1200 correspondents in different parts of the world; they held the personal accounts of the Emperor of the French, Count Chambord, King Leopold of Belgium: 'No House ever had such a business and were I 20 years younger I should delight to conduct it.'[42] Neither the governmental nor the private accounts were necessarily a source of profit – in 1863 Barings found themselves suddenly having to come to the rescue of the Prince of Orange, who had lost his entire allowance and £2000 besides on the Derby[43] – but they gave the house prestige of inestimable value.

But Bates was not twenty years younger, and as he edged into his seventies he became more and more doubtful whether the house had any future after the departure of himself and Thomas Baring. Sturgis was spending £11,000 a year and the amount was increasing even faster than his income. He had only £20,000 in the business and showed no signs of increasing his stake appreciably. Edward Baring lived at the rate of £8400 a year and was far too fond of hunting. Bates remonstrated with them both. After some grumbling Sturgis agreed to give up his house in town, but the economy achieved was trifling and he made such a fuss about it that the word went around that Barings were in financial difficulties. Ned Baring promised to reduce his expenditure to £3000 a year, but signally failed to do so. Bates's preferred solution was to dismiss them both, replacing them by a senior clerk, George White, and his own grandson, Victor Van de Weyer. Whether he put this proposal to Thomas Baring is not clear; if he did he must have been persuaded that it was unduly drastic. The same partners were in charge in 1864; the two managing partners still agreeing that they would have the gravest doubts about leaving the business in the hands of their juniors, but doing nothing very much to put the matter right.[44]

By then Bates's health was clearly failing. Several times in the previous years he had proposed that Barings should go into voluntary liquidation rather than face inevitable decline. When he died in September 1864 it seemed that his suggestion might have to be adopted. Francis Baring ceased to be a partner almost immediately afterwards and the joint effect of these two departures was that the house's capital fell from £1.41 million in 1862 to £0.63 million in 1865, while the Reserve Account was reduced from £0.67 million to £0.13 million. Barings had either to reduce its commitments, rapidly build up its resources, or give up the struggle. It was Thomas Baring who had to find the solution, virtually single-handed.

The firm over which he presided had come a long way since the traumas of 1848. Barings in particular, and the British economy in general, had benefited by the flow of capital from the continent – France and Spain above all – as European capitalists tried to find a safe home for their resources. But to amass these funds was one thing, to deploy them profitably another. The late 1840s and early 1850s were nervous years. There were plenty of openings on the continent – in the last few weeks of 1848 Barings were approached about possible loans for Sardinia, Austria, Tuscany, Denmark and the City of Paris[45] – but none of them seemed possible in the political climate of the day. 'John Bull is in a sort of maze what to do with his money,' Bates told Thomas Baring. '. . . The American stocks are likely to attract his attention.'[46] But here too confidence took time to rebuild and it was to be some years before sales of American securities could be undertaken in London without extreme prudence. Yet somehow business continued buoyant; distributed profit for 1849 was £168,000 and only a little less in 1850. 'What enormous gains,' wondered Bates, and made with little risk, but he characteristically found grounds for despondency about the future: 'There seems abroad a growing indifference and unbelief in regard to Religion which more than anything indicates the decline of nations.'[47]

Barings put at least part of their profit into bricks and mortar. The business had now wholly outgrown the Georgian buildings at 8 Bishopsgate into which they had moved some fifty years before, and early in 1853 Lewis Cubitt, brother of William Cubitt, the architect of Belgravia, and himself responsible for the Great Northern Railway terminus at King's Cross, was called in to remodel the premises. Amazingly, he had completed his work, which included building over the old courtyard and installing gas lighting, within seven months and the imposing new office block was in full operation by the end of the year. 'I hear that you are making yourself very smart and comfortable in Bishopsgate Street,' wrote Charles Labouchère.[48] Bates simply wondered how they had ever managed to make do with the old premises.[49] In accordance with the rules of business procedure throughout the ages, it was a matter of months rather than years before there were discontented murmurs that more space was required.

In January 1854 Baring Brothers gave a dinner at the London Tavern to their forty clerks. 'I hope we are setting a good example,' wrote Bates rather dubiously in his diary. 'They are certainly very excellent clerks.'[50] Ward told his son that they were 'so able in their respective places' that everything ran smoothly. 'Mr Bates says that they have several who are equal to everything required, and know just what to do whatever comes up, and that when anything is wanted of the partners, the matter is placed clearly before them by the Clerk in whose care it is in a few words together with his reasoning on it. The principals only have to assent to the conclusion arrived at, as they do usually, or decide what else shall be done.'[51] One of these super-clerks was presumably the George White whom Bates had wanted to make a partner in place of Russell Sturgis, and who was in time to play an important role in Argentina.

Barings were good employers. Recognizing that the road to the partners' room was all but impassable to those who did not belong to the family, they were always ready to help an ambitious youngster get on elsewhere. Charles Dickens's son Charley, who had been strongly recommended to them, was first put into a broker's and then offered a place in Bishopsgate at £50 a year. 'I suspect the Brokers to have been a device and trial altogether,' wrote his father '– to get a telescopic view of a youth with a double suspicion on him arising out of being an author's son and an Eton boy.'[52] Charley Dickens did well, and a few years later was sent off to set up his own business in Hong Kong with Barings' blessing and financial support. When George Knapp fell ill in 1860 Barings tolerated his frequent absences for almost eighteen months and only then retired him on a pension of £150 a year. His pension was continued to his widow when he died in 1865 and a cash payment was made to his two daughters when she followed her husband.[53]

The Liverpool house never expanded to the extent Bates had once hoped, but it continued to make a useful contribution to profits, usually between £20,000 and £30,000 a year. For twenty years from 1848 it was run by James Price, who became a partner in the London house in 1867. Price was a bachelor, a fact which proved profitable to his second-in-command, Mathias Purton, who found himself responsible for the house's entertainment of American and other visitors. 'I should wish to do the thing in proper style,' he wrote, 'and this I have no doubt you also would expect.'[54] Presumably they did; anyway, they raised no objection when he increased his expenditure by £800 a year and bought a new house for £2850. Price was a prudent man and objected when Bates played with the idea of taking an interest in a line of packet boats to the United States. Cunard had more than enough screw boats to cope with any foreseeable demand and would be formidable competitors. 'The management of steamers is a business of itself and with which the less such Houses as ours have to do, the better.'[55] His words were heeded, Barings' direct involvement in transport by sea was not revived for a decade or more.

Screw boats were one factor that transformed the business of merchant banking, the telegraph was another. 'All news is now made by the electric telegraph common property,' Barings told Hottinguers in 1853, in mingled gratification and alarm.[56] The new development had its influence in every field, but above all in the world of international finance which Thomas Baring had made his own, and which occupied more and more of the house's energies as Joshua Bates lost his grip on the day-to-day business of acceptances and credits. The day of hurried missions and face-to-face negotiations was by no means over, but it became increasingly possible for bankers to appoint representatives abroad and control them closely.

So far as Europe was concerned, Thomas Baring's main preoccupation in the years after 1848 was to practise the art of refusing gracefully. In 1849 Count Tojal, the Portuguese Minister of Finance, asked for a small loan of £45,000 for the repair of roads. Barings replied:

> Nothing would be more agreeable and flattering to us than to be able to co-operate efficiently with advantage to the Government of Portugal . . . That desire on our part has, we can assure Your Excellency, not been diminished when we find that the department of the Finances has been confided to a minister of such acknowledged talents and experience as yourself . . . We have not the slightest distrust of the honour or good faith of the Government of Portugal or of its full determination to keep strictly to its engagements, but we unfortunately had during the last operation a proof that inevitable events may baffle the best intentions, and that perfect reliance cannot be placed on the exact payments at times fixed, and Your Excellency is aware how important such punctuality is in the business of merchants.[57]

In a case like this, Barings concluded, the best solution was to let the local population pay.

Even where the prospects did seem more enticing Barings were hesitant. Towards the end of 1848 they advanced £170,000 to the Spanish government against the delivery of mercury, a safe and profitable business even if it involved tying up capital for a period longer than they really liked. But when the proposal was renewed they proved reluctant. Their correspondent in Madrid, Henry O'Shea, was told that Barings, 'as a matter of delicacy and good feeling', were anxious to avoid 'direct and repeated competition' with their neighbours, Rothschilds.[58] This was the first manifestation of a trend which was to become more and more apparent as the nineteenth century wore on; Rothschilds and Barings no longer seeking to cut each other's throats in every corner of the world, but tacitly accepting that each had a sphere of influence in which they were predominant. Partly this stemmed from recognition of the fact that in a conflict of this kind there could be no winner, only greater or lesser losers; partly it was a banding together of the two oldest and grandest houses against the threat of the joint stock banks and the emergence of new competitors on both sides of the Atlantic.

The new spirit of conciliation wore pretty thin in Spain, however, when the two houses found themselves vying for the 1849/50 mercury contract. The problem for Barings was that the Spanish government was too deeply committed to Rothschilds to shuffle them off altogether, yet wanted to have a rival conspicuously in the offing to ensure that its regular bankers did not exploit it unmercifully. Barings were cast in this dispiriting role. Weisweiller, the Rothschilds' representative, at one point suggested that the two houses should tender for the mercury on joint account, conduct the sales jointly and split the profit fifty-fifty.[59] Thomas Baring, who had gone out to Spain for the auction, was cautiously interested, but negotiations foundered when the Spanish government set a price for the mercury far higher than Barings were prepared to pay, and Rothschilds took the contract for the next two years. From London Joshua Bates complained that Barings' agents, O'Shea and Co., had time and again been outmanoeuvred by Weisweiller and the Rothschilds. Baring defended them: 'They have certainly not the shrewd cunning nor the active talent for intrigue of Weisweiller, but in these qualities Jews beat Christians all over the world. They are, however, honest, straightforward and zealous.'[60] Whether Rothschilds would in fact have gone through with the compromise is an open question; Thomas Baring believed they would only have done so if they had been in sole charge of the negotiations.[61] What is certain is that Rothschilds had no intention of being driven from the field. Baron Lionel told Weisweiller 'to offer $60 in case he has good reason for believing that Baring intends opposing us and making an offer, but if not, he is to offer 53 and to try to get it at 55.'[62]

The Spanish government continued to make overtures to Barings over the next decade but the only time that anything came near a conclusion was in 1853 when Barings were ready to sponsor a £9.5 million loan. Hopes flatly refused to cooperate – 'We have had such repeated proofs of the little faith that can be placed in the assurances of the Spanish Government that we should not wish to place our-selves again in their power'[63] – and were proved right when a politi-cal storm in Madrid led to the government reneging on the deal. It was not until 1867 that Barings again undertook any operation on behalf of Madrid, and then it was on a limited scale and rendered nugatory by a revolution the following year.

Spain was Rothschild territory into which Barings rarely and timidly ventured; the reverse was true in Russia which was to be for seventy years or more the European country with which Barings were most intimately involved. When Baron Stieglitz, the Berlin-born financier who enjoyed a semi-official status in St Petersburg, wished to raise a large loan for the Russian government in 1849, he this time went directly to Barings rather than first approaching Hopes. Barings were sceptical; they wanted Hopes to take the lead and, anyway, felt that 'with the war in Hungary undecided and doubtful, and all European policy uncertain, the chance of profit at 95 does not seem to us at present to compensate for the risk of loss'.[64] Russia at the time was in one of its phases of full-blooded self-assertion, its armies rampant in Poland and Hungary. Barings' calculations were coloured by the fact that Richard Cobden, the influential economist and politician, was being vociferous even by his own high standards in denouncing Rus-sian aggression, and at a well-attended meeting at the London Tav-ern only a few days before had inveighed against any possible loan. 'We do not attribute much importance to the circumstance,' Barings told Stieglitz,[65] but they did.

By the end of the year, however, the war in Hungary was to all intents and purposes over and the loan which the Russian government was seeking was presented as being for the completion of the Moscow–St Petersburg railway and not for any military purpose. Cobden duly denounced it as an 'unholy and infamous transaction,'[66] but the average British investor was more concerned with the prospects of profit. Bates was uneasy – £5.5 million seemed to him too large an amount and 93 too high a price – but he allowed himself to be over-persuaded.[67] His doubts were quickly appeased, the issue was six times oversubscribed and opened at a 2 per cent premium. An anonymous letter received at Bishopsgate which threatened dire consequences to all concerned did nothing to damp the euphoria.[68] The commission earned by Barings, apart from any profits made by dealings in the bonds, was £105,000.[69] Bates's only complaint was that by August 1850 Barings still held £150,000 worth of Russian stock on their own account and Thomas Baring was reluctant to sell it off. It was the old difference of attitude between the two men; in Bates's view, 'the object should be to close an operation and secure the profits – if it can be done without injuring the general impression in regard to the well conducting of the Loan, and as there have been eager buyers I cannot account for the disposition to hold'.[70] But this was a minor blemish; reflecting on the loan Bates concluded: 'I don't know that B. B. and Co. can stand any higher, they are undoubtedly the first Commercial firm in the world which is a great achievement when it is considered that there is no stain on their fame of any kind. We are always liberal to all, honest as a matter of course. We work hard, perhaps too hard.'[71]

Two years after the loan had passed off so successfully, a credit was opened at Barings in favour of the Imperial Court. In effect Barings were now the official agents of the Russian government. It was unfortunate that this happened at a moment when Britain and Russia seemed on the brink of war over Turkish territorial problems. One of Barings' first tasks was to remove the Russian deposit of about £1 million from the Bank of England, retain a third of it for the payment of dividends and ship the rest to Holland in Gold Imperials. 'This will make a sensation when it becomes known,' commented Bates, and a few days later: 'This move is either a political manoeuvre or there must be fear of war on the part of Russia.'[72]

The fears were justified. In March 1854 Britain and France declared war on Russia. Barings' well-known association with the Russian government did not make things easy for them. In the House of Commons Palmerston described Thomas Baring as being the private agent of the Emperor of Russia.[73] The relationship between international finance and foreign policy, or to particularize, between Barings and the Foreign Office, is always hard to define with any precision.[74] Thomas Baring constantly met members of the government in the House of Commons, private houses and the clubs. Often his relations were among them. He was considered by them to be a member of the establishment, whose discretion could be relied on and whose opinion on many issues was well worth eliciting. He, for his part, made it his business to know the main lines of British policy. It is hard to conceive any circumstances in which he would deliberately have taken action likely to frustrate it, and impossible to believe that he would ever have ignored a direct instruction, or even request from the British government – self-interest as well as patriotism would have precluded any such behaviour.

But it did not follow from this that Barings were a docile tool of British policy. On the contrary, they could often take an independent line. Thomas Baring liked to know what the government was about, but he retained the discretion *not* to know if it suited his book. There was in fact nothing ministers could have done to block the transfer of the Russian deposits out of the country, but if there had been and Baring had thought it possible that there might be opposition, he would have been capable of making the transfer first and telling the government later. As for the Crimean War, he never viewed it as anything but a calamity, and an unnecessary one at that. 'Decidedly and foolishly war-like,' was how Barings described the public mood to Hottinguers in February 1854.[75] Of John Russell's peace mission in 1855, Barings feared that 'public opinion may be so goaded by the press and so irritated by the failure of immediate and complete success in the war as had been absurdly anticipated, that national vanity may be a hindrance to a reasonable peace'.[76]

Nor did Barings pretend, even in wartime, that their relations with their commercial contacts in Russia were ever less than cordial. In June 1854 Baron Stieglitz rather bizarrely offered Barings participation in a 50 million rouble war loan. He made it clear he did not anti-

cipate acceptance and Barings duly refused the offer, but 'we are not
the less obliged to you for this evidence of a friendship which we
always value'.[77] When peace came in 1856, Barings were quick to
assure Stieglitz that 'one of the most awful results of the war has been
the interruption of our full and confidential correspondence. We
trust that such a disastrous state of events may not again occur.'[78]

During the war Barings continued to market enough Russian
bonds through Hopes to meet the interest due to British investors on
earlier issues. This activity caused some confusion. 'Only think of the
Russian loan being levied here!' wrote the Secretary of State for
Foreign Affairs, Lord Clarendon, indignantly to his wife. 'In the
ordinary way of business, too, so I don't see how it can be interfered with! £200,000 left London yesterday . . .'[79] It sounds as if
Clarendon was equating payment of interest on the 1850 loan with a
new loan. A surprising number of people, though few of them as
well-informed as Clarendon should have been, imagined Barings
were in some way associated with Stieglitz's 50 million rouble war
loan. Legally this would have been impermissible, economically
injudicious, and politically and socially inconceivable.[80]

As soon as the war was over Barings plunged back into the fray.
The insatiable appetite of the Russian railways for fresh financing
led to negotiations in April 1856 for a huge loan to cover the construction of a network of 2500 miles at an eventual cost of some £40
million. The *Grande Société des Chemins de Fer Russes*, as the enterprise
was called, was to build a line from St Petersburg to Warsaw and
other links, mainly radiating from Moscow. Stimulated in part at
least by the knowledge that Rothschilds were showing interest,
Barings played an unwontedly aggressive role, and in October
Thomas Baring led a group of French and English bankers to St
Petersburg. Bates was initially suspicious; 'Unless they make a very
favourable contract they will, I trust, make no engagement. For my
part I rather wish to have nothing to do with it.'[81] Once the contract
was signed, however, excitement overcame his habitual caution: 'If it
does not prove a brilliant affair I shall be much disappointed.'[82]
Barings agreed to place in London 140,000 shares of £20 each.

An extraordinary outcry greeted the announcement of this agreement, based partly on the argument that British capital was needed
urgently in Britain, partly on the impropriety of helping a country of

autocratic tendencies which had so recently been an enemy, and partly on the alleged riskiness of the investment. In Birmingham Peel made a speech warning the public not to hazard their money in such a field, but his words were dulcet compared with those of the press. Under the headline 'Patriotism and Five Per Cent' the *Illustrated London News* speculated whether Barings could be considered good patriots – 'naturally no direct answer can be given to such a ticklish question'.[83] *Punch* broke into verse:

> Can anybody of the British nation
> Attempt a railway loan's negotiation
>   His countrymen in Russian toils ensnaring?
> No firm in England, sure, could be so base,
> Let us then hope that such is not the case,
>   Although reported of the House of Baring.[84]

But it was *The Times* that produced the most sustained and rebarbative abuse, causing particular offence to Bates by a piece that accused Barings of rigging the market. The newspaper adduced a pair of apparently respectable clergymen who had been put forward as would-be buyers of the stock but in fact were pawns of the unscrupulous promoter. 'False, wicked and malicious,' Bates described it; 'It is inconceivable that malice can invent such falsehoods.'[85] Small wonder that Bates had been outraged when assured in Paris that Barings were proprietors of *The Times*: 'Of course I denied it and informed that it was hostile to the Barings and had abused them from the late Lord Ashburton down to the present Generation.'[86]

The hostility of the press, a shortage of money, the low interest offered by the Russian government, and reasonable doubts about the viability of the project, combined to make the issue a disaster. Under 19,000 shares were applied for, and though others were gradually disposed of in Amsterdam or St Petersburg, Barings were left holding more than 100,000 shares at the end of 1857. They remained obstinately optimistic, however; Thomas Baring told Stieglitz that he was certain the shares would soon win the approval of the British investor while Hottinguers were confidently assured: 'The more we hear and learn of the Grand Russian Railway the better we think of it . . . We hope the opening 100 miles towards Warsaw may make a sensation that the London press will have to notice.'[87]

Unfortunately their optimism proved ill founded. Within a few months they were grumbling about the extravagance of the enterprise and the refusal of the Russians to employ a British engineer.[88] Costs were consistently exceeded, schedules not held to, those lines that were operating were run inefficiently. Thomas Baring tried to withdraw from the Board of the *Grande Société* on the grounds that there were few British shareholders and he had no useful role to play.[89] The foreigners on the council were invariably ignored and 'I do not wish to expose myself to such complete neglect,' he complained in 1868. 'I suppose that the foreign members are considered ornamental but they are evidently of no weight.'[90] For Barings the *Grande Société* meant a lock-up of much-needed capital and much worry and frustration.

Nor did their support for Russian railways guarantee their position when other loans were in question. At the end of 1858, when the Russian government wanted to raise £11 million, it disconcerted Barings by announcing that it proposed to offer the contract to several tenderers. 'We cannot forbear from expressing the painful regret that we experience in observing that the Russian government, in applying to others, should seem to manifest a distrust of the ability and zeal of those who have in past times been entrusted with similar negotiations,' wrote Thomas Baring reproachfully to Baron Stieglitz. 'I cannot help fearing when not an open but private competition is involved . . . that we may be defeated by arts which we could not employ.'[91] The arts he had in mind were of course those of Rothschilds, but when the bids were put in it was found that by far the best came from the respectable but relatively minor firm of Thomson Bonar.

The loan was not a success and Thomson Bonar proved themselves incapable of sustaining the credit of the Russian government. For several years Barings and Rothschilds then boxed and coxed in the favour of St Petersburg; Barings having an expensive time of it in 1860 repairing the damage done by Bonars, Rothschilds managing no better in 1862. Then in 1864 the tide turned; fortunately for Barings on a loan which they and Hopes controlled. The year 1866 proved still better, with Barings harvesting a vast subscription of £18.6 million against a total loan of £6 million which had to be shared with Hopes. It seemed that a prosperous future lay ahead.

But the fickle British public soon concluded that there was a limit to the quantity of Russian stock it was prepared to stomach. The Dutch market too showed signs of being sated. A succession of railway loans proved that the money was more easily raised in Paris, Berlin or Frankfurt, and inevitably the Russians began to look in that direction. Between 1870 and 1886 three fifths of foreign investment in Russia came from Germany.[92] It was a development that left little room for Barings.

While Russia was hungry for foreign capital, France was very capable of looking after its own requirements; indeed French capitalists were more and more in competition with the British in the European money markets. Bates told Lord Shaftesbury that 'he had more hopeful views of French finance than of any other country on earth,'[93] and though the country's wealth was more latent than apparent in the years that immediately followed the revolution of 1848, Louis Napoleon's coup d'état at the end of 1851 restored the confidence of the monied classes.

Barings flattered themselves that they enjoyed a special relationship with the future Emperor. In 1885 they were to write to the *Edinburgh Review*, complaining of a story that in 1866 Louis Napoleon had deposited nearly £1 million with them as a hedge against possible future trouble: 'This statement is entirely erroneous. In 1866 we had neither money nor securities belonging to the Emperor of the French . . . Neither then, nor at any other time during his reign, did the Emperor remit to us any large amount either of money or securities.'[94] The statement was carefully phrased and somewhat disingenuous. Louis Napoleon during his exile in Britain had been a frequent visitor to Joshua Bates's home and during his time as Emperor from time to time deposited a few thousand pounds with Barings, notably after a visit Bates paid to St Cloud in November 1860.[95] Nothing remotely approaching £1 million was involved, but Louis Napoleon was still aware that Barings were his trusted friends.

It must have been in part at least this familiarity which led him in September 1855 to write directly to Joshua Bates with a most singular proposal. There had been a bad harvest in France. If the French government were known to be in the market, prices would soar.

Would Barings procure 3 million hectolitres of corn in the United States? This would be sold in France at the current price: if Barings gained on the deal, it would be their good luck, if they lost, the French government would make up the deficit.[96] It was Ireland and 1845 over again; no one could be better qualified for the task than Barings, Bates assured the Emperor, 'having executed a similar commission for the late Sir Robert Peel'.[97] They would prefer not to make a profit on the deal, but would charge 2 per cent commission on the purchases and 5 per cent on any money they had to advance for the purpose.[98] Louis Napoleon was so far satisfied with this offer that he broke off negotiations with the French houses with whom he had also been treating and entrusted the business to Barings.

The operation could hardly have been better carried out. A poor harvest in Germany and the devastation of the Russian crops by drought and locusts drove prices upward, but in Boston Ward handled the purchases with skill and discretion. 'We repeat our anxiety that this order be executed in the best manner possible,' read Ward's instructions. 'As great confidence has been placed in us by His Majesty the Emperor we should be very sorry that he should in any way be disappointed,' – exemplary sentiments, though rendered a little less inspiring by the fact that the letter was copied to Louis Napoleon.[99] By mid-February, 1856, corn to the total value of £1,864,940.6s.3d. had arrived in France – 'There was a heavy loss on the operation,' reported Barings, 'which however was a gain to the people of France by the influence which our sales had on the general prices.'[100] The only snag was that Barings had to wait a long time for their money. Francis Baring in Paris was responsible for pressing for payment. He found it an ungrateful task. 'This is the shabbiest Government going,' he grumbled. 'After going from one Minister to another I have only half done my job.'[101] The trouble was that if he pressed too hard he gave the impression that Barings were in urgent need of their money and thus not so affluent as generally believed. To be deprived of the money was indeed more inconvenient than they liked to admit; in February 1856 they had to draw on Hopes for £100,000 to tide things over.[102]

Apart from this unusual enterprise, Louis Napoleon's favour did Barings little good in France. When the French government wanted to raise 500 million francs as a loan in 1855, to help pay for the

Crimean War, Barings were the only foreign house to be asked to join the Parisian banks, but the demand in Paris was so great that their list of subscribers was returned to them unused.[103] According to the French financier, Baron d'Eichthal, they suffered more than disappointment. When the French Minister of Finance, Achille Fould, first approached Barings, Thomas Baring apparently argued that, as banker for the Russian government, he could not undertake the issue. He was over-persuaded, and the Russians, attributing the loan's great success to Barings' participation, took their revenge in St Petersburg when their latest loan was put out to tender in 1858.[104] The story seems unlikely; Barings' role in the French loan was in fact insignificant and, if the Russians had felt vengeful, it would presumably have been in 1856 that their displeasure would have been most evident. It is possible, though, that while they accepted that Barings would have actively to support the British government in the Crimean War, they felt it unfriendly to extend that aid to France, and that the memory of this made them more ready to abandon Barings when Thomson Bonar or Rothschild were in contention for a loan.

What small contribution Barings did make to French financing lay in the development of the railways, and here too the French could provide all their own needs and more. Whatever share Barings were willing to take, they found themselves cut down to a tithe or less. They were reduced to arguing that they should at least be placed on a parity with the London Rothschilds, 'that there should be no superiority granted to them, and no power or privilege granted to them which we do not enjoy. That is requisite for our position here.'[105]

Under Louis Napoleon, indeed for the rest of the nineteenth century, foreign capital had little place in France. After the Franco-Prussian war, with French morale shattered and a need to raise an £80 million indemnity loan within a few months, it seemed that outside help would once more be essential.[106] Barings and Rothschilds jointly issued the prospectus and Barings offered to guarantee £2 million for themselves and £2.7 million for 'our friends under our responsibility'.[107] But even this modest contribution proved unnecessary; Paris alone subscribed more than was needed to cover the indemnity, and the French provinces half as much again.

*   *   *

Except for Russia, therefore, Barings' role in international finance after 1848 was concentrated heavily on North and Latin America. They made occasional forays elsewhere. In 1857, for instance, young Hugh Childers was sent out to Australia to act as Barings' confidential representative to negotiate a £7 million loan needed by the Colonial Treasurer of Victoria – 'All is settled with the Barings. They offer very liberally,' wrote Mrs Childers appreciatively. Childers went, negotiated, and returned to report. 'Met Mr [Thomas] Baring and his cousin Mr Edward Baring,' he recorded. 'Norman Court a fine place. Full of curiosities. Edward Baring a capital fellow.' The trip had proved abortive, however. While he was *en route* to Australia the government had changed and the new ministers preferred to deal with the local banks.[108]

Barings were not beyond investing in stocks for which they had no personal responsibility. Thomas Baring rejected as sanctimonious humbug a sentence in a draft letter which stated Barings never speculated in this way. 'Our books would show that we have speculated for our own and for joint account in English, French, Russian, Austrian, American stocks which we did not ourselves bring out, lately in Panama Bonds and Australian Railroad shares. And I presume we should do it again if there was a good prospect of profit.'[109] It was notable that members of the family were decidedly more robust than outsiders like Bates or Sturgis when it came to balancing profit against prestige. Writing about a Mexican loan Francis Baring commented. '. . . the question of dignity remains for the house, which I am less solicitous about if the thing goes down. I don't believe in dignity in our days. See how the Jew gets on!'[110]

Perhaps not surprisingly for a house that every year was concentrating more on the international field, Barings' one large investment at home continued to give trouble. '1858 has certainly been a wonderful year for profits,' Thomas Baring wrote to Bates. 'Luckily it has been an expensive one and we have Grand Trunk and Weardale, or we should become too fat and saucy.'[111] Grand Trunk was the North American railroad which was Thomas Baring's contribution to his house's losses; the Weardale ironworks, losing a regular £10,000 a year, was the cross that Bates had made and now bore manfully. In 1848 he was still hopeful that the situation could be retrieved. Iron was being produced at a little over £2 a ton, which if considerably more than the 16/– predicted by Attwood, was still a competitive price.[112] But to produce iron consistently at a price and quantity which could compete in a glutted market proved beyond Attwood's powers. By 1859 Thomas Baring had largely lost hope. 'I thoroughly deserve my name Thomas for I am incredulous of the existence of miracles . . . I confess that I am not in love with the present system of management and do not think that I disparage the great talents and knowledge of yourself and Mr Attwood when I say that I have not implicit confidence in either as an experienced and practical ironmaster.'[113] The annual loss was a trifling matter, the lock-up of funds far more serious, but there seemed nothing to be done but 'jog on as we best can together'. The moral was that merchant bankers should stick to doing what they knew how to do; something which neither Baring nor Bates would have disputed in principle but sometimes found harder to follow in practice.

What they still did best in practice, though the emphasis was shifting, was the nuts-and-bolts work of international trading. Acceptances were at £1.57 million in 1848, rose above £2 million in 1851, soared to £4.2 million in 1855, fell back in the troubles that followed, but quickly recovered and averaged over £7 million a year towards the end of the 1860s. In 1850 their acceptances were almost four times as large as Rothschilds', figures which contrast strikingly with those for foreign and colonial issues, where the Rothschilds' total was five times that of Barings;[114] Profits mounted proportionately: £11,209 in 1848; £217,863 by 1862; and £480,011 in 1868. There were setbacks, exceptional losses, lean years when international trade withered because of some crisis – but the trend was ever upward.

One such setback came in 1857, with a banking crisis in the United States spreading to Europe, in particular Hamburg and other northern cities. Given their strong American connections it was not surprising that people looked to Barings to see how they were weathering the storm. For some reason, persistent gossip maintained that they were in trouble, so much so that Brown Brothers in New York removed them from the list of houses on which Brown, Shipley might safely take bills. Brown, Shipley protested: Barings were 'among the undoubted English Houses; notwithstanding all the rumours [we] cannot bring ourselves to believe in the possibility of their being in any difficulty'.[115] When George Peabody and Co. came near default, the rumours about Barings redoubled and Brown, Shipley began to trim their sails – 'You need not attach more weight to *our* confidence in them than our assertions warrant, and an additional good name never hurts a Bill.'[116] First thoughts were best; Barings came through almost unscathed, losing only £15,000–£20,000, 'but it will be prudent to leave a considerable sum in Profit and Loss to meet any loss that may happen,' wrote Bates.[117] With a profit of £175,000 in 1857 they could well afford to; Peabody and Co. needed a loan of £800,000 from the Bank of England to carry on. Barings were ready to act as one of the guarantors but previously they had pressed hard for the immediate settlement of outstanding bills and caused the other firm considerable embarrassment. Rancour remained. 'Mr Peabody was so averse to have assistance from Barings . . . that he requested the withdrawal of their names.'[118]

The revolution of 1848 had switched investment from Europe to the United States, now the threat of civil war in the United States moved it back again The war caused schism in Barings – Joshua Bates sturdily supporting the North, Sturgis the South – but more immediately it bit deeply into the cotton trade of the Liverpool house, whose commission income fell from £32,000 in 1861 to £14,000 in 1862.

Fresh turmoil was caused by the joint-stock limited liability banks, whose intervention in matters outside their traditional field of domestic banking threatened the hegemony of the traditional merchant houses. Drawing their capital as they did from any willing investor, these new banks swiftly became larger even than the giants like Barings and Rothschilds. The Crédit Mobilier in Paris was the first great exemplar; Barings gave it a cautious welcome as a potential counterweight to Rothschilds and agreed that Francis Baring should become a director.[119] The movement did not reach London until 1863 in the shape of the International Financial Society. Many of the great names of the City – Junius Morgan of Peabody's, Herman Stern of Stern Brothers, Frederick Huth – were among the directors, but Barings and Rothschilds stayed aloof. Rothschilds were inveterate in opposition, Barings more ambiguous in their attitude.

'You see, Mr Mallet,' Bates said to the envoy of the Crédit Mobilier, 'we consider ourselves a sort of Crédit Mobilier, ourselves, alone.'[120] The argument is not unlike that of the headmaster of Eton contending that his school is really a glorified comprehensive – the same tone of patronizing broad-mindedness is apparent. Bates felt that a joint-stock bank was no more than 'large capital, collected for purposes of speculation'.[121] The idea of limited liability was ungentlemanly, a true Englishman (or American for that matter) should stick by his commitments to the last penny. They were also inefficient; sooner or later, Thomas Baring predicted, the public would appreciate 'that business can be conducted with greater economy, activity and attention by private establishments where every partner has a direct interest, than by boards playing with the money of others'.[122] But in the meantime they were there and notably powerful: 'It appears to me that these sort of Banks will get all the Public Loans and that B.B. and Co. must content themselves with the Commission and Banking business,' wrote Bates gloomily in 1863.[123]

Three years later the bubble was, if not burst, at least partially deflated. Feverish speculation against a background of ancestral voices prophesying war had been the order of the day for more than twelve months, and the more prudent houses like Barings had withdrawn their money from the discount houses and battened down the hatches. Then on 9 May 1866, Overend Gurney suspended payments. This great Quaker house had been by far the largest of the discount brokers, but it had lost heavily for several years and in 1865 had tried to redeem the position by turning itself into a limited liability company. The Bank of England appointed George Glyn, R. C. L. Bevan of Barclays Bevan Tritton and Co. and Kirkman Hodgson, who was soon to join Barings, to judge whether a rescue operation could be mounted. Their conclusion was that things had gone too far. Overend Gurney failed, and in their failing dragged down a host of lesser businesses. The result was temporarily to discredit the limited liability company and to lead to the return to Barings of much of the commercial credit business that they had lost over the previous years.

Joshua Bates was not there to weep crocodile tears over his rivals' misfortunes. With his death in 1864 Thomas Baring depended largely on Russell Sturgis for the running of the business. The thought gave him little satisfaction. His colleague, he felt, was intent on taking profit from the firm and uninterested in the need to build up its depleted capital. Sturgis thought himself quite as capable of managing the concern as ever Bates had been. 'That arises from a constitutional self-esteem which nothing shakes. Of course Americans look more and more to him as the great authority . . . There would be no harm in this if I could always feel perfect reliance on his sound judgement, but he seems to me to be disposed to form too rapid decisions and to act before due reflection, and then never thinks himself wrong.'[124]

Sturgis saw no reason why the house should be reinforced, either in management or in capital, and felt himself fully capable of carrying on if Thomas Baring were to follow Bates. The younger partners, Bingham Mildmay and Ned Baring, agreed. Thomas Baring, supported by Young, thought otherwise. He played with the idea of bringing in another American but was dissuaded by Ward – 'Two Americans would in all probability *quarrel* or *combine*. Equally bad!' What was needed was 'an Englishman of ability and large capital with whom you had a perfect understanding'.[125] By 1867 Baring decided he had found such a man. Ignoring the opposition of his partners – 'It was difficult to oppose Thomas Baring when he had made up his mind,' wrote Mildmay's son Alfred[126] – he forced through an amalgamation of Baring Brothers with the house of Finlay Hodgson and Co. It was, indeed, more like an amicable takeover than a merger: the name of Baring Brothers was retained, and though the result of the new combination was that the capital recovered from £760,000 to £1,390,000, none of the four incoming partners received more than 14/144 of the profits, as against Thomas Baring and Russell Sturgis who took 24/144 each. From Thomas Baring's point of view the most attractive element of the merger was the arrival in the house of Finlay Hodgson's senior partner, Kirkman Hodgson, a former Governor of the Bank of England and long-time colleague on the board of the Grand Trunk Railroad of Canada.

The predominance of the Barings in the new house was emphasized the same year when Thomas's nephew Thomas Charles, son of Charles Baring, the Bishop of Durham, joined the firm. He had been working in the United States for the previous decade and not much was known about him, except that he had been a distinguished classical scholar and was devoted to his old college, Hertford. Thomas was dubious about his nephew's potential, and inclined to wonder whether he was not filling a place that would be more usefully occupied by someone of greater efficiency, 'But there is room enough,' he comforted himself.

The first few years of the new partnership were comfortably successful. Profits rose from £297,000 in 1866 to £446,828 in 1869, but thereafter fell away. By the end of 1871 the capital had swollen to £2.4 million, with acceptances totalling £7.4 million. But it was still, if not a one-man band, then at least a house in which one partner was very evidently predominant. Thomas Baring's share of the capital was £609,000, almost as much as the next two put together – Sturgis and Mildmay with £320,000 apiece. Kirkman Hodgson had £261,000 against his brother J.S. with £251,000. Ned Baring came next with £222,000 while the newest recruit, Thomas Charles, had a mere £71,000.[127] In reputation and influence as well as fortune, Thomas Baring took the lead. There were many who speculated on the future of the house after he had departed.

Not least among these was Thomas Baring himself. From 1870 onwards he had been receding from the direction of the firm. It arose, he wrote, 'in part from age and natural indulgence . . . but also perhaps from the difficulty that may occur in free communications between as many as eight partners'. To the outside world he was still in charge, within the house more and more decisions were being taken without reference to him: 'I do not altogether like when I have been put on the top of the tree, to be regarded as a dead branch,' he complained.[128] Unlike Bates, he had many things to do outside the world of banking and no wish to cling on where he was not welcome. But his readiness to withdraw did not prove that he was entirely happy with what he left behind. About a year before he died, Lady Northbrook asked him whether she should encourage her son Francis to enter the bank. He advised her not to. 'I suspect,' wrote Lady Northbrook, 'from what I picked up that the Halcyon days of the Baring House are past and that there is no talent in the young men that have entered that are of My Boy's standing, and probably Tom Baring with his quiet discernment saw that the House would not keep up its reputation very many more years.'[129]

The testing time was about to come. In the spring of 1873 Thomas Baring was convalescing in Torquay and finding it on the whole beneficial; in the autumn he moved to Bournemouth and, for that or other reasons, lost ground rapidly.[130] On 19 November Bertram Currie of Glyn's wrote to his father, 'Poor old Thomas Baring went off at 4 p.m. yesterday . . . He was certainly a proof, if any were wanting, that a merchant may be as good a gentleman as an acred lord or squire and he was wisely content with and proud of his trade. I don't think he has left his equal behind.'[131] On this point Ned Baring at least was resolved to prove Currie wrong.

11

Riding for a Fall

1873–1890

For the next fifty years of Baring Brothers' history, the house was dominated by a father and son, Edward and John Baring, 1st and 2nd Barons Revelstoke. The two men were in many ways similar. Both were intelligent and cultivated, self-confident to the point of arrogance. They were dignified in manner and imposing in appearance, men accustomed to and demanding the deference of their inferiors, and putting into this category the generality of mankind. They were generous and public-spirited, not over-endowed with a sense of humour but felt by most people to be good company. The indolence that the family were apt to claim as their leading weakness was even less apparent in them than in most of their relations; they had immense application and zest for work. They differed most markedly in that John had the better judgement, more discretion, and a larger share of that most valuable of commodities, luck.

Ned Revelstoke was a man of deeper and more varied intellectual interests than his eldest son. His mother, Cecilia Wyndham, spoke fluent French, German and Italian, loved poetry and had a fine contralto voice which had been trained by Rossini.[1] Her passion for music was transmitted to her son and grandson. Ned was weaker in Italian but spoke excellent Spanish. He greatly enjoyed the theatre and held strong views about it; watching Irving play Romeo he punctuated the performance with indignant snorts of 'Remove that man from the stage'.[2] In this he was no more intemperate than in every other field: sitting next to him at a banquet at Plymouth Lady Monkswell observed with some amusement that when he thought the speeches were going on too long he began to swear to himself in a

186

far from inaudible undertone – 'one really did not know what he would say next'.[3]

His generosity was as unbridled as every other aspect of his character. He used to collect Bréguet watches; not to keep but to give away to people whom he thought would appreciate them. One day, walking in the garden of his Devonshire home with his son Maurice, he announced: 'This is your path; I give it to you and the gate at the end.' It was the inclusion of the little iron gate at the end, recalled Maurice Baring, 'which made that present poignantly perfect'. He had a contempt for half-measures and liked both himself and others to do things on the grandest possible scale. 'So and so,' he used to say, 'has behaved well'; by which he meant 'big and free handed, and above small and mean considerations'. He liked the best.[4] *'C'était magnifique,'* some financial Bosquet might have remarked, *'mais ce n'était pas la haute finance.'*

Nor was his recklessness an attribute generally to be recommended in a banker. His father, Henry, had been a celebrated gambler and was said to have won his house, 11 Berkeley Square, at cards from Lord Orford.[5] Ned Baring was no card player but he had a gambler's instinct which caused frequent distress to his more prudent partners. For a long time the gambles came off. Baring's reputation became ever more established and his renown spread as the first banker of London, and hence the world. In 1885 he was offered a peerage in Gladstone's dissolution honours. His companion in ennoblement was Nathan Rothschild – 'It was thought desirable at this moment to give an addition of commercial strength to the House of Lords,' noted Edward Hamilton, Gladstone's private secretary.[6] Neither the reason nor the company could have been particularly appealing to Baring, but such a gift horse was not to be looked in the mouth. Thanking Gladstone for this 'entirely unexpected and distinguished honour', he assured his patron that the pleasure was enhanced by its coming 'from one so distinguished as yourself, for whom I entertain a sincere admiration and respect'.[7] Lord Revelstoke, as he now called himself, was not the first active banker to become a peer – Lord Overstone had been the first and George Glyn, Lord Wolverton, had followed soon after – but it was still a rarity and he could justly take pride in his achievement. But though his admiration and respect for Gladstone were undoubtedly sincere, they did not stop him accompanying the main weight of the City interest in its drift towards the Tories. When in May 1886 there was a meeting at the Westminster Palace Hotel of dissident Liberals intent on preserving the Union with Ireland, the Lords Rothschild and Revelstoke were among those appointed to the General Committee.[8]

It was shortly after he received his peerage that Revelstoke began the lavish refurbishment of his house in Charles Street, Mayfair. No. 37, an already substantial mid-eighteenth-century terrace house of grey brick which he had bought fifteen years before, was united with No. 38 and £55,000 spent gutting the interiors and creating a rich French-style ensemble with sweeping marble staircase, riotous rococo ornamentation and decorative panelling looted from the houses of France. Into this opulent showcase Revelstoke poured his outstanding collection of French furniture and *objets d'art* – an item typical of his taste was described, in auctioneer's English, as 'Pair of Louis XVI or-molu candelabra, each with an undraped female figure bearing a cornucopia, supporting poppy branches for three lights each, on plinths chased with oak branches, foliage and acorns, by Goullière – on circular pedestals of red and white marble, decorated with festoons of vine foliage and flowers of chased or-molu'.[9] The pictures were less distinguished than the other furnishings: there was a fine Cuyp in one of the two downstairs drawing rooms but a vast Birket Foster view of Venice on the landing outside was more illustrative of the owner's taste.[10] Within this *cadre* Revelstoke entertained in a style as lavish as the furnishing. It was always a home, however: a visitor remembered seeing its splendours tarnished by three small sons of the house lined up on the great staircase, seeing who could pee furthest towards the hall.[11]

As befitted a public figure of his grandeur, Revelstoke became a landowner. The Baring estates were concentrated in Hampshire where they had now accumulated 89,000 acres. There they lived in princely style; in 1887 4076 partridges were shot on Lord Ashburton's land in four days, beating the previous record of 3392 at Holkham in 1885. Revelstoke decided not to compete with his solidly established cousins. He had married Louise-Emily Bulteel, from an old Devonshire family, and it was to the county that had first received the Barings in 1717 that he now returned. He bought the estate of Membland, twelve miles from Plymouth, near the Bulteels of Pamflete and the Mildmays of Flete. There he remodelled the old manor house, converting it into a large, square mansion of Jacobean style built of white brick, with green shutters, ivy and a tower. Houses on the estate were all painted in a distinctive shade somewhat pretentiously described as 'Revelstoke blue'; the 'Bull and Bear Gate', set with figures of appropriate design, commemorated his alliance with the Bulteels; the church at the neighbouring village of Noss Mayo was demolished and rebuilt; Revelstoke's 150-ton yacht, the *Waterwitch*, was berthed in the Yealm river thereby: everything was done in the most lavish style.

Ned Baring had not started rich. In 1873, when Thomas Baring died, the total capital of Baring Brothers was about £2.2 million, of which Thomas Baring owned a quarter. Much of this went to his nephew, T. C. Baring, and thus stayed in the firm; but by 1874 the capital had still dropped to just under £2 million. Of this Edward Baring's share was £222,000, which compared favourably with the pittance with which he had begun but was significantly smaller than the holdings of Sturgis, Bingham Mildmay and J. S. Hodgson. Four years later, so ambitious was his spending, his share of the capital had slipped to a mere £78,000, the smallest of all the partners. It did not even begin to build up substantially until the mid-1880s, and even by 1890 the two Hodgsons, Mildmay and Francis Baring had far larger holdings. But this in no way indicated his importance and activity within the firm, which related more closely to the share he took of the profits. In 1873 this had been $^{18}/_{144}$, against Russell Sturgis's $^{24}/_{144}$; by 1887, with Sturgis departed, he took $^{26}/_{120}$, H. B. Mildmay being the only other partner to receive as much.

Even this did not reflect the extent of his real authority. It was his young brother Evelyn, later Lord Cromer, who earned the nickname 'Over-Baring', but it could as well have been applied to Ned. With the death of Thomas Baring he became increasingly difficult to control and determined to control others. The only effective opposition from within the house came from the senior partner, Russell Sturgis, and the workings of the partnership made it certain that Sturgis would never be more than *primus inter pares* and sometimes not even that. When he retired in 1882, the tone of T. C. Baring's comments was almost contemptuous: Sturgis was physically as strong as ever, he told T. W. Ward's son, Samuel, but 'his nerves have grown weaker of late and he shrinks from the risks that must be met in a business like ours. . . . But we shall lose a genial, kindly and popular partner, who used to work very hard.'[12]

Sturgis's departure was preceded by one of the few serious rows between the partners in the whole of Barings' history. Sturgis insisted that his son Harry should become a partner. His colleagues refused to agree. Harry could be made a partner in the Liverpool office but that was all they would concede. When Sturgis persisted, Ned Baring drew up a grand remonstrance. 'We think it is hardly fair that he should ask us on purely personal grounds to satisfy the expectations of his family to do what has never been done before for anyone and what we all consider is detrimental to the future interests of the House.' If he and Bingham Mildmay had been inclined to behave in the same way they would have sought to reserve the place for their own sons. As it was, his brother Tom had a prior right to a partnership and 'it would be unfair to overlook the claim that the Hodgson interest has to be represented in the House'. Bob Hodgson was at least as strong a candidate as Harry Sturgis. 'I am the last to underrate Mr Sturgis's constant and valuable services to the firm,' Ned Baring concluded his memorandum, 'but supposed that (like the rest of us) he found a fair compensation in an annual accumulation of fortune as well as in the consideration which he enjoys as the head of Baring Brothers and Co.' At the bottom, under a laconic 'We fully agree', were the signatures of J. S. Hodgson, Charles Norman, T. C. Baring and Henry Bingham Mildmay.[13] Robert Hodgson and, eventually, Tom Baring, became partners or directors of Baring Brothers; Harry Sturgis was a managing partner in Liverpool from 1880 but never entered the partners' room in Bishopsgate.

Sturgis's demands on behalf of his son had been inspired by the fact that Francis Henry Baring, son of the 1st Lord Northbrook by his second wife, had recently been granted procuration, a step on the road towards full membership. Francis Baring had dithered for some time before joining the house at all. In March 1874 T. C. Baring reported that he was 'hesitating between a desk here with a large fortune in prospect and a private secretaryship with a view to a life purely political'.[14] Francis did not abandon his political ambitions but concluded: 'Business will, I suppose, lead pretty safely to the House of Commons in good time and is not a bad training for politics or official work if it should come.' He had no anxiety to be very rich, he told his father, 'but it does seem a useful work in the World to keep up a house of high business character'. Besides, if he did not go in, within twenty years there would be little connection between Baring Brothers and the Baring family, and 'this is a prospect that Ned and Charles both seem to dislike very much'.[15] Given the plethora of Baring sons, nephews and cousins available to fill any and every vacancy, this last concern is hard to take too seriously, but the problem of the succession always preoccupied the senior Barings in the house, and anyone who was both able and bore the sacred name would be made to feel welcome.

Francis Baring was exceptionally able. His political career never came to anything and could not have been expected to; his health was poor, his oratorical powers conspicuously lacking and his shy and reserved nature wholly unsuited to the hurly-burly of the hustings or convivial caballing in the clubs or the House of Commons. But he was a classical scholar and a mathematician of real distinction, with a lucid mind and a rare capacity for seeing the essential facts in any situation and holding to them tenaciously. His value to the firm was obvious from the start and was to become more so in the times of crisis that lay ahead.

Ned Baring's brother Tom, whose pretensions had been defended against those of Harry Sturgis, had begun his career in Liverpool, and continued it in the New York firm of Kidder Peabody. His twin passions were classical literature and various types of sporting activity. The latter was the more apparent of the two. A large, red-faced man of blimpish manner, he had been Captain of the Boats at Eton, hunted vigorously when in England, had fished many Canadian rivers and spent his holidays pursuing grizzly bears, moose and wild goats around the Rocky Mountains. When stirred, he could be active and efficient, but the Baring indolence, so absent in his brother, often possessed him. He enjoyed his life in New York but was vaguely disgruntled that he had never been offered a niche in Bishopsgate and regularly awaited a call that was a long time in coming.

Another Baring recruit to the house was Revelstoke's son, John. An oarsman like his Uncle Tom, he achieved the extraordinary feat of coxing the Eton eight one year and rowing stroke the next.[16] At

Cambridge he was master of the University Drag, 'always splendidly mounted,' noted a contemporary, 'and did justice to his horses too, being a fine horseman whose seat in the saddle was akin to perfection'.[17] But at the age of twenty he left university to join Barings, spent two years going through the mill in the counting house, then did an extensive tour of North and South America and finally became a partner early in 1890. To those who studied the fortunes of the house it seemed that he was the most likely of the younger generation to steer it into the twentieth century.

Whether it was – as their father suspected – to keep the line of succession open for John Baring, or because he had doubts about their capacity, Lord Revelstoke flatly refused to take any of Lord Ashburton's sons into the bank, even on a trial basis.[18] Certainly the field was left clear as a result. Charles Norman, one of the old Finlay Hodgson partners, died in 1889 with £600,000 of Barings' capital to his name, to be replaced by his son Archie; but Archie Norman, though well liked and no fool, was not a contender for the leadership. By 1890 he and John Baring were the only two partners who could reasonably expect to survive when Lord Revelstoke and Francis Baring finally departed.

In the meantime T. C. Baring played the part of Revelstoke's right-hand man. Thomas Charles was one of those conscientiously grumpy characters who are always assumed to have a heart of gold but gives few grounds to support such an assumption. His irritability and cantankerousness can be excused by his sufferings from gout, but did not make him appealing in society; indeed, he cultivated few acquaintances, ignoring his neighbours in Roehampton and throughout the year driving the few hundred yards to church in a closed carriage with his children, even on the hottest day, dressed in scarlet comforters and goloshes. When his sons went to Harrow the family moved to the area so that the children could live near by 'and be spared the contamination of other boys'.[19] Two of them were sacked.

Anecdotes abound of T. C. Baring getting the better of other people, and usually jumping on them afterwards. At night when he was being driven back to his house on the outskirts of London he would sleep soundly in his carriage. Suspecting, however, that his coachman was giving an illicit lift to a friend, he one night changed places

Edward Baring (1828-1897), first Lord Revelstoke, by Rudolf Lehmann.

"SAME OLD GAME!"

Old Lady of Threadneedle Street. "YOU'VE GOT YOURSELVES INTO A NICE MESS WITH YOUR PRECIOUS 'SPECULATION!' WELL—I'LL HELP YOU OUT OF IT,—FOR THIS ONCE!!"

A cartoon from *Punch*, 8 November 1890, referring to the Baring Crisis of that year.

with him and donned the cloak and hat. Someone duly signalled to the carriage to stop and prefaced his thanks by saying that he supposed the old so-and-so was safely fuddled inside as usual. Baring threw off his passenger, drove home at full speed and fired the coachman. Another time a clerk made a foolish error in a letter to Hopes. Baring discovered the man responsible and dictated to him a letter to Hopes beginning: 'Owing to the gross carelessness of a member of our staff who has since been dismissed. . . .' To be fair to Baring, this was the last the wretched clerk heard of the incident.[20]

T. C. Baring retired at the end of 1888, aged only fifty-seven. When disaster overtook the firm two years later many people assumed that he had foreseen it and had resigned since he could not change what he regarded as Revelstoke's misguided policies. There is no evidence to suggest this was true and it was denied by other members of the family.[21] Certainly there is nothing in his farewell letter to indicate he was unhappy about the running of the firm. 'I have at least the satisfaction of knowing that I leave the conduct of the firm . . . in exceptionally able hands,' he told Lord Revelstoke, 'and I have great confidence in its new future, as John has shown what I consider great fitness for City life.' Increasing age and failing health were the only reasons he gave for his premature disappearance; 'I have had warnings enough that my powers will not bear the double strain of steady Parliamentary and City work.' Between the two he would have put business before politics, but having only recently been elected for the City of London, he felt that to throw up the seat so soon would not 'have reflected much credit on the firm'.[22]

T. C. Baring was a Member of Parliament, with one brief interruption, from 1874 until his death in 1891. His style was as truculent in the political field as in any other. Standing as a Tory against the Liberal brewer, Edward North Buxton, he took as his slogan 'Barings' brains are best' as a riposte to his opponent's celebrated 'Buxtons' beers are best'. 'Thank God I'm a churchman,' declared Buxton. 'Thank God *I'm* a Christian!' retorted Baring.[23] He was neither offered office nor would have accepted it. He was the last Baring prominent in the bank to combine the task with a parliamentary career, while Ned Revelstoke was the first not to do so. The fact marked a change in the attitude of the partners towards their work. Francis, Alexander, Thomas Baring had all been hard-working professional bankers but they did not see themselves as being merchants first and foremost. The first and second Lords Revelstoke accepted many responsibilities not directly related to their work at Bishopsgate, but they never doubted that Baring Brothers was by far their most important occupation. Banking after the 1880s did not allow of any parallel career.

There were still Barings, however, prominent in public life outside the City. The 2nd Baron Northbrook was appointed Viceroy of India in 1872, became an Earl, was given the Admiralty under Gladstone in 1880 and was as responsible as anyone for sending Gordon to Khartoum. His cousin, Evelyn Baring, younger brother of Ned Revelstoke, was one of the most remarkable public servants of the period, benevolent dictator of Egypt from 1883 to 1907 and created Baron then Viscount, finally Earl of Cromer – fourth of the five extant Baring peerages. In India, where he served before going to Egypt, he was called 'the Vice-Viceroy'; in Cairo he became 'Over-Baring'; after he became a peer he was known simply as 'The Lord'. All three nicknames indicate the strength of character and autocratic disposition which marked his public as much as his private life.

Neither Northbrook nor Cromer was associated directly with the bank, but it did not follow that they took no interest in its concerns. Both were on the short list of 'friends of the house' who could expect a share if some issue was to be floated on advantageous terms, and both felt it entirely natural to brief their relations on events in the public sphere which could bear upon financial developments. This suggests impropriety; none existed. Both Northbrook and Cromer were honourable men, who would never have contemplated taking advantage of their position to feather their own nest or do a good turn for their relations. By the standard of the time their behaviour was wholly proper; even in these more censorious days little would have been found to criticize.

In 1889, for instance, Lord Revelstoke heard that the Egyptian government might soon be seeking to appoint a new agent for the payment of the interest on the loans they had raised in London and Paris. They would like the job, Revelstoke told Evelyn Baring, 'and I think we may say that their interests would be honourably and carefully looked after. If under the circumstances it would not be agreeable to you that our name should be brought forward, we are quite willing to leave the matter entirely alone, but if otherwise, the business is a valuable one and quite in our line, so that it is worth while making an effort to get it. The Jew has no doubt already applied, but perhaps the Government may not be sorry to avoid being entirely in his clutches.'[24] Evelyn Baring replied that he saw no objection to Barings offering themselves for the task. It was not a matter in which he would expect to be consulted, but, 'in order to avoid any possibility of misrepresentation, I will ask the various authorities concerned to settle it in any manner they may think most conducive to the interests of Egypt and without communication with me in any form whatsoever'.[25] There is every reason to suppose that he was as good as his word; Barings did not secure the agency.

Not everyone was ready to assume that the Barings were automatically public-spirited and high-principled. In 1884 Northbrook was despatched to Cairo on a mission to enquire into the state of Egypt's finances. Evelyn Baring, already ensconced in Cairo, was appointed his expert adviser. Randolph Churchill protested in the House of Commons. Traditionally, he said, the public service of the country had been free from any connection with commercial or financial enterprises. This appointment was flagrantly contrary to such a principle. '*Two* members of the great house of Baring are to be entrusted with the sole disposal and almost unlimited control of England's political and financial interests in Egypt. . . . There literally would be no difference whatever in sending out two members of the House of Rothschild. The two are almost equal in greatness and in their great pecuniary interest in the East.' Hugh Childers, the minister responsible, argued that Northbrook had no link with Baring Brothers. His father had been Chancellor of the Exchequer. Would Churchill have objected to *that* appointment? 'Certainly!' interjected Lord Randolph. As usual he spoilt his case by overstatement, yet there were some members of the House of Commons who felt he had a point. But Northbrook was certainly depicting the truth as it was at the time when he told Childers positively: 'I have, of course, nothing to do with Baring Brothers' affairs, and I don't believe they have any concern with Egypt.'[26]

*   *   *

Commenting on a Treasury Bill in 1877, Bagehot discussed the need
for a new kind of security that the Treasury might offer similar to a
bill of exchange, which would be 'the finest security in the world'.
Racking his brain for a phrase that would sum up the splendour of
this new device, he concluded: 'Such a bill would rank before a bill of
Barings'.'[27] Bagehot was far from being typical of the general public
but his words reflected the opinion of the informed man-in-the-
street. As a brand image Barings was unsurpassed: not as glamorous
as Rothschilds, not as thrusting or adventurous as one or two of the
younger Anglo-American houses, but supreme for reliability, stability, honest worth. The *Bankers' Magazine*, referring to that 'unim-
peachable virtue known as first class credit', cited Barings as being
the house which 'have never known, during the present century,
anything but first class credit, into which enters the elements of dignity – moral, personal and commercial alike'.[28] Yet its reputation
concealed certain weaknesses. Now more than ever its prosperity
was built on the shifting sands of international financing, and in this
world of high risks and vast rewards the discretion and good judgement of the man who made the decisions was of paramount importance. In Barings the decisions were increasingly made by Edward
Revelstoke, and the doubts about his judgement first raised by
Joshua Bates had never been totally removed.

   In the last thirty or so years of the twentieth century, British
investment in foreign securities rose from about £775 million to
£4500 million. The greater part of this vast increase was organized
through the agency of a handful of merchant banks, based predominantly in London. Among these Rothschilds still had the largest
share but Barings were catching up. So much business was done in
conjunction with other houses that precise comparisons are impossible, but a rough indication is provided by the fact that between
1860 and 1890 Barings contracted for 62 public issues worth a total
of £560 million; Rothschilds for 43 worth £896 million.[29] Increasingly Hambros and Morgans were featuring as prominent rivals, but
the big two still prevailed. In an article at the end of 1888 *The Statist*
named Barings as being the house most responsible for the drain of
gold resulting from foreign issues. They had raised £95 million in six
years, complained *The Statist*, all for foreign countries except for two
breweries and the Manchester Ship Canal (three pretty substantial

exceptions, as will be seen). 'It will be noticed, too, that Messrs Baring have been growing bolder and bolder in their invitations to the public'; in 1884 they had sought to raise £6.5 million, in 1886 over £18.25 million, in 1888 with a month still to go, £28 million.[30]

This overseas investment was heavily concentrated on the Americas, particularly Argentina and Uruguay, but the traditional European clients were not wholly neglected. The efforts to meet the financial needs of Russia illustrate well Barings' struggle to remain in this field and their comparative lack of success. The opposition was strong and formidably well entrenched, the London market disinclined to participate substantially in Russian investments. In 1877 Hopes approached Barings to ask whether they would be prepared to put up some part of the money needed to tide the Russian government over until a large new loan could be issued. The trouble was that the operation was being set up by Mendelssohn and Co. of Berlin, and the role of the Dutch and English houses would be subsidiary. 'This, it seems to us, as we believe it will to yourselves,' wrote Hopes, 'would be an entirely new mode of coming in contact with the Russian Government.'[31] It was not a mode that appealed to Barings: they excused themselves politely on the grounds that European politics were at the moment too uncertain to permit of any important new commitment being taken on.[32]

The new loan, when it came, was also handled by Mendelssohns, and when in 1884 Barings approached Baron Stieglitz to say that the time had at last arrived when 'the issue of a large Foreign Loan for Russia might be made with every chance of success,'[33] the answer was unenthusiastic. It was not until 1888 that Barings participated in a government loan, this time in conjunction with Hambros, and they then discovered that the British public were so unenthusiastic about Russian securities that they took up only £0.55 million out of a total international loan of nearly £20 million. Even in the financing of rail road building Barings found that continental competition and the indifference of the British investor ensured that they could secure only a small part of the market. In mid-1880 a large loan was raised for the Grand Company, to build a new line. Hopes took it for granted that they and Barings would get first refusal, but to their dismay the stock was sold, without any warning being given them, to the Banque Russe et Française of Paris, and the ubiquitous

Mendelssohns. Hopes and Barings protested jointly to the President of the Grand Company, but got little for their pains. They were not always excluded; several times Barings and Hopes participated in railway loans over this period, but the results were not much to crow over. In 1890, for instance, when a loan of £2.5 million was contracted for, the total subscription in London amounted to a miserable £25,000 – 'We can only regret that we have had so little success,' Barings wrote apologetically to Hopes.[34] Three months later Hopes still had £423,000 worth of unplaced stock, and only the intervention of a French syndicate saved Barings from a lock-up of funds at a particularly awkward time.

Not many people realized how insignificant a role Barings – or for that matter any other British house – were playing in continental financing. In 1871 and 1872 huge loans were floated by the French government to finance the indemnities owing after the Franco-Prussian war. Barings and Rothschilds jointly handled the London end. The loans went conspicuously well. Joseph Laurence wrote to congratulate Barings on 'the marvellous success of the colossal French loan, in great measure due to the influence of your name'. How splendid it was, rhapsodized Mr Laurence, 'in these days of competition' to see 'the house in Bishopsgate maintain its undisputed place as the first Commercial House in the World'.[35] Yet in fact its name was just about all that Barings did contribute. Only about 10 per cent of the £200 million which was raised came from London, and of this modest amount by far the larger part was subscribed by Rothschilds.

For the rest Barings' role was as often as not confined to variations on the theme of saying no. An application for £1 million for the drainage and water supply of Lisbon was rejected on the grounds that the bonds would be issued in Portuguese currency and would therefore not be saleable in London.[36] For Norway in 1876 there was not even that excuse – 'For years past no time has been so unfavourable as the present for introducing new schemes of any kind to the English public.'[37] Six years later, when it was the Spaniards who wanted a loan, things had evidently not improved. In ordinary times Barings would be delighted to employ their money in this way but times were far from ordinary, 'and we, like everybody else, prefer keeping ourselves as strong as we can'. Of course if Barings were official bankers to the Spanish government it would be a different matter. 'I confess I don't quite see why they should not apply to their friends in New Court with whom I believe they have a large account,' wrote T. C. Baring.[38] It would be going too far to say that Barings opted out of Europe in the last quarter of the nineteenth century, but promising opportunities were limited and such as did exist were not pursued with any zest.

This perhaps over-cautious inertia was counterbalanced, however, by a dramatic new departure at home. In 1886 Sir Edward Guinness, whose family had been brewing their dark brown liquid since the mid-eighteenth century, decided to float the business as a public company. According to Lord Rothschild, the business was first offered to his house and turned down. 'When I agree to any proposal, I am immediately filled with anxiety,' he told Frank Harris. 'To say "Yes" is like putting your finger in a machine – the whirring wheels may drag your whole body in after the finger.'[39] Revelstoke was the last man to suffer from such exaggerated timidity. He at once told Guinness that Barings would be happy to undertake the flotation. 'I think Guinness ought surely to yield profit to Baring Brothers and Co.,' wrote Thomas Baring from New York. He agreed it would be absurd to place any of the shares on the American market; London could easily find the money.

Six million pounds' worth of preference and ordinary shares and debenture stock were to be issued, of which the Guinness family elected to keep £800,000. That left £5.2 million, to satisfy what it was clear was going to be a very substantial public demand. Applications were invited for Saturday morning 23 October and extra policemen were brought in to be on hand in case the traffic proved unusually heavy. Nothing prepared Barings for the frenzied tumult that in fact ensued. 'Barings' place was literally besieged,' reported the *Daily News*. 'Special policemen kept back the pushing crowd of clerks, agents, messengers and City men, and pains were taken to have one of the swing doors only partly open, so that none but spectral clerks and Stock Exchange men of the Cassius cut could squeeze in.'[40] Frank Harris wrote that some resourceful applicants wrapped their forms around stones and flung them through the windows.[41] *The Times* reported that applications were said to total somewhere between £60 million and £130 million: 'We have good reason for believing that the latter figure is the more nearly correct of the two.'[42] They were well informed: the actual figure was £114 million. By Monday morning the £10 ordinary shares were changing hands at £16 10/-, the preference shares at £13 10/-.

With people wanting twenty times as many shares as were available, it was obvious Barings would have to apply some kind of rationing. 'It is doubtful whether Messrs Baring have any discretionary powers at all . . . ,' 'Q' wrote to *The Times*. 'Once they allow that they have such power, then they may, if they like, allot the whole of the shares to themselves. I imagine their duty is to divide the shares *pro rata* to the applicants . . . It has been too much the custom to consider that shares may be given away at the sweet will of the issuer.'[43] 'Q' must already have suspected what was indeed the truth, that the sweet will of Barings had been paramount in the allotment of the shares. Of the £4.5 million ordinary and preference shares, where the largest profit was to be found, Barings kept something over £800,000 for themselves. The individual partners took a further slice: £70,000 for T. C. Baring, £20,000 for Thomas Baring. There was an allocation for family and friends outside the house: Lord and Lady Ashburton got £35,000 between them, Lt-Gen. Baring £10,000, Colonel Baring £2000, Lord Rosebery £40,000. Favoured merchant banks and stockbrokers got handsome helpings: Glyn Mills took £250,000; Hambros £105,000; Morgans £100,000; Rothschilds £350,000 – according to the *Morning Advertiser*, in exchange for a large share in a new Chilean loan. Little over a quarter of the shares was available to the general public.

There was nothing illegal in what Barings did. By the standards of the day their behaviour can hardly even be described as immoral. Lord Rothschild – more in admiration than disapproval – said that they had made £1 million profit on the affair.[44] This figure is too high, but the total benefit to the house and individual partners was enormous, probably in excess of £500,000. Their defence would have been that flotations were risky businesses; that when they went badly they accepted their responsibility to maintain the price by holding stock and, if necessary, buying it back when it came on to the market; and it was therefore only fair that they should get a share of the takings if things went well. The defence was not unreasonable, the *Financial News* was doing them less than justice when it wrote that it was convinced 'that if the floating of this company had been no great success the general public would have been favoured with a full allotment and thus have been obliged to hold the baby for all time to come'.[45] The question was, how big a profit was reasonable compensation for the risk? That Barings felt somewhat ashamed of their performance on this occasion was indicated by their reluctance to release the original list of subscribers. Instead, they published the names of those who held shares on 1 March 1887, and the original allocations were released only after they had appeared in considerable detail in the press.

The newspapers and public had no doubt that Barings had been guilty of something approaching sharp practice. *Money* accused them of 'a career of shabby evasion and (in the moral if not in the legal sense) concealment'.[46] Mr R. Cecil, who had applied for Guinness shares and been refused, wrote from the Carlton Club to denounce 'one of the most disgraceful Frauds on the Public that in my experience has ever been concocted'.[47] Mr Charles Hodgson returned a prospectus for an issue of mortgage bonds in the Atchison, Topeka and Santa Fé Railroad, saying he was so outraged by the way his Guinness application had been treated that 'I have resolved if I can possibly help it to have no further dealings with your firm of any kind'. Those who knew rather more about the current practices of the market would not have criticized Barings so harshly, but even among insiders who had benefited from the operation there was a feeling that things had gone a bit too far. Even within the partners' room at Bishopsgate there was some disquiet, if a flotation of a similar nature had come up in 1887 it would have been handled differently. In fact, when a smaller brewery, Combe and Co., was floated in 1888, they were given no chance to repeat their conduct. Charles Combe wrote pointedly: 'For fear of misunderstanding we think it better to remind you that our customers are to have a preferential allotment, even though their applications come in after the close of the subscription list.'[48] Two directors were appointed by the company to sit in Barings when the allotments were decided.

Evidence that Barings had some reason when they argued that flotations were a matter of swings and roundabouts was forthcoming in 1887 when an issue of shares and debentures was made by Barings and Rothschilds to finance the Manchester Ship Canal, a waterway intended to run from the Mersey near Liverpool deep into industrial Lancashire. It was an ambitious and most desirable project but it failed to appeal to the investor. 'Barings' beer is more successful than Rothschilds' water' was a saying of the times, but it was unfair to Rothschilds, for the first £4 million in preference shares were issued at par on joint account between the two houses. Only 18 per cent were subscribed by the public, almost entirely in Manchester and its vicinity. A syndicate had been set up, including Cazenove and Akroyds, Morgans and Hambros, which took a large proportion of the remainder, but Barings were still left with 39,881 shares. By March the following year this total had risen to 42,738 as more shares were acquired on the market to stop the price going to a discount. Only Rothschilds, with 45,317 shares, held more.[49] The issue had been a failure, and locked up capital at a time when it was badly needed.

The routine trading business of the house meanwhile carried on, not in spite of the partners, but without any sustained energy being shown by them. Revelstoke was apt to argue that there was no difference in principle between accepting bills on commission and issuing loans on commission; the bills were private while the loans were public and usually of longer duration, but both called for the same calculations and involved the same risks.[50] No doubt this reflected his views, but he found the loans altogether more glamorous and satisfying and concentrated his attention largely on this side of the business. The strength of Barings and its reputation, and the efficient organization of the house, is shown by the steady growth of its acceptance income during this period in spite of Revelstoke's indifference. Liabilities on acceptances had been £6.7 million at the end of 1870; by the beginning of 1890 they were £15 million. The next largest issuer was Kleinworts, with £4.9 million; Rothschilds had a mere £1.4 million.

The days in which Barings would trade in goods on their own account were almost over. The collapse of Russell Sturgis's family firm in 1875 gravely damaged Barings' traditional network of agents around Asia and nobody was particularly concerned to renew it. The Liverpool office made fitful efforts to get into new lines, rubber and guano among them, but the field was already crowded with specialist firms better qualified to undertake such trade. It was safer and more profitable to provide the money that enabled others to do the work. Not that the task of granting credits was necessarily less oner-ous or risky than the trading which it subsidized. It used to be rela-tively easy for private bankers to know to whom it was safe to lend money, mused Bagehot, but now 'the world has become so large and complicated that it is not easy to tell who is rich and who poor'.[51] There seemed no end to the proliferation of new companies or indi-viduals clamouring for money to finance their favoured projects. Barings took refuge in their habitual caution. 'We have hitherto not even heard the name of the Company mentioned in your letter and therefore can give no advice worth giving as to its merits or demerits,' they typically told Hopes in December 1884. 'But there can be no question that the three noblemen, whose names appear in connex-ion with it, are utterly wanting in business knowledge and commer-cial standing, and none of them is rich.'[52]

One line of business which had been discontinued was now renewed. Finlay, Hodgson had owned two sailing vessels, the *Chaa Sze* and the *Black Prince*. The *Chaa Sze* was soon disposed of, but rather than abandon ship management a second time Barings com-missioned from a Glasgow yard the *Norman Court*, called after Thomas Baring's country house, a clipper ship designed to ply between Britain and Australia or the Far East. The two ships remained in operation throughout the 1870s but the competition of steam proved too strong. The *Black Prince* was finally sold in 1880, the *Norman Court* the following year.

The tradition that Barings, as a merchant house, would deal in anything that might show a profit, was never abandoned. Ventures into strange territory could be risky unless great care was taken. In 1874 the Chinese had urgent need of an ironclad frigate. Barings were asked to purchase one from the Danish government and pro-cured it for £200,000, paying £20,000 of their own money as a deposit. By an aberration which suggests some carelessness on the part of the negotiator, they had agreed to a contract which gave the Danes the right to deliver the ship where and when they wanted. This was unacceptable to the Chinese, who insisted on delivery in China. The Danes argued that the war which was currently raging in the Far East made this impracticable. The delay involved by this toing-and-froing proved disastrous, since the Chinese maintained that there was now no time to get a crew to Copenhagen and to take delivery of the vessel there.[53] They refused to complete the purchase. Barings asked for the return of the deposit from the Danes but were met with a counter-claim for the rest of the purchase price. The Chinese showed no interest in paying anything. All they had accomplished, Barings told their correspondents in Shanghai, was to fall out with the Danish government and risk losing a lot of money.[54] Barings never got back their £20,000, though in the end they were absolved from any other liabilities under the contract. To avoid 'the scandal of a lawsuit with a foreign Government', they cut their losses and called it a day.[55]

The increase of business led to demands for extra staff. The number of clerks continued to grow and the first woman joined the house in 1873. Within a decade there were ten of them, who had of course to be provided with a separate entrance and their own amenities so as to protect them from lascivious male colleagues. Cubitt's work of less than thirty years before had already been found inadequate. Richard Norman Shaw, the architect who was associated above all with the revolt against fashionable Victorian design and a return to the eighteenth-century tradition, was commissioned in 1880 to retain Cubitt's old banking hall but create a new façade in Queen Anne style and expand behind it. His heavy red brick doorway with broad, open pediment and slit-like windows gave the building something of the air of a fortress. 'For myself, I have no objection to its high narrow windows and stony front,' wrote a correspondent of the *Daily News*, 'for that means the safety of valuable property; nor can you cavil at the low, arched doorway, with its two swinging doors, through whose glass panes you look up the long passage into the serene and mystic interior, where gentlemanly clerks deal with heaps of gold as children deal with a handful of hazelnuts.'[56]

Though 'heaps of gold' can hardly have been a common feature of the counting house, the 'serenity' was real. J. Walter Wood joined Barings in the autumn of 1888. The general office was a large room without windows, illumination coming from sky-lights or the single candlestick fixed to every desk.

> The silence was impressive, and the great banking room, with its mellowed features seen through the soft light, was very dignified.

No one seemed in a hurry. Business did not really begin till about 11 o'clock and was usually over by 4 o'clock. For those clerks who remained at work till 5 o'clock, tea with thin slices of buttered bread was served by the liveried 'walkers' [bank messengers]. The partners' room adjoined the general office, and was more like a gentleman's library, with a cheerful open fire in a marble mantelpiece at the end of the room, and a soft red and blue rug. The mahogany desks were massive, and the chairs deeply upholstered in dark leather. In the center of the room was a large table with a limited number of necessary reference books, and from the walls deceased partners of the House looked down from mellowed gilt frames.

In spite of the upheaval caused by the building of Norman Shaw's new offices, changes to the procedural rituals were accepted only after due and sometimes agonizing deliberation. After an important draft had been lost for several hours, Wood suggested the introduction of what were, in effect, In and Out trays. His senior colleague, to whom he put forward the idea, 'after mature reflection admitted advantages but said that such a thing "had never been done" '. The matter was one for the Head Clerk. The Head Clerk listened carefully, added his meed of mature reflection, and said the matter would have to be referred to a partner. A partner eventually appeared and the proposal was expounded for a third time. Whether a partners' meeting was summoned to discuss the issue is uncertain, but the upshot was that the trays were installed and proved notably successful.[57]

As the 1880s wore on, it must have seemed to the outside world that the partners of Barings had every right to be as cheerful as the fire that burnt beneath their marble mantelpiece. Their capital appeared to be large enough for any likely contingency, their profits were more than satisfactory, their reputation as high as ever. Perhaps most remarkable, they had survived the challenge posed by the limited liability joint-stock banks. As *The Statist* argued in 1885, the private banker would always score over the joint-stock bank because he could act with greater promptitude and decision. 'Moreover, he has a skill and training, has accumulated special knowledge, and is possessed of the traditions of the business, in a way and to an extent the directors of a joint-stock bank cannot pretend to; while in addition he is a specialist no more liable to abuse the secrets of his customer than their doctor or solicitor, whereas the joint-stock director may be a competitor in their own trade.' As to the superior resources of the joint-stock bank, *The Statist* dismissed them as unimportant; because his liability was unlimited the private banker, provided he was wealthy, offered security greater than that provided by any but the largest of the joint-stock banks.[58]

That was all true, as far as it went, but it took no account of the possibility that the private banker, because of that very freedom of action which was put forward as being his advantage, might involve himself in commitments greater than his assets. Though almost everyone in the City would have laughed at the idea until the very end, this in fact was what Lord Revelstoke was bringing upon his house by his policy in North and, still more, Latin America.

12

An 'Immense Connection' in America

North America, 1848–1890

'I have pretty well made up my mind,' wrote Joshua Bates in September 1848, 'that the interests of the House will be best consulted by wasting none of our resources on European business but turn[ing] our greatest attention to the United States and to the East.'[1] The following year he visited the United States and was enraptured by all he saw. Business was booming, confidence high, the network of roads and railways spreading with astonishing speed, the States were resolved never to get deep into debt again. 'There never was a country so prosperous. The progress of everything in 8 years is almost incredible.'[2] Though he was better informed than most of them, Bates was doing no more than reflect the views of British investors. The revolutions in Europe had convinced them that their money would not be safe the other side of the Channel; the efforts of the American States to extricate themselves from their difficulties and the ardent championship of Barings had won back confidence in London; money was plentiful and opportunities for investment scarce; the time was ripe for the United States to become once more the fashion.

Bates's visit stirred up speculation in financial circles in America. Belmont, Rothschild's representative, was well informed: Bates's principal object, he wrote, was to find a new general agent, 'Thomas Ward, having made a considerable fortune, being desirous of retiring. He is said to have made $600,000, having had a considerable salary and a share in the business.'[3] Belmont's figures were on the generous side, being no doubt intended to impress his employers with his own comparative ill treatment, but the story was right in essentials. Ward had been talking about retiring since 1845 and was now anxious to go: 'I am growing old, and cannot do what is necessary for Messrs Barings' interest and my own satisfaction.'[4]

Bates was undismayed by the prospect. He was apt to claim that the vast increase in American business had come in spite of and not because of Ward: 'The liberality and high character of the House drew the business and not T.W.W.'s influence, which was rather a drag.'[5] After talking to Ward in Boston he complained that he was so slow and prolix that it took twenty-four hours to establish his views about the future. It was high time he went.[6] But when it came to deciding on a replacement, the problem grew more difficult. The most obvious course was to follow the move of big business to New York and establish a new agency there, but though Bates accepted this, he was a loyal Bostonian and found himself reluctant to take the step.[7] T. W. Ward's son Samuel was put forward as a possible replacement for his father. Bates was at first unimpressed. 'Sam has no energy and the whole agency would be a rickety concern,' he told Thomas Baring.[8] Sam was an unprepossessing figure; small, with a nasal twang and mustachios curling up to his eyeballs. But he was there. Bates's attitude towards him softened. The two men had a long talk and Bates decided Sam was 'not wanting in ability and seems to have the right view of things'. Perhaps T. W. Ward should be persuaded to stay on for a few years longer in partnership with his son. 'The great prosperity of this Country, assisted as it will be by immigration and Californian gold, will lead to hazard, and Ward is just the man to hold people back and keep them safe.'[9]

From London Thomas Baring was sceptical. He declined to give advice – 'How can we at this distance give an opinion as to people we have never seen?' – but wondered whether the retention of Ward would achieve the main objective, that of setting up an agency that would last for many years.[10] Bates persisted, however, and the agency in fact lasted another thirty years. When T. W. Ward finally retired in 1852 Sam Ward was appointed sole agent. It proved an unexpectedly successful solution. Sam Ward was as much a stick-in-the-mud as his father and lacked the latter's knowledge of American business, but he was shrewd, conscientious and much the more affable and approachable of the two. His contacts were excellent and he did much to maintain, if not enhance, the standing of Barings in American trading.

Writing from Havana in 1859 Baron Alphonse de Rothschild told his cousins in London that Barings were the chief among a handful of houses making all the profit from commission, credits and consignation – 'Barings has immense connection everywhere in America and I have no doubt, my dear Cousins, should you enter business in this country with some confidence, you will find enough to extend greatly the already existing sphere of operations in America.'[11] Rothschilds were never to challenge Barings' supreme position in the field of credit. Others did better, notably Brown Brothers. Browns were the more aggressive and picked up much business which Barings either scorned or let slip by. Yet in 1855 Brown, Shipley, Browns' English associates, were still complaining that 'we aim, and with perfect right, at a rank and position equal to Barings,' but were still far from achieving it.[12] Barings' credits on American account rose from £1.3 million at the end of 1848 to £2.6 million in 1852, £3.2 million in 1857 and £3.6 million in 1860. The totals were impressive enough, what was still more remarkable was the quality of the accounts involved. Throughout this period Barings could pick their clients almost as they chose. In 1867, Brown, Shipley reported, Kidder Peabody were beginning to issue credits for use in the East and South America; 'They rely on Barings being able to do less than formerly, which . . . would be a reasonable expectation from Mr Ward's limited powers and not acceptable manner.'[13] Yet, reasonable or not, the following year they were bewailing the fact that they had just lost another customer to Barings.[14] Viewed in terms of the expansion of the American economy and the growth of its rivals, Barings' position was slipping; but the change was self-willed, at any moment they had the ability to take on whatever business they felt judicious. 'The great house of B B and Co [is] now decidedly the first in the world in the estimation of the Americans,' announced Bates smugly in 1849.[15] 'The Administration is entirely in the hands of Barings' friends,' Belmont told Rothschilds in despair.[16] They had their setbacks, and the Administration in particular did not always remain so securely in their hands, but the authority of Barings remained virtually unshaken until the great crash of 1890.

The possibilities for involvement in the flood of new American securities that reached London in the early 1850s were similarly unlimited. Barings had done more than any other house, British or American, to reestablish the credit of the United States in Britain and Europe and they could have participated in virtually any venture that appealed to them. They chose to follow a policy of extreme restraint. In 1852 Thomas Baring visited America on a fact-finding mission. He found a country bursting with optimism, convinced that 'the prosperity would last and encrease'.[17] Ward assured him that all was indeed for the best in the best of possible worlds, that there was wealth enough to take up all that was on offer, 'no overstrained use of credit, no kite-flying, no large circulation of Banknotes, no inability to meet a sudden call for the settlement of pending engagements'. Baring was sceptical. There were too many railway projects and too much speculation, a crash must come, but while Californian gold continued to be produced and England bought cotton and took American bonds, there would be rich pickings for the investor. 'Our policy it seems to me is to take only what is really good and which even if sales are stopped we can hold with perfect security.'[18]

The American railway system was by far the most rapacious consumer of capital and the sector in which fortunes could most easily be lost or made. Increasingly the United States itself found the money needed for such enterprises, but periodic injections of foreign capital were still necessary, if only to give an air of respectability to what might otherwise have seemed an insecure adventure. No name offered greater respectability than that of Barings, yet there were few houses less eager to lend their name, let alone their money. 'I cannot help thinking that there are too many railroads on foot in the U. States . . . and this country is lending too fast,' remarked Bates in 1852.[19] To Ward he criticized those 'go-ahead' people who derided Barings for not promoting the sale of railway bonds. Some of these bonds were undoubtedly sound but 'if we bring forward the good we shall be promoting the bad, and I have great doubts if we should touch them'.[20]

In fact Barings had already touched American railway shares as early as 1839, choosing the Baltimore and Ohio as the favoured exception, in a complicated arrangement which involved exchanging state bonds for iron rails. They believed this to be the safest rail-

road investment in North America and as such fit to be associated
with the name of Barings: 'Before bringing forward this new kind of
Bond here,' they told Ward, 'it is indispensably necessary that the
character of the security should be such as we can offer with credit to
to ourselves and with safety to the public.'[21] Limited investment in
the choicest securities was to be their rule, and in 1853 even this prudent policy was deemed too adventurous. 'We begin to fear that the
Country has already got nearly as many railway Bonds and shares
from foreign Countries as she can hold,' Barings told Ward. 'At any
rate we must see a little clearer into the future before we load ourselves with any more.'[22] But there could be exceptions, especially
when Weardale benefited. In 1855 a transaction involved the Western Railroad Company. Barings took the bonds at a price that
included a 5 to 6 per cent commission and would yield 7 per cent
interest. The rails would come from Weardale, 'the quality being
superior owing to the great strength and toughness of the iron'. The
high commission was justified by the fact that 'we shall not be able to
sell the bonds without our guarantee'.[23] Whether the eventual buyer
was told of the hidden benefit to Barings through the sale of iron
from Weardale, and whether the prospects of such a sale to any
extent affected Barings' judgement of the merits of the Western Railroad, must remain uncertain. In fairness, however, it must be said
that the investors were never given cause to regret their purchase,
and Barings ensured that the interest was paid when the line was in
temporary difficulties.

It was not only over railroads that Barings showed caution. In
October 1850 'a Mr Vanderbilt and Mr J. H. White' were in London
trying to raise money for a canal to link the Atlantic and Pacific
Oceans through the Lake of Nicaragua. The estimated cost was $4
million, Bates believed £10 million would be nearer the mark but felt
it was 'a great work and should be accomplished if possible'.[24] To put
up money for it was another matter, though; Barings agreed with
Rothschilds that a feasibility study by British engineers was an essential first step.[25] By September 1852 the idea had been dismissed as
impracticable and an alternative canal through Panama to cost £14
million was being considered. 'My impression,' wrote Bates in one of
his less prescient moments, 'is that none of these canals will ever be
constructed for the simple reason that they will not pay.'[26]

Thirty years later another equally futuristic opportunity occurred, when in 1881 the United States Electric-Light Co., controlled largely by Grace and Co., and The Edison Company belonging to Drexel Morgan, more or less simultaneously solved the problem of using electric light to replace gas for all purposes. A merger was mooted and Barings were asked to assume the management for England, 'so that you would have a commission on the future use of the invention, in return for the Service it would be to them to have their interests in the best and most influential hands'. It was all very indefinite, Ward apologized, but 'if we wait till the thing is a success it would be too late to take hold of it'.[27]

They waited and it was. Perhaps in this case a fortune was lost, but in general Barings' prudence was amply justified by the crisis of 1857. They had seen it coming for some time and Ward had been busily reducing acceptances and pressing for early remittances. Bates had little sympathy for those less prudent. 'Mr Wildes of Henry Wildes asked if we could assist their House in case they should require it. Their Bankers should assist them,' he noted severely in his diary. 'It is impossible to foresee what inconvenience we ourselves may experience, therefore we cannot promise aid to others.'[28] In fact their practice in the United States was considerably more liberal than this might suggest; they came to the help of several of their long-standing correspondents, one at least of whom would have had to close but for Barings' assistance.[29] They had some uncomfortable moments, but the result of the crisis in the long run was to weaken others and thus to strengthen them. By the beginning of 1858 Bates could claim with justified pride that 'the losses to my house by bad debts arising out of the crisis are not much and will be more than compensated by increased business'.[30]

Any disposition Barings might have had to play a larger part in the financing of America's development was curbed by the increasing likelihood of war between North and South. By December 1860, when South Carolina set the ball rolling by seceding from the Union, Barings had reduced their holdings of American securities to a handful of railroad bonds and had ceased to trade in new issues. Thomas Baring pleaded with the Foreign Secretary, John Russell, to mediate between the two parties, but Russell politely declined the invitation.[31] For the next few months Bates continued to hope that the worst might be avoided,[32] but by May it was plain that a long and bloody war was beginning. 'During its continuance trade must be comparatively at a standstill,' Barings warned Ward. 'Those who considered themselves rich may find themselves poor from the great depreciation of property of all kinds. This will increase the risk of Bill operations.' Ward was advised to 'lessen your operations until it can be seen how things are going, confining your remittances to bills drawn on first class firms' – a counsel which he might reasonably have felt superfluous, since it had been pressed on him repeatedly even in times of peace.[33]

Barings as a house unequivocally supported the North and deplored the British government's policy of non-intervention. So much might have been expected of a staunch New Englander like Joshua Bates, but Thomas Baring was little less enthusiastic. 'People in this country look upon you as a friend of the country,' Samuel Ward assured him. '. . . I was applied to lately for your autograph to go in an album containing autographs of "our friends in Europe".' Benjamin Moran, at the American Legation, noted with approval a speech that Baring made in the House of Commons in May 1864: 'The man is a gentleman. . . . It is mortifying to me that while he is loyal to us, the only citizen of the United States belonging to his firm, Mr Russell Sturgis, is a rebel sympathizer.'[34] Sturgis was indeed a considerable embarrassment to his colleagues. While Samuel Ward deplored the fact that he 'did not take the view of American affairs natural for a Northern man,' he thought Sturgis's 'personal friendliness and efficiency' would make up for this.[35] The American government took the matter more seriously. 'The man's disloyalty has caused the Government to think seriously of transferring its business to some other House,' recorded Moran. The Minister, Charles Adams, formally called on Sturgis to express his displeasure.[36]

Barings sometimes tempered their zeal for the North with financial prudence. In 1875 the *New York Tribune* complained that, in the early 1860s, Barings had sought to embarrass the American government by demanding immediate payment of a small debt of $50,000.[37] The matter was hurriedly cleared up; it was true that the diplomatic account had been overdrawn by that amount but Barings had not been in the least concerned. It was Samuel Ward who, without London knowing, had called on the State Department to draw their attention to the matter. The explanation was accepted, yet on 9 May 1861 Moran had recorded in his journal that Bates had spoken of Barings' doubts 'about letting our Government have more money on account of Diplomatic salaries, as they might not get paid. This is the confidence of Barings after being our bankers for nearly 70 years!'[38]

On the whole, though, Barings proved loyal friends of the Federal government. William Aspinwall visited London to buy ironclads for the Northern government and paid a rousing tribute to Barings' role in the transaction. 'These gentlemen unhesitatingly authorized us to draw on them, at sight, for a very large amount – some millions – and on terms at once liberal and most considerate as to the time of reimbursement by our Government, thus showing a most exceptional degree of confidence and sympathy at a period when the public feeling in London was almost universally in favour of the South. . . .'. From motives of delicacy, no public mention has been made of this honourable act, which certainly no other house in Europe could have or would have done.'[39] In August 1861 Barings advanced $500,000 so that George Schuyler could purchase arms for the American government even though the documents he produced did not authorize any such activity. By the time the proper authorization was received in October the amount had risen to $634,000.[40]

With so creditable a record Barings had reason to feel a little aggrieved when they lost the agency of the United States government in 1871. It was by no means the first time such a setback had seemed possible since they had recaptured it from Rothschilds in 1843. Rothschilds, Peabody, Rothschilds again, and Brown Brothers each in turn thought that the prize was theirs.[41] Yet as late as 1869 the Secretary to the Navy had gratuitously assured Barings that 'we have every reason to be satisfied with the transactions that have taken place between yourselves and the Government, and hope the feeling may long continue'.[42]

It did not. Pressure to transfer the account to an American house was becoming irresistible. That resourceful and well-connected financier Jay Cooke was particularly eager to secure the naval agency, which would 'aid in the cultivation of a very large and profitable business which Barings have monopolized for years, namely the accounts of American merchantmen'. Cooke's desire to rob Barings of the agency was no doubt fomented by the story that, when Barings were asked for an opinion of his house, they loftily replied that they had hardly heard of it, nor any of its directors. In the summer of 1871 he prevailed, and the account was removed from what Cooke described as the 'Anglo-Russian-Chinese' house of Baring to his own London house.[43] At the same time Clews, Habicht and Co. were given the diplomatic and consular account. Who was responsible for the change is unclear; Hamilton Fish, the Secretary of State at the time, was recorded as saying that it was none of his doing and he deplored the decision.[44]

In less than two years Barings had the satisfaction of seeing their rivals in the bankruptcy court. Many people, who felt that they had been hardly used, now clamoured for their recall, and Fish cabled the President to ask that no appointment should be made until he had had a chance of arguing the case for Barings.[45]

'Though we should of course be proud to be once more the agents of the United States Government,' Barings told Ward, 'we can quite understand the difficulty which the existing cabinet would have in appointing us.'[46] They were right, and not only for the existing cabinet. Morton, Rose and Co. were appointed. The days were past when a British bank could represent the American government in London.

Recovery after the Civil War was a slow and painful business. T. C. Baring toured the South early in 1866 and was dismayed by what he saw. He found a population in part hankering after the past, in part dreaming of the future, and in both cases disinclined to face the problems of the present. The old aristocracy, who had lost almost everything, 'sit listlessly in their houses and mourn for the late Confederacy. You would hardly believe that I did not see in Richmond or Petersburg one gentleman's house with the shutters open.' As for the negroes, they were 'gradually being improved off the face of the earth like the red man'. A few worked 'but the lazy ones hang about the bureau for a scanty support. Unfortunately for them they have become possessed by the idea that the U.S. Government is sooner or later going to distribute among them the funds of their former masters and they live, or rather die, in hopes of the good time coming.'[47] America emerged from the war with its cotton production gone to ruin, its countryside devastated, the cream of its youth maimed or dead and a national debt swollen to £555.6 million.

Nevertheless, the corner was turned by 1870. The loss of the government agency coincided with the start of an astonishing boom in American securities in which Barings vigorously participated, undertaking twenty-two new issues in the 1870s and 1880s. The days in which they could operate on important government issues single-handed, however, were over. For Grant's first refunding loan of 1871, five houses were named, including Morgans and Rothschilds as well as Barings. 'Of course these arrangements are not what would be most agreeable to us,' Barings told Hopes, 'nor what we should have recommended as the best mode of bringing the loan under the favourable consideration of the public, but we do not think that it would be becoming to refuse to act. We none of us shall make fortunes out of the agency. . . .'[48]

When the process was repeated in 1873, Barings, Hopes and Morton, Rose were pitted against Rothschilds and Jay Cooke, and the American government asked the two groups to unite in a single syndicate. Belmont, on holiday in Nice, urged Rothschilds to agree. 'I think most favourably of the combination of the five houses,' he told Nathan Rothschild, 'and I am only sorry it was not effected before the two separate offers were handed in, because you would have had, then, the game in your hands, and could have forced the Secretary to better conditions, as no other houses here or in America would have ventured to bid against you.'[49] Barings were by now well accustomed to working in conjunction with Rothschilds and accepted the forced union with equanimity. Hopes were less amenable and protested strongly when they found that the acceptance of subscriptions in Amsterdam was to be made under the instructions of Rothschilds. 'We cannot but regret that we were not aware of the real state of the case,' they declared,[50] though they did not push their dislike of Rothschilds to the point of turning down the business.

Fourteen of the twenty-two issues were for railway companies. Between 1865 and 1890, Barings were responsible for 28.7 per cent of the North American railroad stocks issued through London merchant banks, worth £34.68 million. Morgans were next with 21.6 per cent or £26.09 million. No other competitor took as much as 10 per cent; Rothschilds' share was a mere £800,000.[51] And yet, like England's Indian empire, it happened largely by mistake. The year 1874 found Barings surveying with some dismay the plethora of railway shares for which they had been responsible and those for which financing was now being invited. 'We cannot disguise from ourselves that American Rail Roads in general have lost favour,' they told Ward.[52] They blamed the trouble largely on the lack of discrimination of the British investor, who could not see the difference between good and bad, but the following year they found themselves guilty of the same offence when their much- favoured Louisville and Nashville Railway ran into trouble. 'Not only have we lost a large interest in the Bonds,' they told Ward, 'but, which touches us more nearly, is the fear of loans introduced by us proving other than *first class*.'[53] When the railroad defaulted the following month Barings found the money to pay the balance of the interest. 'You will have understood . . . how deeply we feel the unfortunate collapse of a security we have recommended with so much confidence,' they told Ward.[54]

Not surprisingly this disagreeable experience led them to look sceptically on future railroad offers. They quite agreed with Lee, Higginson in 1876 that the Chicago, Burlington Railroad was secure but declined to participate on the grounds of 'the very unsettled state of European politics' – hardly an argument they would have advanced in 1849.[55] They refused to have anything to do with the New York and New England Railroad the following year: 'There is a feeling of distrust of American Railroads growing out of the condition of several of them.'[56] When Ward, in 1885, pressed them to join a consortium to buy railway land for the North Pacific Railroad Co., they replied bluntly that it 'would not suit'.[57] Ward was indefatigable in his efforts to persuade them that they were missing excellent opportunities. In 1883 he suggested that George Morrison, an authority on railroads, should be recruited as a partner. 'The taking of a new partner is almost as serious a matter as a second marriage,' replied T. C. Baring, 'and the fact that the person is a stranger renders the advantage of the act certainly not less problematical.' They did not want an expert on railways in the partners' room. 'As we have more than once pretty clearly stated, our experience in the business of railway loans in the US, though profitable in the main, has not always been of so satisfactory and smooth a character as to make us very passionately enamoured of it.'[58]

One major issue which slipped through in the early 1880s was the

Atchison, Topeka and Santa Fé Railroad; strongly championed by Barings' closest ally, Kidder Peabody, and endorsed by Sam Ward as being 'unexceptionable, the road finished and earning 12 per cent on its stock, and rapidly developing and without complications'.[59] In 1883 Tom Baring was to be found 'shaking and rattling' along the line and forming an excellent opinion of it. More money would be needed, but it would be found in America.[60] It was, to disastrous effect. Within three years the company's debts had tripled and it was weighed down by interest payments, as well as beset by strikes and involved in a ferocious rate-cutting war with the neighbouring Missouri Pacific Railroad.[61] The quarterly dividend was slashed and the price of the stock tumbled. Things then appeared to mend a little. By early 1889 Tom Baring reported: 'I think we have seen the worst of Atchison.'[62] Once again he was too sanguine. Within a couple of months it was clear that a serious cash shortage lay only a few months ahead. After that horror was piled upon horror: the directors had lied about the floating debt, they had falsified the figures for the payment for cars and locomotives: 'The swindling, extravagance, incapacity, nepotism – as Ward used to say, general wickedness – of the past two years exceeds belief.'[63]

Barings and Kidder Peabody mounted a coup d'état. The old board was forced out of power and a new finance committee set up in New York under the chairmanship of Kidder's expert on corporate reorganization, George Magoun, and with Tom Baring reluctantly recruited as a director. Barings authorized further advances not to exceed $1.5 million and by the autumn of 1889 all seemed to be running relatively smoothly. The two banks congratulated themselves that they had made the best of a bad job and that, though their clients whom they had put into the railroad had certainly suffered, they could have done a great deal worse. Not all the clients agreed. From Stockholm the Duc d'Otrante wrote indignantly to complain about his reduced dividends. Revelstoke's reply was a fine piece of measured disdain. 'I do not wish to avoid any responsibility I may have incurred in recommending the investment to you,' he wrote, 'and you will today receive a letter from my firm crediting you with the sum you paid for the Bonds. As however you think proper to say you think the whole thing is a "swindle" I should prefer that our business relations should cease and I have to request that you will as soon as possible inform my firm to whom they can transfer the Stocks and money they hold for your account.'[64]

Railways seemed constantly to be demanding exertions outside the normal scope of merchant banking. Barings, on the urgent encouragement of Sam Ward, had invested largely in the St Louis and Iron Mountain Railway. Gross mismanagement had reduced the line to chaos and the only recourse was a radical reorganization and the expulsion of the directors. At first it seemed as if the board would go quietly, then the President, Thomas Allen, telegraphed: 'I can before answering only ask you if it means unconditional surrender. If it does, count me out.'[65] It plainly did, and a protracted proxy battle ensued, with Thomas and Francis Baring on a visit to the United States urging on Sam Ward to fresh efforts. Then the battle was transferred to the courts, with the directors trying to rally patriotic sentiment on their side by claiming 'a London party' was aiming to secure control of the line for its own – no doubt nefarious – purposes.[66] Francis Baring became almost as obsessed with the issue as Ward himself: 'It is a scandal to civilization,' he wrote, 'that a good road should not be run to best advantage.' Allen was wholly incompetent, 'stupid, short-sighted and pigheaded'.[67] In the end a compromise was reached, by which the board was remodelled but the stupid, short-sighted and pigheaded Allen allowed to remain President. The result was not notably satisfactory and it took the intervention of Jay Gould, as part of his titanic battle to impose order on the American railways, to allow Barings to escape with credit. 'No railroad can reckon without Jay Gould,' Sam Ward concluded philosophically.[68] 'The man's power is uncomfortably great, whether for good or evil,' wrote Thomas Baring some years later, 'but we must take him as we find him now and thank heaven he is on the side of law and order.'[69]

The Atchison, Topeka and Santa Fé was far from being the only railroad in which Kidder Peabody involved Barings, and the other ventures proved happier. Kidder Peabody were a powerful and ambitious house based in New York and Boston, who believed in playing a more active role in running the enterprises in which they took an interest than was usual in British merchant banking. In particular they specialized in rescuing and reorganizing railways which were in financial trouble, no rarity in America at that period. Barings had been closely associated with them since 1878. Ward's sub-agent in Boston (the headquarters of the agency had now been transferred to New York), perhaps saw a threat to his own position in the connection – at any rate, he deplored it, 'they were not the sort of people you have heretofore corresponded with,' over-sharp, standing low in public esteem, 'the arrangement would create great surprise in Boston'.[70] Barings paid no attention. Even Ward, who had shared his sub-agent's doubts about the future of the house, was impressed by their profits, capital and leadership. 'Mr Kidder is in good health and attends actively to business. He is 59 years old. Peabody, 10 years younger, [is] the genius of the concern; his health suffers from overwork and [he] absents himself a good deal in winter. Magoun . . . is entirely devoted to business yet seems to take it easy and I believe that your experience shows that he does it well.'[71]

On the whole Sam Ward had served Barings well. Extolling his own achievements when it was proposed to cut his pension, he claimed that the credit business had doubled in value during his time as agent. He had maintained a virtual monopoly of the East India business so long as that business existed, sorted out the problems of the Eastern Railroad, carried on the great battle over Iron Mountain: 'What House in the American business can show such a record during all that time?'[72] He had a good case, but by 1884 the days of glory were far behind him. He was a sick man, whose ability to transact business efficiently depended on his taking long and frequent holidays. His brother George suffered from 'softening of the brain' and what Sam described as 'self- interest and mental sluggishness'.[73] His son Tom was very deaf. Tom Baring started with a poor view of his namesake but gradually thought better of him; Magoun, however, described him as 'quite infantile, absolutely incapable of understanding business matters'.[74] Old clients were being lost and new not gained. It was only too plain that if Barings' business in the United States was to survive, rapid changes were essential.

Ward's proposed solution was to bring in the newly appointed sub-agent in New Orleans as reinforcement. To Revelstoke – signing himself thus for the first time – this seemed wholly inadequate.[75] Tom Baring agreed and had no doubt that the future should lie in a closer association with Kidder Peabody – they could not possibly be in safer hands, he commented; a generous verdict, seeing that in the same letter he complained about Kidders' recruitment of a Mr H. L. Griggs, sharp and active enough, to be sure, but 'a disagreeable hog'.[76] Revelstoke was dubious. The sort of arrangement his brother had in mind would entail Barings giving up all their New York and Boston business to another house and abandoning their own individuality. For Kidders to take in Tom Ward as a partner would avail nothing. The only way the new arrangement could be acceptable would be to have 'a partner in New York who would really represent us and safeguard our interests'. Would Tom Baring be that man?[77] With some reluctance Baring agreed he might.

The proposal was duly broached to Mr Kidder, who was disconcertingly unappreciative of the honour being done him. 'He appears altogether to ignore the value of our offer,' wrote T. C. Baring indignantly. 'Perhaps what we should bring to his firm would at the outset not be very much, but it involves the potentiality of the best and largest American credit business, not only in New York but throughout the United States and Canada. His firm would no doubt have to work for this, but it would be *our* standing that would make it attainable.'[78] Kidder flatly refused to accept Tom Ward as a partner – 'he thinks him absolutely useless, even as a clerk' – and did not even seem very gratified by the thought of Tom Baring joining the firm; 'he is afraid of taking in a partner who might very shortly be the chief and controlling influence in the firm,' was Baring's somewhat complacent explanation.[79]

Possibly Kidder wanted not to appear too anxious to grasp at what was, in truth, an enticing proposition. Negotiations were quickly under way and virtually completed by October 1885. Now it was Tom Baring who was anxious not to seem too eager. 'I wish it to be most clearly understood that I do not *ask* to be sent to New York,' he reminded Revelstoke. 'On the contrary I should much prefer to stay here [Liverpool] and I only go to New York because the firm desires me to. Therefore I hope I may assume that by thus going away I do not forfeit or lose any claims or rights that my partnership of 15 years may have given me.'[80] Presumably he received a satisfactory assurance. He joined Kidder Peabody as a full partner taking 20 per cent of the profits (which had recently totalled some £36,000 a year). Tom Ward did not get his partnership but was taken into the office at $7500 a year.[81]

The association proved on the whole fruitful and harmonious. Tom Baring's own role in the enlarged business is more questionable. Peabody was apt to refer to his 'apprehension and uneasiness'. He complained that good business was lost because of Baring's lack of confidence in his partners' 'conservatism and judgment'.[82] To Tom's loyal nephew Cecil, however, the advantage he bestowed on Kidders was of inestimable value. 'There is no doubt that his presence here makes a very great difference to the *tone* as well as to the volume of the business. . . . It is the one thing you want here, a man who is to begin with a gentleman, and who has strength of will enough to have his own way. Of course the ways of doing business are odious and must be distasteful to him, and he frets at not being "boss" of the whole place as he was at Liverpool, but I am perfectly certain that every day he is here makes a difference to the business.' One of his chief contributions was establishing a better relationship between Kidder Peabody and such rivals as Browns or Drexels. 'They used to snarl at each other, but now the partners of both houses have all been in here, and we have dined with them and what not . . . Belmont also, Rothschild's agent – a dog Jew – has been v. civil and appeals to Uncle Tom's stomach – which is more than one can say for any of the others.'[83]

Cecil Baring was much more likeable than this letter might suggest. He was Ned Revelstoke's second surviving son and was academically as formidable as any of his relations, having won the Newcastle Scholarship at Eton and got a first in Greats under Jowett of Balliol. He claimed to base his outlook on life on Aristotle's *Ethics*, but he by no means confined himself to the classics, studied the works of Darwin and Huxley, and took a passionate interest in the flora and fauna wherever he might be. He contrived to be in a lot of far-flung places.[84] He first went to America in the vacations from Oxford, travelling with his Uncle Tom: 'Cecil is a real good fellow and a most pleasant companion, especially for me. We read the *Antigone* through on the steamer and are about to begin on the *Acharnians*. On the 11th we proceed West to Garrison (Montana) and then to Melrose in Idaho. There the guides and horses will be ready and we disappear into the Bitter Root Mountains and Big Hole Basin.'[85] In the course of this visit Cecil found himself inspecting the Niagara Falls with Lord Frederic Hamilton. They saw a plaque commemorating Lord Desborough's feat in swimming the river at that point. 'I looked at Baring, Baring looked at me. "I don't see why we shouldn't do it too," ' he observed. When the two young men emerged naked on the Canadian bank they were confronted by a reporter who tried to interview them but, hearing they had not done it for a bet, said 'Hell!' and walked off.[86]

Cecil Baring drifted into banking for want of an alternative and never really gave his heart to it. He joined his uncle in Kidder Peabody in 1887 – 'Cecil has plunged headlong into work and is doing it all as well as possible,'[87] Tom Baring wrote appreciatively – and was still there when the dual Boston and New York house was dissolved three years later. Two firms took its place: Kidder Peabody in Boston and Baring, Magoun, a partnership of Thomas Baring and George Magoun, the specialist in railways, in New York. Both houses acted as Barings' agents, and in New York Baring, Magoun continued to operate a joint account, with a capital of £1 million or a little more. Cecil Baring went with his uncle, with the promise of a partnership in Bishopsgate in 1891 if all went well.[88] By the time that moment came, the situation of Barings was very different and the future of Tom or Cecil in London looked, to say the least, precarious.

In economic terms Canada was far behind the United States, its industry primitive and kept in that state by the dumping of cheap exports from the south, its agriculture hamstrung by inadequate communications. Politically it was still frail; even in 1848 many people believed it must in the end throw in its lot with the States. It had the same hunger for capital as its neighbour but far less capacity to develop it for itself. If it was not to keep up with the United States, for that was far beyond its powers, but to advance at all, then it urgently required money from abroad. The only source of capital for Canada was London, and all that came was raised by the efforts of Barings and Glyns.

It might be going unnecessarily far to accuse Barings of a crime so heinous as altruism, but their policy towards Canada was consistently generous and liberal. When in 1849 the Inspector General of Public Accounts, Francis Hincks, tried to explain various temporary problems which led to a pressing need for funds, Barings brushed his words aside; the explanations 'were in no wise required by us to confirm our opinion of the honour and resources of the Government or People of Canada'.[89] Barings and Glyns found themselves regularly in advance by £100,000 or more, sometimes as much as £450,000, and charging a rate of interest noticeably lower than they could have got in London. 'We do not wish and we feel we ought not to enforce our full right on such a valued and valuable connection as that with the Province,' wrote Thomas Baring, but the value, whatever it was, was certainly not monetary.[90]

The greatest problem was to persuade the British investor to take an interest in the affairs of this remote and precarious colony. In the late 1850s £400,000 was urgently needed to meet a deficit on current account. Barings and Glyns were in despair. They wrote jointly to assure the Canadian government that debentures could only be sold at a price so low as to alarm every holder of Canadian bonds. 'We are most desirous not only to prevent such an occurrence but to aid to the utmost of our power in the advancement of every work likely to promote the prosperity of the Province. . . . We see no other mode, therefore, than to purchase a portion ourselves and by that means to try to give confidence to others, as well as to meet your immediate wants, and though not anxious to buy a security for which we as yet see no chance of a re-sale, we consent . . . to buy debentures to the extent of £100,000 nominal capital.'[91] At the end of 1858 a powerful delegation came to London to discuss the political and economic future of the provinces. Joshua Bates acted as a kind of unofficial Canadian ambassador, advising the delegates on the people they would be meeting and accompanying them when they called on the Prime Minister and Chancellor of the Exchequer.[92] As one result of the visit Barings and Glyns brought out a £2.8 million loan at the beginning of 1860. They were not particularly optimistic about the prospects – 'our people will not take much interest in it,' they told Hopes gloomily[93] – but in the event it proved a triumphant success. The loan was going 'like hot rolls', Bates noted in his diary, and the issue was ten times oversubscribed.[94]

As in the United States, it was the development of the railway system that needed most capital. Between 1850 and 1870 expansion was particularly feverish, and nearly £30 million was called for to finance the new lines, a demand which the Canadian economy could not begin to meet. The Grand Trunk Railway was the most ambitious of the various undertakings, and from the point of view of Barings at least, the most disastrous. Weardale Iron and the Grand Trunk were Barings' two great blunders of the mid-nineteenth century; the first was primarily the responsibility of Joshua Bates, the second of Thomas Baring.

The Grand Trunk was a noble concept: 1112 miles driving west and opening up the heartlands around Lake Huron. It offered 'the certainty of a great traffic', observed no less an authority than Robert Stephenson; Lord Elgin, the Governor General, eulogized it; it promised a dividend of 11 per cent. Barings supported the idea from the start, but baulked at naming one of their partners to serve on the London board – it was not the sort of thing they did. When the prospectus arrived, however, both Thomas Baring and George Glyn were named among the directors; they protested but gave way on the urging of John Ross, the President of the railway, who pointed out that they would be keeping company with the entire cabinet of Northern Canada.[95]

'The Grand Trunk business will go right, I think,' Bates reassured Baring.[96] His cautious qualification proved all too necessary; within a few years it was going badly wrong. By the end of 1857 funds were exhausted, traffic failed to grow as had been anticipated, the public lost confidence in the securities. Glyns and Barings urged the Canadian government to come to the rescue, otherwise the concern would collapse.[97] The Finance Minister, A. T. Galt, was hardly encouraging; he ruled out any idea of the government taking over the line or providing direct aid; the only long-term solution lay in increased traffic.[98] The line had become an embarrassingly live political issue, and no government was likely to risk the explosion of popular indignation which would have followed intervention. In any case the finances of the Canadian government were almost as precarious as those of the railway. In July 1860 the company made a final appeal. The Grand Trunk 'had scrupulously completed a line of railway of undoubted excellence'; it had bestowed on the province 'incalculable advantages from its expenditure and works'; it had crowned its labours by 'erecting at enormous cost the Victoria Bridge which must always be considered as an honor to Canada'; and yet it was now about to 'sink under the pressing load of present debt'.[99]

Galt's reply was sympathetic but noncommittal. 'Unfortunately the visit of the Prince of Wales absorbs a large share of our time and attention at this moment.'[100] Since the main purpose of the Prince's visit was to open the Victoria Bridge, Galt could have found a happier excuse.

Bates continued to keep a commendably stiff upper lip. When asked whether to sell or keep Grand Trunk shares, he replied, 'Keep to be sure. It will be good property for the grandchildren. Lock up the shares. There is nothing more to pay on them.'[101] To Young, in November 1860, he maintained that the railway was bound to succeed some time or other 'and those who buy at the low price will make money'.[102] But Baring, who felt himself personally responsible and, as Chairman of the London board, was the all-too-visible manifestation of the company in London, took the matter more tragically. Certainly it was hard to find a bright side. By the end of 1860 the Grand Trunk was unable even to cover its running costs, let alone pay interest on its shares. For Barings the consequences were extremely serious. After the first issue they found themselves left with £361,000 worth on their hands and debts from the company amounting to more than £125,000.[103] In 1860, after the second, almost entirely unsuccessful issue, they had more than £800,000 of unsaleable stock and were owed well over £400,000. When Bates was totting up his personal wealth in 1863, he found that his Grand Trunk stock was valued at £219,000, while when Thomas Baring died in 1873 his holding was worth a theoretical £600,000.

By then the railway, though still a drain on Barings' resources, was no longer a total disaster. At the end of 1860 Barings and Glyns took joint action to distrain on the company's property. Their move at last forced the Canadian government to intervene to prevent a disastrous breakdown of communications. A commission was set up and recommended that certain parts of the revenue should be set aside for the payment of creditors; it also proposed important economies in the running of the railroad of a kind which the London board had been urging for years but had wholly failed to impose on their headstrong Canadian colleagues. The Grand Trunk Railway was never to be a favourite of the British investor, nor spoken of with affection inside the partners' room at Barings, but the worst was over.

'Our unpopularity is awful,' wrote Thomas Baring in March 1861 when they were launching their legal action against the railway. 'I hope that *we* may not be the cause of the stoppage of the Road. We should be as much abused in England as in Canada.'[104] One of Baring's stauncher allies in his battle to involve the Canadian government in the affairs of the Grand Trunk had been the Governor General, Sir Edmund Head. 'I believe that the future prosperity of Canada is intimately connected with the speedy and successful conclusion of this great work,' he told Baring.[105] His intervention became well known and the more ardent nationalists deplored what they saw as his subservience to British interests. When, in August 1858, Head somewhat controversially refused a dissolution, the opposition press abused him. Under the headline 'Sir E. Head's Closet Councillors', *The Globe* accused him of taking orders from Barings. Why not, it suggested, do away with all pretence and ask Barings to nominate the Inspector General and the merchants of London, Manchester and Glasgow the two Attorney Generals?[106] Not the least disagreeable feature for Barings of the Grand Trunk affair was that it drew them into Canadian politics and associated them in the public eye with the government as against the opposition.

It was some time before Barings made any other important sorties into the world of Canadian railway finance, but in 1884 George Stephen – later Lord Mount Stephen – reckoned that they should by now be ready to support a yet more grandiose project, the Canadian Pacific Railroad, a line to link east and west and unite the nation. Alexander Baring, a distant cousin who was working for the Canadian Pacific's agents in New York, was dispatched to take the temperature of his kinsmen. He was reasonably well received but reported that at that moment all transatlantic enterprises were viewed suspiciously in London.[107] The following year the Canadian government authorized the Canadian Pacific to raise $35 million, of which they would put up $20 million and the directors must find the rest. This time George Stephen himself took the proposition to Barings. Before he had even completed his exposition Lord Revelstoke interrupted: 'We have been looking into this question carefully, and if agreeable to you, we are prepared to take over the whole issue of £3 million of stock at 92¾.' It was a characteristically flamboyant gesture and Stephen exultantly cabled Canada. His fellow directors were anxiously awaiting the news: 'In the tumult of our feelings we began capering about like schoolboys, even bestowing sundry kicks on the furniture of the board room.'[108]

The story almost missed its happy ending. The London Stock Exchange did not take kindly to the first issue and Barings were left with a great deal of stock on their hands.[109] 'Between ourselves, I doubt if much over half have actually been sold to *investors*,' wrote Stephen. 'There was a dead set against the bonds by Grand Trunk Railroad folks, and there is not another House in London could have done what Barings have accomplished.' Little by little the bonds became established and on 5 November Stephen cabled: 'Railway now out of danger'.[110] The Americans proved more resistant. From New York Cecil Baring reported the Canadian Pacific was little bought, 'and most of the people here abuse it like the devil'. Even if it did well with the eastbound freight, 'all their cars will have to run back empty to the West again without the remotest chance of any compensating traffic'.[111] Undiscomfited, Barings pushed on with fresh issues. A loan for something over £4 million was floated in 1886. They farmed out shares to Glyns, Hambros, Morton Rose and other allies, but once again the market proved sluggish and at one point they had to buy £325,000 worth themselves to support it. The final profit was almost £60,000. A further issue of £3 million in 1888 was still more successful. Over £26 million was applied for and Barings' total profit on expenses and account amounted to nearly £130,000. It was a welcome success after the troubles of the Grand Trunk and provided a moment of satisfaction before the storm broke in Argentina several thousand miles to the south.

13

Overcommitted

Latin America, 1849–1890

Barings' commitments in Latin America between 1850 and 1890 were so heavily concentrated in Argentina and Uruguay that it is easy to ignore their activities in other countries of the region. These did not, in fact, add up to very much. In Mexico their chief function was that of agent for the disgruntled British bondholders who had lost years of interest on their investment as the result of defaults by the Mexican government. The bondholders fondly hoped that tripartite intervention by British, French and Spanish forces would secure them their money, but when an expedition was finally mounted, its object was to benefit only foreign merchants who had claims against the Mexican government.

A French army eventually fought its way to Mexico City in 1863 and it was in an effort to defray the cost of its operations that the French Minister of Finance approached Hottinguers and Rothschilds about a possible loan. Barings were involved from the start, through their close alliance with Hottinguers, but the reluctance of the French government to guarantee the loan ensured that their anyway tepid interest quickly chilled into extinction. Not even a direct appeal to Thomas Baring from 'the great Baron James' had any effect, though Baring told Hottinguers he was perfectly ready in principle to act with Rothschilds; 'since the establishment of the Crédit Mobilier here we must look about us'.[1] He did, however, promise to discuss with Rothschilds any approach made by the French government to either house: *'Cette entente avec M. Baring,'* Rothschild told Fould, *'nous a paru opportune, non seulement à cause de la position difficile où se trouve le Mexique, mais aussi à cause des emprunts antérieurs dont cette maison a été le principal intermédaire.'*[2] In the end Glyns and that threatening new apparition, the Crédit Mobilier, handled the loan.

Barings retained the financial agency for the Chilean government until the 1870s. It was a costly distinction. In November 1858 the house issued a £1.5 million government loan. Thomas Baring, who was abroad at the time, had been pouring cold water on the enterprise, to the chagrin of Joshua Bates. 'I am very sorry that the absence of Francis and myself and our letters should prevent you from concluding what you think right about the Chile loan,' wrote Baring. 'I always consider that the principle of our house is that the partners on the spot, especially when *you* are one of those, should decide all matters of business as they alone can judge of time and circumstances.'[3] Unfortunately a combination of political disorder in Chile and what Baring called 'the uncertainty and languor of the money market' proved damaging. Some half of the loan went the first day but little of this was for permanent investment. 'So small a loan a few years ago would have been taken in a few hours,' Bates wrote in his diary.[4] One million pounds had been allotted a few days later but Barings had already had to buy back £200,000 so as to keep the stock at a premium. Early in 1859 still only half the original amount had been taken, and in 1867 Barings were complaining bitterly that fresh loans issued through Morgans were undermining the value of the earlier issue.

Nor was their experience in Venezuela any happier. In 1862 Barings floated a £1 million loan secured against customs duties, but within two years the government took over all the income from the customs and suspended payments. Barings plagued successive British Foreign Ministers to protest, and in 1867 Thomas Baring headed a deputation that urged Lord Stanley 'to take active and energetic measures'. Stanley had no intention of getting into the same sort of mess as the French had contrived for themselves in Mexico. 'Her Majesty's Government,' he replied, 'do not feel justified in seeking the sanction of Parliament to adopt coercive measures which might involve this country in a war with the Republic of Venezuela.'[5] The bondholders had to wait a long time for their money.

Brazil was Rothschild country and the fact that Barings opened a small credit for the Bank of Brazil in 1879 did not alter the situation.[6] Nor did a £1 million short-term loan for the government of Peru in

1874 establish a pattern for the future.[7] Barings' serious efforts were directed towards Argentina, and the resumption of payments on the 1824 loan in 1859 opened the way for a new and more vigorous expansion of activities. In view of what was to come, it was not without significance that young Ned Baring chose the same year for a first tour of the Americas. 'Edward Baring's . . . news is interesting,' reported Thomas Baring. 'I have a few very sensible lines from him. . . . The youngster promises well.'[8] He was not enamoured by what he found in the various countries he visited. In Mexico he concluded that the real reason for the failure to satisfy the bondholders was 'the antipathy of the majority of the Congress to see so large a sum of money as $4½ million go to pay their just debts to *foreigners*, thus precluding the possibility of any of it going into their pockets'.[9] In Peru he commented, 'an infusion of Anglo Saxon blood into this country would no doubt be of the greatest service; but the intolerance with respect to religion is still so great that it presents a great barrier to any project for immigration'.[10] When he finally reached Argentina he was still further dismayed. 'There is certainly a marked difference between the Argentine Confederation and any other part of S. America as this so called Republic is possibly under a more despotic rule than any other country on the face of the earth.'[11]

Baring found himself seeing a lot of this despot, Juan Rosas, over the next few months. The British Minister, Henry Southern, had been sent out with instructions to get on good terms with Rosas and he performed this task manfully. Southern had a close relationship with Barings, and though Thomas Baring was at pains never to treat him as a supernumerary employee, he larded his letters to the diplomat with casual references to what he had said to Palmerston or Palmerston had said to him when they had met at dinner the previous night. Baring was equally close to Lord Eddisbury, the Under-Secretary of State for Foreign Affairs, who advised him to avoid writing to Rosas on blue paper, which he much disliked; 'whilst on the other hand if your letter were to be made to extend beyond one sheet, and if the sheets were to be tied together with a bit of *Red* Ribbon, Rosas would be more gratified by such a ridiculous bit of homage than if you were to make him a large Loan'.[12] Whatever the colour of the paper and ribbon used, however, it did not alter the fact that by the time Ned Baring arrived in Buenos Aires, all

Rosas had offered was 'promises and a Guano contract, with both of which,' Thomas Baring told Southern, 'I fear that a meeting of bond holders would not be at all pleased'.[13]

Southern and Ned Baring cooperated closely in their efforts to make Rosas improve his offer. Together they regularly visited his country house, where they paid court to the dictator and his formidable, Eva Peron prototype, daughter Manuelita. Baring was not wholly seduced by Rosas, whom he found 'from his vanity and habit of doing just as he pleases' a difficult man to deal with,[14] but he concluded he genuinely wanted a settlement of the debts and would put forward a reasonable proposition as soon as circumstances allowed. Rosas never got a chance to prove his good will. Within two years of Baring's visit the dictator and his daughter were deposed and had fled the country. The news of his downfall arrived in London only a few days before Major Ferdinand White was dispatched to Buenos Aires as Barings' new agent and negotiator for the bondholders.

White was a curious choice. He listed his qualifications as being 'Integrity, Secrecy, Tact, and a knowledge of Spanish',[15] but the last at least was exiguous. He was offered £1000 and expenses for his trouble, and demonstrated his integrity by keeping a low profile and his expenses to a minimum, living in humble lodgings, distributing no bribes and doing no entertaining. He brought out with him a handsome rifle and pair of pistols, purchased originally as a gift for Rosas and subsequently intended for whoever seemed to be in power, but rapidly concluded that all the 'dignitaries and officials I have had to deal with are learned Doctors of Law and peaceful Civilians. The era of the caudillos has passed away: thank God.'[16] He sold the rifle for rather less than had been paid for it to an officer in the Royal Navy and brought the pistols back to England. In this he demonstrated his inadequacy; the new and ferocious military dictator, General Urquiza, would have relished the present, but White never aimed so high. Not that it would have helped much if he had. Urquiza was soon ejected from Buenos Aires and the country lapsed into chaos in which no negotiations over debt settlements could possibly be expected. White sadly left for home: 'I am sorry to say the aspect of affairs is more gloomy than ever.' A protracted civil war seemed inevitable.[17]

It was 1856 before things had mended sufficiently for hopes of a final settlement of the debts to be revived.[18] Zimmerman, Frazier and Co. had become Barings' correspondents in Buenos Aires after the departure of Ferdinand White, and in April Charles Cabot of that firm wrote to report that the situation was now more tranquil, revenues were growing and 'I therefore cannot but think that the Government will be enabled before long to do something more for the English Bond holders'.[19] Ferdinand White's former deputy, confusingly called George White, was sent out to try at last to put a stop to this unhappy saga. He was speeded on his way by a blast of indignation from the bondholders. They considered Barings had been weak and dilatory and nothing would satisfy them but terms substantially better than any so far offered: 'The Committee is so angry that they will throw the whole blame upon Barings.'[20]

Fortunately the improvement was forthcoming. By the time White arrived, indeed, the only point at issue was the rate of interest to be paid on the bonds in lieu of the thirty years or so of lost interest. The bondholders wanted 3 per cent; Roberto Norberto de la Riestra, the Minister of Finance, offered only 1 per cent. Riestra was 'very stiff on the subject,' reported White.[21] In the end he relented, and a sliding scale of interest was agreed which gave the bondholders their 3 per cent from 1871.[22] The settlement meant that the bondholders got only £7000 less than they demanded. 'I have therefore thought it best to close at once,' White told the British Minister, 'and I trust the affair may now be considered as virtually settled.'[23]

After this chastening experience it not surprisingly took some time before Barings were disposed to lend more money to Argentina. The surprising thing, indeed, is that within a few years they were at it again. The fact was that Argentina enjoyed immense natural wealth, and that though incompetence, corruption and political instability might from time to time put foreign investors at risk, in the long run their profit was likely to be secure. The very fact that the risks were there meant that the profits would be greater than those secured in more stable areas. Up to 18 per cent interest could be secured on a well-secured short-term loan. Handled with discretion, investment in Argentina could be an eminently satisfactory enterprise. Barings lost a great deal of money there, but that should not be allowed to obscure the fact that they made a great deal too. They were in a position of peculiar responsibility. The British investor was ignorant of

almost everything to do with Latin America, confusing Argentina
with Chile and Mexico and wholly unable to follow the intricacies of
Argentine internal politics.[24] They depended on the judgement of
Barings as to whether or not the money would be safe. On the whole
their confidence was justified.

Not that the public blindly followed the bankers' bidding. Barings
re-entered the market early in 1866 with a small loan of £1.25 million
to help the Argentine government finance a war the latter and Brazil
were jointly waging against Paraguay. Argentina's 'progress in material resources was rapid and satisfactory,' Barings told Baron
Stieglitz; the security was good, the timing seemed right, yet less
than half the subscription was taken up.[25] Throughout 1866, a year
disastrously marked by the failure of Overend Gurney, Barings kept
up the price of the loan by buying shares as they came on to the market, but the war dragged on, money in London grew no easier, and
1867 found them holding an embarrassingly large amount of unsaleable stock as well as having advanced over £300,000 to meet the
immediate needs of the Argentine government. There was no hope
of issuing the further loan which Argentina now desperately needed.
It was not until June 1868 that a further £1.95 million was offered to
the British investor, and not until the following year, by which time
the war was clearly won, that the full amount was subscribed.

Two years later, with the war against Paraguay over, and the
Franco-Prussian war causing European investors to look farther
afield, it seemed the tide of public opinion must turn. Yet it obstinately failed to do so. In 1873 Barings brought out a small loan for
the province of Buenos Aires. The subscription went well and the
following year the Argentines came back for more. But the British
investor still would not accept that Argentina was a proper resting
place for his money. The 1873 loan was soon at a discount and there
were no buyers to be found. 'It would be impossible to offer a new
loan except at a much lower figure than the last, which would be
derogatory to the dignity of the Government,' Barings told the
Argentine Minister of Finance. 'We may add for your private information that, in order to secure the success of the loan of 1873, we
were obliged to take a considerable amount ourselves, and of this the
principal part remains, still unsold, in our possession.'[26]

Barings did not lose their faith in the long-term future of

Argentina but they had to defend its reputation against ferocious attacks by Stock Exchange speculators and certain financial journalists, particularly from *The Times*. Barings believed that this was a systematic campaign intended to drive down the price of Argentine securities, and it succeeded in lowering the price of the 1873 loan from its original 89.5 to a mere 63.[27] Letters from Barings to the editors of *The Times*, the *Morning Post* and other newspapers to some extent checked the rot, but prices still drifted down. 'We have the strongest interest in seeing the credit of the Republic maintained,' Barings told a new Minister of Finance in August 1876, 'and we have seen with the greatest pain the serious and continued depreciation in Argentine securities . . . We have made large purchases of Argentine Bonds on our own account to endeavour to arrest the fall, but without success.'[28]

Three months later Barings took a step that seemed relatively unimportant at the time but was to have the most direful consequences. It dispatched to act as its agent in Buenos Aires, for an initial three years, Nicholas Bouwer, a clerk of Dutch extraction who had been employed by Barings for some thirteen years. His terms of reference were to urge retrenchment on the Argentine government, but also to look out for suitable mercantile operations, and to pay particular attention to the Buenos Aires Drainage and Waterworks, which had been the beneficiary of the 1873 loan.[29] 'Buenos Ayres on the whole is not a bad place to live, the climate doing much to reconcile a foreigner to the country,' Bouwer told Ned Baring. 'The population however leaves much to desire; the foreign element, generally speaking, is not of the best, and as regards the natives, though exceedingly polite, they invariably betray their descent from the Spaniards.'[30] It was almost the only deprecating phrase about the country that he was to utter; after his first meeting with the Finance Minister he reported: 'It cannot be gainsaid that all the Argentine Republic requires to recover itself from its financial embarrassment is peace and prosperity. The latter appears to be returning and as to the former, I think, from all I hear, that it is decidedly secured.'[31]

It was Bouwer who introduced Barings to the affairs of the well-established Buenos Aires trading house of S. B. Hale and Co. Hales, Bouwer reported, had lost a lot of money recently but were 'honourably run and basically sound'. The principal partner, Mr Pearson, was 'a little too easy in business', but the man who provided most of the management 'I consider to be very active and intelligent'. Bouwer recommended that the house should be given a credit of £40,000 to £50,000. Barings turned down the proposal, but Bouwer later returned to the charge. 'I can assure you from the intimate knowledge I now have of the firm, that your relations with it will be both satisfactory and remunerative, and that you may grant it facilities with perfect confidence.'[32] On the basis of this resounding recommendation Barings granted a credit of £15,000. The intimacy of Bouwer's knowledge is attested to by the fact that he soon after-wards became engaged to Mr Pearson's daughter; its accuracy can be judged by the fact that he was reporting by mid-1879 'with very great regret' that Hales were in serious difficulties and would have to be rescued if they were not to collapse, probably taking the provincial government with them.[33] Against their better judgement Barings agreed to accept the proffered security and enlarge their credit, find-ing themselves by 1880 inextricably engaged with the affairs of this volatile company, and the somewhat perplexed owners of a country house, two ranches and a large quantity of cattle.[34]

It was no time for volatility. After so many years in the doldrums, the Argentine economy found itself on the high seas with a strong wind behind it. The country was as hungry as ever for fresh capital and suddenly the British investor was eager to supply it. 'The Com-mercial crisis which has so long weighed upon your country may be said to have disappeared,' wrote Barings exultantly to the new Presi-dent of the Banco de la Provincia in Buenos Aires, 'and she appears to be entering once more upon a career of prosperity.'[35] When Gen-eral Roca became President of the Republic in October 1880 and Buenos Aires was forcibly and finally integrated with the rest of the country, British investment in joint-stock enterprises in Argentina was worth about £25 million, by 1885 it was £45 million, by 1890 nearly £150 million. In 1889 Argentina absorbed 40–50 per cent of all British funds invested outside the United Kingdom.[36]

By no means all this vast inflow came through Barings but a strik-ingly large proportion did. In the first five years there was some restraint but in the four years beginning in 1886 loans were raised of £4 million, £4.3 million, £3.9 million and £5.3 million, the first two jointly with Morgans. Barings enjoyed a special relationship, even at those times at which they were unpopular for having refused to do all the government asked of them. They supplied the Finance Minister with a complimentary copy of the *Economist* and in 1882 were talked into selecting and sending out a racehorse for the Governor of Buenos Aires. They at first refused this potentially hazardous request and were reproached by Bouwer. The Governor, he told them, was 'very sorely disappointed, as he had hoped that you would have consented to render the country the service of securing a good stallion. He reckoned that some of you being good judges of horses, there would be no objection on your part to undertake the commission, the more as it was intended to leave you entirely free in your choice.'[37] Barings eventually took on the task. The stallion turned out to be ten years older than its proclaimed age, it had bandy legs and the first two foals which it sired were both stillborn.

Barings' close relationship with the government did not assure them a monopoly. In 1881 they refused to accept that the time was yet ripe to launch a new loan in London, whereupon a French syndicate moved in and seized the contract. It seemed as if the French had established themselves so firmly that they would take over the chief role of raising money abroad for the Argentine government, but the Argentines were delighted to play one banker off against the other. Early in 1884 Roca sent for Bouwer and asked whether Barings would take charge of a new $30 million loan to be raised for certain public works. Bouwer pointed out that the French were on the point of raising a $12 million loan in London. Roca said there was no immediate hurry for the larger loan. 'From the manner in which the President spoke I am convinced that he is heartily tired of the way in which the French houses have treated him, and that he very much regrets ever having allowed himself to be induced to place the affairs of the Government in other hands than yours.'[38] There was evidently more hurry than Bouwer thought; Roca got tired of waiting and negotiated the loan with a powerful combination of Morgans and the Crédit Industriel in Paris. It was possibly this rebuff which determined Barings to be more aggressive in future: at all events, in 1886 they combined with Morgans to take the £4 million government loan and added a loan for almost £2 million for Buenos Aires on their own account.

There was still evidence of some restraint in Barings' policies.

When the National Bank in 1886 wanted a credit of £200,000, Barings told Bouwer tartly: 'It is impossible for us to grant all the credits and advances sought for by the Governments, Institutions and individuals in the Republic. The applications we receive are especially numerous just now, while we, from our own point of view, are of opinion that we have already quite as much interest there as we care to have.'[39] Yet the pickings were often sumptuous. In 1887, when they closed the books on two loans of £400,000 for the Western Railway of Santa Fé, the profit that remained from commission and dealings on their own account was £182,334 4s.9d. With fortunes like that to be made, it was hard to blame the partners for yielding to the temptation always to add one more commitment to their existing list.

Meanwhile neighbouring Uruguay was making heavy demands on the resources of the house. At the end of 1887 Bouwer reported that the government in Montevideo wanted Barings to issue a new $20 million loan on their behalf: 'It is willing to leave the time and price of issue to you, and further to bind itself that all future financial operations shall pass through your hands.'[40] The list opened and closed on 5 April 1888 with applications for nearly £30 million. After so heady a success it took some self-discipline to turn down a Montevideo City loan. 'The number of loans and schemes of all kinds connected with the Argentine Republic and Uruguay which are likely to be offered here in the next few months,' Barings told Hales, 'is so great that it seems almost impossible that the European market can absorb them satisfactorily.'[41] The letter ended with a mention of the fact that Hales' director, C. H. Sanford, was expected to call at Bishopsgate after lunch. Barings's self-discipline was about to run out.

There was no prejudice in favour of Sanford within the partners' room at Bishopsgate. He was by origin an American and had come to Argentina as representative of a firm selling 'Florida Water', a proprietary medicine of questionable efficacy made from the flower of the elder tree.[42] Somehow he became a director of Hale and Co. and, almost by default, rose to be its manager. When Hales were heavily in debt to Barings in 1882, it was Sanford who was held particularly to blame in London. 'It is difficult to believe that his two senior partners are unable to control Mr Sanford sufficiently to force him to act honestly,' they wrote indignantly to Bouwer.[43] When Ward asked for a report on Hales some three years later Barings told him that the house had recently been doing well through government loans and that Mr Hale was an old man of whom nobody spoke ill. 'Besides this there is a Mr Pearson, whose daughter our agent married and whom we do not know. The controlling partner is Mr Sanford, in whom we have no confidence.'[44] And yet this man, who could not be induced to act honestly and in whom Barings had no confidence, was not merely received by Lord Revelstoke, but listened to with respect and treated as a sound authority on the Argentine economy.

He seems, indeed, to have been an uncommonly plausible trickster; not, perhaps, consciously a rogue, but carried away by his enthusiasm and with an alarming capacity to carry others away as well. He had greatly impressed the President of Argentina by his business acumen and it was this connection which had secured for Hales the concession to take over and extend the waterworks and drainage system of Buenos Aires. They purchased this concession for $21 million, payable in three annual instalments, and in exchange for this and the construction of the works were to receive £10 million shares and debentures in the newly formed Buenos Aires Water Supply and Drainage Company for sale to the public. If all went well, the construction work proceeded to schedule and to budget, and the public bought the shares and debentures with reasonable alacrity, then an immense profit would be made. If things did not go well, then the loss would be correspondingly calamitous.

Revelstoke saw only the possibilities of profit. He agreed to enter into the business on joint account with Hales, though knowing that that house lacked the substance to give any effective help in case of trouble, and thus committed Barings to a series of enormous payments with no certainty as to where the money was to come from. The first tranche of shares offered to the public gave an indication of the problems that lay ahead. Writing on 16 November to offer Messrs Ephraim and Co. a participation of £25,000, Barings told them that the issue 'was brought out yesterday and owing to various circumstances has not been very favourably received by the Public, which we are bound to say has not much surprised us. We have however every confidence in the future of the undertaking.'[45] Some of Barings' rivals were equally unsurprised but not so confident. Writing in early October about the news that Barings were to issue 'yet another Argentine loan,' Alphonse de Rothschild commented sceptically that 'the Argentine Republic had to grow rapidly very rich indeed, also with a growth of producing, thus enabling her the luxury of these numerous successive big loans'.[46] When the subscription was complete, more than half the preference shares were still held by the syndicate of nine banks and brokers which Barings had set up to handle the issue. Prospects for the second and third tranches seemed increasingly precarious. And yet more or less at the same time Barings and Hales found themselves having to take up £300,000 stock for the Western Railways of Santa Fé and Barings advanced more than £500,000 for the Curamalan Land Company, a vast estate of 600,000 acres in the south of Buenos Aires province.

With reasonable luck things could still have turned out well, but the luck was running out. General Roca's successor as President, Dr Miguel Celman, was a weak man who allowed the railway building mania to get out of hand and ran up debts out of all proportion to the immediately realizable assets of the country. 'The Confederation is piling up liabilities after much too wholesale a fashion, and great as are its resources, it cannot stand such a strain as this threatens to be,' wrote the *Bankers Magazine* at the end of 1888.[47] A year later even Revelstoke was showing alarm. 'The accounts we get from B. Ayres are not very satisfactory,' he told Sanford. 'It seems to us that a crisis is almost inevitable and the consequences may be very serious. Our money market is getting tighter daily, and with the great expansion of trade and continuous outflow of Gold, there will probably be a considerable pinch for money towards the end of the year. Argentine securities of all kinds are depressed and practically unsaleable in any quantity and are likely to remain so for the present.' He ended his letter by saying that his son John was coming out to view things on the spot.[48] John might as well have stayed at home, the damage was already done.

John Baring arrived in Buenos Aires at the very end of 1889. Like so many visitors he found himself divided between wonder at the vast potential of Argentina and dismay at the mess the inhabitants were making of it. 'A glorious country' he considered it – 'I mean exclusively from a financial point of view, aesthetically it is hideous.' If only its rulers would behave decently then the value of its stock would soar sky high. 'There really is no limit to the riches of the republic.' But decency was the last thing to be expected. 'The bribery and corruption is really quite awful,' he told his father. 'After gleaning the principles of business in the moral atmosphere of No. 8 Bishopsgate, I assure you I am perfectly aghast at what goes on.'[49] Yet in spite of the worst that humanity could do, he still felt reasonably confident about the future of the country. 'Of a "crash" I think there is no chance whatever. Business is at an *absolute standstill* as far as brokers etc. are concerned. But I think each day *amejoras* the position of the country. Of their defaulting on their Bonds I do not believe there to be the least chance.'[50]

His initial reaction to the great waterworks project was to be impressed by its efficiency but dismayed by its size. 'I confess I was surprised to see what a big thing this waterwork business is,' he wrote after his first inspection. 'You have no idea, I am sure, of the scale it is on.' Rather in the same way as the Grand Trunk Railroad in Canada, the enterprise had been identified with the government and was therefore abused by the opposition; the company being daily denounced in the press as a monstrous creation designed to benefit a few corrupt Argentine politicians and foreign capitalists at the expense of the inhabitants of Buenos Aires. 'I'm bound to say, the works do not conduce to the comfort of the town,' admitted Baring, 'as they have rooted up most of the streets and excavate huge pits in them. The other day the President was gaily tooling along in a victoria, when his horse disappeared into an abyss and broke its neck. This was rather unfortunate.'[51]

Soon he ceased even to be impressed by the efficiency of the management. Work was almost at a standstill for want of drawings and shortage of materials, labour was extravagantly deployed, money was being squandered. To ensure a safe income for the company it had been provided that the users of its services should pay not in paper pesos, which were swiftly devalued, but at the rate of six gold dollars per house. The householders met this demand either by refusing to avail themselves of the services offered them or by using the water and then failing to pay for it. By the end of October 1890 customers owed the company arrears of $1.65 million.[52] Yet at the same time the company still had to pay interest to the shareholders and the next slice of the purchase price to the government. 'The only chance,' John Baring concluded, as he surveyed the dismal future for Barings in Argentina, 'is to absolutely refuse any new business and to trust to events taking a more favourable turn in the near future.'[53]

Unfortunately there was more than enough old business on hand already. Barings were committed to go on issuing debentures to finance the instalment payments due to the Argentine government, yet did not dare to offer them to the public. Of the £2 million ordinary shares theoretically allotted, only about £150,000 were in fact placed with the public. The greater part remained as a gigantic millstone round the necks of Hales and Barings – which in effect meant the neck of Barings alone. In an article in November 1890 the *Economist* complained about the unscrupulous efforts made by Barings to promote the sale of these securities; 'the market devices that were employed to attract investors' were deliberately calculated to mislead.[54] Sir John Clapham, historian of the Bank of England, agrees that Barings' issuing and underwriting methods were indefensible, 'a great and wealthy house should not have stooped to them'.[55] If Barings were really employing every market device to persuade the investor to take the stock of the Waterworks Company, they were singularly unsuccessful. The impression one gains a hundred years or so later is of a doomed passivity, the resignation of men who see an avalanche about to descend upon them but can do nothing to save themselves.

The disaster was now compounded by a political crisis in Argentina. The grossly inflationary policies of President Celman so alarmed his Minister of Finance that the latter issued an ultimatum – either he would resign or the President of the National Bank must be dismissed. Celman accepted his resignation. The gold premium jumped from 118 to 165 in a single day and Barings were warned that the quarterly dividends on the bonds of the Republic could not be paid.[56] Revolution broke out and the Navy backed the insurgents. Celman fled, and the Vice-President, Carlos Pellegrini, took over. 'The nomination of Dr Pellegrini has had a good effect,' wrote Alphonse de Rothschild, 'and doubtless should restore some calm in the minds of . . . Messrs Barings.'[57] It was too late for any such reassurance. The chaos in Argentina made it more than ever certain that no British investor would hurry to risk his money in such a land. Whether Pellegrini would manage to restore financial order in a year or two was, for Barings, of academic interest.

'Financial affairs critical,' cabled Hales on 20 November 1890. 'Minister of Finance requests us inform you it of the utmost importance loan should be arranged without delay in order to avoid bankruptcy. If conditions are not such as Argentine Government can honourably accept, Minister of Finance and Cabinet will resign. This would be fatal as will probably result in anarchy.'[58] If anyone in the partners' room at Bishopsgate was still capable of raising a wry smile, then surely this cable would have provoked it. They knew by then that not merely could they not provide a new loan, but they could not even find the money to pay the next instalment due under the waterworks agreement. The Argentine ministers were not the only people to be facing bankruptcy.

14

The Baring Crisis

1890

Until the middle of October 1890 there were not half a dozen people in London who suspected that Barings were under serious pressure. Plenty of people were uneasy about what was going on. Within the house T. C. Baring had been predicting disaster in Argentina for several years.[1] Tom Baring was said to have 'spoken very strongly' to Revelstoke some months before.[2] *The Statist* had been particularly prescient. As early as the middle of 1889 it had deplored the huge proportion of the issues made on behalf of Uruguay and Argentina which had had to be taken up by the houses involved; only a few weeks later it stated bluntly: 'The truth is that even the most sanguine can no longer shut their eyes to the fact that a crash is inevitable.'[3] Yet nobody really believed that Baring Brothers could be in danger. Even Revelstoke, who should have known the situation if anyone did, deluded himself that all would be well: 'He of course knew the engagements were very heavy but he had always been confident that money would come in and carry them through as it had on other occasions.'[4]

By 13 October, however, he at least accepted that temporary help was needed. Through the agency of a broker, Mr S. Brunton, Bertram Currie of Glyn, Mills was told that Barings needed a large sum of money immediately and did not wish to cause alarm by appearing in the market as borrowers. On enquiry Brunton established that the gap between Barings' acceptances and the bills in its portfolio amounted to about £1 million. Glyns thereupon made an advance of £500,000 on the security of some of the Guinness stock still held by the house or its partners and subsequently put up a further £250,000. Martins also helped to the tune of £500,000. At the end of the month

Currie was given a statement of Barings' position which showed liabilities of £20.96 million against a shaky list of assets which included £4.16 million for Argentine securities held jointly with Hales, a similar amount for 'Baring Brothers' own securities', and 'Partners' houses, lands, contents etc.' valued at £1 million. Currie at least was left in no doubt that the situation was desperate.

The secret was well kept. When Brown, Shipley cabled Brown Brothers with the news on 12 November, Browns professed their astonishment. 'House referred to much talked about lately,' they replied. 'General impression nothing could be wrong.'[5] The impression that nothing could be wrong with Barings was so general and deeply held that it was to take much disturbing. On Friday 7 November Everard Hambro of C. J. Hambro and Son, a house which was also deeply involved in the affairs of Hales, called on Revelstoke to discuss what was to be done.[6] At 8 a.m. the following day he was with Lord Rothschild in St Swithin's Lane – the first indication for some people that a crisis was afoot was said to be the apparition of so senior a figure in the City on a Saturday morning at so intemperate an hour.[7] Rothschild was inclined to wash his hands of the whole affair; nothing could now be done to save Barings. Undiscomfited, Hambro moved on to visit the Governor of the Bank of England, William Lidderdale. Lidderdale immediately undertook to meet Revelstoke and Francis Baring in Hambro's office that afternoon.

The story Revelstoke had to unfold was darker even than had been expected. Argentina was not Barings' only worry. At the end of June the Russian government had recalled £2 million of the immense deposits they had lavished on Barings the year before.[8] This followed withdrawals of another £3 million in the previous ten months. Barings were already anticipating the blow that was to fall on 11 November, a demand for a further £1.5 million out of the £2.4 million that remained.[9] 'Many people think they see the finger of the Jew in the large Russian withdrawals of cash which were one of the causes of the downfall. I think that there is something in it,' wrote Revelstoke's brother, Colonel Robert Baring.[10] Who the 'many people' were and what grounds they had for their belief is singularly obscure. Only a few days after this letter the Russian Finance Minister was writing to Rothschilds – whom Robert Baring undoubtedly had in mind – to thank them for the contribution they had made 'to assure the safety of a house, in which the Imperial Treasury still had immense interests involved. If anything could add to the renown of the great name you bear as a financier, this would be the assistance which you have just accorded to rivals of yesteryear. This deal will occupy, as I am sure, a place of honour in the annals of the world of finance.'[11] In fact Rothschilds were neither as chivalrous as the Russians claimed nor as base as Colonel Baring believed. Certainly they had played no part in the withdrawal of Russian funds, any more than they could claim credit for a subsequent change of heart in St Petersburg, as a result of which the outstanding £2.4 million was left in entirety with Barings.[12] This decision, probably made at the request of the Bank of England, was to be the first break in the clouds that now enveloped the house of Barings.

Revelstoke's meeting with Lidderdale must have been disagreeable. The Governor took no trouble to hide his indignation at the conduct of affairs. He believed that even without the Argentine imbroglio Barings would have run into trouble sooner or later, and probably sooner, 'because the business was entirely managed by Revelstoke and he did not seem the least to know how he stood; it was haphazard management, certain to bring any firm to grief'.[13] But fume though he might, he could not afford to stand aside; there was too much at stake. As soon as Revelstoke had gone he sent off a message to the Chancellor of the Exchequer, George Goschen – himself a former partner in the financial house of Frühling and Goschen – asking him to stand by for an urgent meeting on Monday morning. 'Mysterious letter from Governor of the Bank, hoping I should be in town early tomorrow – very alarming,' wrote Goschen in his diary; and then the following day: 'Found him in a dreadful state of anxiety. Barings in such danger that unless aid is given, they must stop.'[14] Lidderdale insisted that the government must come to the rescue. If they would put up £1 million, the Bank would do the same and the City could find the rest. Unless something like this was done, banks would be closing all over London and house after house would have to stop. Goschen expressed good will but insisted that the City must find its own solution, there was nothing the government could do to help. When W. H. Smith, the Leader of the House of Commons and First Lord of the Treasury, was brought into the picture he took the same line. There could be no question of government credit, the City magnates must provide the necessary guarantees themselves. 'But do you realize, Mr Smith,' asked Lidderdale, 'what the amount is which has to be guaranteed?' 'Perfectly,' replied Smith, 'and though I have nothing to do with the firm or the interests involved, you can put my name down for £100,000.'[15]

Gallant gesture though this was, it did not go far to solve the problem of Barings' indebtedness. Goschen now involved the Prime Minister, writing in terms of cautious optimism. Smith and he, he told Lord Salisbury, had agreed 'that any direct intervention on the part of the Government would be impossible under any circumstances. . . . Tremendous pressure may be brought on us to help, but I think that it will be necessary for *"la haute finance"* to find its own solution. The Rothschilds are sure to put the screws on, but it won't do . . .'[16] Salisbury, who knew Lord Rothschild well, now sent for him. He found that the great financier was sceptical about the chances of cobbling together a syndicate of City magnates to save Barings. Part of the liabilities was £15 million of bills scattered over the commercial world; any attempt to raise money by a syndicate would reveal the fact that these bills were jeopardized and lead to a general *sauve qui peut*. The government *must* assist, either directly or through the Bank of England.

As to Barings, Rothschild's tone was frankly vengeful. 'He spoke with the utmost certainty that the house must disappear. On the most favourable hypothesis they would only save £2 million of their capital. No one would trust them with large operations again: they could not make more than 5 per cent on the £2 million: and as there were ten partners [in fact there were seven] that would mean an income of £10,000 a year each. He thought they would prefer to cut up their remaining capital and retire into the country on 4 per cent or £8000 a year each.' Rothschild was ambiguous about the effect the disaster would have on his own affairs; he insisted 'that he was quite indifferent – that he had no liabilities', but went on to admit that the accounts of his house, when made up at the end of the year, would not be pleasant reading: and that he should have to live more quietly. 'I thought him very anxious. He said that if the catastrophe came, he thought it would put an end to the commercial habit of transacting all the business of the world by bills on London.'[17]

Rothschild followed up what he described to his Paris cousins as a

'satisfactory interview' by helping Lidderdale build up the reserves
of the Bank of England to support any possible rescue operation. 'I
called on the Governor of the Bank of France and had the satisfaction of sending you a telegram announcing the Bank's readiness to
make a further advance of £1 million to the Bank of England,'
reported Alphonse de Rothschild.[18] This advance was only part of a
larger operation, in which the Bank of England borrowed £3 million
in gold from Paris and purchased a further £1.5 million from St
Petersburg to shore up its inadequate reserves. The fact that the
money was known to be there made it unlikely that it would be
needed; if there had been any suspicion that the Bank of England
was unable to cope with the crisis then the *sauve qui peut* that
Rothschild had predicted would indeed have started. Fortunately
things were calm at the moment in Paris and, as Hottinguers told
Barings, there was a determination to do all that could be done to
avert disaster.[19]

Indeed, the solidarity shown by the financial world was impressive. In London, though Barings were regularly condemned, the feeling was that the City was all in it together. 'What a season of disaster!'
recorded Reginald Brett, future Lord Esher, in his diary. 'Had
Barings been allowed to collapse, Natty [Rothschild] says most of
the great London houses would have fallen with them.'[20] From Paris
Alphonse de Rothschild urged his London cousins to make 'the
greatest effort to forestall a catastrophe'.[21] 'It is frightful to think
what might have been the consequences if Barings had not been
carried through,' wrote Brown Brothers. 'It is sad enough and bad
enough as it is, and with you we are quite ready to make the best of it,
hard as it is to be discredited as every private banker will be because
of their actions.'[22] The *New York Times* proclaimed that this was like
no other banking catastrophe; Barings were 'the greatest banking
house of all the world' whose 'signature has stood always and everywhere for an absolute guarantee'.[23] Only Edward Wagg, the senior
partner of Helbert, Wagg, greeted the disaster with British phlegm.
He was on holiday in Scotland and received a telegram from his partners, 'Barings in difficulties. Return at once.' He replied, 'If by
returning can save Barings will come: otherwise propose finishing
holiday.' He stayed.[24]

But on 11 November the prospects of saving Barings still seemed slight. Rothschilds were opposed to the setting up of a syndicate from within the City unless the government would join in, and the stature of Rothschilds was such that if they abstained the operation would never get off the ground. Yet the government was in principle still opposed to lending assistance. To a nineteenth-century Chancellor of the Exchequer, the idea that he might intervene in a matter of private business was anathema. The government had no money at its disposal, Salisbury told Rothschild; even if it was minded to help, the mechanism did not exist to enable it to do so. The only recourse would be by putting the matter to the House of Commons, which would inevitably provoke acrimonious debate of a kind certain to precipitate rather than avert disaster. 'How defend a supplemental estimate for a loss of half a million?' Goschen asked himself in his diary. 'And would not immediate application put the whole fat in the fire?'[25]

Only one man was in a position to bridge the gap between government and City, and that was Lidderdale at the Bank of England. He was ready, indeed anxious to try, but had first to be sure of his ground. As a preliminary step, he asked Bertram Currie to investigate the exact state of Barings' finances and to report whether the house was solvent – not solvent in the short term, which it was painfully clear they were not, but with assets sufficient to meet their liabilities if they were given time to realize them. At first it was suggested that a partner in Brown, Shipley should share the labour, but Currie objected that then both investigators would be closely involved with the affairs of Barings. Benjamin Buck Greene, another director of the Bank of England, eighty-three years old but singularly sharp and tenacious, was appointed instead.[26] The two men worked with exemplary speed and reported back within three days. Their finding was that Barings' assets exceeded their liabilities, but that many of the securities which formed part of those assets were 'though valuable, virtually unsaleable in any quantity'. If they were to be able to meet all their obligations over the next few weeks, then something over £8 million to £9 million was going to be needed to top up the liquid portion of their assets. Their conclusion, assented to with some reluctance by Greene because he knew that without it the Governor would be unable to take further action, was that: 'On consideration of the whole question we believe that if sufficient time

be given for realizing the assets, the Firm will be left with a substantial surplus after discharging their liabilities.'[27]

Even three days was dangerously long. John Daniell, senior partner of the government brokers Mullens and Co., came into the Bank
of England crying: 'Can't you do something, or say something to
relieve people's minds? They have made up their minds that something awful is up, and they are talking of the very highest names, *the
very highest.*' Lidderdale vividly remembered the words he spoke and
'the way he lifted up his arms when speaking'.[28] As the word spread
that Barings were in trouble, so their paper began to be presented
and anyone who had advances outstanding began to call them in.
The situation cannot have been made any easier by the attitude of
houses like Martin and Co. who, when the crisis was still far from
resolved, asked for the immediate repayment of £150,000 of their
total advance of £500,000, and then demanded the rest the following
day: 'We are under no anxiety as to any of our accounts, but we are
anxious to strengthen our cash as much as possible.'[29]

For the partners of Barings there must have been some consolation in the loyalty shown by family and friends. T. C. Baring was the
first and most conspicuous example. 'When C. T. Baring [sic] heard
of his late firm's disaster he offered them all his fortune to the last
farthing,' reported Reginald Brett. 'This was generous, as he left the
firm two years ago upon differences with Lord Revelstoke in connection with their Argentine speculations. He took the old-fashioned
view.'[30] This story that T. C. Baring had left the house because he disapproved of the house's commitments in Argentina was revived a
year or so later in what Revelstoke's wife described to her son
Everard as an 'odious paragraph' in the *Pall Mall Gazette*; 'Whereas
the truth is he [T. C. Baring] had a *culte* for Papa and wrote a letter on
retiring (*solely on account of bad health*) to Papa, quite the nicest and
most touching letter you can conceive from a man as undemonstrative . . . also as a fact the fresh engagements in Argentina and Buenos
Ayres Waterworks were entered into while he was still a partner –
and not objected to by him.'[31] Lady Revelstoke's comment was fair
enough: though T. C. Baring told Francis Baring that for years he had
been 'shy of S. America' and had thought the house was getting too
deeply involved, the fact remains that he made little effort to check
Revelstoke's madcap course. He must accept some part of the blame.

But legally he was now free of the house and its commitments. He had no obligation to come to its support and most people would have felt he had done his bit if he had merely left in Barings what money he had which was still there. Instead he told Francis: 'Of course what I have is at your disposal to pledge or sell. You have my full power of attorney and may use it.'[32] Legend has it that he went to the Bank of England and withdrew all his cash and securities. Then he proceeded to Bishopsgate with several bulging Gladstone bags, only marring this dramatic gesture by allowing one of the bags to burst open and spill over the road while he was arguing with the cab driver over an alleged overcharge of sixpence.[33] So picturesque a gesture would not have been beyond him. Not merely did he pledge his entire fortune, at the end of November he circulated a memorandum to his future partners:

> As I retired at the end of the year before last I am still rich, as folk count riches. You have been, are not, but, I think, will be again.
>
> Can this inequality be partially remedied in the meantime? I think so. I am prepared from 1 January next to place annually at the disposal of members of the old firm . . . the sum of £23,000 as follows: £5000 a year each to the 3 senior members, £2500 a year each to the 3 junior members, £500 a year to the only bachelor.
>
> The conditions are:
>
> (1) That nothing shall be said about this to anyone, especially to me. Any speaking about it might strain relations, which are naturally a little strange, and which I should like restored to those of 1888.
>
> (2) That this offer ceases in case of my death. . . .
>
> There must be no hesitation on the part of all or any of you in this matter on the ground of delicacy. I don't make this offer as a gift, but as a loan.[34]

Tom Baring in New York was more bitterly critical of Revelstoke's behaviour. He had no responsibility for the disastrous decisions that had been taken and was shocked by the unexpected news. As late as 6 November he was writing: 'I feel in my bones that they will come out all right.'[35] When they came out all wrong, he bewailed his brother's recklessness and folly. 'The name and the glory and the position and everything is gone,' he told Evelyn Baring. 'Ned would have it all – glory and wealth. He might at least have guarded our good name. But it has all gone, offered up to his insatiate vanity and extravagance . . . I never thought I should have to write such a letter as this. Verily "A great Nemesis overtook Croesus." The line has never been out of my head since the Guinness success.'[36] But his rancour did not prevent him cabling his total support for whatever phoenix might rise from the ashes of the old house. Indeed, he hastened home, confident that he would be begged to play an important role in the work of reconstruction, only to find that 'I am asked to take a back seat: to stay as long as I will in New York or take *Liverpool*! where there is nothing to manage. However, I won't cut up nasty.'[37]

Members of the family who had no direct connection with the bank had still less reason to put themselves out to save it, but did so nevertheless. Lord Ashburton was so far out of touch with events at Bishopsgate that when Lord Northbrook arrived at the Grange for a day's shooting and took his host aside to announce with an ashen face that the house was in trouble, Ashburton's mind flew to what he knew to be a regular problem at Stratton Park and he replied: 'Ah, that damned roof leaking again!'[38] But when the time came to put up money as a guarantee of Baring Brothers' liabilities, Northbrook came forward with £250,000 and Ashburton with £50,000. Nor was it just the family who rallied in this way. Markby, Stewart had long been solicitors to Baring Brothers. On 17 November Henry Markby and Charles Stewart wrote to say that their firm had a reserve against contingencies of £10,000. 'We do not know anything . . . beyond what we read in the newspapers. It is possible that we may be totally misapprehending the facts. But we trust that we are not committing any impertinence in saying that we shall feel honoured if you will allow us to place these securities, of comparatively trifling amount though they may be, at your firm's disposal.'[39]

Generous though the gesture was, £10,000 was indeed trifling compared with the sort of sum Lidderdale was looking for. Armed with the imprimatur of Currie and Greene, he on Friday renewed his assault on the government. The Bank, he said, could not alone bear the risk of what might happen if Barings were to founder while a rescue operation was being mounted: 'Unless the Government could relieve us of some of the possible loss,' he said, 'I should return at once and throw out all further Acceptances of the Firm.'[40] In the face of this ultimatum, ministers made a grudging but all-important concession. They agreed to bear half any loss that might result from Barings' bills taken in between 2 p.m. on Friday 14 November and the same time on the 15th. Lidderdale, in fact, had twenty-four hours in which to save Barings.[41]

Imprecise though the promise was, it gave the Governor grounds to act. He summoned a meeting of the Court of Directors of the Bank of England and announced that he was setting up a Guarantee Fund to cover any possible long-term deficit in Barings' finances. Once it was known that the City was backing Barings and that nobody risked loss, then the pressure would be off. The Bank of England, he said, would put up £1 million provided at least £3 million was guaranteed by others. Currie then took over and said that, having investigated the affairs of Barings with Mr Greene, he was prepared to offer £500,000 on behalf of Glyn Mills, provided that Rothschilds would do the same. Lord Rothschild had just arrived. 'When informed of the circumstances of the case and the conditions I had made, he hesitated and desired to consult his brothers,' recorded Currie, 'but was finally and after some pressure persuaded to put down his firm for £500,000.'[42] Word of the hesitation was seized on by those who wished to portray Rothschilds as a half-hearted or even unwilling rescuer. 'I was told that Rothschild had behaved well but I believe that this is not the case,' Tom Baring told his brother. 'He guaranteed £500,000, but only because Bertram Currie shamed him into doing so.'[43] Though Lord Rothschild may not much have relished his role it is hard to believe that he seriously doubted it was inevitable. As Baron Alphonse wrote to him from Paris: 'By saving Barings from this catastrophe [the English house] are serving their own interests, for at this moment the House of Baring is the keystone of English commercial credit and its collapse would provoke terrible consequences for English trade in all parts of the world. You must feel very proud about the contribution you have made, by your personal efforts, towards avoiding the worst misfortune.'[44]

Once it was certain that Glyn, Mills and Rothschilds had joined the Bank of England in a rescue operation, all doubts were put aside. Within half an hour Lidderdale had promises of £3.25 million, with substantial contributions from Brown, Shipley, Antony Gibbs, Morgans, Hambros and all the rest of Barings' former rivals. Not everyone gave gladly. 'The Bank people think there will be no loss, we are not so sanguine,' Raphaels, who contributed £250,000, told their New York agents. They had joined in, they admitted, not from love of Barings but to protect their own interests.[45] But their names were on the list. The following day the joint-stock banks joined in, with £750,000 each from the London and Westminster, London and County, and National Provincial. To be mentioned in the Guarantee Fund became fashionable, though those who had hoped to secure some easy advertisement by appearing in such distinguished company were disappointed when it was decided not to publish the list. By the end of the Governor's twenty-four-hour deadline £10 million had been pledged; the final figure was more than £17 million.

 Lidderdale was the hero of the hour. With a less courageous or less energetic Governor, Barings would certainly have collapsed. 'I don't know what to say or how to thank you but we will do our best not to be unworthy of what has been done,' Revelstoke wrote to him.[46] Goschen recommended him to Salisbury for a GCB – 'He is not rich enough for a baronetcy.'[47] It is pleasant to know that in due course Barings were to return the compliment. In 1897 Lidderdale found himself in financial difficulties, urgently needing £35,000. The security he could offer was inadequate and for £10,000 'my request is for an advance on my bare word that I will repay it if I can'. The money was instantly forthcoming.[48]

Barings were saved, but at a calamitous cost. When Rothschild had told Salisbury that nobody would trust them with large operations again[49] he spoke too soon, but there were few people in the City who would have contradicted him at the time. Sanford, who had done more than anyone except Lord Revelstoke to lead the house to its doom, had the effrontery to remark to a City acquaintance after the crash: 'I made a mistake going to Barings. Had I known that they were such a weak firm, I would have let them alone.'[50] Coming from him the comment was outrageous, but even if Barings could survive they would have to prove that they were not 'a weak firm'. At first even its survival was in doubt. In the eyes of the general public it was written off. When Alice James early in 1891 gave Barings as a reference to a house agent, 'he knew them not; this winter, when the world has rung with their downfall, makes the cessation of his business consciousness just without their radius the more remarkable'.[51]

Clearly the old partnership must be liquidated. Lidderdale had made it a condition of his support that Revelstoke would resign from its management, and this he did on 22 November. 'He is about broken hearted, I think, but now less worried than he was ten days ago,' wrote his son John. 'We have had a ghastly time here. The question now is whether we cannot do something to carry on the business. New capital is necessary, as the liquidation of the old firm must take 2 or 3 years.'[52] Lady Revelstoke bewailed her husband's fate: 'No longer young, to have as it were to begin again. . . . To have to endure this and to cut down every expense *is* very hard for him – coupled with the thought *he* by one mistake has done this.'[53] The saddest thought must have been that for him there would be no beginning again. Discredited as he was, the association of his name with any new firm would have been a guarantee of failure. Henry Mildmay was displaced as well. Some thought that he had been unfairly victimized for a blunder that was not of his creation. He himself contested this. He told his son 'that he had never for a moment doubted the prudence of the firm's policy and that it was humiliating to him that his responsibility as a senior partner should be minimized or that it should be suggested either that he condoned imprudence or that he did not realize what was going on.'[54] Even if he had been wholly innocent, he was the old guard and he would have to go.

Some people frankly rejoiced at Barings' downfall. They had for so long assumed the role of leaders, had wrapped around themselves the imperial mantle, had shown such condescension towards their lesser rivals, that even the most benevolent extracted some satisfaction from the situation. 'Fancy the Barings being brought so low,' wrote Randolph Churchill. 'Lord Revelstoke will not be able to ride the high horse as much as he used to.'[55] But though their judgement had been faulty, their probity was undoubted, and the courage and resolution with which they accepted responsibility for the disaster and set about retrieving it, won the admiration of their sourest critics. Evelyn Baring wrote to his friend C. Moberly Bell, manager of *The Times*, about the affair being 'tricky or dishonourable'. Bell wrote to reproach him. 'The burthen of every comment on all sides was the extreme loyalty and uprightness with which the firm behaved. . . . I am not exaggerating when I say that over and over again I have got up from a dinner with a sort of wish that I should like my name to have been Baring so as to have heard such praise of it.'[56] 'One thing is beyond question,' wrote the future Lord Mount Stephen, 'that is their honor and honesty. . . . Their character stands as high today as it ever did and this of itself will prove as good to them as an extra million of capital.'[57] It was this sympathy that was John Baring's greatest asset when he came to establish the new house.

On 25 November a circular letter announced that Baring Brothers and Company had transferred their business to a new company with limited liability to be called Baring Brothers and Co., Limited. The directors were to be T. C. Baring, Francis Baring, R. K. Hodgson and John Baring. The paid-up capital was said to be £1 million. 'It has been arranged that the whole of Mr T. C. Baring's property shall be liable for the Company's engagements,'[58] read an announcement of the period. T. C. Baring was inevitably the titular senior director. 'I can see that the general feeling here, among people that know me ever so little even, is that *I* should be conducting the new Co.,' wrote Thomas Baring, 'but of course with Charley [i.e. T. C. Baring] here that is impossible. But it is a physical impossibility for his personal management to go on for long.'[59] John Baring would have agreed with the second but not the first part of his uncle Tom's pronouncement. T. C. Baring had to be the leader because of his great financial contribution and the staunch loyalty he had shown the house, but the appointment was not a wholly happy one. He was elderly, ill and curmudgeonly: 'I fear he will drive away what little business there is left,' wrote John Baring gloomily.[60] But it did not follow that because T. C. Baring was to be viewed as no more than a temporary stopgap, Tom Baring should be the heir apparent. To John Baring it was clear that the effective work in the limited company would be done by the new generation and that they – or, to be more precise, he – should lead it.

Of the £1 million capital, T. C. Baring put up by far the largest share, £210,000. Tom Baring produced £25,000, John and Francis Baring and Robert Hodgson, who had been partners in the old house, would have no funds available until it had been liquidated and perhaps not then, but Evelyn Baring contributed £10,000. Hopes and Hottinguers added £50,000 and £40,000 respectively. George Stephen offered £50,000 and said that he could easily raise another £200,000: 'You never in your life saw anything like the effect of this prompt response upon their spirits. It seemed to lift a cloud off their minds and since then all has gone on most swimmingly.' Stephen recommended John Macdonald, Canada's first Prime Minister, to come over personally to consider the question of Barings' replacement as Canada's financial agent, since he feared this might be secured by some second-rate firm; then cabled in relief to report that Barings had set up a new house which would be 'strong beyond question'. There was no need for a change.[61]

> Things have turned out more satisfactorily than we dared hope . . . ,' John Baring told his uncle Evelyn at the end of January 1891. 'My own feeling is that we ought to finish the crying and all buckle to and make a fight for it, so as to circumvent if possible the machinations of these blasted Jews. I would like to see them all crucified upside down, but in the meantime they are reaping a huge advantage from what the newspapers delight in calling the 'Baring smash'. The 'new firm' is fairly started. There is lots of business left. The glory of the past and the prestige of the name have I fear disappeared for ever. But still a great many people *will not* go away. I have no doubt that as far as a financial investment goes, the Company will show a very good return on its capital.[62]

While Baring Brothers and Co. Ltd began to find its feet, the painful task started of liquidating the old house. This work was made more laborious by the degree to which it was involved with recovery, or lack of recovery in the Argentine economy. Before Barings could realize their assets and thus free themselves from their liabilities, their enormous holdings of Argentine securities had to be disposed of; yet the news of Barings' troubles had provoked a catastrophic drop in this market. 'The widespread nature of the disaster and the importance of those who attempted to prevent a panic, brought Argentine matters into a prominence they had never before occupied in the world's estimation,' reported the *Review of the River*

Plate.[63] Prominence proved the last thing that was wanted. Argentine government bonds and railway stock worth an average 100 in March 1889 fell to 60 per cent of that value by March 1891 and 40 per cent by July 1891.[64] If the Argentine government defaulted on its debts for any lengthy period, then the loss would be even worse. All hope of meeting Barings' liabilities would have to be abandoned.

Fortunately the Argentines had no intention of letting this happen. The committee of bankers under the chairmanship of Lord Rothschild which was set up to negotiate a settlement with the Argentine government was met with a request for a new loan to tide them over the next six months and a sensible plan for staggered payments and a gradual resumption of full interest. The committee quickly reached agreement, subject to the proviso: 'This scheme will only be recommended . . . on the understanding that the agreement of the Government with the Buenos Ayres Water Supply and Drainage Company be duly satisfied.'[65] Only when this incubus had been erased from the balance sheet of Baring Brothers would the liquidators be able to see their way towards a final settlement.

In May 1891 provisional agreement had been reached that the waterworks would be sold to the government for £6.325 million in 5 per cent bonds.[66] The works had to be completed and accepted as satisfactory before the agreement would become effective. Unfortunately progress was imperilled by the ineffable Sanford, who made extravagant claims on behalf of Hales. 'Mr Sanford has relapsed into almost open hostility,' Barings told their new agent in Buenos Aires, Essex Reade, 'and his last move is a threat to impede the completion of the Waterworks contract unless we agree to certain conditions. These included the provisos that £50,000 worth of shares should be transferred to him and that he should be paid £5000 immediately and £100 a week for the next three years. It seems to us an outrageous proposal, and we have no intention of yielding.'[67] In the end Sanford got £16,000 in cash and East Argentine railway stock with a face value of £54,000 but in fact worth about half of that.[68]

Unfortunately the government kept finding fault with the building when it was done. Some at least of the criticism was justified, but Barings were in no position to supervise the contractor or speed up the work. Meanwhile the final settlement was held up. The Rothschild committee appealed to the Foreign Secretary, Lord

Rosebery, who in turn cabled the British Minister, instructing him to press for 'equitable and considerate treatment' of Barings and the contractors by the government. 'The matter involves large interests, and on it depends in great measure the issue of the Baring liquidation. A want of good faith on the part of the Argentine government will have the worst possible effect.'[69]

It was as well for Barings that negotiations on the waterworks contract and on a general settlement of Argentina's debts, though theoretically distinct, were in fact intimately connected. At the end of 1892 the Argentine Minister of Finance, Dr Romero, underlined this fact when he put a proposal for further negotiations not to the Rothschild committee but to Barings. Barings suggested politely that it would be better if the minister sent somebody to London, since so many other interests were involved. Romero declined with equal politeness. He wanted to negotiate with someone who could speak Spanish, knew the country and would see for himself how things stood. A representative of Barings, after all, had negotiated the settlement of the 1824 debt. 'I rely,' Romero ended, 'on the recollection of the old link of friendship which has always existed between Messrs Barings and the Argentine Republic.'[70]

It is a measure of the rehabilitation of Barings that John Baring went out to Buenos Aires as de facto representative of the Rothschild committee. The offer that he passed to London as a result of his visit was hardly generous, yet gave a promise of a final solution. Argentina would pay the Bank of England a lump sum of £1.5 million for distribution to creditors over the next five years. Full payment of interest would resume in 1898. Rothschild quibbled over details but in effect accepted the proposal, subject only to his insistence that the waterworks question should at last be settled. The government must take over the works as they stood. The Argentine government, who had as little reason to spin things out as the Rothschild committee, in their turn accepted without demur, only retaining £500,000 in bonds until the claims against the contractors had been settled. The deal was done and heralded a spectacular improvement in the Argentine economy; payment of full interest in fact began a year before the scheduled date. The last serious obstacle in the path of the liquidators had been removed.

*   *   *

Meanwhile the liquidated had been going through what Revelstoke described as 'the Agonies of the Damned'.[71] As partners they were personally responsible for all the debts of Baring Brothers. No one was going to reduce them to a point where they had no roof over their heads or food to eat – T. C. Baring's generosity alone was enough to make sure of that – but the life they had enjoyed in the past was over. 'In reference to the kindness and assistance granted to my firm by the Bank of England,' Revelstoke wrote to the Governor, 'I beg to assure you on my own behalf and that of my partners that we shall hold all our property of every kind at your disposal and be guided in every way by your advice and guidance.'[72] Lidderdale's advice, in a sentence, was that everything had to go: lands, houses, pictures, horses, anything that could make a sensible contribution to liquidating the debts of the partnership.

Revelstoke, who had been the highest, had the furthest to fall. His entitlement to the largest share of the profits now made him responsible for a similar proportion of the losses. To the pain of stripping himself of beloved possessions and the humiliation of feeling himself degraded in the eyes of the world, was added the shame of having almost single-handed brought ruin upon himself, his family and his partners. He was not the most likeable of men, his arrogance and complacency had alienated many who would otherwise have sympathized fully with him, yet it is impossible to contemplate his sufferings at this time without feeling acute pity. There was no question that Membland and the house in Charles Street would have to go, with all the furniture and pictures. Membland, with 4500 acres, was valued at £150,000, with a further £10,000 for the contents; 37 Charles Street at £75,000, with £50,000 for Revelstoke's splendid French furniture, pictures and *objets d'art*. The work of stripping the houses of their rich contents began at once. 'When we went back to Membland at Christmas everything was different,' remembered Revelstoke's son Maurice. 'There was no Christmas party and the household was going through a process of gradual dissolution. Chérie [the French governess] was leaving us, the stables were empty, and the old glory of Membland had gone for ever.'[73]

Revelstoke at first retreated into apathetic misery, then erupted into fresh activity. 'Such a Metamorphosis in the space of one month it is impossible to conceive,' Lady Revelstoke told Everard. 'Tearing spirits – and at the sight of the sideboard with nothing on it, exclaiming "By heaven, I cannot be starved! Let's have enough to eat!" So things *must* be better,'[74] His wife and children not merely refrained from reproaches but defended him fiercely against all criticism. Nor was the more extended family less loyal. Two of Lord Cork's daughters had married into the house – one to a Baring, one to a Hodgson – to the considerable satisfaction of Lady Cork, who thought they would be most handsomely set up. 'They knew what their mother would feel, and went off to break the news to her with cheerfulness and never to this day have said a word of grumbling.'[75] Revelstoke's children, brought up to take it for granted that they would be rich, found themselves abruptly impoverished. 'My darling child, the House is spared at the expense of our being *ruined* for the moment,' Lady Revelstoke wrote to her youngest daughter Susan. 'Papa will not rest until all is paid, and there will be little left. The one of our children we feel for is you, my darling; however you must make eyes at a good rich man! for our *gendre*.'[76] Susan Baring was twenty at the time; nine years later she married James Reid, Queen Victoria's doctor, an alliance which was hardly considered glorious at the time and would have been felt wholly undesirable by Lord Revelstoke before the crash. Susan had been a Maid of Honour at court. The Queen sulked for three days when the engagement was announced, 'but finally laughed when Sir James promised never to do it again'.[77]

Henry Mildmay let his country house, Norman Shaw's majestic fastness at Flete, and in London sacked the under-butler, the two footmen and the schoolroom footman. The governess voluntarily halved her salary. The butler stayed on for a year but then left as there were no guests to give tips and no prospects of a pension. The fine collection of pictures and china was dispersed. Mildmay initially bore the disaster with greater sang-froid than Lord Revelstoke, but in the autumn of 1891 the problems with the Argentine government over the waterworks and a further sharp fall in the value of all South American securities, finally broke his nerve and thenceforward he lived in constant dread of insolvency; a fear rational enough at first but as time wore on less and less close to reality.

Stewart Hodgson, least responsible of the partners of the old house, was nevertheless 'plunged from his riches and beautiful houses at Lythe Hill and in South Audley Street into poverty. His daughter, Ruth, nearly died of a broken heart at having to leave her home and in consequence of the great anxiety they passed through.'[78] In April 1893 he disposed of the last of his pictures to Agnews for £25,000, making the total value of the sale £43,000.[79] Even as far away as Boston Sam Ward suffered in the disaster. For a time Barings kept his and other pensions going but the slow rate of improvement finally forced them to suspend all those where no acute hardship was involved. Ward acquiesced but protested when he saw references to what appeared to be a surplus in Barings' accounts. It was a paper surplus, Francis Baring explained, and produced nothing for the firm. 'To tell the truth *my* conscience has been a good deal strained the last 4 years by continuing any pensions at all and if things had gone hopelessly wrong there would have been a very unpleasant discussion with the guarantors. . . . After all, you must be a richer man at present than any of us and the old arrangements would seem almost absurd.'[80]

The death of T. C. Baring in April 1891 may have eased John Baring's efforts to establish the new house but seriously complicated the liquidation of the old. 'You know he behaved so nobly all through *la crise*,' wrote Lady Revelstoke to Everard Baring, '. . . that it is just possible to wind up the Fairy Tale by his leaving his million to Papa on condition he becomes chairman of the Reconstruction!!! but I fear not even *could such a thing* figure in an *Arabian Nights* story or *Monte Cristo*. . . . Financially I believe it makes no difference as he executed a deed making the whole of his personal estate responsible for the liabilities of the New House for 5 years.'[81] Revelstoke did not get his second chance, nor were the financial consequences as Lady Revelstoke had hoped. When T. C. Baring died he still had £113,000 at Barings, the last part of his capital which had not been due for withdrawal until the end of 1890 and which he therefore considered to be liable to the risks of the business and not to be included among the house's liabilities. His executors, however, were told that the money was as much due to his estate as if he had been an ordinary depositor.[82] They felt themselves '*bound* to take the most strenuous steps' to recover the £113,000 plus interest, even if it meant forcing an immediate bankruptcy. Eventually they were persuaded to accept 50 per cent in full discharge; 'and though we feel that the payment of even this amount is quite contrary to T.C.B.'s intentions,' John Baring told Lidderdale, 'we have no alternative . . . but to recommend it to the Board.'[83]

Early in 1893, with the guarantee due to run out in November, the Bank of England began to press for faster action in disposing of the various assets of the old house: 'We shall be glad to hear from you what you are doing with a view to accomplish this, what sales of securities you can shortly effect, and what arrangements have been made for disposing of the partners' private property, which latter we feel must now be dealt with.'[84] Argentine securities were not the only assets which proved difficult to dispose of. Revelstoke's house in Charles Street was put on the market but found not a single bidder. In the previous three years, said the agents, only two houses of comparable size in London had been sold, Mr Brassey's Bath House in Piccadilly (oddly enough, itself once the property of Lord Ashburton) and Count de Santurce's palace in Carlton House Terrace. Both had been sold at a considerable sacrifice and to foreigners. 'We consider your house quite unique in its way, being freehold in the first place and having been almost rebuilt and then arranged and decorated in a style that is not equalled in any London mansion and having all the modern appliances such as Electric Lighting from its own Dynamos, Hydraulic Lifts etc. There are absolutely no buyers for this sort of House at the present time.'[85] The house was still unsold when Lord Revelstoke died four years later. Nor was it always easy to pick the right moment to sell pictures. A sale of pictures at Christies had to be postponed because a particularly important collection of French pictures came on the market. In the end sales through Christies yielded £215,000 – £50,000 from 37 Charles Street, £40,000 from the Mildmays' house at 46 Berkeley Square, £30,000 from the Hodgsons' at 50 Grosvenor Street, £50,000 from Flete and £10,000 from Membland.[86]

By April 1893 it was clear that more time was going to be needed. The Bank of England recommended extension of the guarantee by a year to November 1894, with the option to renew for a second and final year. On the record of this debate Lidderdale minuted: 'We had a hard fight to get the extension of time – several Banks and the Rothschilds standing out for a long time.'[87] Since the guarantee only needed to be for a quarter of the original amount and it was almost certain that two extra years would be more than enough to meet

what was left of the liabilities, the reluctance of certain of the guarantors seems decidedly unchivalrous. A year later more than £2 million
Argentine waterworks remained unsold; £204,000 Manchester Ship
Canal, £165,000 City of Montevideo, £517,000 Anglo-Argentine
Trams, £529,000 Curamalan Land, £537,000 Uruguay 3½ per cent
bonds, and a bunch of smaller holdings. The Bank of England continued to press for as swift a sale as possible: 'There are still a good
many small amounts of Securities, not of the South American Class,
which could probably be sold at a slight reduction on the quoted
prices, and, bad as the market is, we should be very glad to hear that
progress is being made in the direction indicated.'[88] When the guarantee was renewed for its final year Barings' liability to the Bank had
shrunk to less than £2 million.[89]

The Bank nevertheless continued to insist that Barings should
wind the matter up. Even as the second renewal was effected
Lidderdale told Francis Baring that they would have to reach an end
within six months. It was in their own interests to do so: 'The sooner
the thing is taken seriously in hand the more likely you will be to
escape from being squeezed in the end.'[90] Barings had no doubt that
this was true and had already made their own plans. In November
1894 a new public company, the Baring Estate Company, was set up.
All the capital was owned by Barings. Its *raison d'être* was to issue £1.5
million of debentures, the proceeds of which would be used to take
over the assets of the old partnership of Baring Brothers and Co.
lion of quoted securities, for the most part Argentine, and substantial unquoted assets, mainly what was left of the partners' personal
property. Other assets, including the Uruguay bonds, remained temporarily with the Bank against the balance of the debt, but were to be
taken over within a month or two.[91]

There was no shortage of investors ready to take up these debentures – 'a raging demand', Cecil Baring described it. Finding directors
proved a little more troublesome: 'We want a friendly man, acceptable to the Bank – who will *not interfere.*' Francis Baring proved
exceptionally adroit in ironing out any legal problems while Lord
Revelstoke was 'now in a good temper and does what he is asked'.
Hopes and Hottinguers were prodigal in offers of any help that was
needed. 'Lord Rothschild has been very humane,' reported Cecil
Baring. Only Lord Ashburton disgraced himself, he 'behaved like a

dog and positively refused to see Ned at all!'[92] The Company did not take long in organizing its own demise. The Argentine shares were swiftly disposed of at a good price as soon as the Argentine government announced its resumption of full interest payments in 1897, and the first issue of debentures was redeemed. In December of the same year the final settlement of the waterworks dispute enabled the Company to take up what was left of the debentures. Having done its work the Baring Estate Company formally expired. It was, in the words of the *Daily News*, 'one of the most important and skilfully managed financial operations on record'.[93] The credit for its success, indeed for the whole operation of winding up the old partnership and constructing the new company, belongs to Francis Baring more than to any other individual. His skills, never completely relevant to the career of a merchant banker, were peculiarly adapted to this task. He laid the foundations on which John Baring was to build.

For the Bank of England the operation had concluded in 1895 when the Estate Company took over Barings' remaining assets. 'I congratulate the Sinbad of Threadneedle Street that he is delivered from the Old Man of the Sea,' wrote the Chancellor of the Exchequer, William Harcourt. 'The Baring Guarantee was a bold and probably a necessary stroke. It has ended well. May it never be repeated. Such turns of luck do not often occur in the nature of things.'[94] The word 'probably' strikes a rather grudging note but illustrates well with what distaste politicians of this period looked on such excursions into the private sector. Viewed from the 1980s the bold stroke seems not merely necessary but essential. Disaster was averted and at the end of the day the only victims were the partners in Barings.

For them a nightmare was over. The way ahead was by no means comfortable, but at least they now knew where they were going and could tackle the journey without distractions. 'We should be doing a great injustice to our own feelings,' they wrote to Lidderdale, 'if we allowed the present moment to pass by without expressing to you and to our friend Mr Greene the deep sense of the obligation we feel we are under to you both for your cordial help and advice during the trying years we have gone through – without this continuous and hearty cooperation it would have been most difficult, if not impossible for us to arrive, as we have done, at a satisfactory liquidation of our Debt to the Bank.'[95] Under pressure, the establishment had closed ranks and saved its own. It remained for Barings to prove that they were fit to resume their former place.

15

The Road to Recovery

1890–1914

With the death of T. C. Baring in 1891, formal recognition was made of what was already a reality; a new generation took over Baring Brothers. The Mildmay family hoped that Henry Mildmay might be rehabilitated and put in charge, but even if this could have been done without involving the return of the rest of the old gang, Mildmay was too close to nervous collapse to make the idea practicable.[1] Francis Baring inherited as titular head of the new company. Even if his abilities and temperament had inclined him to become an autocrat in the style of Lord Revelstoke, his frail health would have curbed his ambitions. He remained leader until 1901, but never sought to exercise his authority.

The second of the surviving partners from the old house, Robert Hodgson, was a worthy but curiously dim figure. His role was destined to be a minor one, though it lasted until his retirement in 1908. That left John Baring undisputed master. His only possible rival was his uncle Tom, much richer and with more experience of financial matters, but remote from City affairs and without his nephew's cunning and determination. After his somewhat cool reception in London, Tom Baring returned to New York with moderate good grace and did fine work looking after Barings' interests there. In 1892 he at last joined the partners' room at Bishopsgate. (It could equally, perhaps, have been called the directors' room, since with the creation of the limited liability company the term 'partnership' was more properly applied to the old house. In practice, however, the two terms were used interchangeably and the 'partners' room' was always so called; more justifiably after 1896 when a new partnership, Baring Bros and Co., was set up to control the limited company.)

267

In maturity and old age Tom's mild eccentricity hardened into an almost unbreachable mould. 'A large, red-faced, shrewd, irascible but lovable man,' his great-niece Daphne described him, '[who] concealed considerable erudition and love of literature behind an improbably Blimpish facade.'² Helena Gleichen was one of the several attractive young women with whom he enjoyed a platonic friendship. He taught her about birds and birdsong – on which subject his knowledge was imposing – and they used to visit the 'antiquity dealers' shops' together. 'His presents were an unending joy. An early Ming dynasty bronze horse, a lovely cane with an old Dresden china top, a large comfy sofa for my cottage, and a salmon rod, were among the treasures he gave me.'³ The friendship perished when he startled everyone by getting married at the age of sixty-two. He proposed to Constance Barron at his home in Norfolk. Halfway through his passionate declaration he noticed that she was resting her foot on a precious glass fire screen and broke off to snap, 'For goodness sake, take your foot off my screen!' At the end of his speech, without even waiting for the formality of an acceptance, he pulled five magnificent rings from his pocket. 'Choose one,' he said. The girl hesitated, so he went on impatiently: 'You'd better take them all.' In spite of this somewhat brusque wooing, she took him, bore him two sons, buried him when he was eighty-four and outlived him by a quarter of a century.⁴

Tom Baring was not the man to compete seriously with his ambitious and dynamic nephew. In short bursts he could be formidable. When things went badly wrong in New York in 1904, a new director, Gaspard Farrer, wrote to John Baring: 'Your Uncle Tom has been quite splendid through all the trouble. I had no conception he was such a man and so capable. If only he could be roused, as he has been during the last few days, there is nothing he would not be able to do in the way of business.'⁵ But he could rarely be roused, while his nephew could hardly be induced to rest. John Baring, or Lord Revelstoke as he became after the death of the first baron in 1897, was as autocratic as his father and in time almost as vain, but enjoyed better judgement and a capacity for calculation. If there had been no Baring crisis he might have inherited his father's recklessness as well, but he had learned prudence the hard way and was never to forget it. He hated being in debt or liable for more money than he had immediately available; 'keep down the overheads and know where your own money is,' were the words of wisdom which he imparted to new recruits to the house.[6] In its obituary *The Times* recalled that many years after the crash he was still refusing to take an important role in a certain enterprise. His firm was not yet sufficiently recovered, he said. 'I am going to take no risks.'[7]

He was as much at home in Paris as in London and spoke excellent Spanish and passable German and Italian as well: 'I fancy the Latin mind is one which appeals particularly to your brother,' Gaspard Farrer told Hugo Baring.[8] He was celebrated as a conversationalist, but with a tendency to the pontifical, good sense and wide knowledge more evident than wit or a sense of fun. 'I had a solid regard for John Revelstoke,' wrote W. B. Maxwell, 'because I knew him to be remarkably kind, considerate to his friends, and never wearying in the service of unfortunate people.'[9] But though the benevolence was real it seemed to some that his charity was bestowed in a manner that was intolerably patronizing. The natural hauteur that had been curbed by disaster reasserted itself as prosperity was regained: Jews, the middle classes, almost all Americans, were viewed if not with contempt, then at least in the sublime awareness that they were part of a lower breed. 'I always deprecate the suggestion that any relation of my friends should go on the Stock Exchange,' he told Sir Edward Hamilton; '. . . the whole profession is so very much over-run that I consider it a dangerous and rather demoralizing vocation to suggest for a young man.'[10] He would have been outraged if he had heard the verdict on him of Billy Grenfell – marginally less odious than his brother Julian but still a horror by any standard: 'Dear God, what a man! He has the mind of a haberdasher who reads the social column in the *Daily Mail* every morning before retailing second-hand trowsers and "Modern Society" and Browning on Sunday afternoons.'[11]

Curiously enough this letter was written by the son of Lady Desborough, John Revelstoke's first great love, to Nancy Astor, who was his second. 'Love' is perhaps the wrong word. Revelstoke liked to be seen with attractive and distinguished women. 'Lord Revelstoke is in Paris at the moment, enjoying the Champs Elysées and the boulevards in the company of Mr Arthur Balfour and a large number of beautiful ladies,' wrote Natty Rothschild, his derision

perhaps touched with jealousy.[12] It is hard to believe there was much
more than parade and mutual convenience in his relationship with
Ettie Desborough, that prodigy of synthetic passion. In 1915
Asquith wrote that Revelstoke had been 'more or less' in love with
Lady Desborough for twenty years; 'The years have rattled by, and
every kind of water has passed under the bridge, but *plus ça change,
plus c'est la même chose.*'[13] Nicholas Mosley suggests that the relationship between the two was 'almost certainly sexual'.[14] It would be
impossible to prove him wrong, but what sex there was must have
been suffused by snobbery and etiolated almost beyond recognition.

In his love for Nancy Langhorne it is possible to detect more real
feeling, though she found it hard enough to recognize. At first she
thought him an Apollo but later 'I came to my senses and discovered
that he was an appalling snob'. She was dismayed when she discovered that his affair with Lady Desborough was still in progress and
infuriated when he asked her: 'Do you really think that you could fill
the position that would be required of my wife? You would have to
meet kings and queens and entertain ambassadors. Do you think
you could do it?' She accused him of putting his social and business
interests before his love for her and was not appeased by his denials:
'Nancy *doesn't* come after Russian loans, or 8 Bish (Within) or Aix!
How can you pretend to think so?' His remark about kings and
queens, he explained, had mainly been a warning of the tedium she
might encounter. He probably meant what he said; he formally proposed to her in February 1906, but by that time Waldorf Astor was
on the scene. Revelstoke bowed out in style and possibly with some
relief; his wedding present to them was a diamond bow modelled on
a piece in the crown jewels of Louis XV.[15]

Nancy Langhorne would indeed have had to mix with frequent
ambassadors and the occasional king or queen in Lord Revelstoke's
salons. After a decade of comparative austerity, he indulged himself
by living in the grandest manner. By 1905, within a few weeks, he was
ordering twelve dozen Margaux, a Bechstein grand, a red enamel cig-
arette case and yellow *flacon* from M. Fabergé of St Petersburg and
two jade dogs from Cartier in Paris. He was hunting regularly with
the Pytchley and the Fernie and keeping a house in Market
Harborough for the purpose. The following year he applied for a
licence to drive an Electric Carriage in Hyde Park, and he bought a

series of ever more powerful and luxurious motorcars. Three times within a week a wheel fell off his 60-horsepower, six-cylinder Napier. After the second occasion a mechanic announced it was impossible for the mishap to recur. Revelstoke changed both garage and car.

He leased a splendid house in Carlton House Terrace, furnished it sumptuously and employed the best cook in London, the celebrated Rosa Lewis, who was to go on to still nobler things in the Cavendish Hotel and the pages of Evelyn Waugh. He was, said Edward VII, the 'Prince of Bon Viveurs'. The food and wine were superb but the discipline was also strict; women were only allowed one glass of wine since Revelstoke disliked seeing them with flushed faces. Lady Airlie went to the house for the first time as escort to the Princess of Wales, who was curious to see the *objets d'art*. After dinner more guests arrived and a concert was given: 'The artists were always world-famous – usually brought over from the Continent for fabulous fees. I believe Sarah Bernhardt was the only one who ever refused to appear.'[16] On another occasion he decided to organize a theatrical entertainment in French for the Queen and the Prince and Princess of Wales. The company was to come over from Paris. Rostand's *'Pierrot qui pleure et Pierrot qui rit'* was proposed. This would do, Revelstoke decided, provided it was followed by something light and amusing, 'not too proper, not too improper'.[17] The royal visitors were charmed.

This was not just empty show. Barings had a reputation to regain; the affluence of their senior partner and his acceptance by the greatest in the land was a significant element in their rehabilitation. It would have availed nothing if John Revelstoke had not also been uncommonly good at his job. A somewhat chilly remoteness was not the only Baring characteristic which he had inherited; he enjoyed in large measure the self-evident reliability, the dignity, the *gravitas* of his ancestors. To a friend who was enquiring about a career in the City for his son, Revelstoke observed: 'It is almost a platitude to say that I consider that character and power of application count for more in the City – or indeed in most careers – than brains or brilliant abilities.'[18]

Revelstoke himself had good brains but little brilliance; character and power of application were his hallmarks. They carried him through. 'John . . . is daily gaining power and influence both in

London and in continental financial centres,' wrote Gaspard Farrer. 'If his health remains good then really there seems to be no reason why this house should not come right to the front again, at least as far as English commerce and finance are concerned; but it will need patience and control and a willingness to give up present profits for the sake of the future.'[19] Patience and control were also among Revelstoke's most marked qualities and his influence grew, as Farrer had predicted. It is typical that Sir Edward Hamilton, that most stalwart pillar of the establishment, in 1903 named Revelstoke, Lord Rothschild and Sir Ernest Cassel as his 'first counsellors', the 'representative men' whom he felt it essential to introduce to incoming Chancellors of the Exchequer.[20] It was no mean tribute to a man who, a little over a decade before, had seen his father disgraced and his family firm brought to the verge of bankruptcy.

Gaspard Farrer had been imported into Barings by John Baring from the small merchant banking house of H. S. Lefevre and Co., where he had acquired a reputation as an expert on transport matters in general and American railroads in particular, and in which he remained a partner – a confusing doubling of roles which could have aroused concern if he had not been so patently honourable. He was a man of extraordinary kindness, common sense and humour; tainted by the fashionable anti-Semitism of his time but in most respects humane and liberal: 'he was essentially Aristocratic, socially and economically,' concluded his protégé, Duncan Stirling.[21] Farrer was a genius with figures, who derived delight from the work of reshaping balance sheets and company reports, but he knew that human beings, not statistics, made a business work and he valued friendship highly. 'I am afraid I may be prejudiced in the matter of individuals,' he told Hugo Baring; 'if I like a person I will go far with him, even unreasonably far . . . and equally I am perhaps unreasonably timid where I take a dislike to an individual.'[22] He loved his work and made it his main interest in life, but he would never have allowed its needs to overrule his loyalties. In 1914, though only fifty-four, he decided that he was blocking the promotion prospects of the younger men and should retire; the war disturbed his plans but the fact that he intended such a sacrifice illustrates well the scale of values which shaped his character and career.[23]

Such a man could not, nor would have wished to be a rival to John

The Norman Shaw façade to the Bishopsgate office, built in 1880 and sketched by Geoffrey Fletcher shortly before its demolition.

The senior partners in 1926 (from left to right): John Baring (1863-1929), second Lord Revelstoke; Cecil Baring (1864-1934), later third Lord Revelstoke; Gaspard Farrer and Alfred Mildmay, by Ambrose McEvoy.

The first Earl of Northbrook by Spy

The first Lord Revelstoke by Lib

Cartoons of four distinguished Barings

The second Lord Revelstoke by Spy

The first Earl of Cromer by Spy

Revelstoke. There was, indeed, no one within the house who could come near to challenging his authority. William Bingham Baring, a remote cousin but of the same generation, had been one of the few members of the family to oppose setting up the Estate Company. He had been 'recalcitrant and peevish,' wrote Cecil Baring contemptuously. 'He is indeed a poor thing.'[24] His punishment was to be packed off to Liverpool at £500 a year. Henry Mildmay's son Alfred became a director in 1897 and remained one for forty-three years, but he was not the sort of man to rule, or wish to do so. Apart from Gaspard Farrer, John Revelstoke's most effective support came from his own siblings. Of these the eldest, the most remarkable, and the eventual heir to the title was his brother Cecil.

Cecil Baring was one of the most attractively eccentric members of a family in which unconventionality was no rarity. Long after the fashion had changed he continued to dress in square bowler hat and 'coachman's' topcoat, not from conservatism or any wish to attract attention but because he could not be bothered to adjust his style.[25] A dedicated classicist, he was found at his desk when a financial crisis was raging, peacefully reading Homer. The advice he gave on this occasion was felt to be particularly prescient.[26] His ruling passions, however, were those of the naturalist: he would always walk straight into a rock pool to inspect the contents, without waiting to remove his brogues or to dry them out afterwards. Once he was in Madrid negotiating a loan of particular importance. His partners were waiting anxiously when at last a telegram arrived. It read: 'Have my blackcaps arrived?'[27] He found the routine of the office always tedious and often repulsive; he could rarely bring himself to conform to its shibboleths. Totally unpretentious, while his brother John was conveyed to work top-hatted in an electric brougham, he went in a bowler hat by tube. Yet once at Bishopsgate his mind was as shrewd and his judgement as sound as anybody's.

He had lived and worked in New York, first in Kidder Peabody, then in Baring, Magoun, and had acquired a considerable reputation there. At one point he had been about to marry the future Mrs Cornelius Vanderbilt Junior, but the engagement was broken off – allegedly because he had lost all his money in the Baring crash.[28] Then he eloped with Maude Tailer, née Lorillard, wife of one of his partners in Baring, Magoun. This did not improve his prospects in

New York and he returned to London, where he spent the next decade in semi-retirement, contentedly creating a home on the island of Lambay off Dublin, with a castle extended and remodelled by Lutyens, and gardens planned by Gertrude Jekyll. There he conducted a survey of the wild life: five Lambay species – three worms, a mite, and a bristletail – were new to science; twelve others were additions to the British fauna. He introduced mountain sheep from Corsica, a chamois (which worried the sheep), a kinkajou (which teased the chamois), rheas, bustards, peacocks and, in fine defiance of St Patrick, grass snakes. In 1906 Farrer found him 'entirely blissful and content. . . . He amused us by ordering a thousand new shillings to take back with him, presumably for currency in his own island; though we believe the inhabitants are confined to his family, the nurse and the bootboy.'[29] Though he was used for odd missions by the house, the scandal of his divorce and his own lack of enthusiasm for a long time kept him from playing a full role, and it was not until 1911 that he became a partner.

His younger brother, Hugo, worked with him in New York, mainly because there was no room for him in London.[30] 'He is very young, but it seems to me that he has the makings of a man of affairs,' reported Robert Winsor from Kidder Peabody in 1903.[31] Hugo was twenty-seven, young enough, but at the same age his brother had been grappling with the Baring crisis. His impetuosity and uncertain judgement alarmed his colleagues and were in the end to spell disaster. Everard, the third son, always known in family circles as 'The Imp', had been a soldier and made a reputation for himself as Curzon's Military Secretary. John Revelstoke brought him into the house in 1905: 'He is a person of character and capacity,' wrote Farrer, 'and I think will be useful to us here if not in direct money-making, at least in important negotiations where dealing with fellow creatures plays a more important part than knowledge of markets or businesses.'[32]

Maurice Baring came between Everard and Hugo in the roll call of John Revelstoke's brothers. He had a small but genuine literary talent, a genius for languages, vast exuberance and a wild imagination veering erratically between fantasy and whimsy. He was one of those people of whom it is difficult to see the point unless one actually knows them. He was loved and despaired of by his brother, who was perpetually paying his bills, and trying to impose some order on him. 'I can hardly think that it is necessary for you to patronize so expensive a tailor as Davies?' Revelstoke pleaded with him. 'And Bain's bill of £64 for books could be avoided, could it not? Now that, by your brains, you have acquired a position in the literary and journalistic world, you should be able to make both ends meet.'[33] Once, in St Petersburg and under the supervision of the local Barings' representative, he was allowed to take part in some financial negotiations over a tramways loan. 'You will find him eager and anxious to second your efforts,' wrote Mildmay, 'but he is entirely without business knowledge and we therefore look to you alone to see that our requirements have been satisfied.'[34] The story on which Maurice Baring dined out for many years was that he committed his desired terms to paper, locked himself away and 'sat like the Mikado in the hotel and refused to see a soul, whereby he got the reputation of being an inflexible Lord of Finance,' and prevailed on every point.[35] The truth is not quite so picturesque; Barings' representative conducted the negotiations and had to make several important concessions.[36] Certainly Maurice Baring developed no taste for business and this was his only foray into international finance.

Yet two more members of the family were prominent in the bank's affairs at this period. Windham Baring, Lord Cromer's second son, joined the house in 1903 fresh from university. Like every recruit, of the blood royal or not, he served his time in the galleys before earning promotion. John Revelstoke told Windham's father he had found him late one evening 'engaged in copying one of the yearly statements of account sent to clients. This consists, as you know, in transcribing entries from a ledger to a sheet of paper. He confided to me that he considered it "devilish tricky work".'[37] He made a good impression and three years later was despatched to Buenos Aires; the idea being, Farrer explained, that he would spend ten years at least there; 'It is plain that there will be no room for him here for the present, and his best chance of attaining to the private room is by making himself useful where Baring Brothers and Co. require representation.'[38]

His elder brother, Rowland, had become Viscount Errington when his father Evelyn was created an earl in 1901. Evelyn Baring had taken the first step in the peerage in 1892 when he became Baron

Cromer halfway through his time in Egypt. Sir Edward Hamilton deplored the creation: 'I do not think a peerage to a Baring is the most appropriate of honours. To begin with there is hardly any precedent this reign for ennobling two brothers: the Baring family has already peerages in it; and just now to single out a Baring for a hereditary distinction when the name is in such odium among so many people, is rather a gaucherie.'[39] It seemed that no one else in authority agreed; Cromer continued to progress, becoming a viscount and finally making the Baring family's tally two earls – Northbrook and Cromer – and two barons – Ashburton and Revelstoke. His son, Rowland Errington, spent ten years as a diplomat; was stationed in St Petersburg where he impressed Lord Revelstoke;[40] moved to the bank in 1911; became a director two years later; left for the war in 1914 and thence entered the service of the royal family.

Lord Cromer himself continued his somewhat wary relationship with the family firm. In 1905 he consulted Barings about the sale of some Egyptian bonds. When the time came to sell them, however, he refused to make use of Barings' services, even though he knew 'you would do the business for us much better than anyone else', and 'it is equally clear that I should not gain a farthing by it'. The trouble was, he explained, he was constantly assailed by 'a very vigilant, very hostile and utterly unscrupulous opposition'. If he employed Barings on this business it would give his enemies the opportunity they were seeking. So instead he would use Sir Ernest Cassel. 'Of course, if Cassel likes to associate Baring Brothers and Co. or anyone else in the business, I don't mind. That is his affair. . . .'[41] Since Cassel, as Cromer well knew, was Revelstoke's closest ally, and the two men had already cooperated on Egyptian affairs, Cromer could reasonably congratulate himself on having had his cake and eaten it too. To no one's surprise, Barings participated in the business.

There was one more, and surprising, appointment to the board of Barings before 1914. Patrick Shaw-Stewart had been the most brilliant scholar in an outstanding generation at Oxford, winning the Craven, Ireland and Hertford Scholarships followed by a first in Greats. His contemporaries admired his intelligence, but distrusted his self-interest and aggressive ambition: 'like the electric eel at the zoo,' said Julian Grenfell; 'not quite long enough in the bottle' was

Raymond Asquith's astringent verdict.[42] Ettie Desborough adored him, preached his virtues to Lord Revelstoke, and won the day: 'Bishopsgate is yours if you want it,' she wrote in triumph, 'over Edom shall you cast your shoe.'[43] Shaw-Stewart did want it. 'On Tuesday morning,' he told Ronald Knox, 'I put on my little round black coat, my paper cuffs, and take the tube at Chancery Lane at about 9.15 a.m.' It pleased him, he said, to be in a place 'where you referred to eight thousands of pounds simply as "eight" '.[44] Gaspard Farrer reported that the partners had found him 'charming, very modest and gentle, anxious to learn and, needless to say, extraordinarily intelligent'[45] – a judgement which suggests that Shaw-Stewart was quite as able to advance his own interests as his friends supposed. Early in 1913 he was made a director, a promotion which delighted him though the honour of signing for the firm had its drawbacks: 'My virgin document was a cheque for £100,000, which gave me an exquisite sensation, but since then I have had to sign 500 dividend warrants in 20 minutes, and wished I had taken one of the partners' advice and used "P. Stewart".'[46] The only fault the firm could find in him was that night after night he would stay up till 4 a.m. at fashionable dances, 'which is not a good beginning for a day's work at No. 8'.[47] They tried to cure this weakness by despatching him to New York, a remedy which the war cut short before its efficacy could be proven.

Nobody in the bank played any active part in politics. Lord Ashburton's brother Guy was MP for Winchester and Alfred Mildmay's brother Francis for Totnes; the partners applauded politely and Alfred Mildmay went to canvass for his brother, but, even if they had aspired to a more active role, the demands of their profession would have made it difficult. This did not mean, however, that they had no concern for politics. The City interest had on the whole moved right with the Liberal Unionists and now supported the Conservative party Revelstoke, in particular, was temperamentally akin to Tory ministers and especially close to Arthur Balfour. Cromer found this useful when he wished to get his ideas across to the government without committing himself officially. In 1900 it was rumoured that Kitchener might be appointed to the War Office. Cromer wrote that he personally saw a lot in favour of the idea, and then proceeded to say the opposite to devastating effect.

Kitchener had already produced a mutiny in the army and if he had stayed in the Sudan 'would have stifled trade and have produced a civil upset by over-taxation, and general incapacity to understand that there is a great deal of human nature in men. The only thing which appears really to have interested him was the building (with *forced* military labour) of a ridiculous huge palace wherewith to entertain the Duchess of Portland, Lady Cranborne etc.' Kitchener was 'the most arbitrary and unjust man I have ever met'. If there was a pleasant and unpleasant way to do something he would unfailingly choose the latter. 'He is devoured by personal ambition and, I should say, wholly unscrupulous. . . . Truthfulness and loyalty are not his strong points.' He had no powers of persuasion, no tact, no sense of proportion. In every other way he would do a splendid job at the War Office.[48]

Revelstoke had already had a 'quiet conversation' with Balfour in which he had reported Cromer's limited enthusiasm for Kitchener.[49] Armed with this diatribe he hastened back. Cause and effect are always difficult to establish in politics: all that is certain is that, while on 12 February Balfour had been ready to 'acquiesce with some equanimity' in Kitchener's translation to the War Office, once the South African war was over it was in India and not Whitehall that the newly created viscount found himself installed.

But though Revelstoke was closer to Balfour than any other politician, he considered himself in particular and bankers in general to be above the political conflict. On 20 July 1905 he gave a large dinner party at his house in Carlton House Terrace and invited more people in later to dance to a Viennese band. At 1 a.m. Lord Spencer burst in to announce that the government had fallen. 'He was shortly followed by a jubilant Asquith and by several other citizens, who evidently think they are going to be members of the next Ministry. Margot appeared, as usual very lightly clad, and talked wildly about her approaching occupation of 10 Downing Street.'[50] When the Liberals swept in at the election of 1906 Farrer pronounced that it was inevitable, 'and right as well for the good of the country that there should be a change'.[51] Revelstoke gave a large dinner to introduce Asquith to the senior officials of the Bank of England, and financial heavyweights such as Lord Rothschild, Lord Mount Stephen and Edgar Speyer.[52]

Asquith might be acceptable but Lloyd George went a little far even for the most open-minded banker. Alfred Mildmay noted sceptically that the new Chancellor had said he did not intend to bring in 'any measures of a socialist nature'; the speech was all right as far as it went, 'but it did not seem to me to contain much more than platitudes'.[53] Revelstoke referred gloomily to 'the eccentricities of our Radical Government'.[54] When Lloyd George introduced his controversial budget in 1909, Revelstoke was one of the more well-informed of the peers to oppose it. In his speech, the first after twelve years as a member of the House of Lords, he spoke as 'one brought up in the midst of financial and commercial operations, in the conduct and consideration of which I have endeavoured to follow the traditions and to be guided by the experience of many generations of financiers in my own family'. The Finance Bill penalized capital and destroyed credit. What was being sacrificed was confidence: 'Confidence in financial prudence, confidence in ability to pay, confidence in financial equity, confidence in the sanctity of property.'[55] His speech deserved the highest praise, judged Almeric Fitzroy, 'as it was a maiden effort, and by universal consent an extremely effective contribution to the debate'.[56] But when the issue turned to one of Lords against Commons and the call went out for all moderates to rally to the government, Revelstoke knew where his loyalties lay. He even volunteered to return specially from his beloved Aix to go into the government lobby, 'it being understood, of course, that in that case an opportunity should be given me of registering my protest against the measure in question'.[57]

Though their views on foreign policy might differ from time to time, on one thing all the partners of Barings were united: that if war broke out between two major European powers, then, irrespective of who won or lost, 'as far as banking and commercial circles are concerned, the result would be disastrous'.[58] Gaspard Farrer confessed to an 'old craze of mine of fear of the German and all his works',[59] but he was still convinced that no sane man could contemplate war and ready to deride the various scares which from time to time swept Britain in the early twentieth century. 'If you can come,' he wrote to an American friend in 1906, 'you will find Englishmen who can still sleep soundly in their beds without fear of waking to the boom of German guns and the news of German warships in the Thames. Can anything be more ridiculous than the fuss our newspapers have been making?'[60] But the time came when the fuss was no longer so ridiculous. Revelstoke, at least, was more prescient than the general public, or than many politicians. The ill-feeling which prevailed in Europe, he told Patrick Shaw-Stewart in March 1914, had causes much deeper than any particular squabble in the Balkans: 'This augmentation of European armaments, both by sea and land, is indeed a terrifying thing, and I am more than ever convinced of the want of wisdom in taking on any risks which entail an engagement of a long period.'[61] Less than five months later Britain was at war.

The new limited company that had been set up at the end of 1890 never had many shareholders and members of the Baring family held about 20 per cent of the equity. It had been provided that the Baring partners could buy out the other shareholders by exchanging the voting shares for new preference non-voting shares. At the time this had been a remote contingency. It was not that the sums of money involved were very large but because in 1890 it seemed unlikely that the firm would be able to maintain itself without the overt support of the financial establishment. To the mild chagrin of some of the equity holders, however, who had hoped for a permanent stake in the new house, within five years they had all been bought out by the new partnership.[62] In title as well as reality the Barings were once more in control of their own house. In 1895 the share capital was increased to £1.025 million, a level at which it remained for more than twenty years.

The old house, meanwhile, coexisted with the new; not engaged in active trading but administering its remaining investments. In 1898 the partners were once more able to withdraw capital as all the debts were paid off, and it remained a source of profit until its final demise in 1920. Its relationship with the limited company was close but not invariably harmonious. In 1904 Windham Baring suggested the new firm should take over the country house near Buenos Aires which had been acquired from Hale and Co. Nothing would make the old house more reluctant to sell than the knowledge that the new house was interested, said Gaspard Farrer drily. 'There seems no good reason if it is good business for B.B. and Co. Ltd to buy why the old firm should sell.'[63]

If the recovery of Barings can best be measured by their gross profits – the profits obtained before the deduction of any expenses, writing off bad debts, transfers to reserves etc. – the figures show quiet and on the whole sustained growth from £141,000 in 1891 to £206,000 in 1897; a leap to £315,000 in 1904 and £522,000 in 1905 accounted for by particularly large investment income; a sharp and temporary setback in 1906 and 1907; followed by profits averaging about £450,000 in the years between then and the war. Commission income was far steadier: £98,000 in 1891, it only fell below £100,000 five times between 1892 and 1914, yet only four times exceeded £125,000 and then often only by a few hundreds. Barings' liabilities on acceptances at year end, which had risen to £15 million before the crash, dropped to £3 million, and though they were pushed up again to £6.2 million by 1904 and £7.5 million by 1910 this only represented 5 per cent of the total London figure. Leadership of the market was never recaptured, both Schroders and Kleinworts enjoyed almost twice as large a business and Brown Shipley ran Barings close for third place. Barings tried to see the silver lining in this demotion. 'Personally I am glad to think that Barings' credits are not to be got as easily as Kleinworts' or Schroders',' wrote Cecil Baring, 'because I am vain enough to think that the goodwill represented by our name is in a different class from that represented by the above named and their like.'[64]

The main growth in acceptances came through the joint accounts with Kidder Peabody in Boston and Baring, Magoun or its successors in New York. In 1910, out of a grand total of about £15.5 million, £8.6 million emanated from North America. Three hundred and fifty commercial credits were issued in New York in 1906; among the transactions Barings helped finance were the import of shellac from India, hides from Hamburg, lemons from Italy, slippers from Turkey, skins from Russia, cocoa from Portugal, coffee from Brazil, tin from the Straits and silk from Japan. The house was more ready to seek business than in the old days. 'The old practice here was to sit and wait for applicants,' said Farrer to Hugo Baring in 1905, 'and it is needless to tell you that the result was that the business has fallen to a very low ebb. Of recent years we have reached out to encourage old friends and get new ones, and the results so far seem highly satisfactory.'[65]

But the risks were still there and caution was never thrown

overboard. In 1911 a plausible young man called on the Commercial Credits Department and asked for £10,000 to finance the shipment of Manchester goods to the East. The capital, all owned by him, was said to be £15,000 and was shortly to be raised to £30,000. It took careful enquiry to establish that only £3207 capital was actually paid up and that no confidence was to be placed in the young man or his firm. 'We naturally declined to have anything to do with the business. It was discovered that he was seeking credit all over London, and he failed shortly afterwards.'[66] Precise information was as essential as ever. In the same year Barings lost a substantial sum through the unexpected failure of Messrs Leontieff in St Petersburg. 'It is apparently difficult, if not impossible, to obtain reliable information about firms in Russia,' complained the Credit Department. 'Personal knowledge of members of firms with whom one does business, and frequent personal intercourse is very desirable.'[67]

Any inclination to indulge in more ambitious adventures was sternly curbed. In 1900 Cecil Baring reported from New York that it was said on the Metal Exchange that Barings were at the head of a speculative movement in tin and that they actually controlled three-quarters of the visible supply. The days were long past when Baring Brothers could set out to corner tin, indigo, or any other commodity. Cecil Baring told everyone that the story was a lie, 'and that you and we were only interested in tin from time to time, just as we are in other sorts of merchandise, as Bankers'.[68]

Barings had always done well for themselves as well as for their clients by managing the affairs of the affluent and well connected. In 1891 clients' accounts totalled £2 million; by the end of 1914 the figure was £9.5 million. Sometimes there was a family connection and the motive was to oblige rather than to make a profit. In 1913 Lord Revelstoke found himself called upon to sort out the financial problems of his brother-in-law, Lord Spencer. The difficulty was one of cash flow rather than anything more fundamental. 'I dislike the idea of fine works of art being sold to liquidate deficiencies of income,' Revelstoke told Gaspard Farrer's solicitor brother Henry. 'You are well aware how many beautiful things are at Althorp and in Spencer House, and of all these I believe my brother-in-law has the free disposal without any entail.'[69] Such duties could be troublesome, but at least where no relationship was involved the honour could be declined. When Lady Cunard suggested Barings should look after her affairs, Revelstoke commented: 'She is an extremely tiresome woman, and is mixed up with speculative people, so that, as far as I am concerned, I should consistently refuse to have anything to do with her affairs.'[70] In 1913 Barings took over the small firm of Morris, Prevost, an old, well-established but sleepy house which specialized in looking after bonds and other securities held by foreign customers, collecting interests and dividends and doing any other business that had to be done. Barings' list of foreign clients was thereby embellished by a rich selection of the *noblesse* of France: the Duc d'Abrantes, the Duc de Broglie, the Comte de Fitzjames and many others.

Providing credits for foreign travellers was also an increasing if minor line of business. The most eminent of such clients was undoubtedly Jules Verne's Phineas Fogg, who was entitled to draw on Barings to 'an extent unlimited' in the course of his journey around the world in eighty days. The majority of foreign travellers came from the United States; in 1902 Cecil Baring was reporting from New York that some of his richer clients would like to have 'check books on your esteemed firm bound in a rather more expensive way than the regular paper cover'. Samples of various luxurious forms of binding were asked for.[71] It was the dawn of the traveller's cheque. In 1905 Kidder Peabody reported that the American Express Company was selling a great many such cheques, but for small amounts and at greater cost than those issued by the merchant banks: 'The business which they take from us is the most troublesome and least profitable part of the travelling Credit business.'[72] Barings were not so sure. Gaspard Farrer supposed that, in self-defence, they would have to go in for 'travellers' Circular Notes'. A visiting American lady had just been extolling their delights; 'the womenfolk prefer something that can be easily cashed and easily stolen – to the necessary formalities which a letter of credit entails'.[73]

By the turn of the century it could fairly be said that Barings had recovered. The feat was impressive but needs to be viewed in proportion. Between 1890 and 1914 the City of London was losing its lead as financial centre of the world, the merchant banks were losing ground to the giant joint-stock banks, and Barings were slipping behind certain of the other merchant banks. They were still a big fish, but in a smaller pond and with more and even bigger fish around them.

The competition from Paris was ever more formidable. 'The Crédit Lyonnais,' wrote Farrer, 'is the most powerful institution in the world with investors; we should not care to propose to them a business involving less than $50 million, and they would probably prefer $100 million. . . . The Crédit Lyonnais' yearly power of placement is at least £30 million, and practically every client follows the institution's advice blindly.'[74] But the German banks were equally aggressive. In the United States the opposition became ever more powerful. It is notable that in 1900 Barings employed seventy clerks; the comparable figure for Morgans in New York was twice as great. Within Britain the merchant banks were still powerful but they had shown themselves conservative in the development of new business, had left the financing of the railways largely to contractors, the handling of new industrial issues to company promoters. Their resources were small compared with those of the joint-stock banks, who lured away many of their employees and made incursions into their historic business.[75]

The gulf was wide between the old and traditionally minded merchant banks, among which Barings, Rothschilds, Schroders, Hambros and Gibbs were pre-eminent, and the newer, more aggressive houses, mainly of German origin, Kleinworts, Speyer Bros, Brandts, the French-American Lazards. The partners in the former group sent their sons to public schools, married into the English gentry, spent time on their country estates – a typical August found Revelstoke at Aix, Tom Baring shooting grouse in Scotland and Cecil Baring collecting bugs in the wilds of Mexico. The directors of Kleinworts and Speyers took continental brides and rarely had a country house. They sent their children to learn their job in the German banks, where the clerks worked from sixty to seventy hours a week; in the purely British houses the working day was usually from 10 a.m. to 5 p.m., with one half day a week.[76] A Russian correspondent told Farrer that he only took on young men able to read, write and speak in four languages. 'I told him that in this country we might search from Land's End to Cape Wrath without finding a young man with such qualifications; it is hard enough to find one who can write a decent letter in English.'[77] Rothschilds were no longer Barings' most formidable rival; instead they were an ally, deploring the vulgarity and unscrupulousness of the new wave. Nor did Barings find them particularly effective even in this role. 'New Court is so unreasonable and so lazy that it is difficult to ensure a business being properly carried through under their direction,' complained Revelstoke. 'They refuse to look into new things . . . and their intelligence and capacity is not of a high order.'[78]

Barings in the early twentieth century, then, were a powerful and thriving house, but no longer the innovative force they had been in their youth, nor enjoying the undisputed mastery that had belonged to them in their prime. Their expansion, however, was marked by developments in the offices at 8 Bishopsgate. The first operation of any significance came in 1906 with an attempt to improve the ventilation in what Farrer described as 'our abominable partners' room'. 'It is difficult to please them all,' complained Farrer, and in fact it seemed almost impossible to please any of them. 'Yesterday when every inlet and outlet was hermetically sealed half of them complained of draughts; today when the hot air is on and the fans going Bob [Hodgson] talks of training for another and presumably worse world, while John shivers and suggests that trips to Brighton are no longer necessary.'[79] In 1912 more drastic schemes were afoot. The watchmaker's shop and public house next door had been acquired, the upper part of the house demolished, the general office boarded up, and fierce redevelopment begun. 'We are promised five to seven months of knocking and hammering,' wrote Mildmay gloomily.[80]

But in spite of the knocking and hammering, and in spite – or perhaps because – of the comparatively relaxed atmosphere of the partners' room, Barings remained a good place to work. Whatever the blandishments of the joint-stock banks, most of the staff remained loyal. Mr John Warry was hardly typical, but his attitude was that of many others. 'On 15th May next,' Barings wrote to him, 'you will have completed sixty years service with the Firm and we understand that, now being in your eighty-fifth year, you would be glad to be relieved of your duties.. . . Such a desire is but natural,' admitted Barings handsomely. He was to retire in June, receive full pay until

the end of the year, and then get a pension of £250 a year.[81] One
hopes he enjoyed it for a decade at least.

Two hundred and fifty pounds was quite generous. In 1914 a
junior clerk was taken on probation at £1 a week. A year or so later, if
accepted for the regular staff, this would rise to £70 a year. 'A hard-
working clerk who gives general satisfaction without possessing
exceptional abilities' would expect to work up in the end to about
£400 a year. A thorough knowledge of French, Spanish or German
was very desirable (though if Farrer is to be believed a considerable
rarity) – 'A slight knowledge of a Foreign language is useless.' No
social or educational qualifications were necessary, but 'our experience leads us to the conclusion that the training afforded by the English Public School has the effect of cultivating a wider field of view,
and a greater spirit of self-reliance, than any other type of school at
the present time'.[82] Women were now taken for granted at any
except the highest and lowest levels. They were mostly employed in
the Travellers' Letters Department (which at the peak period in
August might handle as many as 1500 letters in a single day) or the
Coupon Department. The former were in a special category 'in that
they have to pass frequently through the public parts of the office;
we have therefore decided that in future black dresses must be worn.
There is no objection to white collars and cuffs, but the Directors
desire that no coloured trimming or fancy blouses be worn during
business hours.'[83]

The British merchant banks were often criticized for failing to play a
large part in the financing of British industry. Certainly Revelstoke
regarded the business with some caution. In 1911 he disclaimed any
interest in a concern for making use of coal products: 'I confess that
personally I have a horror of all industrial companies, and that I
should not think of placing my hard-earned gains into such a venture.'[84] His attitude may have been coloured by a brush which
Barings is supposed to have had some years earlier with Ernest Terah
Hooley, the most notoriously crooked of the company promoters of
the age. Barings had unwisely been drawn into helping him float his
Trafford Park Estates, and though they had contrived to disentangle
themselves with no more than a nasty scare, the unpleasant memory

lingered on.[85] But though it was rarely indeed that the house partici-pated in any fully-fledged industrial enterprise, their role in what might be called the infrastructure of British industry was by no means inconsiderable.

In 1900 and 1901 came their first association with public transport in London, two issues of £316,000 and £840,000 respectively for London United Tramways. Revelstoke told James Stillman of the National City Bank in New York that, though a small beginning, the first issue was likely to lead to something big. 'Electric traction and surface roads have not reached the same popularity in England as they have in the States . . . the conservatism of my countrymen would seem to render them content with a means of locomotion which would appear quite antiquated to the average American.' This was the first proposition to finance 'electrification for surface roads' in London. 'I am quite convinced that the thing is only in its infancy as far as this metropolis is concerned, and that when the English public is educated to take an interest in such schemes, we shall see a huge development on the lines which have been so successful in your country.'[86] The English public were not the only people who needed education. The Astronomer Royal and the other Observa-tory authorities from Greenwich waged a vociferous campaign to stop the development of the system and it took a long time to con-vince them that 'the disturbances created by the electric currents' were not so damaging as they feared.[87]

From trams to the underground railway was a natural progress. Barings never themselves made an issue for the Central London Railway but they took stock for their own and their clients' account, and Farrer, in particular, had a keen interest in it. He was worried about the increasing competition from the electrified Metropolitan and District Railways and anxious to reduce costs in every way. 'The snipping of tickets at the barriers' he believed to be 'perfectly useless and a great expense'. The occasional fraud would cost little com-pared to the wages of the staff, and inspectors on the trains would be just as effective. He also thought a rise in fares would be justified: 'I do not believe people travel by Tube unless they are obliged. It is not like a surface tram where the sight of the passing car and a very low fare may tempt a man to ride a few hundred yards when he would otherwise walk.'[88]

If neither Revelstoke nor Farrer was personally enthusiastic about an enterprise it did not stand much chance in Barings. British railways came in this category. In 1901 Cecil Baring wrote in high excitement from New York to report that E. H. Harriman was ready to spend $500 million to consolidate and modernize the British system. J. P. Morgan too was interested. 'I am sure this is well worth your thinking about, because we are in an ideal position in the matter, as Harriman would like to be associated with us, and have the whole Jew element behind him without being too conspicuous, while Morgan would come in on such a scheme, and if it ever got as large as it seems to me it might, we could be the leaders with all interests behind us.'[89] Revelstoke was unimpressed by this rosy vision. Clearly there were possibilities, but 'in this small country there are limitations as to the fares and as to the carrying capabilities, impediments created by the Board of Trade, difficulties caused by the Trades unions'. The whole subject was a tricky one and had better be eschewed.[90] Eighteen months later Farrer was ready to concede that the situation seemed more hopeful but he still did not see it as a profitable field for investment. 'We shall be agreeably surprised if in the long run the increase of capital account, and the increase of rates and taxes and labour bills, do not compensate for any increased earnings which more intelligent operation may effect.'[91]

It was different where the Mersey Docks and Harbour Board was concerned. The Board wanted to raise £3.5 million at 3½ per cent. Barings insisted that the price to them could not exceed 94½. It was vital that the first issue should be a success: 'We are proud of our long connection with Liverpool . . . and would strain every nerve to prove our loyalty to you and justify your Board's to us.'[92] This emotional appeal prevailed, and the stock was issued at 96½, the 2 per cent difference being Barings' profit after all expenses including underwriting were deducted. The issue was a success, though not sensationally so, and the house's direct gain on the operation was some £23,000. More important, however, was the fact that Baring Brothers applied for £750,000 worth of stock on its own account and allotted itself £740,000 (in no way an echo of the Guinness affair, since in this case the issue was undersubscribed and Barings' large holding was needed to maintain the price). The investment eventually proved a good one: at the end of 1903 a little over £30,000 was transferred to the Investment Account as profit from the transaction. In January 1906 Barings felt able to contract for a further £500,000 'on terms which give us a reasonable profit and at the same time are very fair to the Dock Board'.[93] By June all the old stock had been sold, almost half the new, and it was expected that what remained would be gone within a few weeks.[94]

There were a few cases in which Barings became involved with those industrial companies which Revelstoke deplored. Usually these rose from his close friendship, or perhaps alliance would be a better word, with the German Jewish financier Sir Ernest Cassel, who by 1900 was a naturalized Briton, one of the dominant forces in the City of London and personal adviser to the Prince of Wales. It was on joint account with Cassel that at the end of 1902 Barings undertook to raise £1 million for the great armaments firm, Vickers Sons and Maxim, though their name was not mentioned in the prospectus. The relationship with Cassel was conducted on the most gentlemanly lines. Cassel wrote to say that he felt he should give the stockbroker Akroyd an interest of £20,000: 'You will understand that as this is in recognition of services rendered in connection with the issue before you had anything to do with it, the cession will fall on my shoulders only.'[95] Revelstoke protested: 'We should very much prefer, if you will allow us to do so, to bear our share of the cession made to him. We should thus be consistent with the idea of a joint account with you, which has been one of the pleasantest features of this particular business.'[96] Another pleasant feature was that everyone concerned made a handsome though not indecent profit; by February all the stock had been taken and Arthur Balfour had received a cheque for £4277.14.9d for the first £4000 of the £10,000 participation which Barings had reserved him.

William Beardmore was another industrial company in which Barings became involved, and the Cunard Steamship Company a third. For Cunards they provided a series of short-term financial credits, totalling about £1.2 million, to finance the building of their new liners of 19,500 tons, the *Caronia* and the *Carmania*, which joined the Cunard fleet in 1905. It was something, but it was not much. Barings' attitude was more often that which they adopted when the German firm of Siemens considered a flotation in London. They *might* be interested, said Barings cautiously, 'though it is only fair to say that it is only in very rare cases that we ourselves issue industrial Stocks'.[97] They saw themselves as they had always been, an international merchant banking house. International trade was their bread and butter; international loans their jam; the financing of British industry was fare for the servants' hall or, worse still, fit only for the dogs.

16

High Finance

1890–1914

By the end of the nineteenth century Barings was once more a force to be taken seriously in the world of national or international financing. The test came in 1900 when the British government, in need of money to finance the war in South Africa and aware of the Bank of England's dangerously depleted gold reserves, turned to the United States for a loan. If the crisis had come five years before, Barings might well have been by-passed and negotiations have taken place by way of J. S. Morgan in London and J. P. Morgan in New York, probably with the participation of Rothschilds and Ernest Cassel. As it was, Revelstoke was from the start consulted by the Chancellor and the Governor of the Bank of England; and when J. P. Morgan in July 1900 showed himself less eager than the Chancellor thought proper to raise the £5 million or so which the government wanted from the United States, it was Barings who were invoked to share the burden. Morgans were most put out – the Chancellor, Hicks-Beach, was 'notoriously stupid and most unbusinesslike,' wrote Morgan's partner in London, Sir Clinton Dawkins – but they had either to swallow the condition or lose the business, and chose the former.[1]

It was some years before this that they had begun to venture back into international financing. From 1895 onwards, somewhat timidly at first, they had begun to handle the London end of minor American issues: $500,000 for the Minneapolis Western Railway, $4.5 million for the Park Steel Company of Pittsburgh. It was the start of greater things; between 1890 and 1914 the house handled twenty United States issues and had a finger in the pie of many more.

It was a battle to become re-established. No British banker commanded the deference in New York that he would have enjoyed twenty years before. Farrer remarked in 1904 that he had seen for a long time 'that it cannot be very long before New York becomes the financial centre of the world; but I fear for our sakes it is coming too quickly'.[2] Barings were doubly devalued. Even after they had rehabilitated themselves in London, they were considered small fry across the Atlantic. In 1901 Dawkins observed that: 'In London, the resuscitated Barings are the only people nearly in the same rank with us. In the US they are nowhere now, a mere cipher, and the US is going to dominate in most ways. The Barings have nobody but Revelstoke [Farrer was recruited a few months later], a man commonly reported to be strong, but a strange mixture of occasional strength and sheer timidity. He has no nerve to fall back on. . . . He has greatly irritated the Morgans once or twice by want of tact and by talking loosely (after they helped Barings largely in 1891) and it cost me a good deal of difficulty this summer to patch up the old alliance between the two houses.'[3]

Even in 1901 Barings were deemed more considerable in New York than this account suggests, but Farrer at least had no illusions about the power they wielded. When Revelstoke returned from the United States in April 1902 enthusing about the warm reception he had encountered, Farrer commented that he wished there 'had been a little more business and a little less civility, but I have no doubt the trip will have done some good'.[4] It did do some good, and every succeeding trip did more, as the position was laboriously retrieved. Barings would not have been Barings if they had not occasionally made the work unnecessarily hard. Only a few months after Revelstoke had returned in such satisfaction an important American client called Charles Alexander visited London. After a few weeks he wrote in indignation to Tom Baring in New York: 'I doubt very much whether Baring Brothers and Company will care to be bothered with my presence at their banking house. I don't believe they very much appreciate me there. . . . While the Union Bank people all called upon my arrival in London . . . and while also Mr Morgan did all that was polite, I have yet to receive a card from anyone connected with your correspondent. . . . My time is very valuable and I don't intend to waste it in trotting down to Bishopsgate unless I have some evidence that they want to have me.'[5]

The issues that put Barings back into the first division in the

United States were those of American Telephone and Telegraph Co. (ATTC) and its subsidiary, the New York Telephone Co. (NYTC). The story began gloomily in 1904, when Kidder Peabody and Barings were unable to secure a slice of the business: '*La maison Speyer devient de plus en plus difficile à combattre*,' noted the Banque de Paris et des Pays Bas.[6] Early the following year, however, Morgans and Kidder Peabody were back in the battle, this time successfully, and it was Speyers, Kuhn, Loeb and Rothschilds who were excluded. Barings were invited to take over the European end of the issue, making themselves responsible for $25 million on joint account with Kidder Peabody. Initially Barings were hesitant, especially since Morgans' London house would have somehow to be accommodated. 'An American bond of this nature would be such a novelty here and on the Continent that the placing would be a matter of work and education. . . . We do not want to educate the old man [J. P. Morgan] to imagine that we are willing to make public issues in conjunction with his present London house, especially as we know that 90 per cent of the work would have to be done in our office.'[7] Courage prevailed, Hopes took $1 million, and the issue was made in early March. The response was cautious – 'We suspect that the voice of your Stock Exchange was influenced by some of your Hebrew friends,' wrote Kidder Peabody, 'as they made a strong *sub rosa* effort, on this side, to discredit the issue'[8] – but soon caught on, and by the end of the month the issue was oversubscribed, with applications 'almost entirely made up of genuine investors'.[9]

The following year, when another ATTC loan was offered, Barings were again hesitant. It was only fifteen years since they had met disaster and they were understandably reluctant to involve themselves in any potentially precarious commitment. Initially they declined to take the lead in Europe on the grounds that money was scarce and investors likely to be backward. The idea of a combination with Speyers and the French Rothschilds was mooted. Yet at the same time they were doubtful about their doubts. Perhaps they were 'actuated by excessive caution', mused Farrer.[10] In the end the robust encouragement of Morgans, and their own fear of losing the position which they had just begun to recapture, prevailed over their timidity. Barings and Morgans' London house took on the $15 million offered in London.

The following year a further $40 million was thrown on to the market. This time it seemed that Barings' scepticism was justified. Everyone agreed that the stock was an excellent long-term invest ment, that no political hurricane could seriously shake the stability of the American investor, yet 'the response made by the public was practically nothing'.[11] Barings had never wanted to make this further issue, explained Mildmay, and had only done so out of loyalty to their friends in the syndicate. Yet though they suffered fleeting embarrassment they were never in real danger. They were not exposed as they had been in Argentina. The ATTC stock continued to sell quietly, and Barings' resolution in sticking by their syndicate was amply rewarded in 1909 when the ATTC subsidiary, the New York Telephone Company, went to the markets for a total of £5 mil lion, of which £2 million was raised by Barings in London. 'There is only one City of New York,' wrote Gaspard Farrer triumphantly; 'only one Telephone Company operating in it, and these bonds are secured on the only First Mortgage which it can issue. In our opinion it is as good as a telephone security can be.'[12] This time the public agreed and there was a hectic struggle for shares. Barings as always protected the interests of their favoured clients: Gordon Cunard, Evan Charteris, the Lords Lansdowne, Allendale, Cromer and Mount Stephen, Robert and Hugo Baring, Revelstoke's favourite, Lady Desborough, were all on the 'red list', as it was called, among the fortunate recipients of allocations of the stock. It was 'one of the best pieces of business we have put through of recent years,' announced Farrer,[13] and psychologically it provided a spectacular boost, announcing to any remaining doubters that Barings were still the house to turn to for a successful American issue.

Not that such reaffirmation was really needed by 1909. The pre vious year Jacob Schiff of Kuhn, Loeb had offered them a large issue for the Pennsylvania Railroad. Revelstoke called in Rothschilds and Cassel, to such effect that he felt able to dispense with underwriting and thus swell an already comfortable profit. The loan 'has exceeded our wildest expectations,' Revelstoke told Windham Baring. The 'ordinary applicant' was getting little more than 3 per cent of what he asked for.[14] The 'ordinary applicants' did not include Lord Lansdowne, Lord Allendale and the rest.

The fact that Kuhn, Loeb put this business in the way of Barings shows both how the latter's standing had been restored and how far the traditional alliances between British and American houses had fluctuated with the years. For the first decade after the crash, such American business as Barings did was conducted through its old ally, Kidder Peabody, in Boston and the partnership of Tom and Cecil Baring and George Magoun in New York. Baring, Magoun was never a total success. Their relationship with their cousin house in Boston veered between the suspicious and the hostile and they were rarely treated as a major contender by their other rivals in New York. Outside the – highly important – work of commercial credits, their independent activities were almost entirely confined to operations with the railroads. Their main value to Barings was as a sort of superior posting house and intelligence agency, reporting on new issues and from time to time negotiating on behalf of the parent house.

When Hugo replaced Cecil in 1902, things got worse. Hugo Baring was a man of outstanding decency who set a high value on his own intelligence and acumen, a judgement that was not entirely shared by the partners in London. Conrad Russell, a young employee, found him kind and generous but 'unattractive and without charm', and marvelled at the lack of discipline within the office – 'very different from the atmosphere of Schroders'.[15] Baring often took a view of business matters radically different from that held in Bishopsgate. In 1903 he was enthusiastic about the prospects of the Wabash Railroad and wanted to make them a $4 million advance for the purchase of equipment. Barings responded coolly: 'Regret Company's past record here makes business unadvisable for us.' 'Regret Wabash decision,' cabled Hugo Baring. 'Would you object our negotiating with Robert Fleming, who seemed interested in such things while here?' If this was a bluff to bring his brother into line it failed signally: 'None whatever,' came the reply. 'Wish you every success.'[16] That Hugo's self-confidence masked doubts about his real stature is indicated by his readiness to take offence. Revelstoke often had to soothe the injured dignity of his younger brother. 'You must I think be affected – even you – by the New York climate, if you are inclined to suggest that we intended any slight to your firm. You know how long-standing a jealousy there has been between the firms in New York; and we also look to your beneficent and independent influence minimizing this as much as possible, so you must realize how much we have in heart your credit and prosperity.'[17] Constantly he urged Hugo to work more closely with Kidder Peabody. 'Looking to the much greater wealth of our competitors,' he wrote early in 1904, 'the only chance for yourselves, Kidder Peabody and ourselves is to work loyally together whenever we can.'[18]

Wealthiest and most powerful of those competitors were Morgans. The received wisdom in London was that New York bankers were devious and unscrupulous. Hugo Baring loved to tell the story of the young man who asked whether he would be able to make an honest living in New York. He was told the chances were excellent, there would be no competition at all. To this Morgans were – somewhat grudgingly – admitted to be an exception. They were the leading Protestant house and prided themselves on it. Talking to Revelstoke in 1904, J. P. Morgan urged him to play a more active part in New York. 'He inveighed bitterly against the growing power of the Jews and of the Rockefeller crowd, and said more than once that our firm and his were the only two composed of white men in New York.'[19] Revelstoke for his part admired J. P. Morgan and wrote of him that he was 'a great, big, large-hearted generous man . . . with a character which is remarkable for straight dealing'.[20] But the real sympathy between the two houses did not alter the fact that they were frequently in conflict. 'We have no wish to act in any way inimical to him,' Revelstoke told Cecil Baring, 'but it is obvious that our interests are such as to render our position one of constant and active competition.'[21] In the past it had usually been Barings who prevailed, now it was more often Morgans, and the older house did not find it easy to stomach this change in their position. To their mind they were constantly going out of their way to conciliate Morgans and not to trespass on their preserves, and met with scant courtesy and a minimum of consideration in return. To Morgans it seemed that Barings were jealously clinging on to a role that they were no longer qualified to play and seeking to exclude others from delights they could no longer experience themselves.

The fiercest clashes between the two houses came in Argentina,* but tension mounted from the beginning of the twentieth century, when J. P. Morgan began to build up his house in London and to

* See pp. 307–10.

bribe up-and-coming City men with promises of partnerships and lavish salaries. It was his intention, said Cecil Baring, 'without regard to expenditure of money, to make the position of said firm un-rivalled for the next generation'.[22] Revelstoke protested that his house were excellent friends with the London Morgans, 'but we real ize their attitude is one of active competition with us, and while we do not suppose that they would act in any manner calculated to take from us any business which is already ours, we feel strongly that a real community of interests with them is impossible'.[23]

Morgans were not the only pebble, or perhaps boulder, on the beach. Revelstoke's remarks were made in response to a query from James Stillman, President of the National City Bank of New York, as to whether Barings would cooperate with him on the British govern-ment's issue business, or whether their existing commitments would prevent such an arrangement. Revelstoke hardly knew what to reply. His instinct was to cooperate whenever possible with the City Bank and to risk the breach with Morgans that might follow, but his brother Cecil was strongly opposed to any such behaviour: 'In any Government loan matter we take it absolutely for granted that we are committed to them [Morgans]. . . . Of course on any really big loan, the City Bank *ought* to be included on the ground floor, and whenever the time comes J.P.M. will be the man to offer Stillman the business.' The relationship with Morgans was all important, 'in culti-vating harmony with them lies our best chance of success'.[24]

Cecil Baring's hurried departure from New York with his former partner's wife precipitated the need for some long-term decision. Tom Baring declared that, with only juniors running the office at Baring, Magoun, he had no intention of leaving his money there for more than a few months. Almost at the same time J. P. Morgan pro-posed a grandiose merger, with Barings closing Baring, Magoun in New York and acting as sole correspondent for the new combination in London.* This would involve sacrificing the London subsidiary, J. S. Morgan and Co., but that did not appear to worry J. P. Morgan, who said cheerfully that J. S. Morgan 'ought to be liquidated and

---

* In his history of Morgans, Vincent Carosso suggests the original initiative came from Lord Revelstoke. No doubt the concept emerged in conversation between the two principals, each being convinced that the other was the more eager (*The Morgans* [Boston, 1987], pp. 446–7).

could not exist without him as a partner'.[25] Revelstoke had been playing with the idea of persuading Kidder Peabody to open in New York, but the partners in Boston were reluctant and he anyway found this new grand design most alluring.

Then J. P. Morgan began to back pedal. He was worried by the future of his protégé, Sir Clinton Dawkins, who would be broken-hearted if any radical change were made to his position. 'There is a berth vacant and likely soon to be filled under the Indian Government, for which he is eminently qualified,' cabled Farrer hopefully, but Dawkins proved most unreasonably reluctant to remove himself to the Orient. J. P. Morgan came to London, but was evasive: 'He has been entirely occupied through the last month with the Archbishop of Canterbury,' reported Bob Winsor of Kidder Peabody, 'and apparently has nothing else on his mind.'[26] Dawkins made up for his obduracy over India by having a heart attack and retiring, but still J. P. Morgan would not move. The real stumbling block, Revelstoke later decided, had been the position of J.P.'s son Jack, who was now spending six months of the year in Britain. 'I expect there is little sympathy and less confidence between father and son. . . . The London lot, as at present constituted, are so entirely useless and so out of touch with anything which is of value in English financial and commercial life that Morgan's people will find their power constantly decreasing on this side.'[27]

In October 1904 Barings decided the matter could no longer be left to drift. Revelstoke wrote Morgan a letter, 'which will necessitate his answering and deciding one way or the other'.[28] J. P. Morgan was assured that Barings would welcome a situation in which they looked after all Morgans' interests in London and Morgans all theirs in New York. The letter was carefully phrased so that it would not do too much damage if shown to Jack Morgan in London, but the implication was clear – there was no room for Baring, Magoun or J. S. Morgan. 'It would be particularly agreeable to me to be able to look forward to opportunities of being brought into closer contact with yourself; I have remembered that you have more than once told me that you considered that your firm and mine should be as intimate as possible in view of the growing power and aggression of our competitors.'[29] But by now J. P. Morgan was committed to the view that while he could to good effect take on the work of Baring, Magoun in

New York, J. S. Morgan should continue to coexist with Barings in London. Early in 1905 he arrived in Europe, resolved to convert Revelstoke to his point of view. 'The old man will have to talk to Doomsday before he convinces John,' said Farrer.[30] He talked until July, or at least desultory negotiations went on until then, but neither man had any real hopes of success. 'We have made up our minds that nothing will come of this alliance, though from no fault of ours,' concluded Farrer regretfully. 'We must therefore look elsewhere.'[31]

Where to look was more difficult to decide. Baring, Magoun must either be reinforced with a new American partner and new capital, reduced to the level of a mere agency as Wards had been, or dissolved altogether and the business handed to some third party. At one moment Lazards were tentatively considered. What reputation did they have in New York? asked Farrer. 'We know the London partner, Kindersley, whom they took in about two years ago, and like him particularly. Are his New York colleagues of the usual repulsive Jewish type, or are they men with whom it would be possible for you or us to work?'[32] James Stillman and the City Bank were canvassed more seriously, and George Baker and the First National Bank were also in contention. In the end, however, and somewhat against their better judgement, Barings set up Hugo Baring with a capital of $1 million in a new firm to be called Baring and Co. He began work to a chorus of anxious voices advising him not to allow his capital to be locked up in speculations. 'Enterprises such as Coal properties or Mexican land thrill us with horror,' wrote Farrer. It was quite unnecessary for Bishopsgate to thrill with horror, replied Hugo Baring rather crossly, he had no intention of risking all his capital in any enterprise.[33] He had, of course. The doings of Hugo Baring in New York and the reactions of his colleagues in London demonstrate vividly the limitations on the role that Barings played in the world after 1890. It was Gaspard Farrer who saw most clearly what could and could not be achieved. 'We are not capitalists,' he emphasized, 'cannot undertake the business of a capitalist, and are only prepared to act as intermediaries between the borrower and the public. . . . We cannot compete with the big capitalists and it is silly and dangerous to pretend we can. Still less will you be able to in New York. . . .'[34] There was nothing in this with which Revelstoke would have dissented, indeed he said much the same thing on several occasions, yet a part of him craved for madder music and stronger wine. Farrer was aware and concerned about the difference between them. Writing about a possible new partner for Barings, he remarked: 'I am not like John – I neither want to have the earth nor to rule – and should be far better content to have a bit of a drudge of high character than the most brilliant financier liable to take chances in morality or business risks.'[35] Hugo Baring was no drudge, and saw himself as a brilliant financier. John Revelstoke had enough of his father in him to sympathize with his younger brother's aspirations. If he had fully supported Farrer's efforts to curb Hugo Baring's exuberance, Baring and Co. might have had a very different history. In 1904 Gaspard Farrer had written Hugo Baring a letter of most prescient advice which he would have done well to heed; if it had come from Lord Revelstoke he might well have heeded it, but it was not a letter Revelstoke could have written:

> I hope you will bear in mind, and bear in mind continuously, that our credit is the only asset which the firm of Baring Brothers and Company possesses, that and character which is part and parcel of credit. We cannot hope to vie with these nimble Jews in point of brains and sharpness, and are not in it for weight of metal in comparison with the rich men of this country and the multi-millionaires of the United States. I have always told John that for his lifetime and mine we must be content to work slowly and build up the business to its former pre-eminence; and if I am content to do that, I am sure anyone of your name should be willing to follow the example. I think only one who has been brought up outside the business like myself can realize how fatal a single mistake would be. Through the efforts of those who have been working here since 1890, mainly through those of John and Francis, a great advance has been made and everywhere people are disposed to be friendly, but I know that the least lapse into speculative finance, even if successful, would immediately raise a storm of criticism.[36]

Speculative finance was just what Hugo Baring now indulged in. Within a few months of the new business opening, Farrer was writ-

ing anxiously to friends in New York of his fears that his young
colleague was lending too rashly: 'If you can do anything to keep
Hugo straight in this matter I shall be eternally obliged, but for
Heaven's sake do not give me away.'[37] By early the following year
alarm became vociferous dismay. Baring was speculating on his own
and on the firm's account in Great Northern Ores, to the extent of
£100,000 or more and was showing a heavy paper loss.[38] Then
Baring's partner, George Hallock, casually reported the firm had
taken an interest of $250,000 in the Union Pacific Syndicate.[39] In
June 1907, when Hugo Baring was in London, the full truth was
revealed. Not merely were there heavy losses on stock purchases for
Baring and Co. but large advances had been taken from the firm to
finance private speculation. A halt was called. E. W. Theobald was
sent out from the Liverpool office to take charge of the firm: Hugo
Baring was allowed to return to New York but only for a few months
and with no effective power – 'our object being, of course, to keep
secret the unfortunate occurrences . . . and to avoid the publicity
which might injure our name and credit".[40]

Hugo Baring had extremely bad luck. He was put into a job for
which he lacked the necessary experience, was given inadequate support from Bishopsgate, and was then unfortunate in his timing. Like
his father before him he had chosen to gamble at a moment when
extreme prudence was called for; 1907 was a year of sharp economic
crisis in the United States. His colleagues in New York pleaded for
him touchingly: 'Let us beg of you that any change that you may
effect will be accomplished in a way that will . . . make sure that his
power and loyalty and affection for and his desire to exalt the name
of Baring, shall not be destroyed.'[41] No one doubted that his conduct
had been honourable and his intentions excellent. But he was in
some disgrace. The Governorship of New South Wales not being
immediately available, he was found a directorship of Parr's Bank
and subsequently served a long and successful stint as Resident
Director in Paris of the Westminster Foreign Bank. His relationship
with his brothers remained affectionate and he was high on the list of
Barings' favoured clients. But he never served again in Bishopsgate,
nor was it contemplated for a moment that he might.

Once again the question of Barings' representation in New York
was for discussion. The idea of handing over all their business to the

City Bank was revived. Then Kidder Peabody decided that, after all, it was not out of the question that they should open an office in New York. Obstacles melted away, and in November 1907 Baring Brothers had the pleasure of informing their correspondents 'that our old and valued friends Messrs Kidder Peabody and Co. of Boston have decided to reopen their house in New York on 1 January 1908, and will represent us there from that date; the firm of Baring and Co. ceasing to exist'.[42]

For what it was worth, Kidder Peabody also concerned themselves with Barings' business in Canada. This was but a shadow of its former glories, however. At the end of 1892 the financial agency of the Canadian government had been removed from Barings and given to the Bank of Montreal. Barings were aggrieved, as they had just offered what they felt to be generous terms for continuing the agency for a further decade and had been ready to put a credit of £1 million at the disposal of the government. Probably the Canadian government's decision represented no more than a desire to employ a national bank, but to Barings, coming so soon after their disaster, it seemed unnecessarily harsh. 'It is a matter of satisfaction to us,' they concluded with some dignity, 'that during the long period of 50 years for which we have acted as Agents for the Dominion of Canada in London, we can recall no occasion upon which we have not been willing to place our services at the disposal of the Government, either by way of temporary advances or by giving very substantial support to the loans which have been issued by us from time to time.'[43]

Barings were not to undertake any more Canadian issues and, though from time to time they took an interest in Canadian financing, the subject provoked a note of rancour in Bishopsgate. In 1908 Farrer was grumbling about Canada's spendthrift ways and deploring the scale of her debts,[44] and three years later he called her 'the most importunate of beggars: £7 million one day for the Canadian Northern, £5 million the next for the Canadian Pacific, besides innumerable other issues of similar dimensions. It will be a miracle if there is not trouble there before long.'[45] The wish, one feels, was father to that thought.

*   *   *

Given the disaster of 1890 it would not have been surprising if Barings had chosen wholly to eschew Latin America in future international financing. The contrary was true. By the early twentieth century they were once more engaged in Argentine loans, and involved to a lesser extent in other countries of the region. But their policies were shaped by an almost exaggerated respect for the susceptibilities and interests of their rivals. In 1902, for instance, when an alliance with the Banque de Paris et des Pays Bas was being forged, Revelstoke stressed that 'it is understood, of course, that the preserves of Brazil and Chile will be respected as belonging to our noble friends in New Court [Rothschilds]'.[46] When the American firm of Grace Brothers wanted them to join in a bid for the construction of a railway in Chile, Barings were happy to undertake it provided that, if a government loan was involved, it should first be offered to Rothschilds: 'This stipulation we made so as to maintain our friendly understanding with them, that we would not interfere with Chile so long as they did not with Argentina.'[47] Unfortunately these elaborate courtesies sometimes meant that the business was snapped up by less gentlemanly rivals. In this case there *was* a government loan, Rothschilds *did* bid for it, but the business ended up with Deutsche Bank. The noble friends in New Court, Mildmay complained, were 'hardly sufficiently active in their business methods to be even with a German firm'.[48]

In some countries syndicates were set up on the understanding that any business acquired would be shared among the participants; in Peru Barings, Morgans, Grace Brothers and the London Bank of Mexico united and agreed with a French group including the Banque de Paris that each would give the other 25 per cent of anything that came out of Lima.[49] Morgans were Barings' most usual American partners, and Revelstoke was even more anxious not to offend them than he was Rothschilds. In 1902 he declined to join the Banque de Paris in a Mexican loan unless Morgans were first invited to participate: 'We should take care not to make ourselves disagreeable to them by endeavouring to take away business to which they might conceive they had a prior claim.'[50]

This genteel and unaggressive approach was very marked when a Cuban loan was mooted late in 1903. Revelstoke refused even to contemplate it unless the operation was placed under the auspices of a powerful American group.[51] Kuhn, Loeb and the National City Bank were powerful enough to satisfy anyone and by February 1904 Barings were telling Hottinguers that 'unless any very untoward circumstances arise we shall find ourselves in the position of controlling the European side of the business'.[52] The untoward circumstance proved to be Edgar Speyer, descendant of a Frankfurt banking family that had once been more eminent than the Rothschilds. Speyer had settled in London but maintained a close relationship with the Deutsche Bank in Berlin. Together these two now put in a bid for the Cuban loan and suggested to Barings that the groups join forces. 'It was obvious that they had only come in at the last moment, and were anxious to gather the fruits of our labours,' wrote Revelstoke crossly.[53] Barings were grudgingly prepared to give Speyer some share, but only if they retained the leadership and issued the prospectus; Speyer insisted on equal participation; the Deutsche Bank suggested that everyone's honour would be satisfied if the firms were both mentioned on the prospectus, but in alphabetical order.[54] Then the Russo-Japanese war broke out and gave Barings a reason – or perhaps an excuse – to quit the field. Speyer persisted, secured the loan, and compounded his offence by making a success of it. 'I can't help feeling, *quite between us two*, that we will appear perhaps a little too conservative in the eyes of our American friends,' suggested Noetzlin of the Banque de Paris.[55] Speyer certainly felt so, though he was effusive when he shortly afterwards met Hugo Baring in New York. 'He said that nothing would please him more than to do business with us and that he wished very much that when I wrote to you I would tell you this!!! Dirty little beast!'[56]

Only in Argentina were Barings prepared to maintain their position with tenacity. Speyers at one point challenged their authority but were bought off after three years of more or less open hostility. The two houses did a deal, 'the basis being,' reported Farrer, 'that they should leave our clients alone and we leave theirs, they keeping out of Argentine government and certain other specified business in that country, and we out of Mexico and Cuba'.[57] Morgans were the only other international house which played a significant role in Argentina. They proved formidable rivals but it was not until 1907 that they achieved parity with the long-established Barings.

Until 1905 Barings' affairs in Argentina were managed by Essex

Reade: 'a charming man, a great reader, rather aesthetic and dainty in his manner of living,' wrote one of the most distinguished of the Anglo-Argentine settlers, Herbert Gibson.[58] Reade was at first much preoccupied with unscrambling the affairs of the old partnership but gradually the possibility of doing new business arose, and by 1898, in collaboration with the Buenos Aires house of Ernesto Tornquist, he was busily negotiating a short-term loan of £300,000. It was not until the Boer War was raging, with the demand it generated for hides, beef, horses, mutton, wheat and wool, that the Argentine economy really expanded, but already the political stability at the end of the nineteenth century was allowing its huge potential to develop.[59]

The only flaw was the incipient war with Chile, which in both countries diverted capital badly needed for other purposes into a wasteful arms race. Anyone who believed that merchant bankers took pleasure in fomenting conflicts for the sake of the pickings to be derived from them would be confounded by Barings' reactions to the possibility of war in Latin America. Like seconds anxious to prevent a duel, Barings and Rothschilds fussed around their respective champions, urging restraint, suggesting compromises, surreptitiously removing the bullets and substituting blanks. 'The views of Messrs Barings and Messrs Rothschilds are in complete accord,' Reade told Tornquist. 'They are both imbued with the friendliest feelings to the respective countries with which they are related in business, but they have naturally no wish to help to keep up the present wasteful competition in expenditure. Of course all they can do is refuse to assist it and to discountenance it in every way they can. This is a very repugnant course to have to take, but it is less repugnant than assisting both countries to cripple themselves to the verge of bankruptcy.'[60]

In this pacifist policy they were consistent. Three years later Chile ordered two ironclads from Maxim and Armstrong. Argentina promptly began to negotiate a similar purchase. 'If these purchases will be effected, it will be financial ruin to both countries,' cabled Tornquist. Could not the British government intervene in the dispute?[61] With Barings already involved with Vickers Sons and Maxim it was a tricky request to make, but Revelstoke faced it manfully. He called on Lansdowne and extracted a promise from the Foreign

Secretary that, if the two governments were to make a formal request, he would do all he could to mediate. But Chile was not the only country to pose a threat to Argentina. In 1906 Brazil entered the field with an expenditure of £10 million on two new battleships. Once again Argentina felt bound to match them and once again Revelstoke was called upon to check the lunatic arms race, perhaps by persuading Rothschilds and the British government to cut off credit to Brazil.[62] He failed, and in 1908 a partner of the shipbuilders, John Brown, called to ask whether Barings would assist if the Argentine government ordered new warships. 'We told him frankly that we should do all in our power to advise the Government against embarking upon warships, but that, if we found building was inevitable, we should . . . be willing to render the Company some financial assistance.[63] The result was that by 1914 Argentina was saddled with three battleships. Barings hoped they might be allowed to sell them on commission elsewhere, but they did not rate the chances very high. 'Argentina will be difficult to deal with in a matter of this kind,' wrote Farrer, 'and even a very large cash insult [would be] probably insufficient to prevail against her sense of dignity. I only wish we could find some way of relieving the country of these useless luxuries. . . . Argentina has no need for a navy, no men to man it, no docks in which to repair it, and no harbour in which it can lie.'[64]

The first important loan to Argentina in the twentieth century came in 1902 with an advance of £1.5 million. The opposition press had a field day over what they called the 'scandalous and ruinous' conditions attached to the loan, but though the 6 per cent interest was unusually high, everything else seemed normal.[65] Certainly it did no harm to Barings' relations with the Argentine authorities: between 1902 and 1914 they were directly responsible for thirteen issues for the country or for Buenos Aires, worth in total a little under £27 million. Any doubts that Barings might have had about this market were now dispelled. 'Have you got anything that you specially recommend?' asked A. J. Balfour. 'Are Argentine Rails desirable?'[66] They were, and another favoured client, Admiral of the Fleet the Earl of Clanwilliam, was urged not to put his money into Uruguay: 'The Governments there are anything but trustworthy and the country a very poor place compared with neighbouring Argentina.'[67]

Nearly all the issues were successful, some remarkably so. One of the few exceptions came in 1907, when Barings were pressed to issue £2.58 million of a larger international loan. It was a difficult year and they put the loan on the market with trepidation. This was more than justified; the public were unenthusiastic and the underwriters left with three-quarters of the stock on their hands.[68] It was on this issue that J. S. Morgan and Co. first appeared with Barings as joint leaders on the prospectus. Revelstoke had initially opposed the proposal but Jack Morgan was obdurate: 'The whole matter most trying and very sorry it has come up now,' he telegraphed to his colleague, E. C. Grenfell, 'but see no reason why we should submit to being squeezed out without saying anything or why all friction should be on our side.'[69]

Barings and Morgans had battled for supremacy in Argentina since the last years of the nineteenth century, but the struggle now reached its climax.[70] Barings were handicapped by the fact that Argentina wanted direct access to the New York market, and that the combination of J. P. and J. S. Morgan could guarantee this in a way impossible for the English house. When in September 1908 the Argentine government opened negotiations with J. P. Morgan and Co. for a new £10 million loan, Morgans insisted that J. S. Morgan should handle the London end of the loan on joint account and deal with Barings on that basis. The Argentines retorted that they proposed to ask Barings for a separate bid and for a time it seemed as if rival syndicates would contest the contract – to the benefit, no doubt, of the would-be borrowers but at the expense of both Morgans and Barings. 'I don't care how we fight him [Lord Revelstoke],' wrote Jack Morgan defiantly, 'but am quite ready to fight him when we need to.'[71] Sanity prevailed, and the two houses did a deal which conceded J. S. Morgan's parity on this and future loans. Barings were relieved but disgruntled. In a letter to G. A. Schwenke of Tornquists, Windham Baring made the best of a bad job. Barings, he insisted, wished 'to do what is absolutely fair, being well convinced that the only way to retain the confidence of successive Argentine Governments is to do their business to better advantage than any other firm. At the same time I wish . . . for you quite clearly to understand the feeling here, which is that we are not running after the business, and we are only too desirous of helping the Minister if he treats us with

due respect and consideration, but if not we are quite content to take
off our hats and say goodbye and leave him strictly to himself.'[72]

Windham Baring, author of this somewhat disingenuous compo-
sition, had gone out to Buenos Aires at the end of 1905. He worked
in the office of Ernesto Tornquist; a difficult role, since though he
found Tornquist not merely well disposed but also 'one of the most
powerful and capable men in the country, having the advantage of
knowing everybody, being a deputy, being rich,' there was no disput-
ing the fact that his first loyalties were to certain German houses.
Farrer had advised Baring to keep his eyes and ears open and his
mouth shut, and this he did to good effect, but he felt inhibited from
seeking business outside since it would seem to be going behind
Tornquist's back.[73] Baring was an activist who itched to better the
position of his house as rapidly as possible. He suggested advertising
in the local press: 'I know it is a practice that *in England* would not be
regarded favourably, especially by my Uncle Tom, but however here
I don't see why it could do any harm and it would show that we are
alive and always ready to take on good business.'[74] Farrer found the
concept quite as distasteful as would Uncle Tom and was sceptical
about the benefits; 'I am in hopes,' he concluded gently, 'that
through your presence in Buenos Aires the idea will get abroad that
we are alive and able to undertake any sound business.'[75] The nearest
thing to advertising Barings could contemplate was a dinner for
General Roca when he visited London. There was a three-line whip
to all senior members of the family, Revelstoke made an excellent
speech, and the only setbacks occurred when the toastmaster
insisted on calling the guest of honour General Roco, and when the
band, called on to play the Argentine national anthem, produced
some tune recognized by neither the British nor the Argentine din-
ers. When Revelstoke expostulated the bandmaster made his men
pack up their instruments and stalked out of the hall in dudgeon.[76]
Banquets for Argentine dignitaries were rather a speciality of
Barings. At a dinner for the Argentine Ambassador in 1910 they infuriated the partners of J. S. Morgan by excluding them from the
planning of the occasion and only inviting them to attend in a very
off-hand way.[77]

After Ernesto Tornquist died in 1908 Barings played with the idea
of acquiring a stake in the company but were not prepared to tie up

the necessary capital when there was so much to be done with it at home.[78] Gradually the interests of the two houses diverged and in 1912 Barings transferred their business to Leng, Roberts, a small house of limited capital, but staffed by 'men of high character', who were English and could be relied on to put Barings' interests first.[79] Everard Meynell, a young man who had been working at Bishopsgate, was sent to join Lengs at a salary paid by Barings of £800 a year. On 1 January 1913 he became a partner of Lengs. Barings offered to put £20,000 into the house on his behalf, but he declined gratefully. The association lasted until the present day, the business being now known as the Banco Roberts.

The break with Tornquists followed abortive negotiations in 1911 for one of the few major loans in which Barings took no interest. They felt that a new loan for £14 million was both more than the market would stand and – at 4½ per cent – insufficiently tempting to attract whatever money there was. 'We know exactly what margin is required to ensure a successful issue,' declared Mildmay with uncharacteristic arrogance, 'and, were we to depart from the lines which experience has taught us are the limit of safe business, we should not only damage ourselves but deprive ourselves of influencing people to invest in future Argentine Government loans.'[80] Instead, the loan was taken by a consortium of French and Belgian bankers, with Schroders, who had previously protested that they were most unwilling to compete with Barings, somewhat shamefacedly taking a share on the grounds that they could not offend their close associate Bembergs. 'If they were a little bigger people,' wrote Revelstoke loftily, 'they might have told Bemberg to go to blazes and come round here to say they had done so, but the semitic blood which runs so freely through their veins does not seem to permit them to take the course which would have been obvious to a good Englishman.'[81] This comment would have been particularly offensive to Schroders, who with reason felt themselves quite as gentile and almost as English as Barings.

Barings regretted the break in their relationship with the Argentine government and felt it 'a great bore losing the commission on the service of the loan, which would have rolled in regularly for the next thirty years,' but they did not doubt that they had made the right decision.[82] Their view was reinforced by the relative failure of the issue.[83] Barings in fact contributed to this happy result. They brought considerable pressure on their friends among the French banks not to help place the loan and made sure that none of the traditional British investors in Argentine stock came forward on this occasion. Something of the sort had to be done, wrote Windham Baring, so as to prove to the Argentine authorities 'the necessity of dealing with first class banking houses'. Otherwise, he concluded, 'our power for any future business will vanish'.[84] It did not vanish: 1912 and 1913 found them involved with substantial loans for Buenos Aires and in March 1914 Farrer was able to announce triumphantly, 'we have apparently collared the Government business for a year to come to the exclusion of our neighbours'.[85]

Barings' inhibitions about trespassing on their neighbours' territory in Latin America were felt still more strongly in Europe. In 1897 they refused to bring out a Spanish loan, since they did not think it would go well in London: 'We should besides be disinclined to incur the hostility of the Jewish Houses, who look on the Spaniard as their exclusive property.'[86] In Portugal they were so anxious not to steal business from the Banque de Paris et des Pays Bas that they gave Speyer and Hambros the chance to slip in and secure a share of the action.[87] They were equally reluctant to break new ground. They rejected a pressing invitation from the Foreign Office to issue a loan for the Turkish government in 1908,[88] brought out a £1 million loan for the City of Constantinople in 1910, but were cool again six years later: 'We are none of us very keen on Turkish things,' said Revelstoke when the Banque de Paris offered him a share of a new loan, though in view of his relationship with the French bank he felt bound to take a token Frs 2.5 million.[89] He resisted even stronger efforts to induce him to raise a loan of £2 million to £3 million for the Romanian railways and in the end sold the idea to Schroders, who took it on with alacrity.[90] Barings did good business in Europe from time to time, notably in Belgium, for which two loans of £6 million each were heavily oversubscribed, but even here they insisted that 'it would be politic and expedient to invite the London Rothschilds to figure in the London issue'.[91] With the exception of Russia, they did not feel that Europe fell properly within their sphere of influence.

Russia was an important exception. Though the French banks provided the bulk of Russia's capital needs, Barings' heavy involvement in Russian railways and long enduring relationship with its government ensured that they would always feel some sort of obligation to help it if help were needed. A complicating factor was Barings' newer but still most friendly relationship with Japan. Barings had discovered Japan in 1898 when they were considering a loan of £1 million to Nippon Tetsudo Kaisha Ltd of Yokohama. 'It has been gratifying to us to have the opportunity of learning the details of such a well-managed business,' they wrote admiringly. 'The accounts seem to us to be kept in a manner which merits warm praise.'[92] They never lost this belief in Japanese efficiency and in 1902 joined with the Hongkong and Shanghai Bank to bring out a 750 million yen (£5.1 million) loan in London to finance the building of railways. It proved a great success, applications pouring in from members of the public who were remote from the City but for some reason warmed to the idea of Japan. The issue was four times oversubscribed.[93]

It was a propitious start to what Barings hoped would be a long and close relationship. The imperialist ambitions of Russia and Japan were, however, on collision course in Manchuria and Korea. At first this did not seem to Barings an impediment to their business, indeed they conceived a splendid scheme by which they would serve the interests of two of their clients and get a handsome commission for their trouble by organizing the sale of the Argentine battleships to Japan. Unfortunately, by the time the proposal was made, war with Russia was so nearly imminent that any such purchase would have come too late.[94] Convinced that they would win an easy victory and thus rally a dissident nation behind them, the Russian government refused to contemplate any compromise. The Japanese struck without the preliminary formality of a declaration of war and Pearl Harbored the Russian fleet in Port Arthur. What seemed likely to be a prolonged war had begun.

Early in 1904 the Japanese came back for a further loan. Barings were in, not two, but at least three minds. Business was business and, as they told the Banque de Paris, this was likely to be 'business of an attractive nature'.[95] On the other hand, they had served the Russian government for many years and were reluctant now to succour its enemies. On a third hand, their sympathies were privately with Japan and they had been more closely associated with the Japanese in recent years. Lord Lansdowne consulted the Prime Minister and reported that the British government had no objection to the loan being made.[96] The Banque de Paris regretted that, 'juicy and safe enough' though the business would be, their relationship with Russia forbade their proceeding.[97] The Jewish houses, delighted that anyone should be at war with Russia, which had pursued a rabidly anti-Semitic line for so many years, were more than ready to take on the loan. Revelstoke wavered, and finally concluded that Barings could not take part in a public issue. 'The fact is,' he told Hugo Baring, 'that there is a feeling here amongst the highest people that it would be well to preserve a more or less neutral attitude.'[98]

He then proceeded to give a masterly demonstration of how to have one's cake and eat it too. Formally Barings had no connection with the loan, their name did not appear on the prospectus; so far as the Russian government knew they disapproved of it. Yet they persuaded Schiff of Kuhn, Loeb to take up a £5 million loan and charged ½ per cent commission for the introduction (£25,000), and they underwrote £300,000 of the loan (£6007). When an additional £30 million was called for at the end of the year Barings again declined to appear on the prospectus – 'for various internal reasons, among them that we have valuable Russian Government Accounts' as Farrer cheerfully admitted[99] – but undertook the negotiations with Kuhn, Loeb, Warburgs in Berlin and Rothschilds. They emerged with a profit of £110,000, having earned the gratitude of the Japanese and left untroubled their relationship with the Russians. 'John seems to have managed the whole matter with great skill,' commented Farrer.[100] The compliment does not seem extravagant.

By mid-1905 the Russian fleet had been destroyed and their defeat was certain. It was now the turn of Russia to be in need of money and their thoughts turned naturally to their tried and trusted friends at Bishopsgate. Barings were at first doubtful whether the British public would look kindly on such an issue,[101] but Lord Hardinge, the British Ambassador in St Petersburg, urged them to do their best, if only in the interest of improving the difficult relations between the two countries.[102] In October Revelstoke was in St Petersburg, escorted by his brother Everard. He found a situation of almost laughable complexity: the German bankers not talking to the French; the Russians at loggerheads with the latter; the Dutch – Hopes – sulking because they had been asked to share their market with another house; the Americans – Morgans – declining to attend a meeting at the Ministry of Finance and, as Revelstoke complained, 'talking, rather "through their hats" if I may say so, of an independent attitude etc. etc.'[103] It was above all due to Revelstoke's efforts, after what he described as 'days of the hardest and most complicated work I've ever experienced',[104] that the broad outlines of an agreement were reached for a loan of £50 million at 4 per cent, of which the British and American share would be £8 million. Public discontent, fanned by the débâcle in the Far East, then exploded. Rail travel was suspended, there was widespread rioting and talk of a general strike. 'If things get worse we shall have something uncommonly like a revolution,' reported Revelstoke, 'in which case it will obviously not be the moment to embark on a public issue.'[105] Things did get worse. The international financiers fled the city. John Revelstoke found a tiny steamer called the *Stave* going to Stettin and paid the captain £100 for the use of his cabin. Morgan did a little better. A passenger liner bound for Stockholm arrived unexpectedly and he took the entire accommodation.[106] It was a sad end to laborious negotiations but Farrer derived some comfort from the thought that the interruption would only be temporary: 'Their visit to Russia,' he told Hugo Baring, 'will be productive of great good to the firm here, and neither of them will have an excuse to regret the work and inconvenience.'[107]

He proved right. The revolution was quickly quashed and by March 1906 the question of the loan was once more under discussion. Revelstoke canvassed his friends in the government and got assurances from Asquith and Grey that they were still in favour – 'Speaking for myself and between ourselves,' wrote Asquith cautiously, 'we shall give all the good will we can.'[108] One complicating factor was that the German bankers were ordered to abstain, partly because the Emperor was displeased with the Russian attitude at the Algeciras conference, partly because the money was needed at home. It did not take too much bargaining to divide up their commitment among the other participants; London's share rose to just over £13 million, the total loan being a massive £89 million.

'I quite agree with you that those that have undertaken to fund the Russian Government this enormous sum of money, are undertaking a huge responsibility,' wrote Lord Rothschild to his French cousins. 'No doubt they are well paid for their trouble and their risk, but I must confess that, anxious as I am for business, quite apart from the Jewish question, I should not care much for the responsibility.'[109] The Jewish banks greeted the loan with dismay, as also did the liberal members of the Duma, who feared that it would reinforce the autocratic tendencies of the Tsar and his ministers. The regrets of Rothschilds turned to rage when the press suggested that they had covertly taken a share of the loan. They indignantly denied the story and the *Jewish Chronicle*, picked up by *The Times*,[110] suggested that the imperial government was responsible for spreading it. Routkowsky, of the Imperial Russian Financial Agency in London, demanded that Rothschild deny 'this astonishing, unwarranted, obviously unfounded and ill-intentioned statement'. Rothschild blandly if evasively replied that Routkowsky's short residence in Britain obviously disqualified him from understanding the workings of free institutions. Routkowsky hastened to Revelstoke to ask for help in drafting a reply. Nothing could have pleased Revelstoke less than to be drawn into a quarrel of this sort. He suggested a temperate response, but Routkowsky elected to pepper the final version with references to lies and dishonour. It is unlikely Rothschild knew that Revelstoke had had any hand in the letter – if he had, the relationship between Bishopsgate and New Court would have grown even more sour than the Russian loan rendered it.[111]

In spite of the ill-timed intervention of the San Francisco earthquake, which induced extreme caution on the part of any investor concerned in the world of insurance, the subscription went well. 'We have a splendid list,' reported Revelstoke. '. . . The Russian government should be pleased to realize that this issue has really appealed to the genuine British investing public.'[112] Most of the Jewish houses refused to participate even in the underwriting, but some took the line that 'the more money they could mulct the Government of the better pleased they would be'.[113] Rothschilds were not among them.

Though they would undoubtedly have prevented it if they could, Barings made an uncommonly good thing out of the Russo-Japanese war. They even derived a little extra benefit from Russia's defeat by financing the ships that brought the troops back to Europe. It had been a troublesome business to get started, wrote Farrer, but it promised to be very profitable and with little risk.[114] By the autumn of 1906 Barings' reputation should have been sky high. Yet in fact rumours abounded that huge amounts of Russian stock had been left unsold and that Barings were in trouble. The Argentine papers trumpeted the story that 1890 was here again.[115] It was a disconcerting but no doubt salutary experience for the partners in Bishopsgate to find that they had not yet exorcized this bogey. 'Our position is that of intermediaries between the public and the borrower,' expostulated Mildmay. 'Our resources are not nearly large enough to enable us to retain any considerable portion of any loan we may happen to bring out.'[116] Farrer, hearing the stories in Canada, wrote that he had no idea what Barings' holdings of Russian stocks might be but that 'if we lost every penny of our holdings it would not hurt us'.[117] Nor would it have, but the man in the street thought he knew better, and the man in the Stock Exchange was almost as ready to believe the worst.

In 1909 came another substantial Russian loan, the British share this time being £6 million and most of the work being done by the French. Once again Barings secured underwriters for the whole issue. 'The underwriting has been a great success here,' Lord Rothschild told his Paris cousins with some regret, but – more hopefully – 'opinions are absolutely divided whether the public will want it or not.' Revelstoke, said Rothschild, was 'very highly pleased, and naturally enough'.[118] He was still more pleased when the public responded hungrily and the lists had to be closed at 4 p.m. on the first day.[119] All applications were scaled down: the larger ones by 50 per cent or more, those under £1000 to an automatic £100. Revelstoke apologized to the Russian Minister of Finance for what he recognized must seem an inexplicable attempt to disadvantage the small investor, but 'the art of "stag-ing" as it is called here, or applying so as to sell instantly at a premium, has been carried to such perfection by the small applicant, that even people who are well off send in countless applications for £100 apiece, without any sense of shame, in the hope of securing a larger proportionate allotment.'[120]

This was the last Russian loan to be brought out before the war. If only because of the dividends they had to pay, however, Barings' links with St Petersburg remained close. One trivial manifestation of their interest in the country arose in 1914 when Commissioner Mapp of the Salvation Army called on Barings' agent armed with a letter in which 'I was requested to show him every civility and to assist him in every way possible. Messrs Baring Brothers further informed me that their house was in close relationship with the Salvation Army.'[121] War and the Revolution sadly put an end to what might have been an interesting experiment.

Russia also was involved, though in a very different role, in abortive negotiations over railways in the Middle East; two episodes which illustrated vividly both Barings' close links with the British government and the frustrations often inherent in any such relationship. First came the Baghdad railway, a project to link the Persian Gulf to the Mediterranean by way of Baghdad. Lord Lansdowne set the ball rolling in February 1903 when he obligingly showed Revelstoke the draft of a letter which the Foreign Office might send to Barings on the subject.* His Majesty's Government, said the draft, attached considerable importance to this enterprise and might even grant a subsidy for the carriage of mails to India and help provide a terminus near Kuwait. 'I am directed by His Lordship to inform you that it would give great satisfaction to His Majesty's Government if the management of the British participation in the scheme were to be placed in your house.'[122] Revelstoke not surprisingly approved this amiable letter with only trivial amendments, and a consortium was quickly set up with Britain, France and Germany all taking 25 per cent of the interest, other countries a total of 15 per cent, and the Anatolian Railway Company – the holders of the previous concession – 10 per cent.[123]

Then things began to go wrong. The first hint of trouble came when Lord Rothschild announced that he had consulted his cousin Alphonse in Paris and that the French house did not 'take a favour-

---

* Given the close relationship between Lord Lansdowne and Barings and the considerable correspondence between them it is interesting to note Lansdowne stating in the House of Lords on 5 May 1903 that it was a 'rare occurrence' for H.M. Government to be in confidential communication with the City – 'probably much rarer in this country than in any other country in the world'.

able view of the operation'.[124] Almost simultaneously the *Spectator* and the *National Review* violently attacked the project on the grounds that it was tailored to favour German rather than British interests, and a debate in the House of Commons gave rise to similar accusations. Joseph Chamberlain was said to be making mischief within the Cabinet. Revelstoke told Cromer that he had no intention of proceeding with the affair unless Downing Street backed him wholeheartedly: 'I have no wish to be gibbeted as promoting a Turkish Railroad for mere motives of cash gain.'[125] To Lansdowne he said that the press reactions must cause everyone to think again: 'I hoped he would not allow any feelings of loyalty he might have for us to lead him to have a tussle with other members of the Cabinet.'[126] Lansdowne acted accordingly and the Cabinet concluded that it could not actively support the scheme or provide any sort of subsidy. 'The decision of the Government not to countenance the Bagdad Railway is wise . . .,' concluded Almeric Fitzroy. 'The scheme was as much financial as political, though no doubt the two elements were inextricably interwoven.'[127] Barings can hardly be blamed for taking a different view. Revelstoke complained that he had been made to 'look small'.[128] He would have echoed his uncle's lapidary judgement: 'I have been serving the British Government all my life,' wrote Cromer, 'but I never yet knew a British Minister who had a policy.'[129]

Much the same thing happened seven years later, when Russia mooted the construction of a railway running 1600 miles across Persia to link Russia with India. The old guard of the India lobby maintained that such a railway would pave the way for a Russian attack on India, but Hardinge, former Ambassador in St Petersburg and now Viceroy of India, dismissed such fears as chimeras. Both the Russians and the French were ready to give the lead to the British, and wanted Barings to look after their interests. The first step would be to set up a Société d'Études to consider the possibilities. At the end of 1910 Revelstoke extracted from the Permanent Under-Secretary at the Foreign Office, Sir Arthur Nicolson, a cautious blessing for the enterprise and the Société was set up, Barings contributing 40 per cent of the £30,000 initially subscribed. The British representatives in the Société kept closely in touch with Whitehall; one of them, Colonel H. D. Napier, was in and out of the Intelligence Department of the War Office, whose attitude was predictably

Janus-faced. They disliked the idea of the railway but, if it had to be, considered it essential that the British should participate and as far as possible control it.[130]

By mid-1912 a point had been reached where the scheme either had to press ahead or die of inanition. In the House of Commons Edward Grey indicated that the government looked with a benevolent eye on the enterprise, but in the Lords the powerful voice of Curzon besought ministers 'to think not once or twice, or even twenty times, but a hundred times, before committing themselves to a project fraught with such grave danger to India'.[131] The reply of ministers, complained Revelstoke, was 'emasculate and unsatisfactory';[132] Lord Morley timidly suggesting that the government was 'in no way committed not to oppose the construction of the railway when the time came'.[133]

Not unreasonably fearful that he was about to be left in the lurch again, Revelstoke tackled the Foreign Office, insisting that the time had come when Barings must know finally 'whether His Majesty's Government view with favour or disfavour the prospect of direct railway communication between India and Europe via Russia'.[134] Favourable in principle, was the reply, but so hedged about with qualifications as to route and timing as to be almost meaningless.[135] From Paris André Benac of the Banque de Paris et des Pays Bas offered sympathy: *'Je comprends que c'est surtout l'attitude de votre gouvernement qui vous cause des inquiétudes. . . . Nous connaissons, hélas! cette situation.'* Patience and diplomacy, he insisted, would see things come right.[136] But Barings felt the time for patience was past. In June 1913 Lord Errington, their representative on the Société, bluntly told Louis Mallet of the Foreign Office that he was going to Paris to announce Barings' withdrawal from the consortium. Mallet 'expressed great surprise and evinced much annoyance', but though Errington's ultimatum produced some movement, the British government could not bring itself to agree to the last link of the railway from Isfahan to Karachi. The most they would contemplate was a temporary line to Bunder Abbas on the Persian Gulf, with the possibility of an extension to India in due course. Long before the course was due, other more pressing considerations supervened. *'Cette question de concession ayant dormi depuis 1912,'* wrote Errington wearily in November 1914 to the President of the Société d'Études, *'il serait peut être possible de la laisser sommeiller jusqu'à la fin de la guerre.*'[137] Like so much other unfinished business, the Trans-Persian Railway went into the pending tray until 1918 and the birth of a very different world.

17

Barings at War

1914–1918

'Austria-Servia grave but not hopeless,' Barings telegraphed their representative in Buenos Aires on 28 July 1914, 'although such war would endanger Russo-German relations. Paris banking situation black. We fear banking troubles inevitable.'[1] It was hardly surprising that a banking house should view the mounting crisis mainly in the light of the financial problem, but at the end of July there were few even in government who foresaw the greater dangers. Even if Russia and Germany went to war, it was by no means certain that France and Britain would be drawn in; if they were it would all be over by Christmas. The day after this telegram was sent, Revelstoke was still debating whether to postpone his annual holiday at Aix. The fact that he contemplated the possibility shows what alarm the situation inspired; the fact it was still a matter for debate shows how little the magnitude of the incipient disaster was appreciated. Yet within forty-eight hours messages were pouring in from the continent reporting that no remittances were available to meet the outstanding debts, brokers were flooded with selling orders, the Stock Exchange closed its doors. With general war more and more certain, it became patent that the machinery of international credit had broken down. 'I do not see how it is possible to guard against such a general cataclysm as we have had,' wrote Farrer, 'but it is none the less mortifying in the extreme to find how instantaneously the credit edifice which we have been building for generations could tumble to pieces in a night.'[2]

Monday 3 August was a bank holiday. Early that morning the leading bankers met at the Bank of England and decided that the holiday must be extended by three days to bring some order into

320

the growing chaos. On Tuesday, reported *The Times*, the only house with its doors actually open was Baring Brothers, though there was plenty going on inside the others.[3] It was not difficult to establish that those banks which relied heavily on remittances from the continent, from Germany and Austria in particular, were going to be in a disastrous plight if nothing was done to help them. If they failed, then the rest of the City would be in an almost equally desperate state. No one doubted that the government would in some way have to shoulder responsibility for the German debts, but how and when were exacting problems: 'If you saw the length of the faces of those who know,' wrote Shaw-Stewart excitedly, 'you would realize this is one of the most terrific things London has been up against since finance existed.'[4]

The bank holiday could hardly be prolonged indefinitely, so as an interim measure a moratorium was declared, permitting the renewal for one month of all acceptances granted before the declaration of war on 4 August. For those whose business was mainly with the continent this provision was essential for survival; even for those like Barings whose acceptances mainly related to other parts of the world it was most desirable, since the outbreak of war briefly interrupted remittances from North and South America as well as the Far East. As much by good luck as by good management, however, Barings were in an extraordinarily strong position. They had just received £200,000 in gold from Kidder Peabody and another £600,000 arrived on 8 August, the proceeds of North Western Telephone Notes and of Austrian Treasury Bills, which had been paid off on 1 July.[5] Though acceptances totalled £5.35 million, only £700,000 of these were at risk and less than half that amount at serious risk. Debts from German firms amounted only to £144,000, just over half of which was an unsecured debt from D. H. Wätjen of Bremen.[6] With payments from the United States being quickly resumed, Barings only availed themselves of the moratorium for two days and then resumed paying in full. They were the only accepting house in London which could afford to behave in such a way. 'We particularly do not wish to herald that we are doing any more than our neighbours or are any better than they,' wrote Farrer. 'The catastrophe that has overtaken the financial world could not have been foreseen, and even if foreseen no effective preparations could have been made against it, so that no one can be fairly criticized for the trials all are undergoing.'[7]

Within Barings the most obvious result of the war was an immediate exodus of staff to join the services. First of the partners to go was Patrick Shaw-Stewart, who started as an interpreter, served in Gallipoli and was finally killed in France at the end of 1917. Windham Baring stayed on with the firm until the outstanding problems with Argentina had been cleared up, during which time he spent every other night on top of some high building manning a searchlight; then in mid-1915 he joined the Navy and saw out the war in the Mediterranean and North Sea. Errington rejoined the Grenadier Guards and went out to India; at the end of 1916 he was lost to Barings for ever when he became Assistant Private Secretary to the King. By 7 October thirty-one of the staff at Bishopsgate had enlisted; none had yet been killed, though Gaspard Farrer had five cousins at the front at the beginning of September and only one left alive a month later. By mid-1915 more than half the male staff had gone and there were more women than men in the office: 'We are now reduced to a very elderly party,' wrote Farrer ruefully, 'old crocks who ought by this time to have been on the shelf.'[8]

So far as the greatly diminished day-to-day banking operations were concerned, a skeleton staff of old crocks could manage very well. But Barings were London bankers for the Russian, Italian and Portuguese governments, and the first of these in particular caused a vast amount of work. The result was that the office as a whole got busier as the war progressed: 5850 letters had been written in January 1914, in 1916 the figure was 7450. Sixty-seven women were employed against forty-three in 1914; sixty men against seventy-five – of whom eighteen were of military age and eight under eighteen. The introduction of conscription early in 1916 alarmed Revelstoke, lest he should lose some of the key men handling the Russian accounts. After a certain amount of prompting, the Russian Ambassador wrote to Revelstoke, hoping that 'the correspondence of a particularly confidential nature should continue to be dealt with by those of your staff by whom it has been conducted since the outbreak of hostilities'.[9] Revelstoke made good use of this letter before the City of London Tribunal, and successfully protected the most cherished members of the staff. The threat was not renewed until almost the end of the war when a new Manpower Bill was introduced. 'It looks as if every clerk of capacity here will be swept off into the service, as well as Alfred Mildmay . . . ,' wrote Farrer gloomily. 'I expect before long John and I will have to take it in turns to sweep the office out.'[10]

It was not only his staff that Revelstoke sought to protect. Late in 1917 the military proposed to requisition his house in Carlton House Terrace. 'I should have the very strongest objection,' wrote Revelstoke. 'My business duties, which are of an important character, necessitate my constant presence for at least eleven months in any year. . . . I trust therefore that the War Department will not find it necessary to inflict upon me what I really believe would be an extreme hardship.'[11] His domestic staff, after three years of war, consisted of housekeeper, three housemaids, one kitchenmaid, one scullerymaid, two parlourmaids, one valet and one odd man. But it was not only his own interests which he sought to defend. An old crony, the Marquise de Villa-Urrutia, was most disturbed because her son at Oxford could not get as much meat as he was used to. Would you please, Revelstoke instructed his doctor, 'send the boy a certificate to the effect that he is suffering from diabetes and therefore entitled to a more generous allowance of meat'.[12]

Conditions at Bishopsgate were not easy, especially when air raids on the City extended from the night to daylight hours. There was a large basement, and a system was introduced which would allow the staff and the more essential records to be evacuated there in three or four minutes from a warning being given – 'I have not yet been told where my own funk hole is,' wrote Farrer, 'but I intend to get there at the double when the time arrives.'[13] The only trouble was that the warning was scarcely ever given: one bomb fell within fifteen and one within thirty yards of the office without any previous indication that a raid was in progress. Neither did damage except to the nerves of the staff. The British guns provided a more serious threat, the head of a shell came through the skylight and would have put paid to anyone who had happened to be below.

The work that was done at Bishopsgate differed largely from that of peacetime. At first it looked as if acceptances would survive more or less unscathed, as the immense demands of the Allied forces for food and material replaced the traditional lines of trade. The second

half of 1914 was not surprisingly poor, bringing total UK acceptances for the year down to £5.5 million. By the end of 1915, though
Mildmay complained that 'business is very quiet and will probably
become quieter'[14] and only twenty-five new credits were opened
against seventy-eight closed, acceptances were at £6.3 million. They
did not maintain this improvement, but in the last few years settled
down at an average of a little over £4.5 million; by no means a negli-
gible figure, though well below that to which Barings had grown
accustomed.

The issuing business, on the other hand, was almost entirely at an
end. One loan for the Argentine government in 1915 was unavoid-
able, otherwise the government vetoed any transaction that might
draw money from the country. As a result, a lot of good and traditional business was lost. In January 1915 Barings got so far as to offer
Kidder Peabody participation in an issue for Toronto Terminals,
only to be told at the last minute that the business was contrary to
public policy. 'I do not think we have ever told you how Treasury-
ridden we are these days,' grumbled Farrer. 'No fresh loan can be
made, and not even a renewal of an old loan carried out, without per-
mission for the issue of fresh loans. . . . No doubt in principle the
Government are right, that we must not place ourselves under fresh
obligations while there are so many calls upon our gold.'[15] Only the
chivalry of Kidder Peabody saved Barings from being totally
excluded. In 1916 they offered Barings participation in a new issue
for the American Telephone and Telegraph Company. Barings were
compelled to decline the invitation, whereupon Kidder Peabody
insisted that the operation had nevertheless been conducted on joint
account and credited Barings with a profit of $32,599.60.[16] 'What a
triumph your Telephone issue was, and how utterly quixotic the
behaviour of your firm to us,' wrote Farrer. 'I do not know what to
say to you about it, but you know we feel a good deal.'[17]

The 1915 Argentine loan was not a success; the passenger liner the
Lusitania has been sunk a fortnight before and, according to
Windham Baring, 'investors in the City were in far too infuriated a
mood with this terrible crime of the Germans to think of paying any
attention to an Argentine issue'.[18] Though the stock was gradually
placed, 88 per cent was initially left with the underwriters. It was the
more disappointing because Barings knew that it was likely to be the

last loan in which they would be able to participate for several years at least. Instead they had to sit back in chagrin and watch the Americans, notably the National City Bank, take over the business. To be forced to quit the field of Argentine finance, which they had for so long dominated, was particularly hard for them to endure. 'For a century past Argentina has honoured us with its confidence,' wrote Farrer in elegiac mood, 'and as a result of intimate association through several generations it has become a proud tradition of our house to sympathize with the country's aspirations, to respect its susceptibilities and to do our best to uphold its credit; and nothing will give us greater pleasure than to see the country regain complete financial independence. But there is only one way to attain this end: Argentina must make up her mind to go slow for some years to come.'[19]

But Argentina did not wish to go slow, and the American banks proved distressingly ready to gratify its ambitions. The National City Bank caused great offence to Barings' agent, H. H. Leng, by sending to Buenos Aires as their representative a certain John H. Allen who was 'not a gentleman, simply a common North American bounder-bully, entirely unscrupulous'. Allen said that the day of Barings was over, the United States would in future provide all the capital Argentina needed. Barings took the news philosophically. Allen was quite as much disliked by the Argentines as by the British; 'We must therefore pray for long life to Mr Allen and for similar successors on his departure.'[20] For better or worse, the immediate future was with the Americans; the best the British could hope was that they could keep the door open for an eventual return. For this reason Barings were relieved when Leng Roberts agreed to work with the National City Bank, Morgans and Kuhn, Loeb in organizing Argentine credit: 'When the London market is once more open to fresh operations on foreign account, it will be of great advantage that you should not meanwhile have been deprived . . . of the close touch with Argentine Government finance and financiers which can only be maintained by active business.'[21]

'We have been doing quite a big business in some ways, wrote Farrer early in 1915, 'genuine commercial business on a large scale and certain banking business connected with allied countries, which has been profitable; otherwise we are idle, did not expect much general business and really do not want it; conditions are so absolutely artificial here that we are scared to death to let any money out of our sight.'[22] But though the bank as such may from time to time have been under-employed, the partners never were. Links between the government and the City, always strong, became doubly so in times of war. Revelstoke told the King's private secretary, Lord Stamfordham, that ministers were closely in touch with City opinion, had set up capable committees to consider all the urgent economic problems of the day, and were giving 'intelligent and expert attention . . . to responsibilities, the magnitude of which were quite unheard of two years ago'.[23] There were no City men more in demand for these capable committees than Revelstoke, Farrer and Mildmay, and the close relationship between Barings and the British government ensured that they were asked to undertake certain odd jobs that could not conveniently be done by any official agency. Indeed, to a great extent Barings between 1914 and 1918 operated as a wing of government.

Both Revelstoke and Farrer had a high respect for Arthur Balfour – 'head and shoulders above any of our statesmen on either side in politics' was Farrer's verdict[24] – and they got on well with Asquith. By 1916, however, like most of the country, they had lost confidence in the Prime Minister's leadership, and they accepted his extinction with equanimity. 'City people dislike a crisis of any kind,' wrote Mildmay, 'but I think that they like the idea of being governed by Mr Lloyd George, who has almost qualified for the post of idol of the Tory party.'[25] With resignation, indeed almost with relish, Farrer announced that he was anticipating a level of super-tax practically amounting to confiscation, and to a great increase in death duties. In terms that would have outraged some of his wealthier clients he admitted that to him 'the very big individual incomes have always seemed a danger in the community and a very moderate blessing to the possessor, and the inheritance of big fortunes an unmixed evil for the inheritors'.[26]

Barings worked with the Bank of England in taking over American securities held by the British to help finance the war – a measure which would have reduced Revelstoke to apoplexy in other times. Observing that most of the partners of Morgans were in London, Farrer announced that he was proposing 'embargoing them and

offering them as collateral for the next loan'.[27] Barings contributed
to the compilation of a black list of German banks working in South
America, particularly Argentina.[28] Cecil Baring was recruited by the
government to assemble information about 'the character, standing
and capacity of suppliers and manufacturers in . . . North and South
America'.[29] Barings were insistent that they intended to keep out of
the direct negotiation of government contracts, a field in which they
felt themselves notably inexpert, but they still hoped that Cecil
Baring's activities would generate a little business for the house:
'There is no reason why we should not undertake all the banking end
of contracts, so long as the end is safe and profitable.'[30]

In fact, with Kidder Peabody, they became more deeply involved
with government orders from United States manufacturers than
they had intended. Insofar as the British government could have
been said to have an agent formally charged with the purchase of war
materials in the United States, it was J. P. Morgan and Co.,[31] but
there was still a lot of business which, particularly in the early stages
of the war, was handled otherwise. In December 1914, for instance,
Kidder Peabody, on Barings' instructions, contracted for the purchase from the American Woollen Company of 250,000 yards of
cloth for jackets, 475,000 for trousers and 750,000 for overcoats.
Other contracts were for telephone cable, hematite ore, picric acid,
oleum, trinitrotoluol, gun cotton and fishing boats. Gradually the
government set up its own purchasing agencies, but there were some
unpleasant contretemps in the meantime. In July 1915 the Director
of Army Contracts complained that Kidder Peabody were claiming
for certain administrative expenses that should properly be to their
own charge. Cecil Baring hotly defended his American colleagues
but could get nowhere. 'I am ashamed,' he told Bob Winsor of
Kidder Peabody, 'that proposals of such incredible meanness should
be made, by a responsible officer of the British Government, to
people who have rendered them such signal service.'[32] Winsor was
unperturbed; American officials were just as bad, he said. Anyway,
the disputed $45,000 was fortunately in their possession and, egged
on by Barings, they refused to part with it.[33]

Kidder Peabody were not the only victims of governmental meanness or chicanery. The Munitions Department contracted to buy one
million Mauser rifles, and put in a clause saying that the supplier

would forfeit his deposit of £10,000 if the rifles were not available for previous inspection. In fact some of the rifles were already in their possession, and so they must have known that they could not be produced for inspection. 'The war is setting many new standards, and apparently a new standard of morality,' commented Farrer. 'Let us hope it will be confined to the Munitions Department.'[34]

'I suppose we ought to be making a mint of money,' wrote Farrer, 'but we have determined we will have nothing to do with any of the Government contracts beyond the purely banking and after a contract has been obtained.'[35] Barings sometimes portrayed themselves as having almost been put out of business, the time of the directors largely taken up with unpaid labours for their country. 'We shut the office now at 4.0 and might almost shut it at 3.0,' Farrer told Winsor. 'I suppose if one took the trouble one could launch in new directions, but we none of us have any desire to make money out of the war.'[36] By 1918, when this was written, it was more nearly true than it had been previously, but inspection of the accounts of Baring Brothers for the period of the war suggests that, if the partners were really reluctant to make money, they had to put up with a good deal. In 1913, the last complete year of business before the war, the gross profit had been £438,000. In 1914 this fell to £282,000. The comparable figure for 1915 was £1.189 million. In 1916 it was £853,000, in 1917 £683,000, and even in 1918 the gross profit was £502,000, higher than in any of the four years before the war. The explanation, in a few words, is the 'banking business connected with allied countries', to which Farrer had referred early in 1915.[37] In that year, 'Certain Russian Accounts' showed a profit of £718,000, the following year the figure was £518,000, and in 1917, the year of the Russian Revolution, the item still contributed £136,000 to the balance sheet.

One of the first indications that war was imminent had come to Barings in July 1914 when M. Routkowsky, Chief of the Imperial Russian Financial Agency in London, asked Barings to withdraw 20 million marks from Mendelssohn and Co. in Berlin. But 20 million marks were not going to last the Russian government long in time of war. It was clear from the start that the Russians would have to borrow vast amounts of money if they were to sustain their armies in the field. For a source of such money they would look first to London. As the official bankers of the Russian government, Barings could not fail to be intimately involved. The first transaction yielded them no profit at all. The British Treasury had agreed to the discount at the Bank of England of £12 million Russian Treasury bills if £8 million in gold was sent over from St Petersburg, against which a further credit of £8 million would be provided. The Russian Treasury contracted to place the bills at Barings, and Barings undertook to have them discounted at the Bank of England, taking no commission or brokerage.

Then the real business began. To meet urgent payments, Barings made a short-term loan of £2 million to the Russian government, borrowed from the Bank of England at 4 per cent and lent to the Russians at 5 per cent with 1 per cent commission. They deposited the Russian gold in the Bank of England, the Bank paid 2 per cent interest, Barings passed on 1½ per cent and retained a modest ½ per cent. When the first big loan of £20 million was negotiated in February 1915, Barings' commission was ¼ per cent. In June 1915, to bridge a gap, they provided a short-term loan of £2.5 million at 5 per cent interest with 1 per cent commission. This was later increased to £4.5 million. A £25 million loan was contracted for in July 1915; Barings' commission was ¼ per cent; modest again, yet worth £62,500. Another £25 million followed. Later in 1915, with Routkowsky ill, Revelstoke found himself negotiating with the British government on behalf of the Russians. He secured a further £30 million, although only £5 million was in fact made available, this being required to settle another temporary advance made by Barings, this time at 6 per cent with 1 per cent commission. All these commitments were dwarfed when in September 1915 the British Treasury agreed to advance a total of £300 million over a twelve-month period. The agreement was negotiated without Barings' intervention, but the Russian government pleaded that things would go more smoothly if their bankers were involved and Barings charged a commission of ¹⁄₁₆ per cent. It was smaller than before, but it still brought in £187,500.

It may sound as if the British or Russian governments were being exploited. That is not the case. The charges, as a proportion of the whole, were reasonable, even modest. Nothing was concealed. Any other bank would have taken as much and probably more. Barings gave good value for their money. It was only because of the immensity of the sums involved that Barings' recompense was high. Yet for a virtually risk-free transaction involving not much in the way of work, the profit was substantial. It is not surprising that some of their rivals felt jealous, and that Gaspard Farrer's protestations about his house's reluctance to make money out of the war might have been somewhat cynically received by Barings' rivals.

Early in 1917 Revelstoke was given the honorary title of Minister Plenipotentiary and dispatched with Lord Milner to St Petersburg. The Russians were demanding economic and military aid on an impossible scale – a further £400 million was their starting point – and the mission was supposed to establish how much was really essential and by what dates it was needed. Revelstoke was dismayed by the sense of incipient chaos that hung over the city. Rasputin had been murdered only a short time before, authority was crumbling from the centre, the mission had grave doubts about the capacity of the imperial government to survive: yet all plans had to be made on the basis that the Russians would continue the war against Germany. The report was completed in a matter of weeks rather than the months that were desirable. 'It is hurried, therefore incomplete, and by no means a good document,' wrote Revelstoke. 'During all the years I have been at Bishopsgate, I have never once allowed so hastily composed a paper to leave the office.'[38]

By the time the mission left St Petersburg the first phase of the Russian Revolution was already under way. Revelstoke had conducted most of his negotiations with M. Bark at the Ministry of Finance; now Bark had gone and his place had been taken by M. Michel Terestchenko, who at once cabled Barings to ask for confirmation that the firm would continue to put their services at the disposal of the provisional Russian government and that all the existing agreements would remain in force. Revelstoke's immediate response was to welcome Kerensky's government. The new ministers, he wrote, 'are said to be honest and upright, and I trust therefore that the risk of disorganization and disorder, which would be the consequence of the direction of affairs by extremists, may be avoided'.[39] He recommended to the Foreign Office that Barings should continue to make payments on the basis of instructions from St Petersburg just as they had done before the Revolution, and got the answer that anything else would be bound to have damaging results.[40]

The Treasury was more sceptical than the Foreign Office; or perhaps more concerned about its balances. By April 1917 most credits were being refused. Cecil Baring called on Sir Robert Chalmers at the Treasury on behalf of Kerensky's provisional government, and got a cool reception. Chalmers was extremely sceptical about the future of the regime and disinclined to pour good money after bad: 'The more roubles you buy, the more orders will be placed here. . . . It is a morass that we have no intention of paving.'[41] Revelstoke would sometimes speculate whether a more generous attitude towards the provisional government might not have helped it to establish itself; it seems unlikely that anything could have checked the march of the better organized and more ruthless Bolsheviks, but Kerensky had grounds for complaint that he was shabbily treated by his allies.

In October 1917 the Bolsheviks struck, Lenin and Trotsky seized power and began to negotiate a separate peace with Germany. Farrer comforted himself with the thought that the regime could not last, but saw much pain for the Russian people in the meantime: 'Starvation and great distress of every kind is inevitable this winter, especially in the big centres, and it is better that this should occur under an anarchical so-called government than under a strong despotic head. The time for the latter has not yet come.'[42] But even as he wrote the despots were establishing themselves. The moment could not long be postponed when Barings would have to decide what to do with the Russian funds in their possession. At the end of 1917 they had nearly £1 million in the Comte Spécial set up in October 1915 for arms purchases in Britain, and well over £1.5 million in other Russian accounts. On 14 December M. Ermolaieff, speaking as a representative of the Treasury of Russia's last and only legal government, told Barings that they should accept no instructions from 'the persons who have temporarily seized the power in Petrograd'.[43] Barings agreed that they would not; but though they did not say so to M. Ermolaieff, the question of whose instructions they *should* accept was more difficult to resolve.

Early in 1918 a firm of solicitors acting for the Bolshevik government notified Barings that Maxim Litvinoff would shortly be arriving as Chargé d'Affaires. All official Russian funds should for the moment be frozen. Barings gave an equivocal reply, but equivocation was no longer possible when a telegram arrived from Petrograd, purporting to come from the Chancellery of Credit and signed Axelrod, which instructed them to make a dollar payment to the Guaranty Trust of New York. Barings appealed to the Treasury, who on 1 February 1918 formally ordered them to hold all transactions on the Russian accounts in abeyance until the situation had evolved. The British government would indemnify them fully against any consequences. Fortified by this, Barings ignored Axelrod's telegram, and the stream of subsequent instructions that arrived from Petrograd.

But though Barings were ready to freeze the Russian funds, they were more reluctant to countenance their confiscation. In March 1918, after the Russians had left the war, the possibility was raised that their funds should be distrained and in some way applied to the war effort. Farrer wrote in dismay to the Chancellor of the Exchequer: 'I am convinced such a seizure would be considered as a blot on the past record of this country as the safest centre for banking funds.' If it had to be done, then let it at least be done by all the allies acting in unison. 'It would be grievous if this country were placed at a disadvantage with our competitive neighbours.'[44] For this or for other reasons the idea was dropped. Peace came with Barings still in possession of approximately £3.5 million of Russian money and no very clear idea what to do with it.

18

'The Concern Remains a Family Affair'

1918–1929

Barings at the end of 1918 was dominated by Lord Revelstoke even more than had been the case before the war. He had been on the Court of the Bank of England since 1898 and a Privy Councillor since 1903. He had become Receiver-General of the Duchy of Cornwall in 1908, was George V's closest financial adviser as well as being a personal friend, and became Lord Lieutenant of Middlesex in 1926. He was the indispensable man of British financial life; indispensable, that is to say, until he died, when – like all indispensable men – he was rapidly dispensed with. 'The Chancellor of the Exchequer is overwhelmed,' Thomas Jones told Hankey in 1919. 'One feels he is fighting a losing battle. Ought he not to have at his elbow someone of the calibre of Reading or Revelstoke?'[1] His rule at Barings was autocratic; though he never ignored his partners as his father had done, he generally considered that he knew best and was reluctant to accept the contrary.

On his normal working day he would come in to lunch at Barings, and be served a sole. He would open it and peer suspiciously at the backbone. If it seemed to him darker than it should be, he would push it to one side and march off to the Bank of England in search of better pickings.[2] His life in Carlton House Terrace was as grand as his demands in the office were simple. The new 'concealed electric lighting' in the reception rooms illuminated gatherings even more magnificent than those before the war, royalty was still more often present, the artists who performed after dinner yet more distinguished. People rarely felt at home with Revelstoke, not many even

333

felt at ease – his niece Daphne Pollen recalled the 'chill atmosphere' of the great rooms, with their 'well-varnished and discreetly lit Canalettos and polished parquet floor' – but in his own style he did it very well. In 1922 he was thinking seriously of adding a country house to his other possessions, sending inter alia for the particulars of Mereworth, a Palladian villa in Kent, but the impulse passed before he had indulged it.

One day in Bishopsgate he wanted to speak to the book-keepers and got the postal department by mistake. He asked the boy who replied to let him know the balance of Princess Troubetskoy's account. There was a baffled silence. Revelstoke repeated the question. 'Who are you?' asked the boy cautiously. 'Lord Revelstoke!' 'Lord who?' Revelstoke in his turn now asked, 'And who are you?' 'I am Barings,' replied the boy with some magniloquence. 'So am I!' retorted Revelstoke. So, in the eyes of the outside world, and indeed in the eyes of his partners, he was.

The only one among them who could hold his own was Gaspard Farrer, and he reserved his fire for occasions that he felt of real importance. But Farrer was almost sixty at the end of the war, and it was five years since he had first announced his intention to retire. At the beginning of 1924 he handed over virtually all his interests in Barings to the younger generation, and though he did not formally cease to be a partner until the end of the following year, his attendance in the partners' room became more erratic and he devoted himself to his work with his first love, H.S. Lefevre and Co. Alfred Mildmay soldiered on, did not retire as a director until 1940, and was indeed technically a partner when he died aged seventy-three in 1944. His influence on Revelstoke had never been great, however, and did not increase with the years. When asked what Mildmay did all day, an unkind colleague remarked that he used to spend his time adding up his money on a piece of blotting paper, but had had to renounce this pursuit when the blotting paper became too small.[3] Cecil Baring too remained from the older generation, but he regarded his elder brother with a certain amount of awe and rarely took a different line to him.

Of those others who had been partners or near-partners before the war, Shaw-Stewart was dead, Errington – now Lord Cromer – was at court, and Everard Baring had gone back to the army and ended up

as Chairman of the Southern Railway. Windham Baring was the
only partner to return. He was one of the first to be demobilized,
having had the good fortune to be serving on a ship that was paid off
in November 1918. He was in the office before Christmas: 'It seemed
rather strange coming back to this life again,' he told Leng in Buenos
Aires, 'but nevertheless I can assure you I am very glad to return.'[4] He
took responsibility for Latin American affairs again, and also for the
office in Liverpool, where Alan Tod was put in charge the following
year. In due course he would probably have become senior partner.
Then, at the end of 1922, he was convalescing after an operation for
appendicitis. A blood clot reached his heart and he died suddenly,
aged forty-one. 'We were devoted to him and he to us and we shall
miss him sadly,' Farrer told Leng. 'He was too young to die. . . . His
great interest in life was his business here and most particularly its
connexion with Argentina.'[5]

Even before he died it was obvious that new blood was needed.
'We shall have to bestir ourselves and try to make arrangements for
the Future here,' wrote Farrer in 1919, 'as we are all getting old and
past work, and I at least am certainly not fit to cope with the new conditions in business which we shall all have to face. We badly need
men here of sound sense and strength, who are not afraid to tell
unpleasant truths, but sympathetic enough to command attention.'[6]
Arthur Villiers was sympathetic enough, though perhaps not too
eager to tell unpleasant truths. He had joined Barings before the war
but had been lured away to help George Schuster set up an investment company and excelled in this arcane science. Two wounds and
a DSO later he returned to Barings. He professed dislike of Jews and
foreigners, particularly Germans, but went to France to be best man
at Antony de Rothschild's wedding and did more than anyone else
to strengthen his house's relationship with Rothschilds and
Schroders.[7] Villiers was thirty-six when he rejoined Barings in 1919;
ten years older than Evelyn Bingham Baring, a descendant of Sir
Francis's fourth son, William, who became a director in 1923. Evelyn
Baring – 'little Evelyn', not to be confused with Lord Cromer's third
son, Evelyn, who served briefly in the bank but made his name in the
public service and ended as Lord Howick – was said by Cecil Baring
to be 'gifted with ability and insight'.[8] He went with Windham Baring to Argentina in 1921 and was described as 'getting on first class

and is a great help to me, talks Spanish whenever he gets an opportunity and makes friends wherever he goes'.[9] He never seems to have made any marked impression, however, and did not stand out as the natural leader who would take Barings into the 1930s and 1940s.

Still younger blood was introduced in the next decade. Edward Reid was the son of John Revelstoke's sister Susan. He became a director in 1926, one year before his cousin Alexander, who was to succeed as 6th Lord Ashburton and remain with Barings till 1969. 'Both shew great capacity for work,' wrote Cecil Baring, 'and one feels sure that when it comes to their turn to exercise judgment, there need be no lack of confidence as to the outcome.'[10]

All of these except Villiers were members of the family, and all of them were out of the same intellectual and social mould. Revelstoke could not see among his junior partners any who were suitable to take on the leadership when he died or retired: some were too old, some too young, and those that were neither were too deeply imbued with the values and shibboleths of establishment merchant banking to grapple with the problems that lay ahead. Barings needed a new Joshua Bates, and like Alexander Baring before him Revelstoke looked for him from the New World.

Edward Peacock was the son of a poor Presbyterian minister in Ontario. He worked his way through college, had a few months as motorman on a streetcar, taught English for five years, and in 1902 joined Dominion Securities, a Toronto financial company, which sent him to manage its affairs in London.[11] His already considerable reputation was enhanced when Dr Pearson, the international financier, was drowned in the *Lusitania* and Peacock was put in charge of a motley collection of ill-managed and under-funded enterprises and 'brought them through in a marvellous way'.[12] Revelstoke was much struck by him and was instrumental in securing his election to the Court of the Bank of England in 1921: 'I shall look forward to the certainty of having gained a most esteemed new colleague,' he wrote in congratulation.[13] He then proceeded to get his protégé out of the Court again by persuading him to join Barings – tradition dictating that two partners from the same house should not serve with the Bank simultaneously. Peacock made up his mind at the end of 1923: 'He is another man since the decision was made,' wrote Farrer, 'comes in here fairly often and in the highest spirits.'[14]

John Baring (1863-1929), second Lord Revelstoke, by Ambrose McEvoy.

The partners' room at 8 Bishopsgate, designed by Lewis Cubitt in 1853,
as it appeared shortly before its demolition in the early 1970s.

Thomas ('Tom') Baring (1839-1923) by Sidney Kent.

Sir Edward Peacock by James Gunn.

Windham Baring (1880-1922) photographed in naval uniform during the First World War.

Hugo Baring (1876-1949).

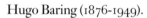

He joined Barings on the implicit understanding that, whoever the senior partner might be in title, he would effectively run the house after Revelstoke's departure. Whether some of the partners felt chagrin at this appointment is unknown. Cecil Baring certainly welcomed it from the start. 'Peacock is a man of strong character and wide experience,' he told the King's secretary, Lord Stamfordham, after Revelstoke's death. 'The principal driving force in our management now resides in him and it is inevitable that a large share of the work and responsibility will devolve upon his shoulders.'[15] An outstandingly clear mind, integrity, determination and a readiness to suffer fools, if not gladly, at least with a measure of patience, were Peacock's most marked characteristics. Taciturn and largely indifferent to the delights of London society, he did not fit readily into Lord Revelstoke's gilded soirées, but his good looks and natural dignity carried him through such occasions as he felt it is duty to attend.

The house which he joined was still a gentlemanly affair. In his diary in March 1929 Lord Revelstoke wrote with some wistfulness of Barings' closest allies in France, the house of Hottinguer. 'Their life seems to be one happy unity. They are extremely rich, they have beautiful houses with fine works of art, and have such a solid position in the banking world that they seem to be content to manage their fortunes and those of their many rich (Protestant) clients without any nervous desire to compete with more modern conditions, or to be tainted by the "get-rich-quick" feeling which is so prevalent nowadays.'[16] He recognized that Barings could not survive on such a basis, yet part of him hankered for it. He introduced an internal telephone system into Bishopsgate, but could rarely make it work and preferred to stump around the building seeing people for himself. Statements of account were still sent out in longhand. 'They also impressed me by the simple grandeur of their notepaper,' wrote one young correspondent. 'Thick, cream, of beautiful quality, it carried as the sole heading, die-stamped in square, black letters: "8 Bishopsgate Within. London E C". Doubtless it reflected the conviction that the letter was a private communication from one gentleman to another.'[17]

With such a disposition it would have been surprising if Revelstoke and the other partners had not been conservative in politics. So, indeed, they were, but their approach was pragmatic and they were remarkably ready to contemplate working with a Labour government if need arose. In the election of 1918 Mildmay admitted to a lack of enthusiasm for the Conservative/Liberal coalition but concluded that 'the Labour party, which includes many patriotic and disinterested men, is clearly too inexperienced to take over the government of the country at the moment'.[18] In 1922 Farrer rejoiced at the setback experienced by Lloyd George and said of the greatly increased Labour vote: 'I for one do not regret their large representation in Parliament. If, as is probable, some day they will be in actual control, it is better that they should have this preliminary training in opposition.'[19] Even Revelstoke, as close to being a diehard as was to be found in the partners' room, noted with some amusement that Ramsay MacDonald, so recently the bugbear of the capitalists, had only been Prime Minister for a few weeks when he found himself 'the hero of the hour'.[20] He seemed, said Mildmay, 'a cautious man, very well-intentioned and of a rather sympathetic personality'.[21]

Open-mindedness did not extend to taking the side of the unions in the General Strike. Barings hired hotel rooms to accommodate those of their staff who lived out of London, and motorcars to fetch in those in the suburbs. 'We have also been able to encourage some of our young men to take up emergency work, as of course the volume of business has very much diminished.' One of the not-so-young men was Evelyn Bingham Baring, who paraded the streets of Bow and Hounslow in the guise of a special constable.[22] In Liverpool Alan Tod was busily distributing posters and copies of Churchill's brainchild, the *British Gazette*: 'There are very few "dismal Jimmies" and good spirits showing everywhere,' he wrote proudly.[23]

The 'new conditions in business' which Gaspard Farrer had said would need new men to cope with, were most notably the decline of Britain's economic standing in the world and the readiness of the government to interfere in matters that had traditionally been dealt with entirely in the private sector. It was a matter for conjecture whether the merchant banks would be able to thrive, or even survive, in these new circumstances. Farrer confided his thoughts and worries to C. E. ter Meulen of Hopes, Barings' ally for nearly 150 years.

My own feeling is that the private firms are on their trial; if they have not gone back during the war, they have at least not made the progress of the Joint Stock Banks. . . . Nevertheless, I am convinced that there is still room for the private firms, but they must be sure of themselves, and I think such as yours and ourselves must not only set their own houses in order but make fast their alliances with houses similarly situated in other countries. Houses such as Hottinguers, Kidder Peabody, Morgans or whoever they may be. You will notice that I include ourselves among the private houses, for such we still consider ourselves; though we think that our constitution gives us a great advantage, not only from the fact of publishing our accounts yearly, but from the nature of our constitution, which provides for a continuing capital which remains irrespective of death. . . . At the same time the control of the firm is absolutely in the directors' hands. You would perhaps be amused to hear that during my sixteen years here, we have only once had a shareholder at our Annual Meeting, and he came at our special request.[24]

The interference of government was mainly confined to those transactions which involved the export of British capital – particularly in the financing of international issues. What money there was, was needed at home. Barings admitted a patriotic duty to abide by the spirit as well as the letter of the law. When Maurice Jenks wanted Barings' help in transferring £150,000 of Hong Kong money to New York and undertaking its management there, the business was refused. 'Even if the operation were not found to be contrary to existing regulations, we should not wish to facilitate the removal of so large a sum from London to the United States.'[25] Control of trade was another matter, and Barings deplored any restraint put upon the free market forces. Not surprisingly it was acceptances that were the first part of Barings' peacetime business to recover. In 1918, by far the worst war year, the annual total granted had fallen away to £14 million, of which only £3.9 million related to British trade; in 1919, aided by the boom as European industry rebuilt its depleted stocks, the British figure rose to £7.7 million; while in 1920, the London acceptance figure rose to £12.1 million and the grand total including Boston and New York to £30 million. There was a sharp drop when the postwar boom ended, a gradual recovery, another sharp relapse in 1926 caused by lower prices for wool, cotton and rubber and the increasing ability of German banks to finance their own national trade, then a resurgence in 1928 to £22.6 million in Britain alone – a figure which would not be surpassed for many years as the Wall Street Crash of 1929 led to the world's most calamitous slump.

It was the growth in continental credits – 'insatiable', Farrer described the demand in 1925[26] – which contributed most to the excellent figures for the 1920s; American acceptances fell away as more and more of their trade was financed through dollar credits. Barings viewed the trend without too much regret: 'We have watched the falling-off with some equanimity,' wrote Farrer, 'in view of the rates of commission at which US credit business is now being generally done.'[27] They valued the connection with Kidder Peabody more than the credit business they did on joint account. 'Our Joint Account operations have not only been eminently remunerative,' declared Revelstoke, 'but have been conducted in a manner which has made the business a pleasure for us all.'[28] It was this, more than any possible profit, which led Barings to increase their existing stake of $2.5 million, when Kidder Peabody developed a more or less dere-lict concern, called first the New England Yarn Company and then the New England Investment Company, into the Kidder Peabody Acceptance Corporation. For a time it did remarkably well and by 1929 its outstanding acceptances had risen to $40 million, making it the second largest specialized acceptance house in the United States.[29] Then the business was overwhelmed in the disasters of 1929 and 1930, Kidder Peabody retreated from the field of acceptances, and the joint account was wound up. Barings at least were able to repay some of the support Kidder Peabody had offered during the war by contributing $600,000 to the operation that Morgans organ-ized to rescue its old friend and rival.

Barings were as conservative as ever when it came to advancing money to industrial concerns or trading houses. They had an almost inviolable rule against advancing cash against shares, and would only do so against goods in store if the margin was satisfactory and the facility requested by a first-class firm. In general, they felt that they could not compete with the joint stock banks and did not intend to try. When they offered to advance up to £500,000 against cotton they emphasized that this was an exception, undertaken only 'to keep up our connection with our cotton friends in Liverpool'.[30] They were restrictive of credit even to an international company as well established as Lever Brothers. 'I cannot believe that sensible business people such as the Directors of Messrs Lever would take umbrage at a refusal which is based on our unwillingness to increase our acceptances,' wrote Farrer in what one assumes was feigned surprise.[31] Levers had indeed taken umbrage and their indignation was redoubled when Barings not only refused to double their existing £200,000 credit, but withdrew even this on the ground that Levers were drawing bills 'upon nearly every institution in London'.[32] Barings knew that they were taking a different line to many of their rivals – Kleinworts, in particular, were conspicuously more liberal in their grants of credit – but, wrote Farrer, 'I do not think that any action of our neighbours should influence us in our policy'.[33] Barings always had been prudent in such matters and they were not going to start changing their attitude after more than 150 years.

In other respects Barings could be curiously gullible, or perhaps more accurately, had a weakness for a particular type of flamboyant adventurer. The first Lord Revelstoke had had his Sanford, the second his Albert Loewenstein. Loewenstein was a Belgian stockbroker who had made a fortune in dealing in various Latin American shares and was habitually referred to in the popular press as 'The Belgian Croesus' or 'The Mystery Millionaire'. In May 1926 he fell on his head from a horse, became prone to mystical experiences, and began to behave with marked eccentricity. He acquired a large number of shares in the Brazilian Traction Co., a concern in which Barings were interested, and then began to plan a gigantic merger without any prior consultation with the boards concerned.[34] 'He is adopting his usual peculiar, theatrical methods which are very unpleasant to me and harmful to the business,' complained Revelstoke. 'Nevertheless, from what I can learn, I should think he has a reasonably good chance of putting the business through and if he succeeds in doing so, the new Company will be a strong one.'[35]

It was a marked misjudgement. Barings put £300,000 into the group which backed Loewenstein, but soon regretted it. By early 1927 Peacock was trying to set up a syndicate to take over

Loewenstein's vast and ramshackle shareholdings and thus save a market collapse: Loewenstein, or people acting on his behalf, was meanwhile busily manipulating the market, forcing up the price of one share and undermining another to suit his own advantage. 'No doubt we shall come through in the end,' wrote Peacock philosophically, 'but we are having a new experience meanwhile which is far from pleasant. It involves also having L or his accountant in our office day by day, all day, and as he is in a state almost of collapse and the accountant much the same, and as his accounts are of the strangest order, we are making the slowest kind of progress.'[36] The omelette was still largely unscrambled when Loewenstein, theatrical to the last, disappeared from his personal Fokker aircraft over the Channel. His body was eventually picked up off Cap Gris-Nez. He must have jumped, but whether to commit suicide or as the result of another mystical experience has never been established.

The government's embargo on foreign issues impelled Barings to take more interest than they had done previously in British industry. Early in 1919 they were struck by the fact that both Kuhn, Loeb and the City Bank were prowling around London looking for profitable enterprises in which to invest. 'It looks as if some business should be possible,' wrote Farrer, 'and we for our part will assuredly keep our eyes open.'[37]

They did, but not always to good effect. The most protracted and painful saga was that of Armstrong Whitworth, the engineering and armaments firm. A central figure was Montagu Norman, Governor of the Bank of England, who saw himself as the man who would rescue British industry from its decline.[38] It was Norman who early in 1924 introduced Armstrongs to Barings, originally with the proposal that a joint company should be formed to set up and develop promising enterprises. Barings declined this honour but were happy to act as financial advisers.[39] Armstrongs were short of capital, mainly because they owned an exceedingly costly paper company in Newfoundland, which they believed would eventually yield handsome profits but currently produced nothing but headaches and a crippling loss. Barings raised £2 million for Armstrongs, and at the end of 1924 a further £3 million – 'The fact is,' commented Farrer, 'they require a *very stout* Godmother that can hold babies till they are well grown . . . and this takes time and money.'[40]

By 1925 the situation had deteriorated so far that Barings felt bound to intervene. At Peacock's instigation, the Bank of England imported and placed on the board a tough Aberdonian called Frater Taylor, so cautious that his most enthusiastic recorded reaction was 'I'm not against it', and so cheeseparing that, when the chairman of Armstrongs was eventually forced from office, Taylor refused him the use of a company car to travel home after the decisive meeting.[41] Sir Glyn West, the chairman in question, accepted Taylor's original arrival with apparent equanimity, but the Aberdonian met with stiff resistance when he tried to pry too deeply into the company's accounts. It was in February 1926, with Armstrongs more than £5 million in debt to the Bank of England, that a balance sheet was finally approved. 'The story is going to be a very unpleasant one and must result in drastic action,' commented Peacock grimly.[42] First drastic action was to evict the chairman; the second might have been to put the company into receivership but this would have resulted in the loss of all its government contracts and destroyed any chance of its rehabilitation. Instead, the Bank of England was persuaded to put up yet another £500,000 and to allow a further twelve months' breathing space. 'The time has come when we should establish the relations between Armstrong and Barings on a more business-like basis,' wrote Peacock. Hitherto Barings had received not a penny for all their trouble, in future they would work on commission.[43]

They certainly gave service for their money. Throughout 1926 and 1927 Revelstoke and Peacock tried to secure Armstrongs contracts in a variety of countries and enterprises: a floating dock for the St Lawrence, locomotives for Argentina, Rhodesia and the Great Western Railway, destroyers and frigates for the Royal Navy, liners for Cunard, steamers for the Canadian lakes, a tanker for the British Molasses Company, steel sleepers for Rhodesia. A merger of shipbuilding interests was arranged with Vickers, and the joint Board had its first meeting in January 1928. The search for a chairman proved particularly taxing. Lords Southborough and Verulam came and went. 'I have heard from an intimate friend of Sir John Reith, Managing Director of the British Broadcasting Company, that he would like additional work and has plenty of time to look after another job,' reported Peacock. 'I have been told that he is very able and has many of the qualities of a good chief.'[44] Possibly the BBC proved more time-consuming than Reith had expected; anyway, the job in the end went to General Dawnay.

Early in 1929 a drastic reorganization was put in hand. Fourteen million pounds in accumulated losses were written off; the Newfoundland paper mill was at last disposed of. If the scheme goes through, declared the *Economist*, it will be 'the greatest achievement of financial salvage ever recorded'.[45] It did go through, though there were angry shouts at the shareholders' meeting and Mr W. J. Smith complained that the proposals 'simply weren't cricket'.[46] It would be pleasant to record that recovery followed rapidly, but in mid-1931 Peacock was admitting that: 'Vickers Armstrong has been a great disappointment. . . . The whole difficulty, of course, is based upon very much wider considerations than those affecting Armstrongs directly. The deterioration in the industrial position of England . . . has been even greater than that of Armstrong and is mainly responsible for the whole of the difficulties.'[47] It was 1936 before the Bank of England recovered the greater part of its losses.

Compared with this the Underground Electric Railway was a model enterprise. In 1926 Lord Ashfield asked Barings to raise the capital for and tender advice on the expansion and reconstruction of the underground railway. Peacock went on to the board and took a keen interest in the railway's running, complaining that the curved platform at the Bank Station meant that an unacceptably large gap was left between carriage and *terra firma*. There *were* solutions, replied the manager, but they were all extremely expensive. 'I had a look at it again this morning,' retorted Peacock, 'and quite expect to break my leg there some day.'[48] He had still not done so when he died in 1962. An issue of £4 million was made in May 1928 in conjunction with Rothschilds, Schroders and Speyers. Barings kept all the underwriting to themselves on the grounds that 'our profit on the issue is so small that we have perforce had to eke it out by making what we could out of the underwriting ourselves'.[49] Fortunately for them the issue was subscribed ten times over, though Lord Revelstoke still managed to reserve £50,000 for Lady Desborough and suitable amounts for other cronies.

'Compared with foreign Government loans, an issue such as this seems to involve a great deal more work at a great deal less profit,' complained Evelyn Bingham Baring.[50] He could hardly have said the same of the flotation of the brewing company, Taylor Walker. Early in 1927 Barings agreed to place £600,000 ordinary shares and £414,000 debentures. For these Taylor Walker would receive £912,000, the £102,000 difference covering Barings' costs and profit. Lady Desborough for some reason was not among those allotted ordinary shares but Princess Troubetzkoy, Lord Lansdowne, Lord Allendale and other close friends of Barings or Lord Revelstoke were given a slice of what promised to be an appetizing cake. The only condition made was that the shares should not be resold within six months, but Revelstoke in fact sold Lansdowne's after only two – making a profit of £4300 on an investment of £10,000: 'It was my opinion that the shares were a good investment at 20/–, but the present quotation would seem to discount to a marked degree the prospects of prosperity which the Company undoubtedly has.'[51] A few weeks later Barings financed Taylor Walker's takeover of a smaller brewery, Smith Garrett and Co., for a little over £900,000. Barings' commission on this transaction was £37,500, and their profit on the sale of shares £82,000.

These were by no means the only excursions made by Barings into the field of British industry, though they were cautious about enterprises on which they felt themselves inadequately informed. Yardleys, the scent and soap manufacturers, approached them in 1927 about a projected financial reorganization. 'It is only in very exceptional cases that Baring Brothers undertake the responsibility of sponsoring an industrial concern,' wrote Arthur Villiers, 'but in view of the high standing and excellent record of your company we should be very happy to look further into the matter.'[52] Evidently the further look was displeasing, the approach was not followed up. The Goodyear Tire and Rubber Co., the American firm that was the world's biggest tyre manufacturer, got a better hearing when they asked Barings to raise money to pay for a British subsidiary. Farrer was sceptical – 'Such a business is good so long as tyres are required and can be made and sold at a profit and almost valueless unless'[53] – but the other partners took a rosier view of the prospects for the motorcar and Barings agreed to place £800,000 of 6½ per cent debentures provided Goodyear would take up the same number of ordinary shares at par. The public subscribed £955,000, and the enterprise flourished. Mild alarm was experienced when Firestone opened its sumptuous new Art Deco factory on the Great West Road but the managing director of Goodyear reassured the partners that, though the site had great advertising value, the costs of the final product would certainly be too high.[54]

Barings were cautious when Mr Ullner of the Deutsche Erdoel Aktiengesellschaft approached Arthur Villiers about stopping a price-cutting campaign which was damaging the coal industries of both Britain and Germany. Ullner wanted Barings to set up a new Anglo-German company which would, *inter alia*, investigate the potential of producing oil from coal. He was convinced that this was the way of the future. 'It was calculated that existing supplies of oil in the USA, Persia and elsewhere would not last much longer than 12 years, and that when they were exhausted the only method of obtaining oil would be to extract it from lignite and coal.'[55] Villiers was sufficiently interested in the possibility to try to set up a meeting between Ullner and a colliery owner, but not to pursue it further when the British coal producers proved conspicuously unenthusiastic.

It was in the field of international financing that Barings felt most markedly the changed world conditions. Determined to protect a weakened sterling and to prepare the way for a return to the gold standard, the Treasury in 1918 imposed an almost complete embargo on the issuing of foreign loans. When loans did again become permissible it was only under licence, and they were directed above all to the monetary reconstruction of Europe.

A radical change in the direction of Barings' business inevitably resulted. The United States was now a creditor nation on a majestic scale, able to finance its own needs and much else besides. To a lesser extent the same was true of Canada, which anyway looked more and more to its southern neighbour for finance. Schroders were anxious to involve Barings in the development of Ontario, arguing that the potential of the province was so enormous that it would not matter if the underwriters were landed with the stock for a year or two. Revelstoke demurred and Peacock, for all his Canadian loyalties, fully supported him: 'This is undoubtedly a very rich and progressive province but it has been adding to its debt rather rapidly and its bonds sell upon a basis which would make it very difficult to offer them in London.'[56] A loan to Canada was, indeed, one of the few issues for a country outside Europe that the Bank of England would have tolerated before the end of 1925. Montague Norman 'says he cannot possibly bar a Colonial issue on this market,' reported Revelstoke.[57] Australia would have been equally favoured, but there was little likelihood of Barings chancing their arm in that direction. Farrer had an especial dislike of the Antipodes. Denouncing the 'spendthrift democracies' who would go on borrowing till nobody was left to lend, he concluded, 'I have always thought our Australian cousins a particularly vicious example and do not believe for a moment that they would continue to pay even their interest if we were unable or unwilling to continue to lend'.[58]

Despite his caution over Ontario, Peacock's membership of Barings did lead in the end to an increased interest in Canada. In 1927 a small company was set up, with a capital of $1 million – half British, half Canadian – to take advantage of any promising investment opportunities that might develop in Canada. Of the British $500,000, Revelstoke put up $200,000, Cecil Baring, Mildmay and Peacock $50,000 each and Robert Fleming, of the eponymous banking house, $100,000.[59] The hope was that the capital would build up substantially out of profits, and with holdings in enterprises like the Ford Motor Co., Massey-Harris and the Canada Cement Co. it would certainly have done so swiftly if the recession after 1929 had not set back investment prospects in Canada, and indeed the world.

Of Barings' other traditional clients, loans to Russia ended with the Bolshevik Revolution and the prospect of recovering money already lent seemed remote. Barings had no inclination to plunge deeper into this morass and early in 1919 refused to advance money on the security of vineyards in the Crimea. 'I confess that the idea of discharging the debts of the Grand Dukes leaves me absolutely cold,' Revelstoke told Stamfordham.[60] Their sympathies, however, were with the White Russian government in Omsk, and when this government proposed to export £10 million in gold to Hong Kong as security against a loan to finance the forces of the Omsk government and General Denikin in South Russia, Barings were ready to help. Alfred

Holt and Co. provided steamers to pick up the gold but were uneasy about their strongrooms – eventually it was decided to put the bullion in the deep tank and then to pour in water; 'this treatment would in their opinion entirely eliminate the risk of theft'.[61] The Omsk government refused to sell the gold and Barings made themselves responsible for placing £3 million of the loan at 7 per cent per annum for eighteen months. The largest shares went to the joint-stock banks, though Revelstoke personally took £300,000 and Farrer £100,000. It was a silly way for the White Russians to do business. 'The expense . . . to our friends seems to me a crime,' commented Farrer. 'At the end of the period they will have disbursed some £1.2 million in interest and expenses without any advantage that I can foresee which they would not have obtained by selling their gold now.'[62]

By early 1920 it was clear that the Omsk government was in disarray. The Foreign Office declined to say whether it was still in existence or not and for some months no instructions of any kind were received, but finally it became clear that Denikin was *de facto* in control of whatever White Russian government was left and his representative authorized the selling of the gold. Barings offered it to the Treasury but Norman would pay only a very low rate of exchange between sterling and the dollar on the amount due to be remitted to New York. Farrer indignantly refused: 'I told him we could never justify such a transaction to our clients, and that it was most unreasonable of the Treasury to hold us up because we wished to behave like white men.'[63] Norman increased his price, but not enough, and Farrer threatened to sell the gold elsewhere. 'Don't do that,' said Norman. '[The Treasury] would be dreadfully upset, so would I, and so I believe would you.' Reluctantly Farrer accepted the Bank's offer. 'It is not as good a settlement as I had hoped to make nor as good as I think we had a right to make, but we concluded it would be unwise to go our own way and leave Norman and the Treasury with sore heads.'[64] It was May before Denikin's successor, General Wrangel, retrospectively authorized the sale, and it was not long afterwards that he and what was left of his army were driven back to the Crimea and fled to Constantinople.

So far as the Bolshevik government was concerned, Barings considered that until they would acknowledge and put forward some

scheme for repaying the imperial debts, then there could be no further dealings with them. They remained convinced that in the end
economic forces would make a settlement inevitable: 'It is as certain
as night follows day,' wrote Farrer in 1923, 'that before long the
people of that country will of themselves acknowledge the necessity
of recognizing the debt.'[65] It was a long time before Farrer's logic was
accepted in Moscow. Meanwhile Barings retained the £3.5 million-
odd of Russian funds that had been in their possession at the end of
the war, paid the interest regularly and wondered when they would
be relieved of the responsibility. It was not until 1986, by which
time the total had risen to some £48 million, that a settlement
was reached with the Soviet government and Barings' stewardship
was over. The imperial treasure which it was so often alleged was
mouldering in the cellars at Bishopsgate existed only in the popular
imagination: the Russian royal family had no account with Barings
and deposited no assets there.

There could be no equally abrupt severance with Argentina; too
much unfinished business needed to be done. From 1918, however,
Barings were fighting a rearguard action against the superior power
of the American banking houses. At first they could not even get into
the fight. Late in 1919 a gloomy Windham Baring reported that
Buenos Aires was making overtures to New York bankers, including
Barings' traditional allies Morgans and the City Bank. 'There is no
getting away from the fact that the Americans will have the field to
themselves as far as Argentine finance is concerned, as it will certainly be some time before our Government allows us to take part in
any Argentine finance on a large scale.'[66] When he visited Buenos
Aires in 1921, however, he found that the name of Barings still
enjoyed a prestige in Argentina which he feared would long have
been lost.[67] The Americans seemed chivalrously reluctant to take
advantage of Barings' temporary disablement – 'Morgans . . . have
been particularly civil and anxious to defer to us,' reported Farrer.[68]
It seemed that one day Barings might after all be able to reclaim their
former fief.

The prospects seemed even brighter when in 1923 Barings, in conjunction with Morgan Grenfell (as J. S. Morgan had now become),
were exceptionally allowed by the Treasury to issue £2.5 million 5
per cent bonds for the development of the Port of Buenos Aires. The

issue was heavily oversubscribed and went immediately to a premium of 1½ per cent. For Barings this happy result was doubly gall-
ing. In Argentina it gave rise to bitter complaints that the price was
too low and Barings had made extravagantly large profits – the premium was, indeed, striking, admitted Mildmay, 'but the margin
between success and failure is very small. That is to say, either people
throng to apply for a loan or people do not apply at all.'[69] In London
it showed how much money there was waiting to be invested in
issues of this kind. Yet Barings were not allowed to bring the horse to
the water. In 1925, when the Argentine government offered Morgans and Barings the chance to bring out a $40 million loan on most
generous terms, Barings had to refuse: 'The embargo on foreign
issues is stronger than ever.'[70] 'Barings must of course cooperate with
those who have the good of our country at heart,' commented
Mildmay sanctimoniously, but doing so left a sour taste in the
mouth.[71]

It was not until the end of 1925, with a return to the gold standard,
that the merchant banks were once more free to raise money for any
part of the world that took their fancy. Lord Beaverbrook characteristically marked the occasion by sending a messenger to Barings with
a bill for which he demanded payment in gold. 'His action was only
taken, of course, to embarrass us,' wrote Revelstoke, 'and he must
have been disappointed to have had his £25 paid to him in gold without demur. But it is a vicious move on his part, and shows an
unnecessarily unreasonable, vindictive spirit.'[72]

What the Treasury gave with one hand, it took away with the
other. The unkindest cut came in 1926, when another $25 million of
Argentine bills had to be placed. This time the British Treasury formally placed no obstacle, but the stamp duty which they levied
forced Barings to tender at a price 1½ per cent worse than that available in New York, a difference which the Argentines could hardly be
expected to ignore. In 1927 Barings for the same reason had to refuse
to participate in a number of issues where they knew they could not
compete with the American price. Still the Argentines remained
remarkably loyal to their old friends. In 1929 a request was made for
an immediate advance of £5 million. Mildmay for the first time
talked to Everard Meynell in Buenos Aires by telephone. The result
was not wholly satisfactory; Mildmay knew that it was Meynell by

the tone of his voice but: 'What you said was indistinguishable; it sounded as if you were trying to shout with pebbles in your mouth.'[73] The attitude of the Argentine President, on the other hand, could not have been bettered. He had, reported Evelyn Bingham Baring, who was visiting Buenos Aires, 'an insane desire to deal with London and Baring Brothers and Co. Ltd at all costs'. He had turned down a multiplicity of offers from New York. 'Cannot we and Great Britain profit by this unique opportunity?'[74] This time all went well; after a frantic flurry of telegrams, terms were agreed by the end of the year. It did not represent a real turn of the tide, but it was comforting to find that after more than a hundred years so much good will persisted.

This falling away of Barings' traditional issuing business was in part compensated for by the great increase in loans raised for Europe. It was not until after 1926 that this really gained its full momentum – between 1926 and 1928 Barings made twelve issues in London for continental governments, Hambros thirteen and Morgan Grenfell six[75] – but a new pattern had long before been established. 'I am sure that if private firms are to survive amidst the constantly increasing competition of companies, the more friendly terms on which they are with each other, the better it will be for their wellbeing,' Farrer told J. S. Morgan.[76] Barings acted on this precept by forging the closest possible alliance with two other veterans of merchant banking, Rothschilds and Schroders. Forgotten – or at any rate concealed – was the animosity of the nineteenth century; together these three banks established a powerful cartel which competed for business as a unit, one bank taking the lead in each country and dividing up the liabilities and the profits between them. So close was the relationship that Barings practically refused to join a syndicate raising a French loan in 1927 unless Schroders were also included. Lazards, another participant, pleaded that Schroders were a German house, with no standing in this business, but Barings were obdurate. Only the fact that Lionel Rothschild told Arthur Villiers that his house had agreed to Schroders' exclusion induced Barings reluctantly to give way.[77]

Czechoslovakia was a country in which Barings took the lead and controlled the negotiations, and since it was also the first country in Central Europe to receive a loan, the case deserves a little study.

Barings first heard of the possibility in November 1921 from Michael Spencer-Smith, a former colleague of Farrer's and a Director of the Bank of England, who had promised the premier, Dr Beñes, that he would try to help him raise money in London. Spencer-Smith did not pretend that it would be easy, and Farrer was also without illusions. Czechoslovakia seemed more likely to prove solvent than any other of the Central European states but the political risks would make the public chary of investing in such an area.[78] Anyway, the country had only recently been conjured from the old Austro-Hungarian empire and the man in the street hardly knew what or where it was. The man in the bank was not much better informed; as late as April 1922 Barings were having to instruct Kidder Peabody that Czechoslovakia should be written as one word and with a small 's'.

In February 1922, while Barings were still hesitating, Dr Beñes arrived in London. 'A nice little man,' Farrer judged him, 'bright, quick on the uptake, very human, and so far as we can see entirely simple and straightforward.'[79] Serious negotiations then began, made more troublesome by the fact that the Czech negotiator, Dr Vilem Pospisil, spoke no English and very little French; considering this, said Farrer handsomely, 'it is creditable to him to have got through at all'.[80] The Czech team needed as much education as the British public. Seeing that would-be underwriters were quick to come forward, they assumed the loan could be for as much as they wished. 'It is hard to get them to realize that selling loans to underwriters is a very different matter from placing a loan with the permanent investor. At the first breath of an adverse wind, every underwriter is a seller and the credit of a country may be damaged for months or years to come.'[81]

In the event Barings apportioned the first tranche of what was eventually to be a £10 million loan so that $14 million was issued by Kidder Peabody in the United States, £2.8 million in conjunction with Schroders and Rothschilds in London and £500,000 by Hopes in Amsterdam. The issue got away to an excellent start and was soon at a premium of 2 per cent. Masaryk, the President of Czechoslovakia, called personally on the British Minister in Prague, Sir George Clerk, to express his pleasure. The success had been almost too great, Clerk told Revelstoke, 'for besides increasing an already sufficiently developed conceit [in the Czechs], it has led some people to think that the terms might have been less stringent'. With a bluntness that was something less than diplomatic Clerk pointed out that Czechoslovakia had to pay 'for being a fraction of Central Europe – not an encouraging field for the British investor – and for its comic opera name, and so on'.[82]

The advice was ineffective. Within a few weeks Helbert, Wagg were back in the market with a £1.5 million loan for the City of Prague. The State of Czechoslovakia stock promptly went to a discount, and though Barings propped it up for a while they were not at all dissatisfied by the chagrin which this setback caused the Ministry of Finance in Prague. Farrer read Dr Pospisil a stern lesson when it was rumoured at the end of the year that enquiries were being made about a further national loan. 'Even in London millions do not grow like cherries on a cherry tree . . . ,' he wrote. 'We and our associates would not for a moment pretend to claim the monopoly of Czechoslovak business, but we do think it was due to us, if such an operation was contemplated, that we should have been first consulted in the matter.'[83] Pospisil denied that any such move was in the air, and it was not until mid-1923 that Barings were asked to bring out the second tranche of the loan.

Politics then intervened. The British Foreign Office had been instrumental in urging Barings to take up the loan in the first place, now they were displeased with the attitude of the Czechs on the Reparations Committee. The government 'would not go so far as to veto our raising further money for the Czechs,' Farrer told ter Meulen of Hopes, but 'it would no doubt be sorry to see us doing it'.[84] Barings urged the Czechs to discuss the matter direct with the Foreign Office, and only when this had been sorted out did they feel free to proceed with the second tranche. It went even better than the first. Barings paid 91 and offered the bonds to the public at 96½, yielding interest of 8.3 per cent. Of the £1.85 million issued in London, Rothschilds were allotted £337,000 and received applications for £1.7 million and Schroders £236,000 against £1.4 million. 'Messrs Barings have undertaken all the negotiations and arrangements for the loan, including the underwriting,' Lionel Rothschild told his cousins in Paris.[85] Though they had exacted a substantial payment for the trouble and the risk, they had given value for money and established the credit of the fledgling republic in a way few other houses could have matched.

Of the other loans raised in London for the continental countries, those for Hungary were managed by Rothschilds: 'We value very highly your unfailing friendship and much of the success of the loan was due to your wise and able guidance,' Lionel Rothschild assured Revelstoke.[86] With a £3.5 million loan for the City of Berlin it was Schroders who led. But they were not the only London houses with whom Barings worked. Morgan Grenfell and the Westminster Bank were the partners when a loan for Belgium was mooted in 1926. Here, as so often in this period, Barings found themselves expected to act in part as an arm of British foreign policy. The British government were preoccupied by the risk that Belgium might slip into chaos and, perhaps, then into communism, and felt a loan might save the day. Peacock saw the force of this, 'but I cannot help thinking a good deal also of the danger to Barings and our colleagues if we should issue something that is not sound that might come to grief in the very near future'.[87] In the end a £7.25 million loan was issued and heavily oversubscribed: the profits from underwriting alone netted Lord Revelstoke's various accounts (including the assets he managed for other people) £15,000, Lord Lansdowne £300, and Sir Edwin Lutyens £37.10/–.

The fact that Barings were almost always working in partnership with at least one other house did not diminish the conviction of the partners that there was something very special about their status. In 1928 a loan to the Portuguese was in question but was being viewed with some suspicion in London because of the doubtful constitutional standing of their government. 'We must remember,' wrote Mildmay, 'that in American as well as British opinion, the Baring Brothers and Co. trade-mark will be regarded as sufficient evidence of legality, as good or better than the League of Nations.'[88]

Outside Europe it was Brazil that provided the most business. This was traditional Rothschild territory and Barings were scrupulous about taking no initiative which might suggest they were anything but junior partners. Such an attitude might have caused embarrassment when the Permanent Under-Secretary at the Foreign Office in 1926 tried to use his friendship with Peacock to stop the issue of a loan to Brazil. The British government were annoyed with the Brazilians for blocking German entry to the League of Nations. 'It is obvious we can do nothing except to restrain, for the moment only I hope, any intempestive enthusiasm on the part of Messrs N.M.R. and Co.,' Revelstoke commented. 'It would be well to keep in close touch with the F.O.'[89] The enthusiasm was duly restrained and the business lost to the United States, but Barings were still involved in seven Brazilian issues between 1921 and 1930. A £25 million Japanese loan to repair the damage done by the earthquake of 1923 was also a formidable success. For this Morgan Grenfell and other banks were added to the more usual triumvirate of Barings, Schroders and Rothschilds: the result was 'quite satisfactory to us from a pecuniary point of view,' said Farrer; a modest representation of what had been an extremely profitable operation.[90]

In the Middle East the Société d'Études for the Trans-Persian railway lingered on as loth to die. After characteristic shilly-shallying the Foreign Office in 1919 finally committed itself to a blunt: 'Present circumstances certainly render desirable the dissolution of the Société in question.'[91] Inexplicably, the following year Revelstoke assured Routkowsky: 'I have had no indication that the British Government has expressed a desire to see the Société d'Études wound up.'[92] Possibly there had been a change of heart in Whitehall. Certainly Barings could not have been playing some deep game on their own behalf, since they had no interest in the Société's preservation and welcomed the death of its chairman in 1932 as a reason for giving the enterprise its final quietus. This did not imply a lack of interest in Persia. In mid-1925 Villiers wrote to Sir Percy Lorraine, the British Minister in Teheran, to deplore the fact that 'the Americans are endeavouring to retain the Persian business for themselves to the exclusion of British interests,' and that the restrictions on foreign issues imposed in London made their task lamentably easy. Could not some help be given under cover of development by the Anglo-Persian Oil Company?[93] Lorraine cautiously replied that the worst thing for Persia would be cut-throat Anglo-American competition. Barings persisted, and armed the local representatives of Anglo-Persian with a letter stating that in principle Barings and Schroders were disposed to help develop the national transport system. 'I cannot give you a very encouraging account of conditions over here,' Villiers told Lorraine. 'We are lending abroad more than would appear to be justified by the amount of goods which we export, and our home trade has hardly fulfilled expectations.' But things were looking up; 'every year since the war we have made distinct progress towards sounder and more settled conditions'.[94]

Unfortunately the sounder conditions were never established, in part because of the speculative fever in the United States and the scale of their foreign lending. Revelstoke wrote in alarm of a situation in which, even in the more remote hamlets of the West, the 'ticker' buzzed busily all day as the speculators gambled on perpetual growth,[95] while Farrer remarked that they were 'aghast at the size and number of their foreign loans. . . . How can these borrowers fulfil such obligations? or is London judging from her past experiences as complete a back number as I feel and know I am myself?'[96]

It was against this background of incipient disaster that Revelstoke, at the end of 1928, accepted Winston Churchill's invitation to join Sir Josiah Stamp as British delegate at the forthcoming conference on German reparations in Paris. Revelstoke was by then sixty-six, and had been carrying the brunt of the responsibilities at Barings for almost forty years. He must from time to time have contemplated retirement, but he showed no signs of any such intention when he wrote to Peacock from Paris urging his partner to accept the task of Chairman of the Channel Tunnel Committee. The conference could not last much longer, he wrote: 'I hope and think that at any rate by the end of April I ought to be free, and in that case I can assure you that it will be with particular pleasure that I shall return to my Penates at Bishopsgate.'[97]

The work in Paris was gruelling. Moreau, the head of the French delegation, refused to modify the existing reparation terms by one iota – 'he shuts his mouth like a steel trap when Schacht pleads poverty and inability to pay'.[98] Schacht, the German delegate, was equally intransigent: 'with his hatchet, Teuton face and burly neck and badly fitting collar . . . ,' wrote Revelstoke in his diary, 'he reminds me of a sealion at the Zoo, which is half out of the water on a rock, and is waiting to catch a fish thrown to him by his keeper'.[99] The Italians felt it their duty to be as difficult as the French. J. P. Morgan, for the Americans, was 'like a wild bison in a shop that sells

Dresden china'. Revelstoke, in atrabilious mood, deplored the power of the United States and the unhappy lot of the British who, 'in spite of their loss of blood and treasure since 1914, find themselves ground under the iron heel of the insolent wealth of a Trans-Atlantic people who must be considered the greatest profiteers that the World has ever seen'.[100] Finally the representatives of the British Treasury drove Revelstoke to despair, with their 'supercilious manner and sneering attitude for the whole of the rest of mankind' and their 'impossibly inelastic preconceptions'.[101]

Most of these disobliging observations, it is only fair to say, were written when Revelstoke had fallen prey to the virulent flu epidemic that was ravaging Europe. He was ill and tired but the demands of the conference did not allow him to relax. Sometimes the leaders of the delegation would convene at his bedside to argue acrimoniously over his ailing body. By mid-April a complete breakdown of negotiations was imminent. On 18 April the committee sat until 6.45 p.m. and the Germans walked out in high anger: 'Schacht was quite impossible today,' Revelstoke wrote in his diary in a shaky hand. It was his final entry. He suffered a major heart attack in the early hours of 19 April and was dead when his servant came to call him in the morning. His body was brought back to England and buried at Membland. A special trainload of family and friends travelled to Devon for the funeral. 'It seemed to be a matter of course,' wrote his niece Daphne, 'that Lady Desborough and her daughter Imogen should take their places as chief mourners.'[102]

Lord Revelstoke left unsettled estate of £2,492,000, of which £1,087,000 was paid in duty. To the National Gallery he left his Guardi, his Van de Capelle and the 'well-varnished Canalettos'; the National Portrait Gallery got his pictures by Hone and Chandler. He left £100,000 to King Edward's Hospital, whose Treasurer he had been for many years; £50,000 to Guy's; £25,000 to St Mary's, Paddington, Medical Schools and £5 to a Baring godchild. Though his death inevitably diminished the money immediately available to the house for day-to-day operations, it did not affect the capital or reserves. Besides the £2 million or so which figured in the published balance sheet there was, Cecil Baring told Lord Stamfordham, 'at least as much more money in the business which might, if the need for strict accounting arose, be set down as "surplus or undivided profits" '.[103] The growth of Barings over the previous decade had not been spectacular, especially when compared with certain of their rivals, but the business was sound and prosperous. Alfred Mildmay was now the senior partner, but everyone accepted that it was to Peacock that the house looked for its future direction.

'You will see,' Cecil Baring, now Lord Revelstoke, wrote to Stamfordham, 'that the concern remains, as a whole, a family affair, although it has always been laid down here, and we of the family constantly recognize, that there can be no place for one of our members unless he shews the requisite character and brains. It is a team that I feel sure will pull together, and to which the term "happy family" can unhesitatingly be applied. In spite of the loss which we have suffered, which cannot in its entirety be made good, we are going to do our best to meet the responsibilities which are entrusted to us, and to conduct our business with the same impersonal ends which have guided our predecessors.'[104]

Stamfordham in his reply spoke for George V, who had profited so signally from Lord Revelstoke's advice throughout his life. The King was confident, he wrote, that 'with the varied personnel of the Baring family, strengthened by the addition of Mr Peacock, the Board of Directors will not only be "family" in character, and a united "happy family", but remain a powerful national institution, animated by the great traditions of which John was so justly proud'.[105] Those traditions, established towards the end of the eighteenth century, had been carried through for almost one hundred and fifty years with astonishing consistency. The language was different, the sums of money vastly greater, but the spirit of Francis Baring's partners' room still ruled in Bishopsgate. Intelligence was desirable, clubability no defect, but integrity was indispensable. Lord Revelstoke had done as much as anyone to ensure that this scale of values had survived. He had good reason to be proud of his accomplishment.

Epilogue
1929–1987

It is now nearly sixty years since the death of Lord Revelstoke, some-thing over a quarter of Barings' total life span to date. The period between 1929 and 1939 was marked by a radical reshaping of the house's activities in the field of issues. The slump between 1929 and 1934 shook still further the strength of sterling and disrupted the world's monetary order. New issues for overseas borrowers were less than half what they had been in the previous decade, while issues for British borrowers were three times as numerous. Peacock made a speciality of corporate finance, and under his direction Barings played an important part in financing and reorganizing British busi-ness. The formation of the Lancashire Cotton Corporation, the reconstruction of the Royal Mail Group, the electrification of the Southern Railway and the extension of the Piccadilly Line to Finsbury Park in the north and Hammersmith in the west, the takeover by Charringtons of Hoare's Brewery, were only some of the larger enterprises in which Barings were involved.

During the Second World War, as between 1914 and 1918, tradi-tional merchant banking was almost impossible to practise. Issuing stopped altogether, the credit business collapsed, and with all the partners involved in some kind of war work, the house was con-cerned mainly with routine banking business such as the payment of dividends and the management of client accounts. Though Bishops-gate never closed, most of the remaining staff moved down to Lord Northbrook's old family home, Stratton Park – acquired from the school which by then occupied it – where they stayed for the dura-tion of the war.

After 1945 Peacock continued to lead the house. He was assisted

by Howard Millis, a solicitor formerly with the City firm of
Slaughter and May, who specialized in corporate finance. Investment expertise was supplied by Arthur Villiers and Evelyn Baring.
Sir Edward Reid looked after the banking business and Lord
Ashburton played an important general role with responsibility for a
number of orporate relationships. Lord Errington and John Phillimore respectively represented the younger element of the family
and brought Argentine experience. Errington, who succeeded his
father as Lord Cromer in 1953, was to take leave of absence from the
firm in 1959 to become Minister at the Embassy in Washington and
without returning to the firm went on to become Governor of the
Bank of England at the age of forty-three. When Millis retired in the
1950s, his place was taken by Andrew Carnwath who with A. W.
Giles led the house team in many important mergers and takeovers
during the 1960s. It was Giles who was above all responsible for
keeping alive Barings' connection in South-East Asia – particularly
with Jardine Matheson, a significant holding in which was acquired
in the late 1950s.

When Peacock retired in 1954 his role as senior partner was taken
over by Evelyn Baring. He in turn was succeeded in 1963 by Sir
Edward Reid, followed in 1967 by Lord Cromer, at the end of the
latter's five-year term of office as Governor of the Bank of England.
In 1971 Cromer was appointed British Ambassador in Washington.
His place as senior partner was filled for brief periods, first by John
Phillimore and then by Sir Andrew Carnwath. John Baring, the
eldest son of Lord Ashburton, was appointed Chairman of the Ex-
ecutive Committee on Lord Cromer's departure and on Sir
Andrew's retirement in 1974 was named the first Chairman of
Baring Brothers.

The change in the traditional business of Barings became still
more accentuated after 1945. With sterling far weaker even than
before the war, issues for overseas borrowers became a rarity in the
1950s, 1960s and 1970s. The sterling market was opened to overseas
borrowers, however, on a number of occasions during this period.
Barings led sterling debt issues for the World Bank on two occasions
in the 1950s and again in 1972, for the Inter American Development
Bank in 1964 and for the Government of Japan in 1963. It was a particular feather in the firm's cap to be selected as lead manager for the

two international agencies; in the case of the World Bank, Barings were unanimously put forward as lead manager by the group of six banks (Barings, Hambros, Lazards, Morgan Grenfell, Rothschilds and Schroders) whom the World Bank had selected.

While the sterling market was only opened to foreign borrowers as an exception between 1945 and 1979, Barings remained active as a manager of new issues of equity and debt securities for UK issuers during this period – though the market for new issues of debt saw little marked activity in the 1970s. The firm also featured among those London houses who took part in the development of the Eurobond market, and kept its relationship with foreign clients alive in that way. It was not until 1979 that exchange controls were abandoned and Barings availed themselves of the possibility of issuing long- or medium-term sterling debt for countries like Finland and Sweden. The house has since emerged as a leader in new issues of sterling debt securities.

Acceptances, the other pillar on which the prosperity of Barings traditionally rested, have remained a feature, though far less significant than in the past as a measure of business activity, since they are today just one of a number of facilities offered to clients. Liabilities on acceptances at the end of 1987 stood at over £350 million. In 1981 Barings, with Rothschilds and Samuel Montagu, were responsible for setting up a syndicate of more than fifty banks to finance an acceptance credit of £365 million for Petroleos Mexicanos, at that time the largest acceptance credit ever arranged in London.

Corporate finance has played an increasingly significant part in the bank's activities. Most of the acquisitions and mergers which Barings have organized have taken place with relatively little bother, but from time to time contested bids have commanded the headlines for weeks or even months at a time. A particularly conspicuous example was the great battle in the early 1960s, when Barings advised Courtaulds in their fierce and finally successful resistance to a takeover bid from ICI. Breweries, textiles and overseas trading companies were the industrial sectors in which Barings were particularly active. They were involved in takeover transactions for Watneys and Whitbreads, and played an important part in the building up of Allied Breweries, now Allied-Lyons. Another *cause célèbre* was the takeover of AEI by GEC in which Barings managed to achieve an increase in the value of the offer, though AEI lost its independence at the end of a hard-fought battle.

The corporate finance business has never been more active than it is now. The roll of clients for whom the firm has recently acted, or whom it has advised, includes national and international names such as Royal Insurance, Pirelli, Blue Circle Industries, Cathay Pacific Airways, Allied-Lyons, Ferranti, Philips, W.H. Smith, Bank of England, H.M. Government, Royal Bank of Scotland, Union Bank of Switzerland, The World Bank, and this is but a selection of some of the better-known names.

Investment management is a part of the business in which growth had been outstanding. Before 1939 this was done on an informal basis for friends and clients; by the mid-1950s the securities managed on a discretionary basis for clients were valued at some £15 million. The growing complexity of the securities market, together with an immense upsurge in the amount of money available for investment, especially in pension funds, has led to a wide range of charities, trusts and funds, as well as private clients, concluding that their affairs would be better looked after by professionals. At the end of 1987 Barings managed about £10.7 billion for a wide range of clients through companies in London, Boston, Tokyo and Hong Kong.

Compared with the British clearing banks, Barings is a minnow among whales. In comparison with the other merchant banks, it can hold up its head, but is not among the largest. Yet in 1987 its balance sheet stood at some £2.7 billion, having grown from £276 million in a little over a decade. The old offices in Bishopsgate have vanished, replaced by a twenty-storey tower block. The worldwide staff of the Barings Group is not far short of two thousand and growing.

In the mid-1960s existing inheritance tax laws and the possibility of a wealth tax being introduced by the ruling Labour Government were seen to pose a threat to the continuity of Barings in its then form. Partly in order to meet this threat it was decided in 1969 to transfer a majority stake in the equity of the business to a newly-formed charity called The Baring Foundation. In 1985 a major capital reorganization took place with a new top company, Barings plc, being set up and the balance of the equity being transferred to the Foundation. Baring Brothers remains the merchant banking subsidiary, with the investment management business being grouped in a parallel operating company. Control of the policy of the Barings Group rests with the directors of Barings plc while the economic interest in its equity is owned by the Foundation, which applies the flow of dividends to charitable purposes. In 1987 it made grants totalling £2.6 million to a wide range of national and other charities with particular emphasis on social welfare.

Two hundred and twenty-five years after Francis Baring opened his agency in London, his four-times great-grandson, John, is Chairman of the house, and his three-times great-grandson, Nicholas, is Deputy Chairman. Nicholas's brother Peter is group finance director and another Baring is a director of Baring Brothers & Co. Limited, while three more are working in the house. Of the eight men and women who sit on the board of The Baring Foundation, five are members of the family. Sixty years ago Cecil Baring told Lord Stamfordham, 'The concern remains, as a whole, a family affair.' Immense though the growth has been in the business and in the number of individuals involved, there is still strong family representation at the top level today working in partnership, as has so often been the pattern in the past, with non-family colleagues of great ability. There is nothing in the constitution of Barings or of the Foundation which requires family involvement, and its continuation depends on a flow of suitable individuals. However, there is no lack of up-and-coming Barings in the wings, and this, together with the interest of other members of the group in seeing the traditional spirit of the house maintained, gives good reason to hope that the business will continue to have a distinctive feeling for some time yet.

APPENDIX I

Abridged Baring Family Trees

FIG. 1

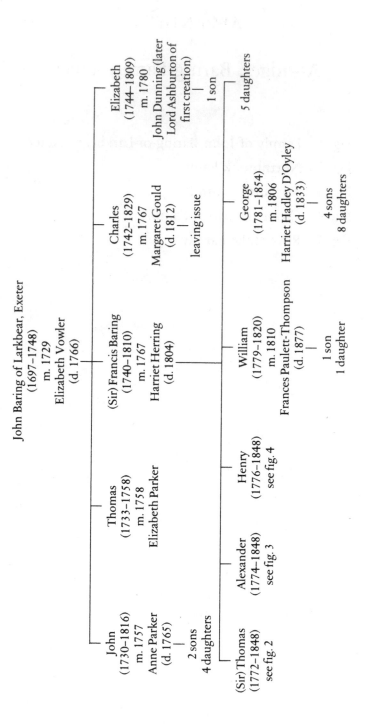

John Baring of Larkbear, Exeter
(1697–1748)
m. 1729
Elizabeth Vowler
(d. 1766)

Thomas
(1733–1758)
m. 1758
Elizabeth Parker

(Sir) Francis Baring
(1740–1810)
m. 1767
Harriet Herring
(d. 1804)

Charles
(1742–1829)
m. 1767
Margaret Gould
(d. 1812)

leaving issue

Elizabeth
(1744–1809)
m. 1780
John Dunning (later
Lord Ashburton of
first creation)

1 son

John
(1730–1816)
m. 1757
Anne Parker
(d. 1765)

2 sons
4 daughters

(Sir) Thomas
(1772–1848)
see fig. 2

Alexander
(1774–1848)
see fig. 3

Henry
(1776–1848)
see fig. 4

William
(1779–1820)
m. 1810
Frances Paulett-Thompson
(d. 1877)

1 son
1 daughter

George
(1781–1854)
m. 1806
Harriet Hadley D'Oyley
(d. 1833)

4 sons
8 daughters

5 daughters

FIG. 2

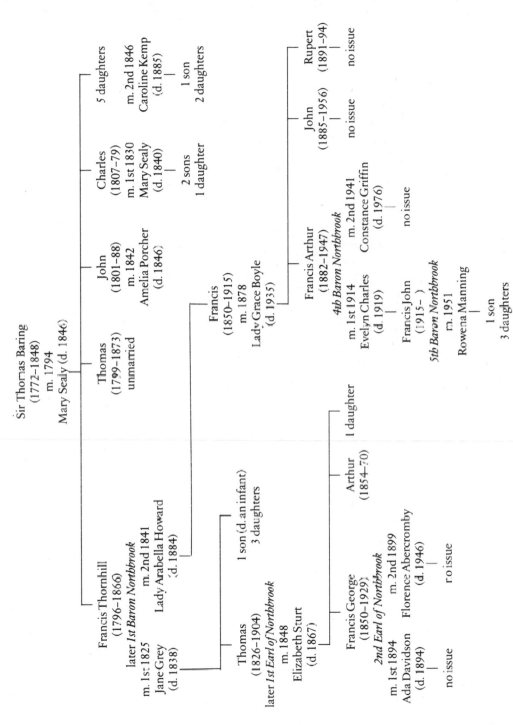

Sir Thomas Baring
(1772–1848)
m. 1794
Mary Sealy (d. 1846)

Francis Thornhill
(1796–1866)
later *1st Baron Northbrook*

m. 1st 1825   m. 2nd 1841
Jane Grey   Lady Arabella Howard
(d. 1838)   (d. 1884)

Thomas   1 son (d. an infant)
(1826–1904)   3 daughters
later *1st Earl of Northbrook*
m. 1848
Elizabeth Sturt
(d. 1867)

Francis George   Arthur   1 daughter
(1850–1929)   (1854–70)
2nd Earl of Northbrook
m. 1st 1894   m. 2nd 1899
Ada Davidson   Florence Abercromby
(d. 1894)   (d. 1946)

no issue   no issue

Thomas
(1799–1873)
unmarried

John
(1801–88)
m. 1842
Amelia Porcher
(d. 1846)

Francis
(1850–1915)
m. 1878
Lady Grace Boyle
(d. 1935)

Francis Arthur
(1882–1947)
4th Baron Northbrook
m. 1st 1914   m. 2nd 1941
Evelyn Charles   Constance Griffin
(d. 1919)   (d. 1976)

Francis John   no issue
(1915–)
5th Baron Northbrook
m. 1951
Rowena Manning

1 son
3 daughters

Charles
(1807–79)
m. 1st 1830
Mary Sealy
(d. 1840)

2 sons
1 daughter

John
(1885–1956)

no issue

5 daughters

m. 2nd 1846
Caroline Kemp
(d. 1885)

1 son
2 daughters

Rupert
(1891–94)

no issue

FIG. 3

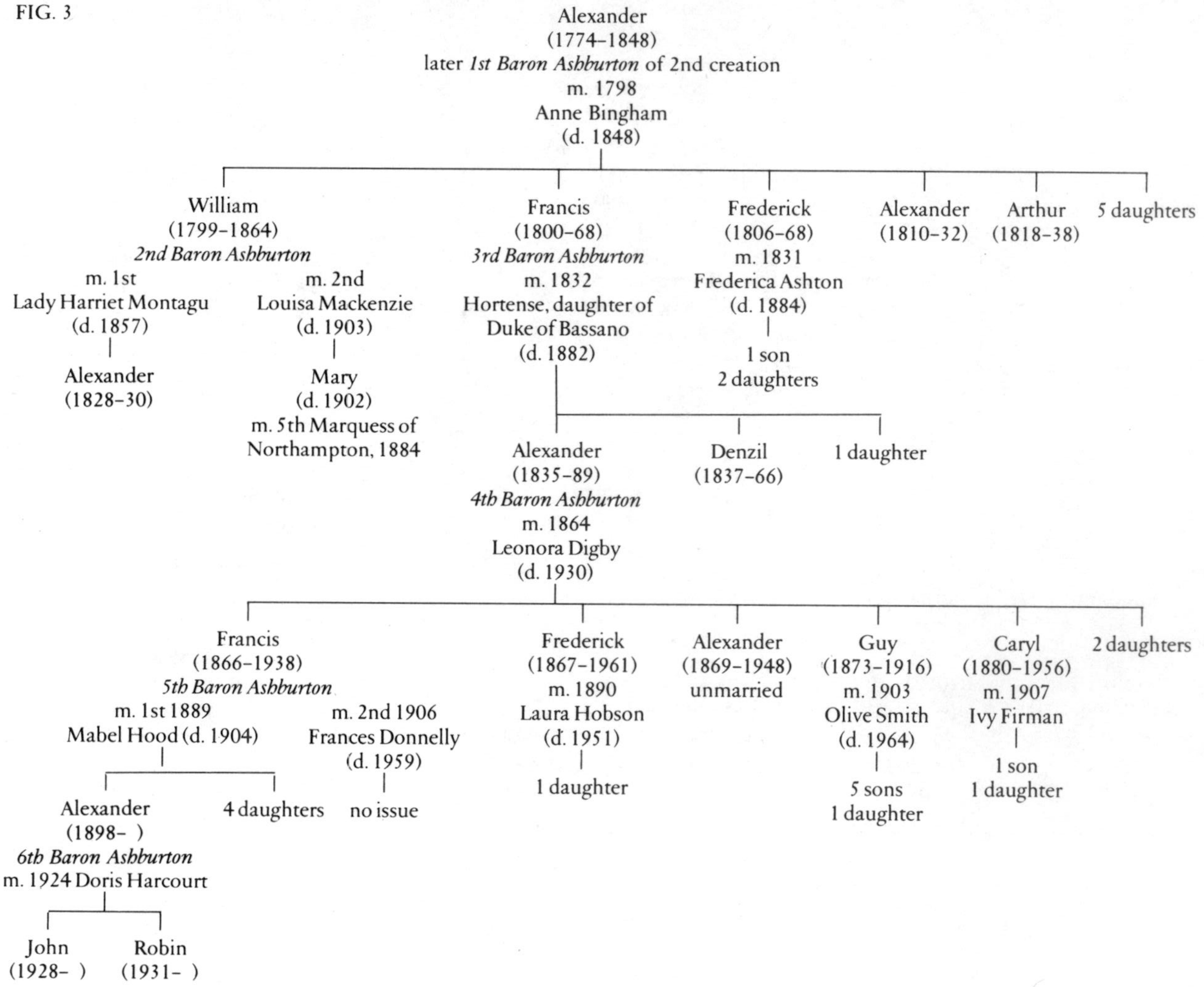

Alexander
(1774–1848)
later *1st Baron Ashburton* of 2nd creation
m. 1798
Anne Bingham
(d. 1848)

William
(1799–1864)
2nd Baron Ashburton

m. 1st
Lady Harriet Montagu
(d. 1857)

m. 2nd
Louisa Mackenzie
(d. 1903)

Alexander
(1828–30)

Mary
(d. 1902)
m. 5th Marquess of
Northampton, 1884

Francis
(1800–68)
3rd Baron Ashburton
m. 1832
Hortense, daughter of
Duke of Bassano
(d. 1882)

Frederick
(1806–68)
m. 1831
Frederica Ashton
(d. 1884)

1 son
2 daughters

Alexander
(1810–32)

Arthur
(1818–38)

5 daughters

Alexander
(1835–89)
4th Baron Ashburton
m. 1864
Leonora Digby
(d. 1930)

Denzil
(1837–66)

1 daughter

Francis
(1866–1938)
5th Baron Ashburton

m. 1st 1889
Mabel Hood (d. 1904)

m. 2nd 1906
Frances Donnelly
(d. 1959)   no issue

Frederick
(1867–1961)
m. 1890
Laura Hobson
(d. 1951)

1 daughter

Alexander
(1869–1948)
unmarried

Guy
(1873–1916)
m. 1903
Olive Smith
(d. 1964)

5 sons
1 daughter

Caryl
(1880–1956)
m. 1907
Ivy Firman

1 son
1 daughter

2 daughters

Alexander
(1898–)
6th Baron Ashburton
m. 1924 Doris Harcourt

4 daughters

John
(1928–)

Robin
(1931–)

FIG. 4

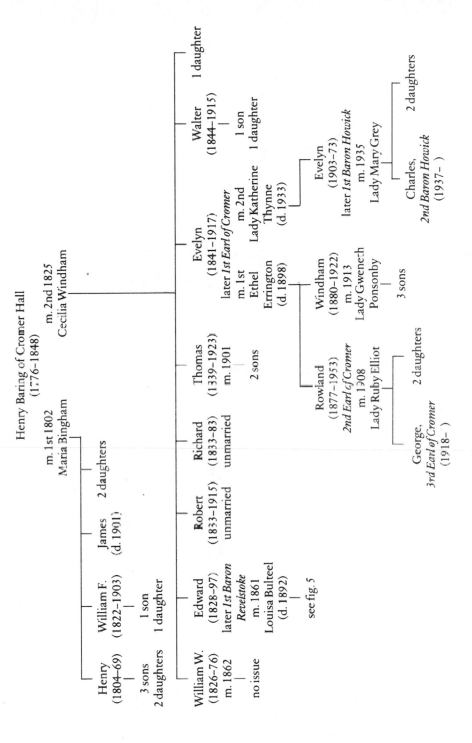

Henry Baring of Cromer Hall
(1776–1848)

m. 1st 1802   m. 2nd 1825
Maria Bingham   Cecilia Windham

Henry
(1804–69)
3 sons
2 daughters

William F.
(1822–1903)
1 son
1 daughter

James
(d. 1901)

2 daughters

William W.
(1826–76)
m. 1862
no issue

Edward
(1828–97)
later 1st Baron
Revelstoke
m. 1861
Louisa Bulteel
(d. 1892)

see fig. 5

Robert
(1833–1915)
unmarried

Richard
(1833–83)
unmarried

Thomas
(1839–1923)
m. 1901

2 sons

Evelyn
(1841–1917)
later 1st Earl of Cromer
m. 1st
Ethel
Errington
(d. 1898)

m. 2nd
Lady Katherine
Thynne
(d. 1933)

Walter
(1844–1915)
1 son
1 daughter

1 daughter

Rowland
(1877–1953)
2nd Earl of Cromer
m. 1908
Lady Ruby Elliot

Windham
(1880–1922)
m. 1913
Lady Gweneth
Ponsonby

3 sons

Evelyn
(1903–73)
later 1st Baron Howick
m. 1935
Lady Mary Grey

George,
3rd Earl of Cromer
(1918–)

2 daughters

Charles,
2nd Baron Howick
(1937–)

2 daughters

FIG. 5

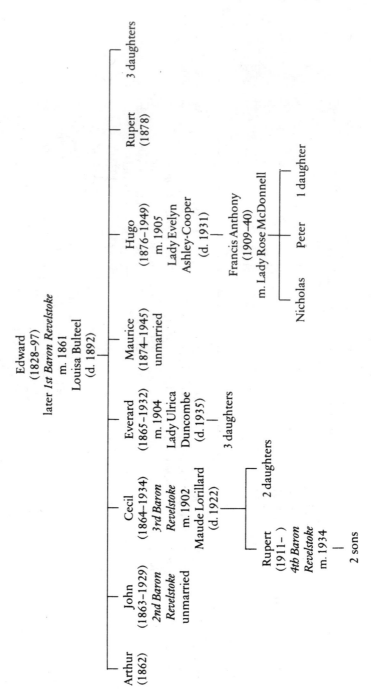

Edward
(1828–97)
later *1st Baron Revelstoke*
m. 1861
Louisa Bulteel
(d. 1892)

Arthur
(1862)

John
(1863–1929)
*2nd Baron
Revelstoke*
unmarried

Cecil
(1864–1934)
*3rd Baron
Revelstoke*
m. 1902
Maude Lorillard
(d. 1922)

Rupert
(1911–)
*4th Baron
Revelstoke*
m. 1934

2 sons

2 daughters

Everard
(1865–1932)
m. 1904
Lady Ulrica
Duncombe
(d. 1935)

3 daughters

Maurice
(1874–1945)
unmarried

Hugo
(1876–1949)
m. 1905
Lady Evelyn
Ashley-Cooper
(d. 1931)

Francis Anthony
(1909–40)
m. Lady Rose McDonnell

Nicholas   Peter   1 daughter

Rupert
(1878)

3 daughters

APPENDIX II

Partners of Baring Brothers & Co., 1762–1890 and Managing Directors of Baring Brothers & Co. Limited, 1890–1929

PARTNERS

Charles Baring	1762–1776
John Baring	1762–1800
Francis Baring (later Sir Francis, 1st Bt)	1762–1804
James Mesturas	1781–1795
Charles Wall	1781–1809
Thomas Baring (later Sir Thomas, 2nd Bt)	1804–1809
Henry Baring	1804–1823
Alexander Baring (later 1st Baron Ashburton)	1804–1830
John Deacon	1809–1823
Thomas Nixson	1809–1828
Swinton Holland	1815–1827
The Hon. Francis Baring (later 3rd Baron Ashburton)	1823–1864
Humphrey Mildmay	1824–1847
John Baring	1828–1837
Joshua Bates	1828–1864
Thomas Baring	1828–1873
Charles Baring Young	1843–1867
Russell Sturgis	1851–182
Edward Baring (later 1st Baron Revelstoke)	from 1856*
Henry Mildmay	from 1856*
Thomas C. Baring	1867–1888
James Price	1867–1870
William Moir	1867–c.1872
Kirkman Hodgson	1867–1878
Charles Norman	1867–1889

James Hodgson   from 1867*
The Hon. Francis Baring   from 1882*
Robert Hodgson   from 1882*
Archibald Norman   from 1890*
The Hon. John Baring (later 2nd Baron Revelstoke) from 1890*

MANAGING DIRECTORS

Thomas C. Baring   1890–1891
The Hon. Francis Baring   1890–1901
Robert Hodgson   1890–1908
The Hon. John Baring (later 2nd Baron Revelstoke) 1890–1929
Thomas (Tom) Baring   1892–1912
Walter Gair   1897–1920
Alfred Mildmay   1897–1940
Gaspard Farrer   1902–1925
Sydney Ward   1904–1933
The Hon. Windham Baring   1910–1922
The Hon. Cecil Baring (later 3rd Baron Revelstoke) 1911–1934
Patrick Shaw-Stewart   1913–1917
Viscount Errington (later 2nd Earl of Cromer)   1913–1916
The Hon. Arthur Villiers   1919–1954
Evelyn B. Baring   1923–1966
Edward Peacock (later Sir Edward, GCVO)   1924–1954
Sir Edward Reid (2nd baronet)   1926–1966
The Hon. Alexander Baring (later 6th Baron
    Ashburton)   1927–1969

* Continued beyond 1890 as partners of Baring Brothers & Co. but were not
necessarily directors of Baring Brothers & Co. Limited.

Baring Brothers & Co.
Capital, Profits and Losses, Commission Income and Total of Trial Balance, 1762–1890

Year	Capital	Distributed profit	Profit and loss	Total of trial balance	Accepting and other commission
1762	4200	—	—	—	—
1763	4765	423	423	13,879	49
1764	4368	353	353	11,421	258
1765	4500	601	601	23,564	414
1766	8237	−3091	−3091	26,878	584
1767	11,302	—	264	31,748	554
1768	13,075	900	900	47,947	849
1769	17,200	—	—	56,661	892
1770	17,016	—	—	81,402	1172
1771	19,687	3000	3000	87,289	1517
1772	17,849	−1500	—	93,241	1654
1773	19,323	—	—	86,708	1906
1774	19,296	—	—	91,517	2315
1775	19,718	600	1100	72,772	3002
1776	19,452	—	500	134,873	3105
1777	20,071	3000	3363	173,412	4248
1778	20,595	2400	1037	159,151	4563
1779	23,321	4000	4426	113,205	4484
1780	28,091	8000	7574	132,646	5021
1781	34,171	10,000	10,297	162,757	6289
1782	41,261	10,000	11,506	129,296	5894
1783	43,951	5000	7547	132,434	4645
1784	43,318	3000	532	185,835	5945
1785	46,477	5000	10,258	191,463	6839
1786	53,726	7000	8,374	205,276	5735
1787	59,797	8000	6153	333,149	5580
1788	74,923	16,160	11,854	277,161	3633
1789	71,997	600	4092	286,018	6236

Year	Capital	Distributed profit	Profit and loss	Total of trial balance	Accepting and other commission
1790	72,591	6300	3730	384,089	8237
1791	74,940	8400	9170	378,104	8043
1792	75,891	14,000	13,268	412,000	9868
1793	66,177	3500	8537	365,821	10,448
1794	76,317	16,100	13,696	407,852	12,573
1795	99,731	28,000	32,383	765,063	19,913
1796	130,156	40,000	37,746	1,875,167	20,732
1797	117,920	42,000	40,729	1,660,534	27,918
1798	138,223	40,000	40,833	1,845,699	20,485
1799	183,675	44,000	45,115	1,136,973	21,119
1800	220,445	66,018	66,753	1,690,966	16,781
1801	225,337	80,034	55,419	1,716,201	28,353
1802	413,576	210,352	211,166	2,260,930	28,237
1803	428,594	80,400	91,465	2,187,751	48,453
1804	399,168	20,000	18,352	1,923,101	20,969
1805	378,413	32,000	38,743	1,749,441	24,296
1806	449,899	50,000	51,874	1,795,895	29,204
1807	428,053	40,000	46,077	1,799,115	32,242
1808	274,843	40,000	36,115	2,585,934	25,078
1809	350,701	44,000	25,744	3,182,378	31,759
1810	413,606	26,000	39,718	3,421,615	37,373
1811	366,054	—	9811	2,927,419	27,193
1812	288,540	—	1006	2,810,508	30,894
1813	302,151	—	61,447	3,173,930	42,599
1814	322,192	80,000	53,968	3,284,573	50,958
1815	374,365	60,000	100,276	3,876,853	54,409
1816	355,823	9000	26,784	3,891,109	55,345
1817	416,060	45,000	87,875	3,633,173	48,351
1818	429,318	84,000	67,404	4,631,614	44,456
1819	484,022	20,000	39,175	3,777,842	45,152
1820	578,193	36,000	−6664	2,851,330	32,910
1821	621,943	72,000	133,107	3,127,263	28,507
1822	502,412	36,000	36,438	2,666,968	25,496
1823	226,146	46,200	36,456	2,004,815	17,783
1824	286,342	50,000	103,142	2,842,246	25,788
1825	452,654	120,000	135,374	2,424,997	31,414
1826	445,126	−65,000	−56,087	2,110,983	27,666
1827	384,429	20,000	35,378	1,846,278	29,666
1828	309,803	—	47,106	2,254,518	20,672

Year	Capital	Distributed profit	Profit and loss	Total of trial balance	Accepting and other commission
1829	392,459	68,996	25,655	2,195,373	26,294
1830	292,390	60,000	64,913	3,370,693	47,644
1831	326,424	48,000	53,612	3,795,927	47,611
1832	405,818	96,000	97,651	4,236,557	80,701
1833	525,542	132,000	118,766	4,592,313	110,800
1834	605,608	84,000	91,160	4,591,385	64,933
1835	674,018	84,000	129,220	4,886,608	85,261
1836	776,650	126,000	164,312	6,102,441	113,535
1837	776,798	18,000	−167,976	3,927,226	76,579
1838	637,746	72,000	64,413	3,666,675	71,549
1839	691,489	108,000	71,548	4,492,319	97,243
1840	756,201	162,000	121,085	3,685,164	103,423
1841	620,212	−100,000	118,111	3,770,390	69,178
1842	546,835	−36,000	9375	2,992,120	64,033
1843	497,767	—	−112,669	3,100,216	56,772
1844	501,944	36,000	50,294	3,050,421	62,619
1845	529,082	192,000	181,098	3,333,904	73,210
1846	589,908	108,000	30,812	3,756,499	78,073
1847	469,588	—	98,573	3,308,388	106,456
1848	477,055	114,000	11,209	3,238,857	88,128
1849	499,024	168,000	230,102	3,648,392	103,489
1850	589,613	144,000	159,441	4,546,428	115,989
1851	624,306	108,000	134,256	4,792,239	104,259
1852	865,235	192,000	286,486	6,106,027	127,395
1853	928,727	120,000	140,925	6,661,165	129,504
1854	1,007,142	120,000	180,811	6,424,494	156,692
1855	1,099,122	168,000	190,204	7,926,698	144,408
1856	1,182,535	96,000	210,456	6,957,396	191,732
1857	1,233,684	120,000	175,343	8,149,021	163,169
1858	1,349,550	192,000	181,609	7,754,924	168,799
1859	1,409,365	120,000	123,378	7,718,404	166,102
1860	1,266,451	145,043	125,777	9,385,914	148,714
1861	1,268,769	144,000	194,962	9,860,331	152,335
1862	1,409,061	216,000	217,863	9,234,183	139,503
1863	772,344	96,000	4944	9,228,457	138,297
1864	682,195	185,759	204,052	10,525,571	165,450
1865	627,597	240,000	299,096	11,477,768	161,341
1866	759,245	336,000	297,233	10,630,337	210,860
1867	1,388,379	360,000	438,572	12,186,022	269,994

Year	Capital	Distributed profit	Profit and loss	Total of trial balance	Accepting and other commission
1868	1,824,234	504,000	480,011	17,565,415	315,471
1869	2,072,413	360,000	446,828	n.a.	262,929
1870	2,098,772	144,000	293,749	n.a.	265,960
1871	2,403,129	504,000	334,153	n.a.	—
1872	2,498,130	266,000	376,716	n.a.	244,229
1873	2,193,845	388,500	242,352	n.a.	212,854
1874	1,991,244	140,000	237,958	n.a.	218,022
1875	1,628,765	—	141,757	n.a.	203,943
1876	1,724,293	210,000	102,553	n.a.	187,877
1877	1,725,362	280,000	149,573	n.a.	218,926
1878	1,811,082	280,000	278,630	n.a.	158,466
1879	1,904,063	350,000	264,440	n.a.	215,059
1880	1,855,269	175,000	223,642	n.a.	209,691
1881	2,222,495	210,000	218,728	n.a.	198,953
1882	2,159,904	240,000	237,410	n.a.	204,930
1883	1,981,200	120,000	173,779	n.a.	206,179
1884	1,898,745	90,000	124,970	n.a.	199,826
1885	2,157,368	300,000	218,556	n.a.	224,403
1886	2,463,719	480,000	515,445	n.a.	294,261
1887	2,620,292	360,000	319,142	n.a.	171,571
1888	3,102,368	600,000	643,165	n.a.	219,458
1889	2,452,438	362,000	442,915	27,987,327	282,756
1890	2,954,025	—	368,135	24,095,982	302,185

Baring Brothers & Co. Limited, 1890–1930
Balance Sheet and Profit and Loss Figures (1)

Year	Share capital at year end	Client accounts at year end	Bills accepted at year end	Gross profits (2)	Expenses (3)	Net profits (4)	Balance sheet total
1891	1,000,000	2,129,970	3,455,927	140,643	15,181	125,462	6,712,205
1892	1,000,000	2,251,041	3,876,582	221,684	42,626	179,058	7,379,094
1893	1,000,000	2,161,173	3,037,728	169,884	63,188	106,697	6,462,160
1894	1,000,000	2,901,571	3,608,382	150,366	41,351	109,015	7,750,963
1895	1,025,000	2,409,231	4,893,919	175,213	61,627	113,586	8,617,340
1896	1,025,000	2,551,920	4,515,542	192,400	45,172	147,228	8,459,742
1897	1,025,000	2,823,071	4,678,974	206,450	46,775	159,676	8,998,909
1898	1,025,000	3,201,575	3,557,178	220,677	45,814	174,863	8,296,458
1899	1,025,000	3,514,189	3,900,266	241,127	46,340	194,787	9,260,488
1900	1,025,000	3,382,858	4,532,186	205,408	50,320	155,088	9,577,939
1901	1,025,000	3,770,478	4,490,105	200,433	51,343	149,090	9,955,781
1902	1,025,000	5,201,506	4,714,587	202,212	55,024	147,188	11,634,016
1903	1,025,000	4,627,592	3,833,856	164,439	62,585	101,854	9,882,503
1904	1,025,000	4,835,183	6,201,543	315,322	57,341	257,981	12,593,064
1905	1,025,000	7,114,411	7,422,989	521,849	65,310	456,539	16,450,734
1906	1,025,000	11,415,022	7,373,608	257,357	65,608	191,748	20,810,151
1907	1,025,000	4,425,168	5,391,253	256,121	74,507	181,614	11,982,917
1908	1,025,000	4,863,246	6,938,568	607,254	68,573	538,682	14,328,409
1909	1,025,000	5,404,440	7,771,615	658,673	62,046	596,628	16,099,090
1910	1,025,000	7,526,339	7,498,544	448,571	70,592	377,980	17,813,790
1911	1,025,000	6,412,558	6,263,429	319,412	74,869	244,543	—
1912	1,025,000	5,840,123	6,810,846	289,718	79,117	210,602	15,518,288
1913	1,025,000	6,011,766	6,636,588	437,870	78,197	359,673	15,815,001
1914	1,025,000	9,481,297	3,723,682	282,200	103,387	178,813	16,238,785
1915	1,025,000	12,483,038	6,781,991	1,188,773	94,337	1,094,436	23,193,245
1916	1,025,000	14,484,896	4,613,591	852,667	88,475	764,192	23,353,310
1917	1,025,000	17,517,268	5,939,554	683,214	93,302	589,913	28,011,822
1918	1,025,000	15,728,333	3,077,331	502,048	89,039	413,008	23,469,826

Year	Share capital at year end	Client accounts at year end	Bills accepted at year end	Gross profits (2)	Expenses (3)	Net profits (4)	Balance sheet total
1919	1,025,000	23,240,711	11,257,865	441,592	183,550	258,042	38,701,625
1920	1,025,000	15,532,070	4,157,670	895,477	133,407	762,070	24,271,031
1921	1,025,000	16,977,543	8,283,430	697,889	133,067	564,822	29,765,651
1922	1,025,000	15,113,012	6,785,757	920,826	141,794	779,032	26,936,797
1923	1,025,000	13,469,571	5,512,430	823,650	133,786	689,863	23,727,350
1924	1,025,000	17,003,047	9,004,163	894,586	137,236	757,351	31,174,516
1925	1,025,000	23,044,315	10,205,631	767,164	142,122	625,042	38,477,181
1926	1,025,000	19,125,898	7,868,871	738,504	232,000	506,504	32,214,916
1927	1,025,000	18,897,751	7,780,572	809,841	233,496	576,344	32,142,596
1928	1,025,000	18,411,419	9,411,511	720,438	251,283	469,155	33,392,229
1929	1,025,000	16,366,036	6,780,601	646,724	240,761	405,963	28,807,904

NOTES

(1) The figures are extracted from the private balance sheets, and not the published balance sheets, but the two are broadly similar.

(2) Total gross profit is profit prior to deduction of counting houses expenses (salaries, office costs, etc.), bad debts written off, and transfers to reserves.

(3) These include counting house expenses, certain bad debts written off and Liverpool office losses but not transfers to reserves.

(4) Net profits are gross profits less expenses.

APPENDIX V

Baring Brothers & Co. Limited
Analysis of Gross Profits, 1890–1930

Year	Total gross profit (1)	Invest- ments (2)	Commis- sion (3)	Interest+ discount (4)	Russian accounts (5)	Barings' Liverpool office (6)	Other
1890–91	140,643	3255	98,061	38,431	—	192	704
1892	221,684	47,800	136,102	35,128	—	1154	1500
1893	169,884	4277	118,117	44,093	—	146	3251
1894	150,366	45,619	77,320	25,109	—	—	2318
1895	175,213	20,312	128,313	20,395	—	—	6193
1896	192,400	40,443	103,770	39,390	—	—	8797
1897	206,450	45,558	111,838	44,613	—	—	4441
1898	220,677	43,076	116,506	56,516	—	—	4579
1899	241,127	57,032	105,593	67,180	—	—	11,322
1900	205,408	47,504	92,170	56,933	—	—	8801
1901	200,433	35,251	106,051	55,679	—	—	3452
1902	202,212	8055	114,417	67,820	—	—	11,920
1903	164,439	—	93,506	61,855	—	—	9078
1904	315,322	148,232	110,558	49,700	—	—	6832
1905	521,849	334,099	122,679	54,774	—	—	10,297
1906	257,357	4203	124,341	67,700	—	—	61,113 (7)
1907	256,121	84,887	85,766	69,892	—	—	15,576
1908	607,235	253,411	83,970	97,307	—	—	172,547 (8)
1909	658,673	413,109	125,858	87,119	—	—	32,587 (9)
1910	448,570	220,785	120,027	96,407	—	—	11,351
1911	319,412	88,814	109,753	112,909	—	—	7936
1912	289,828	40,074	112,797	128,928	—	110	7919
1913	438,098	160,000	117,410	149,357	—	228	11,103
1914	282,200	18,026	126,651	130,799	—	—	6724
1915	1,188,772	153,061	149,043	142,253	718,089	—	26,326
1916	852,666	6433	160,818	148,045	517,992	—	19,378
1917	683,214	6326	172,563	366,987	135,555	—	1783

Year	Total gross profit (1)	Invest- ments (2)	Commis- sion (3)	Interest+ discount (4)	Russian accounts (5)	Barings' Liverpool office (6)	Other
1918	502,048	13,881	109,008	284,251	—	—	94,908 (10)
1919	441,592	—	171,501	266,594	—	—	3497
1920	895,495	51,036	303,111	505,430	—	—	35,918 (11)
1921	697,889	62,184	173,501	455,451	—	811	5942
1922	920,826	475,706	160,128	262,809	—	1836	5947
1923	823,650	249,739	165,380	324,929	—	4276	79,326 (12)
1924	894,586	345,799	198,911	299,568	—	7022	43,286 (13)
1925	767,164	106,108	276,462	367,525	—	3039	14,030
1926	738,504	94,016	218,513	419,174	—	937	5864
1927	809,841	233,105	203,451	364,571	—	1250	7464
1928	720,438	117,310	215,099	371,534	—	1937	14,558
1929	646,724	—	198,506	391,011	—	1180	56,025 (14)
1930	675,877	200,000	170,540	296,239	—	1182	7918

NOTES

(1) Total gross profit is profit prior to the deduction of counting houses expenses (salaries, office costs, etc.), bad debts and transfers to reserves.

(2) Investment income was derived from the issue, placing and dealing in securities. As from 1922 the account was known as British Government securities when commission arising out of issuing etc. was included as commission income.

(3) Commissions result from accepting, work as paying agents, purchase and sale of securities for clients, charges on client accounts, trusteeship work, provision of guarantees and bail bonds, etc.

(4) Interest and discount represents interest received on loans made less interest credited to client accounts, and monies received as a result of discounting bills of exchange.

(5) Commissions were regularly received for business undertaken for the Russian Government. These commissions were so large during the war years, they are shown separately.

(6) Barings' Liverpool office represents profits made by the Liverpool office and transferred to the profit and loss account.

(7) Inclusive of £43,000 transferred from Russian loan 1906 Account.

(8) Inclusive of £160,831 transferred from Russian loan 1906 Account.

(9) Inclusive of £19,784 recovered as a result of the liquidation of Baring & Co.

(10) Inclusive of £90,857 transferred from the Italira Reserve Account.

(11) Inclusive of £31,386 transferred from the Omsk Government Loan Account.

(12) Inclusive of £43,352 commission on coffee sales re Brazil loan and £35,583 re Government of Brazil advance.

(13) Inclusive of £27,649 and £6833 re above respectively.

(14) Inclusive of £50,000 transferred from Income Tax Account.

APPENDIX VI

Purchasing Power of the Pound Sterling, 1750–1980

In order to obtain an impression of the current value of sterling figures provided in the text, the following price index of consumer goods and services may be helpful. It should be used with caution and provides no more than the roughest of guides.

Jan. 1974=100

Year	Index	Year	Index
1750	6.6	1870	12.3
1760	7.2	1880	11.6
1770	8.0	1890	9.9
1780	8.2	1900	9.7
1790	9.8	1910	10.7
1800	17.6	1920	27.7
1810	18.8	1930	17.6
1820	15.2	1940	—
1830	12.9	1950	35.6
1840	14.5	1960	49.6
1850	10.9	1970	73.1
1860	12.1	1980	263.7

SOURCES
1750–1849: 'Seven Centuries of Price Consumables', *Economica* (Nov., 1956), p. 311; 1850–1913: Layton & Crowther, *The Study of Prices*, appendix E, table 1, p. 265; 1914–1980: *Long-term Index of Prices of Consumer Goods and Services*, Central Statistical Office.

BIBLIOGRAPHIC NOTES

The archives of Baring Brothers must surely be the most complete and extensive of any merchant bank in the British Isles. The first component, including many of the most important papers from the first fifty years of the bank's history, are not in fact properly part of the Baring archives at all. These are the papers deposited in Bishopsgate by Lord Northbrook, described in the reference notes as *Northbrook papers*. Most of the other Baring papers dating from before 1870 are at the time of writing to be found in the Guildhall and are described as *Baring Mss (G)*. Subsequent papers are still at Bishopsgate (*Baring Mss (B)*) and also at Bishopsgate are various collections, some earlier than 1870, some later, some most extensive and some consisting of only one or two documents, catalogued under *Baring Mss (B) DEP*. At one stage in the 1920s the archive was pillaged by a Canadian professor who removed several thousand pages, mainly papers of Canadian interest but some relating to the United States or Latin America. These are now in the Public Archives in Ottawa (*Baring Mss (O)*). A further small but important batch of Baring papers is in the possession of the Marquess of Northampton at Compton Wynyates (*Northampton papers*), while the Bank of England holds a number of papers concerning the Baring Crisis of 1890 (*Bank of England papers on Baring Crisis*). A copy of the diary of Mr Joshua Bates, one of Barings' most durable partners, is to be found in *Baring Mss (B) DEP*.

Outside the Baring archives the most relevant papers are undoubtedly those of Messrs Rothschilds. The papers of the London House are at the bank's headquarters at New Court in St Swithin's Lane (RAL). Though they have been sadly emasculated, the papers of the French house are also of limited use. They now form part of the Archives Nationales in the Cité des Archives contemporaines at Fontainbleau (RAF). Other manuscript collections of more than fleeting relevance are those of Lord Milner in the

Bodleian Library at Oxford; the Peel, Gladstone and Liverpool papers and the Hamilton diaries in the British Library; the papers of the 3rd Marquess of Salisbury at Hatfield House; the Gallatin collection in the Library of Congress; the Simon Gratz, Cadwalader and Bingham Collections in the Historical Society of Pennsylvania; the Rufus King and Brown Brothers papers in the New York Historical Society; and the Thomas W. Ward papers in the Massachusetts Historical Society.

Among published works John Orbell's *Baring Brothers and Co. Limited. A History to 1939* (privately printed, 1985) provides a lucid and reliable introduction to the history of the house. Ralph Hidy's *The House of Baring in American Trade and Finance* (New York, 1949) is the somewhat indigestible fruit of a heroic trawl through the documents relating to this aspect of Barings' affairs. Professor Platt's *Foreign Finance in Continental Europe and the USA 1815–1870* (London, 1984) makes excellent use of Barings' archives for this period. Professor Fern's *Britain and Argentina in the Nineteenth Century* (Oxford, 1960) deals extensively with the affairs of Barings and in particular has a chapter on the 1890 Crisis which he is now developing into a book – some of which he has most generously allowed me to see in typescript. On a more personal level, Daphne Pollen's *I Remember, I Remember* (privately printed, 1983) and Bernard Mallet's *Thomas George, Earl of Northbrook* (London, 1906) both add useful information about the banking members of the family.

It would be a work of supererogation to list all the books which are referred to in the notes. Among the general studies which I found of particular value are Stanley Chapman's *The Rise of Merchant Banking* (London, 1984), P. L. Cottrell's *British Overseas Investment in the Nineteenth Century* (London, 1975), Leland Jenks's *The Migration of British Capital to 1975* (London, 1927) and D. C. M. Platt's *Finance, Trade, and Politics in British Foreign Policy 1815–1914* (Oxford, 1968). Sir John Clapham's *The Bank of England* (Cambridge, 1944) and R. S. Sayers's *The Bank of England 1891–1944* (Cambridge, 1976) were both highly relevant. Among the studies of other banks I would mention Aytoun Ellis's *Heir of Adventure. The Story of Brown, Shipley and Co.* (privately printed, 1960); E. H. Allman's *William Deacon's* (Manchester, 1971); Roger Fulford's *Glyn's* (London, 1953) – most pleasantly written of all such books; Bo Bramsen and Kathleen

Wain's *The Hambros* (London, 1979); Martin Buist's *At Spes non Fracta. Hope and Co.* (Amsterdam, 1974), Vincent Carosso's *More Than a Century of Investment Banking. The Kidder, Peabody and Co. Story* (New York, 1979) and *The Morgans* (Boston, 1986); Frederick Allan's *The Great Pierpont Morgan*; Bertrand Gille's *Histoire de la Maison Rothschild* (Geneva, 1965) – much the most considerable of the innumerable studies of this bank, and Richard Davis's *The English Rothschilds* (London, 1982) – most interesting but concentrating heavily on the family's political and social role.

NOTES

CHAPTER 1 (pp. 13–24)

1. Northbrook papers. D.
2. *Public Characters of 1805* (London, 1805), p. 30.
3. The early history of the Baring family has been painstakingly assembled by Miss Anne-Cecilia Baring.
4. Charles Wilson, *Anglo-Dutch Commerce and Finance in the Eighteenth Century* (Cambridge, 1941), p. 40. See also W. G. Hoskins, *Industry, Trade and People in Exeter* (Manchester, 1935).
5. Hoskins, op. cit., p. 42.
6. Northbrook papers. G3.
7. Robert Dymond, *History of the Suburban Parish of St Leonard, Exeter* (Exeter, 1873), p. 19.
8. *He Knew He Was Right* (London, 1868; World's Classic Edition, 1948), p. 58.
9. *He Knew He Was Right* (London, 1868; World's Classic Edition), p. 65.
10. Elizabeth Baring to Nath. Paice, 13 Dec. 1763. Northbrook papers. G11.
11. *Public Characters of 1809* (London, 1809), pp. 590–1.
12. Northbrook papers. G1. 1.
13. Northbrook papers. G6. 1.
14. Northbrook papers. G3.
15. Francis Baring's Account Book. Baring Mss (B) HC1. 204. 31.
16. Elizabeth to Francis Baring, 31 March 1766. Northbrook papers. G11.
17. *The Farington Diary*, ed. James Greig (London, 1926), vol. VI, p. 137.
18. Memorandum by Francis Baring. Northbrook papers. D1.
19. Northbrook papers. G3.
20. Charles to Francis Baring, 22 March 1800. Northbrook papers. D8.
21. Francis to Charles Baring, 14 April 1800. Northbrook papers. D8.
22. Northbrook papers. A14.
23. Francis to Charles Baring, 14 April 1800. Northbrook papers. D8.
24. Francis to Charles Baring, 14 April 1800. Northbrook papers. D8.
25. Memorandum by Francis Baring. Northbrook papers. D1.
26. Memorandum by Francis Baring. Northbrook papers. D1.
27. Francis to Charles Baring, 14 April 1800. Northbrook papers. D8.

CHAPTER 2 (pp. 25–42)

1. Francis Baring's Account Book. Baring Mss (B) HC1. 204. 31.
2. Northbrook papers. G3.
3. *Public Characters of 1805* (London, 1805), p. 38.
4. John Lewis Mallet, unpublished 'Autobiographical Retrospect'. Baring Mss (B), p. 3.
5. John Lewis Mallet, unpublished 'Autobiographical Retrospect'. Baring Mss (B), pp. 4–5.
6. See chapter 4 below. Ralph W. Hidy, *The House of Baring in*

American Trade and Finance (New York, 1949) provides the fullest picture of this development.

7. Viscount D'Abernon, *Portraits and Appreciations* (London, 1931), pp. 14–15.

8. Bernard Mallet, *Thomas George, Earl of Northbrook* (London, 1908), p. 291.

9. Christopher Sandeman, *No Music in Particular* (London, 1943), p. 82.

10. *The Letters and Private Papers of William Makepeace Thackeray, Vol II*, ed. Gordon Ray (London, 1945), p. 647.

11. Mallet, *Northbrook*, op. cit., p. 15.

12. 4 Nov. 1787. Northbrook papers. N4. 5. 17.

13. Martin G. Buist, *At Spes Non Fracta. Hope and Co. 1770–1815* (Amsterdam, 1974), pp. 33–4.

14. John Mallet, 'Autobiographical Retrospect', op. cit., pp. 3–4.

15. William Hope to Francis Baring, 26 Jan. 1790. Northbrook papers. A 1.

16. Lansdowne to Francis Baring, 5 Aug. 1786. Northbrook papers. N4. 4.

17. Adam Shortt, 'The Barings', unpublished thesis. National Archives, Ottawa. MG 30. D101. Vol. 60, p. 58.

18. Buist, *At Spes Non Fracta*, op. cit., pp. 33–4.

19. Jan. 1786. Northbrook papers. N4. 4. 337.

20. Lord Brougham, *Historical Sketches of Statesmen who flourished in the Time of George III. Vol. II* (London, 1856), pp. 325–34.

21. *Farington Diary*, op. cit., vol. III, p. 259.

22. Northbrook papers. B1.

23. Shelburne to Francis Baring, 16 Sept. 1782 and Baring to Shelburne, 24 Sept. 1782. Northbrook papers. N4. 3.

24. Francis Baring to Shelburne, June 1783. Northbrook papers. N4. 3.

25. 13 Dec. 1784. Northbrook papers. N4. 3. 231.

26. *Cobbett's Weekly Register* (17 July 1824), p. 132.

27. Memorandum of May 1783. Northbrook papers. A 23.

28. Francis Baring to Shelburne, 4 Dec. 1784. Northbrook papers. N4. 4. 224.

29. Northbrook papers. N4. 4. 346.

30. John Ehrman, *The Younger Pitt. Vol. I* (London, 1969), pp. 242–5.

31. 4 Aug. 1784. Bowood Mss.

32. Francis Baring to Dundas, 7 April 1793. Northbrook papers. N4. 5. 225.

33. 6 Feb. 1806.

34. Lansdowne to Francis Baring, 11 Nov. 1785. Northbrook papers. N4. 4. 318.

35. Hoskins, *Industry, Trade and People in Exeter*, op. cit., p. 44.

36. Northbrook papers. G3. cf. Baring Mss (B) DEP 17.

37. Baring Mss (B) DEP 17.

38. *The Correspondence of George, Prince of Wales*, ed. A. Aspinall (London, 1964), vol. II, p. 112.

39. Baring Mss (B) HC1. 204. 3a.

40. 7 May 1785. Northbrook papers. N4. 4. 295.

41. *Daily Advertiser, Oracle and True Briton* (12 Oct. 1805).

42. *Public Characters of 1805* (London, 1805), p. 34.

43. 'Notes on a Commercial Treaty with the United States'.

44. 20 Nov. 1783. Northbrook papers. N4. 4. 127.

45. Sir N. W. Wraxall, *Posthumous Memoirs of His Own Time. Vol. 1* (London, 1836), p. 118.

46. C. H. Philips, *The East India Company 1784–1834* (Manchester, 1961), pp. 25–63.

47. Dundas to Pitt, 18 Oct. 1792. PRO 30/8/157.

48. Ehrman, *The Younger Pitt*, op. cit., vol. I, pp. 458–66.

49. May 1793. Northbroook papers.

N4. 4. 293.

50. ? Jan. 1786. Northbrook papers. N4. 4. 337.
51. Hidy, *The House of Baring*, op. cit., pp. 20-1.
52. cit., Norman Baker, *Government and Contractors* (London, 1971), p. 242.
53. Northbrook papers. N4. 4. 255.
54. Baker, *Government and Contractors*, op. cit., pp. 146-7.
55. Baker, *Government and Contractors*, p. 140.

CHAPTER 3 (pp. 43-60)

1. Copy of memorandum in Bingham Collection. Historical Society of Pennsylvania. f64.
2. *Farington Diary*, op. cit., vol. III, p. 261.
3. *Farington Diary*, op. cit., vol. VI, pp. 187-9.
4. Charles to John Baring, 3 March 1801. Northbrook papers. D7.
5. Charles to Francis Baring, 4 March 1801. Northbrook papers. D7.
6. Francis to Charles Baring, 7 March 1801. Northbrook papers. D7.
7. Francis Baring to William Bingham, 6 Jan. 1803. Northbrook papers. B3. I.
8. Francis Baring to William Bingham, 6 Jan. 1803. Northbrook papers. B3. I.
9. Voûte to Francis Baring, 4 June 1793. Northbrook papers. A I.
10. General David Cobb to Bingham, cit. Robert C. Alberts, *The Golden Voyage. The Life and Times of William Bingham* (Boston, 1969), pp. 270-1.
11. Robert Gilmor, *The Golden Voyage*, op. cit., p. 311.
12. *Extracts of the Journals and Correspondence of Miss Berry*, ed.

Lady Theresa Lewis (London, 1905), vol. II, p. 344.
13. Francis Baring to William Bingham, 6 Jan. 1803. Northbrook papers. B3. I.
14. Alexander to Francis Baring, 13 Oct. 1801. Baring Mss (B) DEP 3. III.
15. Francis Baring to William Bingham, 6 Jan. 1803. Northbrook papers. B3. I.
16. *The Memoirs of Vincent Nolte*, translated from the German (New York, 1931), p. 158.
17. Alexander to Thomas Baring, April 1824. Northbrook papers. E7 c.
18. *The Journal of the Hon. Henry Edward Fox*, ed. Earl of Ilchester (London, 1946), p. 131.
19. David Lance to Francis Baring, 3 Nov. 1803. Northbrook papers. B3. IV.
20. William to Francis Baring, 3 Jan. 1806. Northbrook papers. B3 i.
21. Henry to Thomas Baring, 28 Sept. 1815. Northbrook papers. B3. VIII.
22. Alexander to Thomas Baring, 10 June 1827. Northbrook papers. E7 d.
23. *The Journal of the Hon. Henry Edward Fox*, op. cit., p. 318.
24. 14 Jan. 1806. Baring Mss (B) DEP 3. Part III.
25. Francis Baring to Count Louis Stahremberg, 8 Oct. 1807. Northbrook papers. A21.
26. Baring Mss (B) DEP 22. VII.
27. Edwyn and Josephine Birchenough, *The Manor House, Lee, and its Associations* (Lewisham, 1971). cf. A. W. Wood, 'Lee and the Northbrook family'. Copy in Baring Mss (B) DEP 22. VII.
28. H. R. Fox-Bourne, *English Merchants. Vol. II* (London, 1866), p. 240.
29. A. W. Wood, 'Lee and the

Northbrook family', op. cit.

30. F. M. L. Thompson, *English Landed Society in the Nineteenth Century* (London, 1963), p. 89.

31. John Francis, *Chronicles and Characters of the Stock Exchange* (Boston, 1850), p. 75.

32. *Farington Diary*, op. cit., vol. III, p. 261.

33. Northbrook papers. A21.

34. *Farington Diary*, op. cit., vol. III, p. 303.

35. *Farington Diary*, op. cit., vol. IV, p. 134.

36. *Farington Diary*, op. cit., vol. V, p. 114.

37. Francis Baring to Pierre César Labouchère, 9 Oct. 1804. Northbrook papers. A4. 3.

38. Northbrook papers. A9.

39. Francis Baring to Rufus King, 4 Jan. 1808. Rufus King papers. New York Historical Society. Box 1805–8.

40. Philips, *The East India Company*, op. cit., p. 148.

41. Philips, *The East India Company*, op. cit., p. 9.

42. Thompson, *English Landed Society*, op. cit., p. 51.

43. 1 Oct. 1809. *The Letters of Sydney Smith*, ed. Nowell C. Smith (Oxford, 1953), p. 153.

44. *Gentleman's Magazine* (1810), p. 293.

45. Francis Baring to William Bingham, 17 Sept. 1799. Northampton papers.

46. Undated memorandum. Northbrook papers. B.

47. Northbrook papers. A23.

48. 23 Oct. 1802. *The Life and Letters of William Cobbett*, ed. Lewis Melville (London, 1913), vol. I, p. 172.

49. Barings to William Bingham, 11 Sept. 1801. Northampton papers.

50. Francis to John Baring, 13 Nov. 1805. Northbrook papers. D4.

51. 10 Jan. 1794. Northbrook papers. A1.

52. Henry Hope to Francis Baring, 10 Jan. 1794. Northbrook papers. A1. cf. Buist, *At Spes Non Fracta*, op. cit., pp. 48–50.

53. Nolte, *Memoirs*, op. cit., p. 112.

54. Nolte, *Memoirs*, op. cit., p. 50. cf. Algar Thorold, *The Life of Henry Labouchère* (London, 1913), pp. 11–12.

55. See p. 46.

56. Otto Wolff, *Ouvrard: Speculator of Genius* (London, 1962), pp. 112–13. cf. Thorold, *Labouchère* op. cit., pp. 6–11.

57. Alexander to Sir Thomas Baring, 4 Jan. 1817. Northbrook papers. E 7a. I.

58. 9 March 1797. Northbrook papers. A19.

59. Francis Baring to William Stephens, 14 March 1797. Northbrook papers. A19.

60. Francis Baring to William Stephens, 12 Dec. 1801. Northbrook papers. A19.

61. Labouchère to Francis Baring, 17 Feb. 1802. Northbrook papers. A19.

62. Francis Baring to Labouchère, 12 March 1802. Northbrook papers. A19.

63. Francis Baring to Stahremberg, 13 Feb. 1800. Northbrook papers. A21.

64. Francis Baring to Stahremberg, 21 June 1809. Northbrook papers. A21.

65. Canning to Stahremberg, 23 June 1809. Northbrook papers. A21.

66. Francis to Alexander Baring, 20 May 1799. Baring Mss (B) DEP 3. III.

67. 29 Oct. 1803. Northbrook papers. A20.

68. C. Gore to Rufus King, 16 Nov. 1803. Rufus King papers, op. cit. Box 1803–1804.

69. J. C. Herries to A. Rosenhagen, 25 Nov. 1813. RAL X1/T37/4.

70. I am indebted to Professor Platt for these statistics, who derived

them from P. K. O'Brien's unpublished D.Phil. thesis, 'Government Revenue, 1793–1813' (Oxford, 1967).

71. A. F. Fremantle, *England in the Nineteenth Century* (London, 1930), pp. 316–18. cf. Denis Gray, *Spencer Perceval* (Manchester, 1963), pp. 370–5.

72. 29 Sept. 1810.

73. *Weekly Political Register*, vol. XVIII, no. 16 (3 Oct. 1810).

74. Francis Baring to Burke, 17 Oct. 1792. BM Add Mss 29172. f458.

75. William Foster, *The East India House* (London, 1924), p. 176.

76. William Foster, *The East India House* (London, 1924), pp. 137–8.

77. 2 April 1800. Northbrook papers. N4. 5.

78. Philips, *The East India Company*, op. cit., p. 157.

79. Philips, *The East India Company*, op. cit., p. 164.

80. 12 June 1802. Rufus King papers, op. cit. Box 1798–1802.

81. *Journals and Correspondence of F. T. Baring*, ed. Lord Northbrook (London, 1905), p. 10.

82. *Illustrated London News* (21 Oct. 1843).

83. Henry Baring to Robert Peel, 4 Feb. 1846. Peel papers. BM Add Mss 40584. f26.

84. See Leland Jenks, *The Migration of British Capital to 1875* (London, 1927), p. 18.

85. Richard Kellett, *The Merchant Banking Arena* (London, 1967), p. 10.

CHAPTER 4 (pp. 61–77)

1. Robert Morris to John and Francis Baring, 17 April 1783. Baring Mss (O) MG 30. D101.

2. Bingham to Thos. FitzSimons, 29 Nov. 1783. Gratz Collection. Historical Society of Pennsylvania. Case 1. Box 3.

3. Barings to Rufus King, 28 Aug. 1796. Rufus King papers, op. cit. Vol. 39, f5.

4. Barings to Rufus King, 28 Dec. 1796. Rufus King papers, vol. 39, f12.

5. Barings to Rufus King, 6 June 1797. Rufus King papers, vol. 39, f17.

6. Barings to Rufus King, 20 July 1797. Rufus King papers, vol. 39, f19.

7. Rufus King to Barings and Co., 6 Oct. 1798. Rufus King papers, vol. 51, f461.

8. Barings to Rufus King, 22 Dec. 1799. Rufus King papers, vol. 39, f62.

9. Hidy, *The House of Baring*, op. cit., p. 32.

10. Baring Mss (B) DEP 3. cf. Alberts, *The Golden Voyage*, op. cit., pp. 229–50.

11. Alexander Baring to Barings, 12 Dec. 1797. Baring Mss (B) DEP 3. II.

12. Alberts, *The Golden Voyage*, op. cit., p. 252.

13. Nolte, *Memoirs*, op. cit., p. 159.

14. Alberts, *The Golden Voyage*, op. cit., p. 265.

15. Alexander Baring to John Williams Hope, 30 April 1798. Baring Mss (B) DEP 3. II.

16. Alberts, *The Golden Voyage*, op. cit., p. 276.

17. Alexander Baring to Hopes. Baring Mss (B) DEP 3. I.

18. Memorandum by Lord Ashburton of Nov. 1846. Northbrook papers. G8. 1.

19. 29 Nov. 1796. Baring Mss (B) DEP 3. II. 40.

20. 1 June 1797. Baring Mss (B) DEP 3. II. 40.

21. Obituary of Lord Ashburton (15 May 1848).

22. J. A. Froude, *Thomas Carlyle. Vol. I* (London, 1884), p. 348.

23. 'Notes and Recollections'. Baring Mss (B) DEP 135.
24. Alberts, *The Golden Voyage*, op. cit., p. 346.
25. *Spectator* (30 April 1864).
26. Alexander Baring to John Williams Hope, 8 Dec. 1795. Baring Mss (B) DEP 3. III.
27. Alexander Baring to Henry Hope, 9 Jan. 1797. Baring Mss (B) DEP 3. II. 43.
28. 20 Jan. 1799. Baring Mss (B) DEP 3. III.
29. Alexander Baring to Hopes, 31 Dec. 1797. Baring Mss (B) DEP 3. II.
30. Alexander to Francis Baring, 29 March 1801. Baring Mss (B) DEP 3. III.
31. Alexander Baring to Hopes, 10 Jan. 1797. Baring Mss (B) DEP 3. II.
32. Alexander to Francis Baring, 20 Jan. 1799. Baring Mss (B) DEP 3. III.
33. Francis to Alexander Baring, 9 March 1799. Baring Mss (B) DEP 3. III.
34. Alexander to Francis Baring, 20 Jan. 1799. Baring Mss (B) DEP 3. III.
35. Francis Baring to Thomas Willing, 3 July 1793. Gratz Collection, op. cit. Case 13. Box 20/3.
36. Francis Baring to Thomas Willing, 13 Aug. 1795. Gratz Collection, op. cit. Case 13. Box 20/3.
37. Alexander to Francis Baring, 1 Feb. 1799. Baring Mss (B) DEP 3. III.
38. 17 Feb. 1803. Rufus King papers, op. cit. Vol. 55. ff378-9.
39. 12 Nov. 1800. Northampton papers.
40. Alexander to Francis Baring, 19 Nov. 1797. Baring Mss (B) DEP 3. II.
41. Willing to Bingham, 22 June 1802. Northampton papers.
42. 4 Feb. 1804. Gallatin Collection. Library of Congress. Reel 9.
43. Bingham to Willing, 22 May 1802. Gratz Collection, op. cit. Case 13. Box 20.
44. *L'Annexion de la Louisianie. Revue d'Histoire Diplomatique* (1916) vol. XXX.
45. King to Robert Livingston, 16 May 1803. Rufus King papers, op. cit. Box 1803-1804.
46. J. E. Winston, 'How the Louisiana Purchase was Financed', *The Louisiana Historical Quarterly* (April, 1929), vol. 12, no. 2.
47. Francis Baring to Henry Addington, 12 Nov. 1803. Northbrook papers. A4.
48. 15 Feb. 1803. Northbrook papers. A4/1.
49. 21 April 1803. Northbrook papers. A4.
50. Note by Francis Baring, 19 June 1803. Northbrook papers. A4.
51. Francis Baring to Robert Gilmor, 15 Aug. 1803. Northbrook papers. A4.
52. Henry Addington to Francis Baring, 16 Dec. 1803. Northbrook papers. A4.
53. 23 Dec. 1803. Northbrook papers. A4.
54. 26 Dec. 1803. Northbrook papers. A4.
55. Alberts, *The Golden Voyage*, op. cit., p. 434.
56. 21 July 1804. Northbrook papers. A4.
57. Nolte, *Memoirs*, op. cit., p. 92.
58. Alexander Baring to C. W. Hare, 21 Oct. 1807. Cadwalader papers. Historical Society of Pennsylvania. Box 2.
59. Alexander Baring, *An Inquiry into the Causes and Consequences of the Orders in Council and An Examination of the Conduct of Great Britain towards the Neutral Commerce of America* (London, 1808), pp. 4, 21 and 177.

60. Baring, *An Inquiry into the Causes
. . .*, op. cit., p. 1.
61. 10 March 1808, *Hansard*, vol. X.
1058–62. cf. Gray, *Spencer
Perceval*, op. cit., p. 173.
62. 6 August 1808.
63. 2 May 1809. Rufus King papers,
op. cit. Box 1809–13.
64. Hidy, *House of Baring*, op. cit.,
pp. 51–2.
65. 22 July 1813. *A Great Peace
Maker. The Diary of James
Gallatin*, ed. Count Gallatin
(London, 1914), pp. 281–3.
66. Henry Adams, *The Life of Albert
Gallatin* (New York, 1943),
pp. 496–9.
67. 11 April 1814. *A Great Peace
Maker*, op. cit., p. 14.
68. 3 July 1815. *A Great Peace Maker*,
op. cit., p. 14.
69. Adams, *Gallatin*, op. cit., p. 552.
70. Instructions of 19 June 1817,
Cadwalader papers, op. cit. Box 2.
1.
71. Hidy, *House of Baring*, op. cit.,
p. 71.
72. Thomas Payne Govan, *Nicholas
Biddle* (Chicago, 1959), p. 81.
73. Hidy, *House of Baring*, op. cit.,
p. 69.
74. Gratz Collection, op. cit. 'Baring
Brothers'.
75. Jenks, *Migration of British Capital*,
op. cit., p. 75.
76. Baring Brothers to Gen. T.
Cadwalader, 25 June 1824.
Cadwalader papers, op. cit. Box
15.
77. Baring Brothers to Gen. T.
Cadwalader, 14 Dec. 1825.
Cadwalader papers, op. cit. Box
15.
78. Baring Brothers to Gen. T.
Cadwalader, 18 Feb. 1826.
Cadwalader papers, op. cit. Box
15.
79. Baring Brothers to Gen. T.
Cadwalader, 14 May 1827.
Cadwalader papers, op. cit. Box 15.
80. Jenks, *Migration of British Capital*,

op. cit., p. 67.
81. Kenneth Porter, *John Jacob Astor.
Vol. I* (New York, 1966), p. 310.
82. Nolte, *Memoirs*, op. cit., p. 286.
83. Joshua Bates to T. W. Ward, 7
Nov. 1830. T. W. Ward papers.
Massachusetts Historical Society.

CHAPTER 5 (pp. 78–99)

1. 4 Aug. 1801. Northbrook papers.
A9.
2. D. C. M. Platt, *Foreign Finance in
Continental Europe and the USA
1815–1870* (London, 1984), p. 6.
3. *Mémoires de la Comtesse de Boigne.
Vol. II* (Paris, 1907), p. 246.
4. Francis Baring to J. L. Mallet, 14
Sept. 1826, cit. *Journals and
Correspondence of Francis Thornhill
Baring, Lord Northbrook*, ed.
Thomas, Earl of Northbrook
(London, 1905), vol. I, p. 49.
5. Otto Wolff, *Ouvrard*, op. cit.,
p. 137.
6. Paul Emden, *Money Powers of
Europe in the 19th and 20th
Centuries* (London, 1937), p. 9.
7. *Mémoires de la Comtesse de Boigne*,
op. cit., p. 247.
8. J. E. Cookson, *Lord Liverpool's
Administration* (Edinburgh, 1975),
p. 27.
9. Nolte, *Memoirs*, op. cit., p. 265.
10. *Mémoires de la Comtesse de Boigne*,
op. cit., p. 254.
11. Talleyrand to the Duchesse de
Courlande, 30 Jan. 1817, cit.
Lacour-Gayet, *Talleyrand. Vol. III*
(Paris, 1947), p. 72.
12. 6 Dec. 1816. *Supplementary
Despatches of the Duke of
Wellington. Vol. XI* (London,
1864), pp. 562–5.
13. Castlereagh to Wellington, 17
Jan. 1817. *Supplementary
Despatches . . ., Vol. XI*, pp. 600–1.
14. Wellington to Castlereagh, 3 Feb.
1817. *Supplementary Despatches
. . ., Vol. XI*, p. 619.

15. See, in particular, Professor Platt's lucid exposition in *Foreign Finance in Continental Europe*, op. cit., pp. 7–11.
16. Baring to Wellington, 4 Dec. 1817. *Supplementary Despatches . . ., Vol. XII* (London, 1865), p. 171.
17. 16 Jan. 1817 and 17 Dec. 1816 respectively, cit. Jenks, *Migration of British Capital*, op. cit., p. 36.
18. 4 Feb. 1818. *Supplementary Despatches . . ., Vol. XII*, pp. 247–9.
19. 1 March 1817. RAL T27/212.
20. James to Salomon Rothschild, 3 March 1817. RAL T27/213.
21. 9 Aug. 1817. RAL T27/292.
22. James to Nathan Rothschild, 11 Oct. 1817. RAL T27/297.
23. James to Nathan Rothschild, 17 Dec. 1817. RAL T63 46/1.
24. James to Nathan Rothschild, 9 Feb. 1818. RAL T64/174.
25. James to Nathan Rothschild, 14 Feb. 1818. RAL T64/174.
26. Salomon Rothschild to London Cousins, 24 Feb. 1818. RAL T64/158/2.
27. Bertrand Gille, *Histoire de la Maison Rothschild* (Geneva, 1965), p. 64.
28. Baring to Wellington, 27 May 1818. *Supplementary Despatches . . ., Vol. XII*, op. cit., pp. 526–8.
29. Liverpool to Wellington, 9 June 1818. *Supplementary Despatches . . ., Vol. XII*, pp. 539–40.
30. Baring to Wellington, 30 Oct. 1818. *Supplementary Despatches . . ., Vol. XII*, p. 789.
31. Elizabeth Longford, *Wellington, Pillar of State* (London, 1972), p. 59.
32. 16 July 1819. Ms Autobiographical Memoirs of Swinton Holland. Baring Mss (B) DEP 22. XV.
33. 13 Nov. 1825. Rufus King papers, op. cit. Box 1825–26.
34. Thomas Moore, *Memoirs, Journal and Correspondence*, ed. Lord John Russell (London, 1854), vol. V, p. 66.
35. 6 Nov. 1814. *The Letters of Richard Brinsley Sheridan*, ed. Cecil Price (Oxford, 1966), vol. III, p. 203.
36. Emily Eden to Miss Villiers, July 1827. *Miss Eden's Letters*, ed. Violet Dickinson (London, 1919), p. 128.
37. 28 Dec. 1826. *A Great Peace Maker*, op. cit., p. 624.
38. 18 Jan. 1826. *The Diary of Colonel Peter Hawker. Vol. 1* (London, 1893), p. 290.
39. Thompson, *English Landed Society*, op. cit., pp. 36–8.
40. William Cobbett, *Rural Rides*, ed. Pitt Cobbett (London, 1885), vol. I, pp. 251 and 396.
41. Mallet, *Northbrook*, op. cit., p. 10.
42. Thompson, *English Landed Society*, op. cit., p. 38.
43. *Rural Rides*, op. cit., vol. I, pp. 129–30.
44. Emily Eden to Miss Villiers, 4 June 1819. *Miss Eden's Letters*, op. cit., p. 35.
45. Marianne Thornton to Hannah Moore, 29 Dec. 1825. *William Deacon's 1771–1970*, ed. A. H. Allman (Manchester, 1971), p. 81.
46. W. D. Rubinstein, *Men of Property* (London, 1981), p. 92.
47. *The Creevey Papers*, ed. Herbert Maxwell, vol. II (London, 1904), p. 11.
48. 6 April 1826, *Hansard* NS.15. 100–3.
49. Cookson, *Lord Liverpool's Administration*, op. cit., p. 21.
50. Chester New, *Life of Henry Brougham* (Oxford, 1961), pp. 163–6.
51. 6 March 1828, *Hansard* NS. 18. 1033–40.
52. cit. Stanley Chapman, *The Rise of Merchant Banking* (London, 1984), p. 30.
53. Lord Houghton, *Monographs Personal and Social* (London, 1873), p. 234.

54. Roger Fulford, *Glyn's* (London, 1953), p. 69.

55. Alberts, *The Golden Voyage*, op. cit., p. 437.

56. 12 May 1823. *Elizabeth Lady Holland to her Son*, ed. The Earl of Ilchester (London, 1946), p. 23.

57. Nolte, *Memoirs*, op. cit., pp. 281–2.

58. Labouchère to Thomas Baring. Undated. Northbrook papers. A13.

59. Alexander Baring to T. Cadwalader, 11 Oct. 1823. Cadwalader papers, op. cit. Box 2.

60. Alexander to Thomas Baring, 4 Jan. 1817. Northbrook papers E7. 1.

61. Thomas to Tom and John Baring, 3 Oct. 1825. Baring Mss (B) DEP 193. 39.

62. Thomas to Tom and John Baring, probably Nov. 1825. Baring Mss (B) DEP 193. 39.

63. Autobiographical Memoir. Baring Mss (B) DEP 22 XV.

64. Cobbett, *Rural Rides*, op. cit., vol. II, p. 151.

65. James de Rothschild to Alexander Baring, 13 March 1824. Baring Mss (G) MS 18321. HC7. 7. 1.

66. Gille, *Maison Rothschild*, op. cit., pp. 136–9.

67. May 1824. Baring Mss (G) MS 18321. HC2. 576.

68. James to Nathaniel Rothschild, 9 April 1818. RAL T64/338/3.

69. Carl to James Rothschild, 13 April 1818. RAL T64/202/3.

70. H. Sillem to Alexander Baring, 25 June 1822. Baring Mss (G) Ms 18321. HC8. 3.

71. Autobiographical Memoir, op. cit., 18 July 1821.

72. Chapman, *Rise of Merchant Banking*, op. cit., p. 40.

73. Gille, *Maison Rothschild*, op. cit., p. 67.

74. *Don Juan*, Canto XII, verse V.

75. Chapman, *Rise of Merchant Banking*, op. cit., p. 40.

76. *Hansard* NS 41. 906.

77. Emden, *Money Powers of Europe*, op. cit., p. 38.

78. Sir John Clapham, *The Bank of England. Vol. II* (Cambridge, 1944), pp. 93–4.

79. Thomas Love Peacock, 'Paper Money Lyrics', *Collected Works. Vol. III* (London, 1875), p. 226.

80. Thomas Love Peacock, 'Paper Money Lyrics', *Collected Works. Vol. III*, p. 222.

81. *The Greville Memoirs*, ed. Lytton Strachey and Roger Fulford (London, 1938), vol. I, pp. 154–5.

82. 18 Oct. 1825. Baring Mss (B) HC1. 204. 3f.

83. Autobiographical Memoir, op. cit.

84. Comte de Bertrand to Barings, 8 June 1818. BM Mss 20122 f465.

85. Baring Mss (G) MS 18321. HC1. 82.

CHAPTER 6 (pp. 100–11)

1. 30 May 1807. Copy in Baring Mss (B) DEP 193. 75. 3. 47.

2. 13 March 1817. *Hansard* NS 35. 1026.

3. D. C. M. Platt, *Latin America and British Trade 1806–1914* (London, 1972), pp. 4–10.

4. Baring Mss (G) MS 18321. HC4. 1. 3. 1A.

5. Monypenny and Buckle, *The Life of Benjamin Disraeli. Vol. I.* (London, 1910), p 59. cf. Robert Blake, *Disraeli* (London, 1966), p. 26.

6. Claudio Veliz, 'The Irisarri Loan'. *Boletin de Estudios Latinoamericanos y del Caribe*, no. 23 (December, 1977).

7. Reinhard Liehr, 'La Deuda exterior de la Gran Colombia frente a Gran Bretaña. 1820–1860'. Instituto Ibero-Americano y Universidad Libre de Berlin, pp. 12–14.

8. H. S. Ferns, *Britain and Argentina in the Nineteenth Century* (Oxford, 1960), p. 132.
9. Vera Blinn Raber, *British Mercantile Houses in Buenos Aires 1810–1880* (Harvard, 1979), p. 116.
10. 24 Oct. 1824. Baring Mss (G) MS 18321. HC4. 1. 3. 1B.
11. 'El Primer Empréstito Argentino', *Revista de Economia Argentina.* Tome XIII. Nos 75–76 (Sept.–Oct. 1924).
12. e.g., R. Scalabrini Ortiz, *Política Británica en el Rio de la Plata* (Buenos Aires, 1965) or Eduardo Duhalde, *Baring Brothers y la Historia Política Argentina* (Buenos Aires, 1968).
13. e.g., Juan Carlos Vedoya, *La verdad sobre el Empréstito Baring Brothers* (Buenos Aires, 1971) and Arnando Chiapella, *El Destino del Empréstito Baring Brothers. 1824–26* (Buenos Aires, 1975).
14. Baring Mss (G) MS 18321. HC4. 1. 13. 18. cf. Ernesto J. Fitte, *Historia de un Empréstito: La Emisión de Baring Brothers en 1824* (Buenos Aires, 1962).
15. Robertson to Holland, 5 May 1825. Baring Mss (G) MS 18321. HC4. 3. 6.
16. Robertson to Holland, 14 Dec. 1827. Baring Mss (G) MS 18321. HC4. 3. 6.
17. I am indebted to Dr Samuel Amaral of the Instituto Torcuato di Tella for drawing my attention to this fact.
18. 23 April 1825. Baring Mss (B) DEP 193. 74. 2.
19. Henry Ward to Canning, 30 Oct. 1825. PRO. FO. 50/15.
20. Francis to Thomas Baring, 22 July 1817. Baring Mss (G) MS 18321. HC 20. 5/1.
21. Reinhard Liehr, 'La Deuda exterior de México en la primera mitad del siglo XIX y los merchant bankers británicos', Instituto Ibero-Americano y Universidad Libre de Berlin.
22. 27 Aug. 1825. Simon Gratz Collection, op. cit. 'Francis Baring'.
23. 18 Oct. 1825. Baring Mss (B) HC1. 204. 3f.
24. *Annual Register*, 1844. p. 348.
25. Sydney Smith to Lady Grey, 17 July 1844. *Letters of Sydney Smith*, op. cit., p. 841.
26. Bates to T. W. Ward, 3 July 1844. Ward papers. Massachusetts Historical Society.
27. Barings to Manning and Marshall, 22 Oct. 1832. Baring Mss (G) MS 18322. Vol. III.
28. 15 June 1824. *Hansard*. NS2. Vol. 174. 1404.
29. 6 July 1847. *Hansard*. NS3. XCIII. 1298–1306.
30. Ferns, *Britain and Argentina*, op. cit., p. 209.
31. Ferns, *Britain and Argentina*, pp. 220–2.
32. 'El Primer Empréstito Argentino', op. cit., p. 14.
33. García to Parish, 31 Dec. 1831. Baring Mss (G) MS 18321. HC4. 1. 6.
34. 30 June 1832. Baring Mss (G) MS 18322. Vol. III.
35. 6 Feb. 1833. Baring Mss (G) MS 18322. Vol. III.
36. 1832 and 1835, undated. Baring Mss (G) MS 18321. HC1. 11.
37. Barings to Francis Falconnet, 5 Oct. 1842. Baring Mss (G) MS 18322. Vol. III.
38. Instructions of 30 March 1842. Baring Mss (G) MS 18321. HC4. 1. 13. 18.
39. Falconnet to Barings, 15 June and 12 July 1842. Baring Mss (G) MS 18321. HC4. 1. 14.
40. Falconnet to Barings, 24 Oct. 1842. Baring Mss (G) MS 18321. HC4. 1. 14.
41. Falconnet to Barings, 20 Feb. 1843. Baring Mss (G) MS 18321. HC4. 1. 14.

42. Falconnet to Barings, 20 March 1843. Baring Mss (G) MS 18321. HC4. 1. 14.

43. Falconnet to Barings, 20 March 1843. Baring Mss (G) MS 18321. HC4. 1. 14.

44. For a lucid exposition of this imbroglio see Ferns, *Britain and Argentina*, op. cit., pp. 122–4.

45. 29 Oct. 1845. Ward papers, op. cit.

CHAPTER 7 (pp. 112–26)

1. Ward to Bates, 4 Jan. 1831. Ward Papers, op. cit.

2. Bates to Ward, 7 Nov. 1830. Ward papers, op. cit.

3. Bates to Ward, 5 April 1831. Ward papers, op. cit.

4. Bates to Ward, 24 Nov. 1830. Ward papers. cf. Nolte, *Memoirs*, op. cit., p. 287.

5. Roger Fulford, *Glyn's*, op. cit., p. 199.

6. Edward Strutt, 1st Baron Belper. Ralph E. Pumphrey, 'The Introduction of Industrialists into the British Peerage', *American Hist. Rev. LXV* (1959), pp. 1–16.

7. F. M. L. Thompson, *English Landed Society*, op. cit., p. 100.

8. 19 Oct. 1829. *Miss Eden's Letters*, op. cit., p. 185.

9. *The Journal of Mrs Arbuthnot*, ed. Francis Bamford and the Duke of Wellington (London, 1950), vol. II, p. 369.

10. *Gentleman's Magazine*. New Series, vol. XXX, p. 89.

11. 9 Feb. 1830. *The Correspondence of Daniel O'Connell*, ed. Maurice O'Connell (Dublin, 1971), vol. IV, p. 124.

12. Feb. 1831. *Three Early Nineteenth Century Diaries*, ed. A. Aspinall (London, 1952), p. 9.

13. 13 March 1831. *Hansard*. Third Series. Vol. II. 1305–17; and 14 July 1831. Ibid. Vol. IV. 1286–8.

14. 12 Nov. 1830. *Northbrook. Journals and Correspondence*, op. cit., p. 70.

15. John Gore, *Creevey* (London, 1948), p. 339.

16. Monypenny and Buckle, *Disraeli*, op. cit., vol. I, p. 204.

17. Bates to Colonel Thomas Perkins, 14 May 1832. Baring Mss (G) MS 18321. HC8. 1. 10B.

18. Michael Brock, *The Great Reform Act* (London, 1973), p. 294.

19. 13 May 1832. *Three Early Nineteenth Century Diaries*, op. cit., p. 251.

20. *The Taylor Papers*, ed. Ernest Taylor (London, 1913), p. 344.

21. *Greville Memoirs*, op. cit., vol. II, p. 299.

22. *Letters of Sydney Smith*, op. cit., p. 590.

23. Alexander Baring to Peel, 15 Dec. 1834. BM Add Mss 40405 f221.

24. Disraeli to Sarah Disraeli, 15 Nov. 1834. Monypenny and Buckle, *Disraeli*, op. cit., vol. I, p. 265.

25. Obituary of 15 May 1848.

26. Ashburton to Croker, 7 April 1844. *The Correspondence and Diaries of John Wilson Croker*, ed. Louis Jennings (London, 1844), vol. III, pp. 17–18.

27. 15 March 1843. *Life and Letters of the Fourth Earl of Clarendon*, ed. Sir Herbert Maxwell (London, 1913), vol. I, p. 241.

28. Ashburton to Peel, 9 May 1839. BM Add Mss 40426 f262; and 29 Aug. 1841. BM Add Mss 40486 f209.

29. Peel to Ashburton, 3 Sept. 1841. BM Add Mss 40487 f150.

30. 24 Dec. 1841. *The Letters of Queen Victoria. 1837–1861*, ed. Arthur Benson and Viscount Esher (London, 1907), vol. I, p. 462.

31. 12 Feb. 1843. *Letters of Queen Victoria*, vol. I, p. 579.

32. Melbourne to John Russell, 7 Oct. 1842. *Lord Melbourne's Papers*, ed. Lloyd Sanders

(London, 1889), p. 515.

33. Ashburton to Peel, 18 Oct. 1842. BM Add Mss 40492 f250.

34. Peel to Ashburton, 16 and 22 Oct. 1842. BM Add Mss 40517 ff5 and 9.

35. Peel to Ashburton, 4 Nov. 1844. BM Add Mss 40553 f244 and Ashburton to Peel, 6 Nov. 1844. BM Add Mss 40576 f41.

36. Ashburton to Peel, 30 Jan. 1846. BM Add Mss 40584 f18.

37. Peel to Ashburton, 30 Jan. 1846. BM Add Mss 40584 f20.

38. G. D. H. Cole, *The Life of William Cobbett* (London, 1924), p. 367.

39. George Harding to Lady Ashburton, 23 Nov. 1864. Baring Mss (B) DEP 37.

40. Francis Baring to his wife, 23 Nov. 1830. *Northbrook Journals*, op. cit., p. 75.

41. *Greville Memoirs*, op. cit., vol. III, p. 213.

42. *Greville Memoirs*, vol. VI, p. 62.

43. 2 Sept. 1841. *Letters of Queen Victoria*, op. cit., p. 395.

44. 2 Aug. 1841. *Northbrook Journals*, op. cit., p. 179.

45. 8 Aug. 1839. *Northbrook Journals*, op. cit., p. 142.

46. 8 Aug. 1839. *Northbrook Journals*, op. cit., p. 147.

47. Francis to Thomas Baring, 21 Oct. 1843. *Northbrook Journals*, op. cit., pp. 192–3.

48. Nolte, *Memoirs*, op. cit., 287–8.

49. Francis Baring to Barings, 21 May 1845. Baring Mss (G) MS 18321. HC 7. 17.

50. Francis Baring to Barings, 28 Nov. 1845. Baring Mss (G) MS 18321. HC 1. 20. 5. 1.

51. John to Francis Baring, 1 Dec. 1845. Baring Mss (G) MS 18322. Vol. 15.

52. Bates to Ward, 10 July 1833. Ward papers, op. cit.

53. Joshua Bates's diary, 2 Oct. 1835. Copy in Baring Mss (B) DEP 74.

54. John Baring to Bates, Dec. 1837.

Baring Mss (G) MS 18321. HC 1. 20. 7.

55. Bates's diary, 1 Jan. 1838, op. cit.

56. Bates's diary, 1 Nov. 1838, op. cit.

57. Thomas Baring to Barings, 17 Aug. 1832. Baring Mss (G) MS 18321. HC 1. 20. 4. 1.

58. Bates to Ward, 31 Jan. 1843. Ward papers, op. cit.

59. Bates to Ward, 18 Oct. 1843. Ward papers, op. cit.

60. *The Correspondence of Lord Overstone*, ed. D. P. O'Brien (Cambridge, 1971), vol. I, pp. 338–40.

61. Bates to Ward, 2 May 1844. Ward papers, op. cit.

62. Bates to Ward, 3 Feb. 1845 and T. W. Ward's diary, 31 Aug. 1845. Ward papers, op. cit.

63. B. Disraeli, *Lord George Bentinck. A Political Biography* (London, 1852), pp. 87–8.

64. B. Disraeli, *Lord George Bentinck. A Political Biography*, op. cit., p. 526.

65. Bates to Ward, 19 April 1847. Ward papers, op. cit.

66. Samuel to T. W. Ward, 21 Sept. 1846. Ward papers, op. cit.

67. Bates's diary, 3 Jan. 1836, op. cit.

68. Ward to Bates, 25 July 1853. Baring Mss (B) DEP 193. 26. 1.

69. Bates to Ward, 4 Jan. 1832. Ward papers, op. cit.

70. 26 Sept. 1864. *The Journal of Benjamin Moran*, ed. Sarah Wallace and Frances Gillespie (Chicago, 1948), vol. II, p. 1331.

71. 25 April 1831.

72. Bates's diary, 16 May 1853, op. cit.

73. Bates's diary, 14 Oct. 1833, op. cit.

74. T. W. Ward's diary, 30 Aug. 1841, op. cit.

75. 6 May 1858. *The Journal of Benjamin Moran*, op. cit., vol. II, p. 308.

76. Ward's diary, 30 Aug. 1841, op. cit.

77. Bates to Ward, 21 Dec. 1831. Ward papers, op. cit.
78. Bates's diary, 24 June 1844, op. cit.
79. Bates's diary, 30 April 1836, op. cit.
80. Bates's diary, 17 Feb. 1838, op. cit.
81. Charles to George Sumner, 30 April 1842. *Memoirs and Letters of Charles Sumner*, ed. Edward La Pierce (London, 1878), vol. II, p. 207.
82. John A. Munroe, *Louis McLane* (New Jersey, 1973), pp. 281–2.
83. Nolte, *Memoirs*, op. cit., p. 287.
84. Bates's diary, 1 Nov. 1835, op. cit.
85. Bates's diary, 27 Dec. 1835, op. cit.
86. Bates's diary, 3 Sept. 1837, op. cit.
87. Ward's diary, 30 Aug. 1845, op. cit.
88. Francis Baring to Barings, 10 Aug. 1847. Baring Mss (G) MS 18321. HC 1. 20. 5.
89. Bates to Ward, 3 Nov. 1847. Ward papers, op. cit.

CHAPTER 8 (pp. 127–42)

1. 24 Jan. 1830. Baring Mss (B) DEP 193. 13.
2. Chapman, *Rise of Merchant Banking*, op. cit., p. 13.
3. 13 Jan. 1831. Ward papers, op. cit.
4. Bates's diary, 24 May 1834, op. cit.
5. Charles Blake to Thomas Baring, 11 Nov. 1848. Baring Mss (G) MS 18321. HC 1. 14. 3. 18.
6. 31 Dec. 1832.
7. Regulations of 1 June 1845. Baring Mss (B) PF 323. Staff Memoranda.
8. Eleanor F. Rathbone, *William Rathbone. A Memoir* (London, 1905), p. 94.
9. Alfred Mildmay, 'Notes and Recollections'. Baring Mss (B) DEP 135.

10. *From the Books and Papers of Russell Sturgis*, ed. Julian Sturgis (Privately printed, Oxford), p. 108.
11. Ronald Knox, *Patrick Shaw-Stewart* (London, 1920), p. 81.
12. Ward's diary, August 1828, op. cit.
13. April 1838. Cit. Hidy, *The House of Baring*, op. cit., p. 138.
14. Bates's diary, 4 March 1837, op. cit.
15. Cecil Woodham-Smith, *The Great Hunger* (London, 1962), pp. 54–7.
16. Minute of Board of Treasury of 9 Dec. 1845. Copy in Baring Mss (B) DEP 193. 74. 9.
17. C. E. Trevelyan to Barings, 26 Aug. 1846. Baring Mss (B) DEP 193. 74. 11.
18. Bates to Ward, 7 Nov. 1830. Ward papers, op. cit.
19. Bates to Ward, 20 April 1833. Ward papers, op. cit.
20. Chapman, *Rise of Merchant Banking*, op. cit., pp. 25–6.
21. Bates to Ward, 13 Jan. 1831. Ward papers. Bates's diary, 6 Dec. 1830, 15 Dec. 1830, 9 Jan. 1831, op. cit.
22. Bates's diary, 5 Feb. 1831, op. cit.
23. Barings to Stieglitz, 18 Feb. 1831. Baring Mss (G) MS 18322. Vol. I.
24. Bates's diary, 30 Nov. 1831, op. cit.
25. Bates to Ward, 30 Jan. 1832. Ward papers, op. cit.
26. Bates's diary, 8 Sept. 1833, op. cit.
27. Bates's diary, 14 Oct. 1833, op. cit.
28. Instructions to Francis Booth Wells of 12 Dec. 1839. Baring Mss (O) MG24. D21. Vol. 124.
29. Bates's diary, 28 Feb. 1835, op. cit.
30. Hidy, *The House of Baring*, op. cit., p. 359.
31. Bates's diary, 30 July 1832, op. cit.
32. Thomas Ashton, *Iron and Steel in the Industrial Revolution*

(Manchester, 1924), pp. 2–3.
33. Bates's diary, 25 April 1845, op. cit.
34. Bates's diary, 6 May 1845, op. cit.
35. Mildmay to Thomas Baring, 16 Nov. 1845. Baring Mss (G) MS 18321. HC 1. 20. 2. 18.
36. Thomas Baring to Bates, 11 Dec. 1844. Baring Mss (G) MS 18321. HC 1. 20. 4.
37. 3 Aug. 1846, Ward papers, op. cit.
38. 4 Oct. 1846, op. cit.
39. Bates to Ward, 6 Feb. 1831. Ward papers, op. cit.
40. Bates to Ward, 6 Feb. 1831. Ward papers, op. cit.
41. Bates to Ward, 21 June 1832 and 6 July 1833. Ward papers.
42. Baring Mss (G) MS 18321. HC 3. 52. 1B. cf. Emden *Money Powers of Europe*, op. cit., p. 73.
43. 23 July 1839. Baring Mss (G) MS 18322. Vol. 9. cf. Clapham, *The Bank of England*, op. cit., pp. 168–70; Gille, *Maison Rothschild*, op. cit., vol. I, p. 292.
44. 2 Dec. 1839. RAL T35/85.
45. Bates to Ward, 5 April 1846. Ward papers, op. cit.
46. 13 Sept. 1847. Baring Mss (G) MS 18321. HC 1. 20. 4. 2.
47. Bates to Ward, 3 Nov. 1847. Ward papers, op. cit.
48. Bates to Ward, 3 Nov. 1847. Ward papers, op. cit.
49. 21 Aug. 1848. Baring Mss (G) MS 18321. HC 1. 20. 7.
50. John Baring to Bates, 30 Dec. 1847. Baring Mss (G) MS 18321. HC 1. 20. 7.
51. Bates to Ward, 13 Jan. 1831. Ward papers, op. cit.
52. Barings to Hottinguer and Co., 1 March 1847. Baring Mss (G) MS 18322. Vol. 17.
53. Jenks, *Migration of British Capital*, op. cit., pp. 127–30.
54. Disraeli, *Endymion* (London, 1881 edition), p. 356.
55. 24 Jan. 1836, op. cit.
56. Barings to Hopes, 28 Oct. 1842. Baring Mss (G) MS 18322. Vol. 12.
57. Mildmay to Bates, 13 Dec. 1846. Baring Mss (G) MS 18321. HC 1. 20. 2.
58. Bates's diary, 31 May 1835, op. cit.
59. 26 June 1848. RAL T8/83.
60. 7 Dec. 1844. Baring Mss (G) MS 18321. HC 1. 20. 4.
61. 7 Dec. 1844. Baring Mss (G) MS 18321. HC 1. 20. 4.
62. Francis Baring to Barings, 8 March 1847. Baring Mss (G) MS 18321. HC 1. 20. 5. 1.
63. See, in particular, Platt, *Foreign Finance in Continental Europe*, op. cit., pp. 18–24.
64. Anselm de Rothschild to London Cousins, 6 May and 8 May 1843. RAL T18/128 and 129.
65. Bates to Ward, 29 Oct. 1845. Ward papers, op. cit.
66. Platt, *Foreign Finance*, op. cit., p. 20.
67. 25 March 1846. Baring Mss (G) MS 18322. Vol. 16.
68. 11 Oct. 1831. Baring Mss (G) MS 18322. Vol. 2.
69. Barings to Hopes, 30 Nov. 1832. Baring Mss (G) MS 18322. Vol. 3.
70. Hopes to Barings, 5 Feb. 1842. Baring Mss (G) MS 18321. HC 8. 1. 4.
71. Mildmay to Thomas Baring, 1 Dec. 1846. Baring Mss (G) MS 18321. HC 1. 20. 2. 26.
72. Ashburton to Thomas Baring, 30 Nov. 1846. Baring Mss (G) MS 18321. HC 1. 20. 1. 9.

CHAPTER 9 (pp. 143–57)

1. J. N. Vaughan to James Madison, 21 Oct. 1829. Baring Mss (B) DEP 36.
2. Bates to Ward, 30 Oct. 1833. Ward papers, op. cit.
3. Bates to Thomson, Bonar and Co., 2 Feb. 1828. Baring Mss (O)

MG24. D21. Vol. 3.

4. Thomas Baring to Barings, 30 June 1829. Baring Mss (G) MS 18321. HC 1. 20. 4.

5. Thomas Baring to Barings, 21 Sept. 1829. Baring Mss (G) MS 18321. HC 1. 20. 4.

6. Bates to C. B. Young and Thomas Baring, 18 May 1849. Baring Mss (G) MS 18321. HC 1. 20. 8.

7. T. W. Ward diary, 30 Aug. 1841, op. cit.

8. T. W. Ward diary, 19 Oct. 1829, op. cit.

9. Ward to Bates, 12 Aug. 1829. Baring Mss (G) MS 18321. HC 5. 1. 2.

10. Memorandum for 1833. Baring Mss (G) MS 18321. HC 5. 1. 5.

11. Ward to Barings, 11 Feb. 1840. Baring Mss (O) MG24. D21. Vol. 31.

12. Hidy, *The House of Baring*, op. cit., pp. 185, 285-8.

13. Barings to Ward, 18 June 1831. Baring Mss (O) MG24. D21. Vol. 7.

14. Levi Woodbury to Rothschilds, 2 July 1834. RAL T49/6.

15. Bates's diary, 26 Sept. 1834, op. cit.

16. Gille, *Maison Rothschild*, op. cit., vol. I, p. 405.

17. Barings to Ward, 29 Sept. 1834. Baring Mss (O) MG24. D21. Vol. 9.

18. Bates's diary, 26 Sept. 1834, op. cit.

19. Belmont to Rothschilds, 25 June 1843. RAL T54/173.

20. Belmont to Rothschilds, 29 Nov. 1843. RAL T54/190.

21. Ward to Bates, 8 Dec. 1835. Baring Mss (G) MS 18321. HC 5. 1. 5.

22. Ward to Bates, 20 Nov. 1835. Baring Mss (O) MG 24. D21. Vol. 26.

23. Ward to Bates, 7 June 1833. Baring Mss (O) MG 24. D21. Vol. 24.

24. Ward to Bates, 4 April 1835. Baring Mss (O) MG 24. D21. Vol. 25.

25. Ward to Bates, 29 May 1832. Baring Mss (G) MS 18321. HC 5. 1. 4.

26. Barings to Ward, 30 Jan. and 14 Feb. 1833. Baring Mss (G) MS 18322. Vol. 3.

27. P. Perit to Ward, 16 Dec. 1836. Ward papers, op. cit.

28. Clapham, *Bank of England*, op. cit., vol. II, pp. 151-4.

29. *Journal of Thomas Raikes. Vol. III* (London, 1857), p. 157.

30. Ward to Barings, 21 May 1837. Baring Mss (O) MG24. D21. Vol. 27.

31. Alexander Baring to Barings, 27 Nov. 1828. Baring Mss (G) MS 18321. HC1. 20. 1.

32. Irene D. Nev, 'Edmond J. Forstall, Banker of New Orleans.' Copy in Baring Mss (B) DEP 22 (ii)c.

33. Bates to Ward, 21 June 1832. Ward papers, op. cit.

34. Bates to Ward, 10 July 1833. Ward papers, op. cit.

35. 24 Nov. 1839. RAL T35/81.

36. 14 June 1838. Baring Mss (O) MG24. D21. Vol. 122.

37. Bates to Stockmar, 1 Sept. 1838. Baring Mss (O) MG24. D21. Vol. 122.

38. Jenks, *Migration of British Capital*, op. cit., pp. 88-90.

39. Mildmay to Thomas Baring, 22 July 1829. Baring Mss (G) MS 18321. HC1. 20. 4.

40. Bates's diary, 8 May 1831, op. cit. Ward to Barings, 17 Oct. 1831. Baring Mss (G) MS 18321. HC5. 1. 3.

41. Bates's diary, 24 April 1836, op. cit.

42. Thomas Payne Govan, *Nicholas Biddle* (Chicago, 1959), p. 318.

43. Jenks, *Migration of British Capital*, op. cit., pp. 95-6.

44. Barings to Jaudon, 23 Aug. 1839.

Baring Mss (O) MG24. D21. Vol. 122.

45. Overstone to G. W. Norman, 11 Nov. 1839. *Correspondence of Lord Overstone*, op. cit., vol. I, p. 245.

46. Ward to Barings, 5 Nov. 1839. Baring Mss (O) MG24. D21. Vol. 27.

47. 19 and 20 Dec. 1839.

48. 13 Jan. 1840.

49. E.g., Barings to Prime Ward and King, Hopes, and Hottinguers, 6 Jan. 1840. Baring Mss (O) MG24. D21. Vol. 124.

50. 9 Feb. 1841. Ward papers, op. cit.

51. 15 Feb. 1841. Baring Mss (O) MG24. D21. Vol. 32.

52. Bates to Ward, 3 Nov. 1841. Ward papers, op. cit.

53. Ward to Bates, 13 Nov. 1841. Ward papers, op. cit.

54. Smith to Lady Grey, 19 Sept. 1842. *Letters of Sydney Smith*, op. cit., p. 765.

55. Bates to Ward., 26 April 1843. Ward papers, op. cit.

56. Ward to Barings, 31 May 1841. Baring Mss (O) MG24. D21. Vol. 32.

57. Cit. Jenks, *Migration of British Capital*, op. cit., p. 105.

58. Hopes to Barings, 5 Jan. 1841. Baring Mss (O) MG24. D21. Vol. 3.

59. 10 Aug. 1842. Baring Mss (G) MS 18321. HC1. 20. 4.

60. Hidy, *House of Baring*, op. cit., pp. 313-20.

61. Bates to Ward, 26 April 1844. Ward papers, op. cit.

62. Bates to Ward, 4 Nov. 1844. Ward papers, op. cit.

63. Ward to Barings, 4 May 1839. Baring Mss (O) MG24. D21. Vol. 27.

64. Ward to Barings, 15 Sept. 1843. Baring Mss (B) DEP 193. 10.

65. Prime Ward and King to Barings, 30 June 1895. Baring Mss (B) DEP 193. 10.

66. John Davis to Thomas Baring,

28 Jan. 1846. Baring Mss (B) DEP 193. 10.

67. 16 May 1845. Ward papers, op. cit.

68. Alexander Baring to Hopes, 31 Dec. 1797. Baring Mss (B) DEP 3. 2.

69. Fulford, *Glyn's*, op. cit., pp. 144-8.

70. 31 Aug. 1841. Baring Mss (O) MG24. D21. Vol. 32.

71. Thomas Baring to Francis Hincks, 12 Jan. 1849. Baring Mss (G) MS 18321. HC1. 20.

CHAPTER 10 (pp. 158-85)

1. Northbrook, *Journals and Correspondence*, op. cit., p. 244.

2. *Greville Memoirs*, op. cit., vol. VI, p. 147.

3. Froude, *Carlyle*, op. cit., vol. I, p. 444.

4. *Greville Memoirs*, op. cit., vol. VII, pp. 286-7.

5. Houghton, *Monographs*, op. cit., p. 231.

6. *The Journal of Benjamin Moran*, ed. Sarah Wallace and Frances Gillespie (Chicago, 1948), vol. I, p. 632.

7. Mrs T. B. Laurence to her mother. Baring Mss (B) DEP 187.

8. 1 Jan. 1858. Baring Mss (G) MS 18321. HC1. 20. 5. 2.

9. T. W. to Samuel Ward, 30 June 1853. Ward papers, op. cit.

10. Bates to Ward, 3 April 1857. Ward papers, op. cit.

11. Bates's diary, 13 Jan. 1850, op. cit.

12. Bates's diary, 7 Aug. 1851.

13. Bates's diary, 16 June 1850.

14. Bates's diary, 15 April 1853.

15. T. W. to Samuel Ward, 4 July 1853. Ward papers, op. cit.

16. Bates to Ward, 13 May 1852. Ward papers, op. cit.

17. Monypenny and Buckle, *Disraeli*, op. cit., vol. III, p. 94.

18. Monypenny and Buckle, *Disraeli*, op. cit., vol. III, pp. 307–8.

19. *Greville Memoirs*, op. cit., vol. VI, p. 276.

20. Bates's diary, 22 Feb. 1852, op. cit.

21. Baring Mss (B) DEP 185.

22. *Greville Memoirs*, op. cit., vol. VI, p. 403.

23. 30 April 1852, *Hansard*. Third Series. Vol. CXXI, pp. 47–8.

24. Monypenny and Buckle, *Disraeli*, op. cit., vol. III, p. 78.

25. *Memoirs of Henry Reeve*, ed. John Laughton (London, 1898), vol. II, p. 154.

26. 25 March 1838. *The Letters of Samuel Palmer*, ed. Raymond Lister (Oxford, 1974), vol. 1, p. 181.

27. Alfred Mildmay, 'Notes and Recollections', op. cit., p. 165.

28. *A Descriptive Catalogue of the Collection of Pictures belonging to the Earl of Northbrook* (London, 1899).

29. T. W. Ward to Samuel Ward, 14 July 1853. Ward papers, op. cit.

30. Cit. Hidy, *House of Baring*, op. cit., p. 420.

31. Thomas Baring to Bates, 10 Nov. 1849. Baring Mss (G) MS 18321. HC1. 20. 4.

32. Bates to Ward, 9 Jan. 1849. Ward papers, op. cit.

33. Bates's diary, 27 July 1849, op. cit.

34. Bates's diary, 10 Sept. 1849.

35. Bates's diary, 22 Dec. 1850.

36. Bates's diary, 21 Oct. 1856.

37. Bates's diary, 4 Oct. 1863.

38. Bates's diary, 5 Nov. 1853.

39. Bates's diary, 8 June 1853.

40. Bates's diary, 5 Nov. 1853 and 1 Jan. 1856.

41. Bates's diary, 12 Dec. 1853.

42. Bates's diary, 1 April 1858.

43. Bates's diary, 24 May 1863.

44. Bates's diary, 5 Oct. 1858; 11 Dec. 1859; 4 Feb. 1860; 3 June 1860; 13 April 1862; 17 Oct. 1863.

45. Barings to Hopes, 5 Jan. 1849. Baring Mss (G) MS 18322. Vol. 19.

46. 26 Dec. 1849. Baring Mss (G) MS 18321. HC1. 20. 4. 3.

47. Bates's diary, 10 March 1850, op. cit.

48. J. Charles Labouchère to Bates, 20 Sept. 1853. Baring Mss (G) MS 18321. HC1. 22.

49. Bates's diary, 20 Nov. 1853, op. cit.

50. Bates's diary, 1 Jan. 1854.

51. T. W. Ward to S. G. Ward, 15 Aug. 1853. Ward papers, op. cit.

52. Edgar Johnson, *Charles Dickens. Vol. II* (New York, 1952), p. 848.

53. Baring Mss (G) MS 18322. Vol. 34 and MS 18321. HC1. 14. 3. 49.

54. M. Purton to Bates, 7 Dec. 1850. Baring Mss (G) MS 18321. HC3. 35. 16.

55. J. Price to Bates, 10 Feb. 1859. Baring Mss (G) MS 18321. HC3. 35. 22.

56. 2 July 1853. Baring Mss (G) MS 18322. Vol. 25.

57. 30 Oct. 1849. Baring Mss (G) MS 18322. Vol. 20.

58. Barings to O'Shea, 18 Dec. 1848 and O'Shea to Barings, 28 Dec. 1848. Baring Mss (G) MS 18321. HC4. 8. 6.

59. Thomas Baring to Barings, 21 Nov. 1849. Baring Mss (G) MS 18321. HC1. 20. 4. 2.

60. Thomas Baring to Barings, 23 Dec. 1849. Baring Mss (G) MS 18321. HC1. 20. 4. 2.

61. Thomas Baring to Barings, 16 Nov. 1849. Baring Mss (G) MS 18321. HC1. 20. 4. 2.

62. Baron Lionel to Mayer Rothschild, 26 Nov. 1849. RAL T8/188.

63. Hopes to Barings, 28 March 1852. Baring Mss (G) MS 18321. HC8. 1. 7.

64. Barings to Hopes, 8 Jan. and 22 Jan. 1849. Baring Mss (G) MS 18322. Vol. 19.
65. Barings to Stieglitz. 24 July 1849. Baring Mss (G) MS 18322. Vol. 19.
66. *The Times* (16 Jan. 1850).
67. Bates's diary, 13 Jan. 1850, op. cit.
68. Bates's diary, 17 Jan. 1850.
69. Bates's diary, 23 Jan. 1850.
70. Bates's diary, 18 Aug. 1850.
71. Bates's diary 30 Jan. 1850.
72. Bates's diary, 18 and 24 Nov. 1853.
73. 2 Aug. 1854, *Hansard*. NS3. 777–9.
74. For an interesting discussion of the relationship between government and bankers see Platt, *Finance, Trade and Politics*, op. cit., pp. 10–12.
75. 1 Feb. 1854. Baring Mss (G) MS 18322. Vol. 26.
76. Baring to Hottinguers, 20 Feb. 1855. Baring Mss (G) MS 18321. Vol. 27.
77. Barings to Stieglitz, 20 June 1854. Baring Mss (G) MS 18321. Vol. 26.
78. Barings to Stieglitz, 1 April 1856. Baring Mss (G) MS 18321. Vol. 28.
79. Lord to Lady Clarendon, 19 Dec. 1855. Cit. Herbert Maxwell, *Life and Letters of the Fourth Earl of Clarendon. Vol. II* (London, 1913), p. 107.
80. Clive Anderson, 'The Russian Loan of 1855', *Economia* (Nov. 1960), pp. 368–71 and Frank Whitson, 'The Russian Loan of 1855: a Postscript', *Economia* (Nov. 1961), pp. 421–6.
81. Bates's diary, 19 Sept. 1856, op. cit.
82. Bates's diary, 28 Dec. 1856, op. cit.
83. 29 Nov. 1856.
84. 2 May 1857.
85. *The Times* (21 and 22 April 1857). Bates's diary, 22 April 1857, op. cit.
86. Bates to C. B. Young, 16 Aug. 1855. Baring Mss (G) MS 18321. HC1. 20. 8.
87. Thomas Baring to Stieglitz, 19 May 1857; Barings to Hottinguers, 5 Sept. 1857. Baring Mss (G) MS 18322. Vol. 29.
88. Thomas Baring to Hottinguers, 4 Jan. 1858. Baring Mss (G) MS 18322. Vol. 30.
89. Thomas Baring to Hottinguers, 22 Oct. 1859. Baring Mss (G) MS 18322. Vol. 31.
90. Thomas Baring to S. Gwyer, 14 Jan. 1868. Baring Mss (G) MS 18322. Vol. 40.
91. Thomas Baring to Stieglitz, 13 Dec. 1858. Baring Mss (G) MS 18322. Vol. 30.
92. Platt, *Foreign Finance in Continental Europe*, op. cit., pp. 65–7.
93. Edwin Hodder, *The Life and Work of the Seventh Earl of Shaftesbury. Vol. II* (London, 1886), p. 384.
94. Barings to the *Edinburgh Review* (16 March 1885). Baring Mss (B) Letter Books.
95. Bates's diary, 9 Nov. 1860 and 25 March 1861, op. cit.
96. Louis Napoleon to Bates, 2 Sept. 1855. Baring Mss (B) DEP 193. 11.
97. Bates to Louis Napoleon, 3 Sept. 1855. Baring Mss (B) DEP 193. 11.
98. Bates to Louis Napoleon, 4 Sept. 1855. Baring Mss (B) DEP 193. 11.
99. Barings to Samuel Ward, 21 Sept. 1855. Baring Mss (B) DEP 193. 11.
100. Barings to Louis Napoleon, 27 Dec. 1856. Baring Mss (B) DEP 193. 11.
101. Francis Baring to Barings, 11 Nov. 1856. Baring Mss (G) MS

18321. HC1. 1. 20. 5.

102. Barings to Hopes, 12 Feb. 1856. Baring Mss (G) MS 18322. Vol. 28.

103. Platt, *Foreign Finance in Continental Europe*, op. cit., p. 16.

104. E. d'Eichthal to Barings, 5 April 1891. Baring Mss (B) HC7. 67.

105. Barings to Hottinguers, 24 Dec. 1851. Baring Mss (G) MS 18322. Vol. 22.

106. Platt, *Foreign Finance in Continental Europe*, op. cit., pp. 16–17.

107. Barings to Rothschilds frères, 24 June 1871. Baring Mss (B) Letter Books.

108. *The Life and Correspondence of the Right Hon. Hugh C. E. Childers*, ed. Lt Colonel Spencer Childers (London, 1901), pp. 81–5.

109. Thomas Baring to Barings, 11 July 1853. Baring Mss (G) MS 18321. HC1. 20. 4. 3.

110. Francis to Thomas Baring, 21 March 1864. Baring Mss (G) MS 18321. HC1. 20. 5.

111. 30 Jan. 1859. Baring Mss (G) MS 18321. HC1. 20. 4. 4.

112. Bates's diary, 8 June 1848, op. cit.

113. 2 Sept. 1859. Baring Mss (G) MS 18321. HC1. 20. 4. 4.

114. Chapman, *Rise of Merchant Banking*, op. cit., p. 17.

115. Brown, Shipley to Brown Bros, 1 Dec. 1857. Brown Brothers papers. New York Historical Society.

116. Brown, Shipley to Brown Bros, 5 Dec. 1857. Brown Brothers papers, op. cit. cf. Vincent Carosso, *The Morgans* (Boston, 1987), p. 65.

117. Bates's diary, 13 Feb. 1858, op. cit.

118. Brown, Shipley to Brown Bros, 5 Dec. 1857. Brown Brothers papers, op. cit.

119. Thomas to Francis Baring, 27

Jan. 1855. Baring Mss (G) MS 18322. Vol. 27.

120. Chapman, *Rise of Merchant Banking*, op. cit., p. 29.

121. Bates to Thomas Baring, 16 Aug. 1855. Baring Mss (G) MS 18321. HC1. 20. 8.

122. Thomas Baring to Henri Hottinguer, 2 April 1864. Baring Mss (G) MS 18322. Vol. 36.

123. Bates's diary, 5 May 1863, op. cit.

124. Thomas Baring to Ward, 1 July 1865. Baring Mss (B) HC1. 204. 28.

125. Ward to Thomas Baring, 6 Nov. 1864 and 9 June 1865. Baring Mss (B) HC1. 204. 28.

126. 'Notes and Recollections', op. cit., p. 60.

127. Baring Mss (B) DEP 193. 39.

128. 1 Oct. 1870. Baring Mss (B) HC1. 204. 3k

129. Arabella, Lady Northbrook to Lord Northbrook, 27 Nov. 1873. Northbrook papers, vol. III.

130. Barings to Ward, 1 March and 8 Nov. 1873. Baring Mss (B) Letter Books.

131. Roger Fulford, *Glyn's*, op. cit., p. 208.

CHAPTER 11 (pp. 186–206)

1. The Marquess of Zetland, *Lord Cromer* (London, 1932), pp. 20–1.

2. Maurice Baring, *The Puppet Show of Memory* (London, 1922), p. 31.

3. *A Victorian Diarist. Extracts from the Journals of Mary, Lady Monkswell* (London, 1944), p. 152.

4. Baring, *Puppet Show of Memory*, op. cit., p. 72.

5. Zetland, *Cromer*, op. cit., p. 20.

6. *The Diary of Sir Edward Walter Hamilton*, ed. Dudley Bellman (Oxford, 1972), p. 880.

7. 25 June 1885. Gladstone papers. BM Add Mss 44491 f163.

8. Arthur D. Eliot, *Goschen. Vol. II* (London, 1911), appendix 1.

9. Memorandum by Susan Beattie of the Historic Buildings Division of the GLC.
10. Baring, *Puppet Show of Memory*, op. cit., p. 20.
11. Daphne Pollen, *I Remember, I Remember* (privately printed, 1983), p. 31.
12. 14 Dec. 1882. Baring Mss (B) Letter Books.
13. 5 Nov. 1878. Baring Mss (B) HC1. 204. 3L.
14. T. C. Baring to Lord Northbrook, 5 March 1874. Northbrook papers, 8. 1.
15. Francis Baring to Lord Northbrook, 15 and 22 Jan. 1874. Northbrook papers, 8. 2.
16. Sydney James, *Seventy Years* (London, 1926), p. 49.
17. Ralph Nevill, *Unconventional Memories* (London, 1923), pp. 84–5.
18. Oral information from Lord Ashburton.
19. Unpublished memoirs of Mrs Constance Hugh Smith. In the possession of Mrs Fortune Stanley. Vol. III, p. 84.
20. Baring Mss (B) DEP 22 (XX).
21. E.g., Alfred Mildmay, 'Notes and Recollections', op. cit., pp. 148–9.
22. Undated. Dec. 1888. Baring Mss (B) HC1. 204. 33.
23. Baring Mss (B) DEP 22 (XX).
24. 12 March 1889. Baring Mss (B) Letter Books.
25. 23 March 1889. Baring Mss (B) HC1. 182.
26. *The Life and Correspondence of the Right Hon. Hugh C. E. Childers*, op. cit., pp. 207–11.
27. *The Collected Works of Walter Bagehot*, ed. Norman St John Stevas (London, 1978), vol. XI, p. 407.
28. No. XVIII (1888), p. 609.
29. Chapman, *Rise of Merchant Banking*, op. cit., p. 17.
30. 1 Dec. 1888.
31. 25 April 1877. Baring Mss (B)

HC8. 1. XVI.
32. Barings to Hopes, 26 April 1877. Baring Mss (B) Letter Books.
33. T. C. Baring to Stieglitz, 24 March 1884. Baring Mss (B) Letter Books.
34. Barings to Hopes, 12 July 1890. Baring Mss (B) HC8. 1. Vol. XVIII.
35. Joseph Laurence to Thomas Baring, 17 Aug. 1872. Baring Mss (B) HC1. 168.
36. Barings to Torlades and Co., 16 March 1876. Baring Mss (B) Letter Books.
37. Barings to Joachim Ebbell, 25 May 1876. Baring Mss (B) Letter Books.
38. T. C. Baring to Mr Buck, 11 Feb. 1882. Baring Mss (B) Letter Books.
39. *Frank Harris. His Life and Adventures* (London, 1947), pp. 336–7.
40. 27 Oct. 1886.
41. *Frank Harris. Life*, op. cit., pp. 336–7.
42. 25 Oct. 1886.
43. 26 Oct. 1886.
44. *Frank Harris. Life*, op. cit., pp. 336–7.
45. 28 Oct. 1886.
46. 19 Jan. 1887.
47. 19 Jan. 1887. Baring Mss (B) HC3. 130.
48. Charles Combe to Barings, 27 June 1888. Baring Mss (B) HC3. 139.
49. Baring Mss (B) HC3. 135 and 143.
50. e.g., *Bankers' Magazine of 1888*, No. XLVIII, pp. 607–8.
51. Walter Bagehot, *Lombard Street: a Description of the Money Market* (London, 1874).
52. Baring Brothers to Hopes, 29 Dec. 1884. Baring Mss (B) Letter Books.
53. 5 Sept. 1874. Baring Mss (B) Letter Books.
54. Barings to Messrs Russell and

Co., 30 Oct. 1874. Baring Mss (B) Letter Books.
55. 12 March 1875. Baring Mss (B) Letter Books.
56. 27 Oct. 1886.
57. Baring Mss (B) DEP 115.
58. 17 Jan. 1885.

CHAPTER 12 (pp. 207–28)

1. Bates to Young, 23 Sept. 1848. Baring Mss (G) MS 18321. HC1. 20. 8.
2. Bates to Hottinguer, 7 Sept. 1849. Baring Mss (G) MS 18322. Vol. 19.
3. Belmont to N. M. Rothschild, 15 May 1849. RAL T54/290.
4. T. W. Ward diary, 22 June 1848, op. cit.
5. Bates to Thomas Baring, 20 Jan. 1862. Baring Mss (B) DEP 193. 39.
6. Bates to Thomas Baring, 8 May 1849. Baring Mss (G) MS 18321. HC1. 20. 8.
7. Bates to Thomas Baring, 15 May 1849. Baring Mss (G) MS 18321. HC1. 20. 8.
8. 15 May 1849. Baring Mss (G) MS 18321. HC1. 20. 8.
9. Bates to Thomas Baring, 2 June 1849. Baring Mss (G) MS 18321. HC1. 20. 8.
10. Thomas Baring to Bates, 1 June 1849. Baring Mss (G) MS 18321. HC1. 20. 8.
11. 14 Jan. 1849. RAL T8/125.
12. Brown, Shipley to Brown Brothers, 9 Feb. 1855. Brown Brothers papers, op. cit.
13. Brown, Shipley to Brown Brothers, 2 Aug. 1867. Brown Brothers papers, op. cit.
14. Brown, Shipley to Brown Brothers, 2 Nov. 1868. Brown Brothers papers, op. cit.
15. Bates to Young, 4 June 1849. Baring Mss (G) MS 18321. HC1. 20. 8.
16. Belmont to N. M. Rothschild, 27 Nov. 1849. RAL T54/310.
17. Thomas Baring to Bates, 14 Sept. 1852. Baring Mss (G) MS 18321. HC1. 20. 4/3.
18. Thomas Baring to Bates, 2 Nov. 1852. Baring Mss (G) MS 18321. HC1. 20. 4/3.
19. Bates to Thomas Baring. 7 Sept. 1852. Baring Mss (B) DEP 193. 39.
20. Bates to T. W. Ward, 13 May 1852. Ward papers, op. cit.
21. Hidy, *House of Baring*, op. cit., p. 412.
22. 14 Jan. 1853. Baring Mss (G) MS 18322. Vol. 25.
23. Barings to S. Ward, 23 March and 13 April 1855. Baring Mss (O) MG24. D21. Vol. 154.
24. Bates's diary, 6 Oct. 1850, op. cit.
25. Bates's diary, 15 Oct. 1850, op. cit.
26. Bates to Thomas Baring, 7 Sept. and 10 Sept. 1852. Baring Mss (B) DEP 193. 39.
27. Ward to Barings, 20 April 1881. Baring Mss (B) HC5. 2. 30.
28. Bates's diary, 25 Oct. 1857, op. cit.
29. Hidy, *House of Baring*, op. cit., pp. 463–4
30. Bates's diary, 10 Jan. 1858, op. cit.
31. Russell Sturgis to Thomas Baring, 31 Dec. 1860. Cit. Hidy, *House of Baring*, op. cit., p. 474.
32. 22 April 1861. Baring Mss (G) MS 18322. Vol. 33.
33. Barings to Ward, 25 May 1861. Baring Mss (G) MS 18322. Vol. 33.
34. *Journal of Benjamin Moran*, op. cit., vol. II, p. 1297.
35. Ward to Thomas Baring, 2 Jan. 1865. Baring Mss (B) HC1. 204. 28.
36. *Journal of Benjamin Moran*, op. cit., vol. II, pp. 1401–2.
37. 15 Oct. 1875.

38. *Journal of Benjamin Moran*, op. cit., vol. II, p. 807.
39. *New York Tribune* (15 Oct. 1875).
40. Baring Mss (G) MS 18322. Vol. 33.
41. T. W. Ward to Bates, 26 Jan. 1851. Ward papers, op. cit. Bates to Ward, 14 Feb. 1851. Ward papers, op. cit. Brown, Shipley to Brown Brothers, 22 Sept, 1860. Brown Brothers papers, op. cit. Brown, Shipley to Brown Brothers, 17 May 1865. Brown Brothers papers, op. cit.
42. 18 March 1869. Baring Mss (O) MG24. D21. Vol. 23.
43. Ellis Oberholtzer, *Jay Cooke. Financier of the Civil War, Vol. 2* (Philadelphia, 1907), pp. 209–10.
44. *The Herald* (9 Oct. 1875).
45. Ward to Barings, 26 Sept. 1873. Baring Mss (B) HC5. 2. 30.
46. Barings to Ward, 11 Oct. 1873. Baring Mss (B) Letter Books.
47. T. C. Baring to Thomas Baring, 2 Feb. 1866. Baring Mss (O) MG24. D21. Vol. 23.
48. Barings to Hopes, 27 Feb. 1871. Baring Mss (B) Letter Books.
49. Belmont to N. M. Rothschild, 23 Jan. 1873. RAL T58/134.
50. Hopes to Barings, 1 Feb. 1873. Baring Mss (B) HC8. 1. XV.
51. Chapman, *Rise of Merchant Banking*, op. cit., p. 97.
52. Barings to Ward, 6 June 1874. Baring Mss (B) Letter Books.
53. Barings to Ward, 17 Aug. 1875. Baring Mss (B) Letter Books.
54. Barings to Ward, 23 Dec. 1875. Baring Mss (B) Letter Books.
55. Barings to Lee, Higginson and Co., 13 Oct. 1876. Baring Mss (B) Letter Books.
56. Russell Sturgis to Mr Roosevelt, 22 Feb. 1877. Baring Mss (B) Letter Books.
57. Barings to Ward, Nov. 1882. Baring Mss (B) Letter Books.
58. T. C. Baring to Ward, 2 Aug. 1883. Baring Mss (B) Letter Books.
59. Ward to Barings, 14 Dec. 1880. Baring Mss (B) HC5. 2. 30.
60. Tom Baring to Revelstoke, 18 April 1886. Baring Mss (B) HC5. 1. 27.
61. Vincent P. Carosso, *More Than a Century of Investment Banking. The Kidder Peabody and Co. Story* (New York, 1979), p. 22.
62. Tom Baring to Revelstoke, 1 Feb. 1889. Baring Mss (B) HC5. 1. 27.
63. Tom Baring to Revelstoke, 6 Oct. 1889. Baring Mss (B) HC5. 1. 27.
64. 20 Nov. 1889. Baring Mss (B) Letter Books.
65. 1 Feb. 1877. Baring Mss (B) HC5. 2. 30.
66. Thomas Baring to Barings, 13 Feb. 1877. Baring Mss (B) HC5. 2. 30.
67. Francis Baring to Barings, 8 Sept. 1877. Baring Mss (B) HC5. 2. 30.
68. Ward to Barings, 14 Dec. 1880. Baring Mss (B) HC5. 2. 30.
69. Thomas Baring to Revelstoke, 12 Nov. 1890. Baring Mss (B) HC5. 2. 30.
70. Ward to Barings, 24 Aug. 1878. Baring Mss (B) HC5. 2. 30.
71. Ward to Barings, 28 Feb. 1882. Baring Mss (B) HC5. 2. 30.
72. Ward to Barings, 19 Feb. 1891. Baring Mss (B) HC5. 2. 30.
73. Thomas Baring to Revelstoke, 4 Aug. 1885 and Sam Ward to Revelstoke, 18 June 1885. Baring Mss (B) HC1. 145 and HC5. 2. 30.
74. Thomas Baring to Revelstoke, 4 and 6 Aug. 1885. Baring Mss (B) HC1. 145.
75. Revelstoke to Ward, 9 July 1885. Baring Mss (B) Letter Books.
76. Thomas Baring to Revelstoke, 3 June 1886. Baring Mss (B) HC5. 1. 27.

77. Revelstoke to Thomas Baring, 25 Aug. 1885. Baring Mss (B) Letter Books.

78. T. C. Baring to Thomas Baring, 29 Aug. 1885. Baring Mss (B) Letter Books.

79. Thomas Baring to Revelstoke, 9 Aug. 1885. Baring Mss (B) HC1. 145.

80. Thomas Baring to Revelstoke, 8 Oct. 1885. Baring Mss (B) HC1. 145.

81. Barings to Kidder Peabody, 15 Oct. 1885. Baring Mss (B) Letter Books.

82. Carosso, *Kidder Peabody Story*, op. cit., p. 20.

83. Cecil Baring to Revelstoke, 26 Jan. 1886. Baring Mss (B) HC5. 1. 27.

84. An admirable portrait of Cecil Baring is to be found in Daphne Pollen's *I Remember, I Remember*, op. cit.

85. Thomas Baring to Revelstoke, 9 Aug. 1885. Baring Mss (B) Letter Books.

86. Lord Frederic Hamilton, *The Days Before Yesterday* (London, 1920), p. 251.

87. Thomas Baring to Revelstoke, 5 April 1888. Baring Mss (B) HC5. 1. 27.

88. Thomas Baring to Revelstoke, 7 Nov. 1890. Baring Mss (B) HC5. 1. 27.

89. Barings to Hincks, 12 Jan. 1849. Baring Mss (G) MS 18322. Vol. 19.

90. Thomas Baring to W. Cayley, 8 Jan. 1858. Baring Mss (O) MG24. D21. Vol. 24.

91. Fulford, *Glyn's*, op. cit., p. 152.

92. Bates's diary, 10 Nov. 1858, op. cit.

93. Barings to Hopes, 3 Jan. 1860. Baring Mss (G) MS 18321. HC8. 1. 9.

94. Bates's diary, 5 and 18 Jan. 1860, op. cit.

95. Thomas Baring to John Ross, 8 April 1853. Baring Mss (O) MG24. D21. Vol. 19.

96. 27 Aug. 1853. Baring Mss (B). DEP 193. 39.

97. George Glyn to A. T. Galt, Nov. 1857. Cit. Fulford, *Glyn's*, op. cit., p. 154.

98. Galt to Thomas Baring, 26 June 1859. Baring Mss (G) MS 18321. HC5. 15. 24.

99. 14 July 1860. Baring Mss (G) MS 18321. HC5. 15. 24.

100. Galt to Thomas Baring, 3 Aug. 1860. Baring Mss (G) MS 18321. HC5. 15. 24.

101. Bates to Thomas Baring, 30 July 1858. Baring Mss (G) MS 18321. HC1. 20. 8.

102. Bates to Young, 2 Nov. 1860. Baring Mss (G) MS 18321. HC1. 20. 8.

103. Bates to Young, 25 Aug. 1858. Baring Mss (G) MS 18321. HC1. 20. 8.

104. Thomas Baring to Bates, 26 March 1861. Baring Mss (G) MS 18321. HC1. 20. 8.

105. D. G. G. Kerr, *Sir Edmund Head. A Scholarly Governor* (Toronto, 1954), p. 214.

106. D. G. G. Kerr, *Sir Edmund Head. A Scholarly Governor*, op. cit., p. 190.

107. Heather Gilbert, *Awakening Continent. The Life of Lord Mount Stephen. Vol. I* (Aberdeen, 1965), pp. 160–1.

108. Beckles Wilson, *The Life of Lord Strathcona and Mount Royal. Vol II* (Boston, 1915), p. 120.

109. Hopes to Barings, 24 July 1885. Baring Mss (B) HC8. 1. XVII.

100. Gilbert, *Awakening Continent*, op. cit., p. 179.

111. Cecil Baring to Revelstoke, 26 Jan. 1886. Baring Mss (B) HC1. 1. 27.

CHAPTER 13 (pp. 229–43)

1. Thomas Baring to Hottinguers, 24 June 1863. Baring Mss (G) MS

18322. Vol. 35.

2. Gille, *Maison Rothschild*, op. cit., pp. 414–17.

3. Thomas Baring to Bates, 14 Nov. 1858. Baring Mss (G) MS 18321. HC1. 20. 4/4.

4. 26 Nov. 1858, op. cit.

5. Jenks, *Migration of British Capital*, op. cit., pp. 287–8.

6. Barings to Luiz Alves de Silva Porto, 7 May 1879. Baring Mss (B) Letter Books.

7. Hopes to Barings, 30 April 1874. Baring Mss (B) HC8. 1. XVI.

8. Thomas Baring to Barings, 28 Nov. 1849. Baring Mss (G) MS 18321. HC1. 20. 4/2.

9. Edward Baring to Barings, 13 Aug. 1849. Baring Mss (G) MS 18321. HC1. 20. 13. 1.

10. Edward Baring to Barings, 12 Dec. 1849. Baring Mss (G) MS 18321. HC1. 20. 13. 1.

11. Edward Baring to Thomas Baring, 15 May 1850. Baring Mss (G) MS 18321. HC1. 20. 13. 1.

12. Lord Eddisbury to Thomas Baring, 14 April 1849. Baring Mss (G) MS 18321. HC4. 1. 18.

13. 4 May 1849. Baring Mss (G) MS 18322. Vol. 19.

14. Edward to Thomas Baring, 28 June 1850. Baring Mss (G) MS 18321. HC4. 20. 13. 1.

15. 'Journal of Major White's Mission to Buenos Ayres, 1852–53'. Baring Mss (O) MG24. D21. Vol. 193, p. 20.

16. 'Journal of Major White's Mission to Buenos Ayres, 1852–53'. Baring Mss (O) MG24. D21. Vol. 193, p. 182.

17. 'Journal of Major White's Mission to Buenos Ayres, 1852–53'. Baring Mss (O) MG24. D21. Vol. 193, p. 240.

18. By far the best account of British involvement in Argentine history is to be found in H. S. Ferns, *Britain and Argentina in the Nineteenth Century* (Oxford, 1960).

19. Cabot to Barings, 30 April 1856. Baring Mss (G) MS 18321. HC4. 1. 9. 14.

20. David Robertson to George White, 7 April 1857. Baring Mss (G) MS 18321. HC4. 1. 3. 4.

21. White to Barings, 3 April 1857. Baring Mss (G) MS 18321. HC4. 1. 3. 4.

22. David Robertson to White, 1 Oct. 1857. Baring Mss (G) MS 18321. HC4. 1. 3. 4.

23. White to W. D. Christie, 27 Sept. 1857. Cit. Ferns, *Britain and Argentina*, op. cit., p. 320.

24. Ferns, *Britain and Argentina*, op. cit., p. 330.

25. 11 Jan. 1866. Baring Mss (G) MS 18322. Vol. 38.

26. Barings to Dr Huergo, 17 Sept. 1874. Baring Mss (B) Letter Books.

27. Barings to Sr Eduardo Madero, 2 Sept. 1875. Baring Mss (B) Letter Books.

28. Barings to Don Roberto de la Bicestra, 8 Aug. 1876. Baring Mss (B) Letter Books.

29. Barings to Bouwer, 1 Nov. 1876. Baring Mss (B) HC4. 1. 65. I. and Letter Books.

30. Bouwer to Edward Baring, 19 Oct. 1877. Baring Mss (B) HC4. 1. 65. I.

31. Bouwer to Barings, 26 Dec. 1876. Baring Mss (B) HC4. 1. 65. I.

32. Bouwer to Barings, 19 Jan. 1878. Baring Mss (B) HC4. 1. 65. I.

33. Bouwer to Barings, 23 June 1879. Baring Mss (B) HC4. 1. 65. I.

34. Bouwer to Barings, 17 Oct. 1879. Baring Mss (B) HC4. 1. 65. I.

35. Barings to Dr Lopez, 3 May 1879. Baring Mss (B) HC4. 1. 65. I.

36. Ferns, *Britain and Argentina*, op. cit., p. 397.

37. Bouwer to Barings, 18 Oct. 1882. Baring Mss (B) HC4. 1. 65.

38. Bouwer to Barings, 14 Feb. 1884. Baring Mss (B) HC4. 1. 65.

39. Barings to Bouwer, 18 June 1886.

Baring Mss (B) Letter Books.
40. Bouwer to Barings, 31 Dec. 1887. Baring Mss (B) HC4. 1. 71.
41. Barings to Hales, 18 Sept. 1888. Baring Mss (B) Letter Books.
42. H. Osborne O'Hagan, *Leaves from My Life. Vol. I* (London, 1929), p. 377.
43. Barings to Bouwer, 17 Jan. 1882. Baring Mss (B) Letter Books.
44. Barings to Ward, 20 Aug. 1885. Baring Mss (B) Letter Books.
45. Baring Mss (B) Letter Books.
46. Alphonse de Rothschild to London Cousins, 12 Oct. 1888. RAL T14/39.
47. Vol. XLVIII. 1888. p. 382.
48. 25 Oct. 1889. Baring Mss (B) Letter Books.
49. John Baring to Revelstoke, 20 Jan. 1890. Baring Mss (B) Uncatalogued.
50. John Baring to Revelstoke, 7 Feb. 1890. Uncatalogued.
51. John Baring to Revelstoke, 4 Jan. 1890. Uncatalogued.
52. 'The Baring Crisis in Anglo-Argentine History'. Chapter from an as yet unpublished book by Professor H. S. Ferns, pp. 23–4.
53. John Baring to Revelstoke, 14 Jan. 1890. Baring Mss (B) Uncatalogued.
54. 22 Nov. 1890.
55. Clapham, *Bank of England*, op. cit., vol. II, p. 327.
56. Ferns, *Britain and Argentina*, op. cit., p. 453.
57. Alphonse de Rothschild to London Cousins, 7 Aug. 1890. RAL T15/37.
58. Baring Mss (B) HC4. 1. 71.

CHAPTER 14 (pp. 244–66)

1. Francis to T. C. Baring, 11 Nov. 1890. Baring Mss (B) DEP 193. 75. 1. 134.
2. Philip Currie to Evelyn Baring, 21 Nov. 1890. Baring Mss (B) DEP 84.
3. XXIV (1889), p. 100 and XXV (1890), p. 257.
4. B. W. Currie's account of the Crisis. Fulford, *Glyn's*, op. cit., pp. 209–12.
5. 12 Nov. 1890. Brown Brothers papers, op. cit.
6. Bo Bramsen and Kathleen Wain, *The Hambros* (London, 1979), p. 319.
7. Clapham, *Bank of England*, op. cit., vol. II, p. 328.
8. Revelstoke to Tom Baring, 23 April 1890. Baring Mss (B) Letter Books.
9. Francis Baring to T. C. Baring, 11 Nov. 1890. Baring Mss (B) DEP 193. 75. 1. 134.
10. Colonel Robert to Evelyn Baring, 25 Nov. 1890. Baring Mss (B) DEP 84.
11. Wischnegradny to Rothschilds, 28 Nov. 1890. Copy in Baring Mss (B) DEP 150.
12. Clapham, *Bank of England*, op. cit., vol. II, p. 334.
13. Cit. L. S. Pressnell, 'Gold Reserves, Banking Reserves and the Baring Crisis of 1890', in *Essays in Money and Banking in honour of R. S. Sayers*, ed. G. R. Whittlesey and J. S. G. Wilson (Oxford, 1968), p. 195. My attention was drawn to this, as to much else in this chapter, by Ferns, 'The Baring Crisis', op. cit.
14. Eliot, *Goschen*, op. cit., p. 170.
15. Lord George Hamilton, *Parliamentary Reminiscences and Reflections* (London, 1916), p. 79.
16. 11 Nov. 1890, Hatfield House papers. 3M/E. Goschen.
17. Salisbury to Smith, 12 Nov. 1890. Hatfield House papers. 3M/DXV.
18. 13 Nov. 1890. RAL T15/43.
19. Rodolphe Hottinguer to Revelstoke. 11 Nov. 1890. Baring Mss (B) HC7. 1. 16. 14.
20. *Journals and Letters of Viscount Esher*, ed. Maurice Brill (London, 1934), vol. 1, p. 145.

21. 12 Nov. 1890. RAL. X1. 101/21/ 37.
22. Brown Brothers to Brown, Shipley, 21 Nov. 1890. Brown Brothers papers, op. cit.
23. 16 Nov. 1890. Cit. Carosso, *The Morgans*, op. cit., p. 299.
24. L. E. Jones, *Georgian Afternoon* (London, 1958), pp. 71–2.
25. Eliot, *Goschen*, op. cit., p. 172.
26. Fulford, *Glyn's*, op. cit., pp. 209–12.
27. Bank of England papers on Baring Crisis. G15/189/2.
28. Clapham, *Bank of England*, op. cit., vol. II, pp. 330–1.
29. 17 Nov. 1890. Baring Mss (G) MS 18321. HC3. 38.
30. Esher, *Journals and Letters*, op. cit., p. 145.
31. 9 April 1891. Baring Mss (B) DEP 47.
32. 9 April 1891. Baring Mss (B) DEP 47.
33. Baring Mss (B) DEP 22 (XX).
34. Baring Mss (B) DEP 193. 74. 13.
35. Thomas to Evelyn Baring, 6 Nov. 1890. Baring Mss (B) DEP 84.
36. Thomas to Evelyn Baring, 14 Nov. 1890. Baring Mss (B) DEP 84.
37. Thomas to Evelyn Baring, 4 Dec. 1890. Baring Mss (B) DEP 84.
38. Oral information from Lord Ashburton.
39. Baring Mss (B) HC3. 103.
40. Minutes of the Court of the Governor of the Bank of England, 26 Nov. 1890.
41. Clapham, *Bank of England*, op. cit., vol. II, p. 332.
42. Bank of England papers on Baring Crisis. G15/192.
43. Thomas to Evelyn Baring, 21 Nov. 1890. Baring Mss (B) DEP 84.
44. 15 Nov. 1890. RAL 101/21/ 40.
45. Cit. Chapman, *Rise of Merchant Banking*, op. cit., p. 79.
46. Bank of England papers on Baring Crisis. G15/189/12.
47. 9 May 1891. Hatfield House papers. 3M/E Goschen.
48. Baring Mss (G) MS 18321. HC1. 29. cf. Baring Mss (B) Letter Books. 3 Dec. 1897.
49. See p. 247.
50. O'Hagan, *Leaves From My Life*, op. cit., vol. I, p. 381.
51. *The Diary of Alice James*, ed. Leon Edel (London, 1965), p. 205.
52. John to Evelyn Baring, 21 Nov. 1890. Baring Mss (B) DEP 84.
53. Lady Revelstoke to Everard Baring, 30 Nov. 1890. Baring Mss (B) DEP 47.
54. Alfred Mildmay, 'Notes and Recollections'. Baring Mss (B) DEP 135.
55. Lord Randolph Churchill to Alfred de Rothschild, 17 Nov. 1890. RAL T15/58.
56. 28 Jan. 1891. Baring Mss (B) DEP 84.
57. Stephen to John Macdonald, 22 Nov. 1890. Gilbert, *Mount Stephen*, op. cit., vol. II, p. 256.
58. Baring Mss (B) DEP 193. 26. 2.
59. Thomas to Evelyn Baring, 17 Dec. 1890. Baring Mss (B) DEP 84.
60. John to Evelyn Baring, 21 Nov. 1890. Baring Mss (B) DEP 84.
61. Gilbert, *Mount Stephen*, op. cit., vol. II, pp. 255–6.
62. 30 Jan. 1891. Baring Mss (B) DEP 84.
63. 16 Jan. 1892. P. 3.
64. Platt, *Latin America and British Trade*, op. cit., p. 284.
65. *Economist* (6 Dec. 1890).
66. Barings to Governor of Buenos Aires, 3 Oct. 1892. Baring Mss (B) Letter Books.
67. 17 Oct. 1891. Baring Mss (B) Letter Books.
68. Barings to Lidderdale, 5 Jan. 1892. Baring Mss (B) Letter Books.
69. 27 Jan. 1893. Cit. Ferns, *Britain and Argentina*, op. cit., p. 475.

70. Luis Dominguez to Barings, 28 Dec. 1892. Baring Mss (B) HC4. 1. 115.

71. Revelstoke to Tom Baring, 15 Nov. 1890. Baring Mss (B) DEP 84.

72. Revelstoke to Lidderdale, 15 Nov. 1890. Baring Mss (B) Letter Books.

73. Maurice Baring, *Puppet Show of Memory*, op. cit., p. 147.

74. 26 March 1891. Baring Mss (B) DEP 47.

75. Unpublished autobiography of Mrs Constance Hugh Smith, op. cit., vol. III, p. 118.

76. 15 Nov. 1890. Baring Mss (B) DEP 193. 75. 2. 239.

77. *Life with Queen Victoria. Marie Mallet's Letters from Court*, ed. Victor Mallet (London, 1968), p. XXI.

78. Constance Hugh Smith, op. cit., vol III, p. 118.

79. Bank of England papers on Baring Crisis. G15/191/65.

80. 12 Dec. 1894. Baring Mss (B) Letter Books.

81. 9 April 1891. Baring Mss (B) DEP 47.

82. Barings to Lidderdale, 5 Jan. 1892. Baring Mss (B) Letter Books.

83. 2 Feb. 1893. Baring Mss (B) Letter Books.

84. 12 Jan. 1893. Bank of England papers on Baring Crisis. G15/191/1.

85. 9 March 1893. Bank of England papers on Baring Crisis. G15/191/49.

86. Barings to D. Powell, 3 Feb. and 11 July 1893. Baring Mss (B) Letter Books.

87. Bank of England papers on Baring Crisis. G15/192/178 and 179.

88. Powell to Barings, 26 July 1894. Bank of England papers on Baring Crisis. G15/192/71A.

89. 25 Oct. 1894. Baring Mss (B) HC1. 204. 38.

90. 6 Nov. 1894. Baring Mss (B) HC3. 52. 10.

91. Barings to A. G. Sandeman, 4 Dec. 1894. Bank of England papers on Baring Crisis. G15/192/112.

92. Cecil Baring to Lord Cromer, 23 Nov. 1894. Baring Mss (B) DEP 193. 42.

93. 14 Dec. 1897.

94. 11 Jan. 1895. Bank of England papers on Baring Crisis. G15/192/167.

95. 11 Jan. 1895. Baring Mss (B) HC1. 204. 38.

CHAPTER 15 (pp. 267–90)

1. Mildmay, 'Notes and Recollections', op. cit., p. 159.

2. Daphne Pollen, *I Remember, I Remember*, op. cit., p. 37.

3. Helena Gleichen, *Contacts and Contrasts* (London, 1940), p. 36.

4. Baroness de Stoeckl, *My Dear Marquis* (London, 1952), p. 86.

5. 6 April 1904. Baring Mss (B). Lord Revelstoke's Private Letters.

6. 'R.F.S.K.' 'Arthur Villiers. A private memoir', p. 82. Baring Mss (B). DEP 22 (XXXV)

7. 20 April 1929.

8. 4 May 1905. Baring Mss (B) PF 6.

9. *Time Gathered* (London, 1937), p. 256.

10. 19 April 1906. Private Letters, op. cit.

11. W. Grenfell to Nancy Astor, cit. Christopher Sykes. *Nancy, The Life of Lady Astor* (London, 1972), p. 103.

12. Lord Rothschild to French Cousins, 5 June 1906. RAL XI/130A/0.

13. 11 May 1915. *H. H. Asquith. Letters to Venetia Stanley*, ed. M. and E. Brock (Oxford, 1982).

14. *Julian Grenfell* (London, 1976), p. 42.

15. Sykes, *Nancy Astor*, op. cit., pp. 71–87.
16. Mabel Countess of Airlie *Thatched with Gold* (London, 1962), pp. 103–4.
17. Revelstoke to Gaston Meyer, 9 March 1910. Private Letters, op. cit.
18. Revelstoke to Arthur Lawley, 25 May 1909. Private Letters, op. cit.
19. Farrer to John Sterling, 14 April 1905. Baring Mss (B) DEP 33/9.
20. Hamilton diaries, 16 Nov. 1903. BM Add Mss 48658.
21. Oral information from Mr Duncan Stirling.
22. 22 Aug. 1905. Baring Mss (B) PF 6.
23. Farrer to John Sterling, 1 Jan. 1914. Baring Mss (B) DEP 33/15.
24. Cecil to Evelyn Cromer, 23 Nov. 1894. Baring Mss (B) DEP 193. 42.
25. Daphne Pollen, *I Remember, I Remember*, op. cit., pp. 49–50.
26. Obituary by Maurice Baring in *The Times* (27 Jan. 1934).
27. Daphne Pollen, *I Remember, I Remember*, op. cit., p. 47.
28. Cornelius Vanderbilt, *The Vanderbilt Feud* (London, 1957), pp. 24–5.
29. Farrer to Windham Baring, 25 Jan. 1906. Baring Mss (B) PF 181.
30. Farrer to Hugo Baring, 7 June 1905. Baring Mss (B) DEP 33/9.
31. Winsor to Farrer, 2 Sept. 1903. Baring Mss (B) PF 2.
32. Farrer to Sterling, 16 March 1906. Baring Mss (B) DEP 33/10.
33. 23 May 1907. Baring Mss (B). Private Letters, op. cit.
34. Alfred Mildmay to James Whishaw, 24 Feb. 1908. Baring Mss (B) PF 220.
35. Ethel Smyth, *Maurice Baring* (London, 1938), p. 40.
36. Whishaw to Mildmay, 12 March 1908. Baring Mss (B) PF 220.
37. Revelstoke to Cromer, 3 Nov. 1903. Baring Mss (B) COF 05. 1. 1.
38. Farrer to Mildmay, 25 Aug. 1906. Baring Mss (B) DEP 33/9.
39. 26 May 1892. Hamilton diaries, op. cit.
40. Revelstoke to Cromer, 7 Nov. 1903. Baring Mss (B) COF 05. 1. 1.
41. Cromer to Revelstoke, 15 Nov. 1905. Baring Mss (B) COF 05. 1. 1.
42. Philip Ziegler, *Diana Cooper* (London, 1981), p. 18.
43. Mosley, *Julian Grenfell*, op. cit., p. 174.
44. Knox, *Shaw-Stewart*, op. cit., pp. 71–3.
45. Farrer to Robert Winsor, 21 Jan. 1914. Baring Mss (B) DEP 33/15.
46. Knox, *Shaw-Stewart*, op. cit., p. 81.
47. Farrer to J. W. Sterling, 21 Jan. 1914. Baring Mss (B) DEP 33/15.
48. Cromer to Revelstoke, 22 Feb. 1900. Baring Mss (B) COF 05. 1. 1.
49. Revelstoke to Cromer, 12 Feb. 1900. Baring Mss (B) COF 05. 1. 1.
50. Revelstoke to Thomas Baring, 21 July 1905. Baring Mss (B) Private Letters, op. cit.
51. Farrer to Windham Baring, 16 Jan. 1906. Baring Mss (B) PF 181.
52. Farrer to Windham Baring, 7 Feb. 1906. Baring Mss (B) PF 181.
53. Mildmay to Windham Baring, 26 June 1907. Baring Mss (B) Windham Baring Correspondence.
54. Revelstoke to Hugh O'Beirne, 10 July 1907. Baring Mss (B) PF 211.
55. 22 Nov. 1909, *Hansard* (Lords). 9 Edward VII. Vol. IV, 794–9.
56. *Memoirs of Sir Almeric Fitzroy, Vol. I* (London, 1925), p. 388.
57. Revelstoke to Lord Hindlip, undated. Baring Mss (B). Private Letters, op. cit.
58. Farrer to Howard Elliott, 17 Feb. 1912. Baring Mss (B) DEP 33/12.
59. Farrer to Adolf Boissevain, 20

June 1902. Baring Mss (B) DEP 33/6.

60. Farrer to Arthur Gwinner, 13 Feb. 1906. Baring Mss (B) DEP 33/10.
61. 18 March 1914. Baring Mss (B). Private Letters, op. cit.
62. Kellett, *Merchant Banking Arena*, op. cit., pp. 113-14.
63. Farrer to Windham Baring, 20 Feb. 1904. Baring Mss (B). Windham Baring Correspondence.
64. Cecil Baring to Revelstoke, 3 Nov. 1900. Baring Mss (B) PF 3.
65. 12 July 1905. Baring Mss (B) PF 6.
66. Baring Mss (B) Credit Department CRD. 22. 7. 1911.
67. Baring Mss (B) Credit Department CRD. 22. 7. General Remarks.
68. Cecil Baring to Revelstoke, 5 Oct. 1900. Baring Mss (B) PF 3.
69. 1 September 1913, Baring Mss (B) Private Letters, op. cit.
70. Revelstoke to Hugo Baring, 23 Oct. 1906. Baring Mss (B) Correspondence with Baring, Magoun.
71. Cecil Baring to Revelstoke, 25 Jan. 1902. Baring Mss (B) HC5. 2. 39.
72. Kidder Peabody to Baring, Magoun, 9 Sept. 1905. Baring Mss (B) PF 6.
73. Farrer to Hugo Baring, 6 Dec. 1905. Baring Mss (B). Correspondence with Baring, Magoun.
74. Farrer to J. J. Hill, 15 Dec. 1905. Baring Mss (B) COF 05. 2. 5
75. Chapman, *Rise of Merchant Banking*, op. cit., pp. 173-7.
76. Chapman, *Rise of Merchant Banking*, op. cit., pp. 170-1.
77. Farrer to Windham Baring, 30 Jan. 1906. Baring Mss (B) PF 181.
78. Revelstoke to Cromer, 3 April 1903. Baring Mss (B) COF 05. 1. 1.
79. Farrer to Windham Baring, 19

Jan. 1906. Baring Mss (B) PF 181.
80. Mildmay to Everard Meynell, 26 Sept. 1912. Baring Mss (B) PF 189.
81. Barings to John Warry, 22 Feb. 1896. Baring Mss (B) Letter Books.
82. Barings to the Educational Officer, 22 July 1914. Baring Mss (B) PF 323.
83. Undated directive. Baring Mss (B) PF 323.
84. Revelstoke to Gordon Cunard, 11 Dec. 1911. Baring Mss (B) Private Letters, op. cit.
85. E. T. Hooley, *Hooley's Confessions* (London, 1925), pp. 26-31.
86. 31 Oct. 1900. Baring Mss (B) Letter Books.
87. Revelstoke to George White, 27 Dec. 1900. Baring Mss (B) Letter Books.
88. Farrer to James Ross, 16 Jan. 1904 and to Robert Fleming. 11 March 1909. Baring Mss (B) DEP 33/7.
89. Cecil Baring to Revelstoke, 5 Oct. 1901. Baring Mss (B) PF 4.
90. Revelstoke to T. S. Tailer, 17 Oct. 1901. Baring Mss (B) Private Letters, op. cit.
91. Farrer to J. H. Thors, 17 Feb. 1903. Baring Mss (B) Banque de Paris et des Pays Bas. Uncatalogued.
92. W. B. Gair to H. R. Robertson, 14 Jan. 1905. Baring Mss (B) Mersey Docks and Harbour Board.
93. Farrer to Windham Baring, 16 Jan. 1906. Baring Mss (B) PF 180.
94. Mildmay to Windham Baring, 8 June 1906. Baring Mss (B) PF 181.
95. Cassel to Revelstoke, 6 Feb. 1903. Baring Mss (B) PF 157.
96. Revelstoke to Cassel, 10 Feb. 1903. Baring Mss (B) PF 157.
97. Barings to Deutsche Bank, Berlin, 26 Jan. 1899. Baring Mss (B) Letter Books.

CHAPTER 16 (pp. 291–319)

1. Kathleen Burk, *Morgan Grenfell, 1838–1988* (Oxford, 1988). I am most grateful to Dr Burk for allowing me to see this book in typescript. Cf. Carosso, *The Morgans*, op. cit., p. 511.
2. Farrer to Sterling, 31 Dec. 1904. Baring Mss (B) DEP 33/8.
3. 22 March 1901. Milner papers. Bodleian Library. 214/42. 41.
4. Farrer to Sterling, 26 April 1902. Baring Mss (B) DEP 33/6.
5. Copy sent to Revelstoke by T. S. Tailer, 4 Aug. 1902. Baring Mss (B) PF 1.
6. Banque de Paris to Barings, 13 April 1904. Baring Mss (B). Banque de Paris et des Pays Bas. Uncatalogued.
7. Revelstoke to Winsor, 10 Feb. 1905. Baring Mss (B) PF 19.
8. Kidder Peabody to Barings, 3 March 1905. Baring Mss (B) PF 19.
9. Barings to A. Spitzer, 22 March 1905. Baring Mss (B) PF 19.
10. Farrer to Winsor, 6 Feb. 1906. Baring Mss (B) PF 20.
11. Mildmay to Windham Baring, 8 Feb. 1907. Baring Mss (B) PF 182.
12. Farrer to Oliver Baring, Oct. 1909. Baring Mss (B) PF 25.
13. Farrer to Winsor, 30 Oct. 1909. Baring Mss (B) PF 25.
14. 30 April 1908, Baring Mss (B) PF 184.
15. *Letters of Conrad Russell*, ed. Georgiana Blakiston (London, 1987), pp. 31–2.
16. 23, 28 and 29 Dec. 1903. Baring Mss (B) HC5. 2. 39.
17. Revelstoke to Hugo Baring, 2 Feb. 1904. Baring Mss (B) PF 5.
18. Revelstoke to Hugo Baring, 5 Feb. 1904, Baring Mss (B) PF 5.
19. Revelstoke to Farrer, 19 April 1904. Baring Mss (B). Private Letters.
20. 14 Feb. 1929, Revelstoke diary. Baring Mss (B) DPP 2. 4. 4.
21. 23 Nov. 1900. Baring Mss (B). Letter Books.
22. Cecil Baring to Revelstoke, 28 Dec. 1900. Baring Mss (B) PF 3.
23. Revelstoke to Cecil Baring, 23 Nov. 1900. Baring Mss (B). Letter Books.
24. Cecil Baring to Revelstoke, 27 Nov. 1900. Baring Mss (B) PF 3.
25. Winsor to Farrer, 10 Sept. 1904. Baring Mss (B) COF 05/2/2.
26. Winsor to Revelstoke, 10 Oct. 1904. Baring Mss (B) COF 05. 2. 2.
27. Revelstoke to Hugo Baring, 8 Aug. 1905. Baring Mss (B) COF 05/2/2.
28. Farrer to Winsor, 18 Oct. 1904. Baring Mss (B) DEP 33/8.
29. Revelstoke to J. P. Morgan, 18 Oct. 1904. Baring Mss (B) COF 05/2/2.
30. Farrer to Winsor, 12 Jan. 1905. Baring Mss (B) COF 05/2/2.
31. Farrer to Winsor, 29 July 1905. Baring Mss (B) COF 05/2/2.
32. Farrer to Hugo Baring, 12 Feb. 1907. Baring Mss (B). Correspondence with Baring, Magoun.
33. Hugo Baring to Farrer, 1 May 1906. Baring Mss (B). Correspondence with Baring, Magoun.
34. Farrer to Hugo Baring, 11 Jan. 1906. Baring Mss (B). Correspondence with Baring, Magoun.
35. Farrer to John Sterling, 20 Oct. 1905. Baring Mss (B) PF 5.
36. Farrer to Hugo Baring, 11 Oct. 1904. Baring Mss (B) DEP 33/8.
37. Farrer to John Sterling, 30 April 1906. Baring Mss (B) DEP 33/10.
38. Farrer to Hugo Baring, 12 Feb. 1907. Baring Mss (B). Correspondence with Baring, Magoun.

39. Farrer to Hugo Baring, 28 May 1907. Baring Mss (B). Correspondence with Baring, Magoun.

40. Baring Brothers to Baring and Co., 17 June 1907. Baring Mss (B) COF 05/6/3.

41. Baring and Co. to Baring Brothers, 2 July 1907. Baring Mss (B) COF 05/6/3.

42. Circular of 19 Nov. 1907. Baring Mss (B). Correspondence with Baring, Magoun.

43. Barings to Hon. George Firton, 21 Nov. 1892. Baring Mss (B). Letter Books.

44. Farrer to R. Meighan, 3 Nov. 1908. Baring Mss (B) DEP 33/7.

45. Farrer to J. W. Sterling, 14 Dec. 1911. Baring Mss (B) DEP 33/7.

46. Revelstoke to Mildmay, 9 Oct. 1902. Baring Mss (B). Private Letters.

47. Farrer to Windham Baring, 6 Jan. 1906. Baring Mss (B) PF 180.

48. Mildmay to Windham Baring, 22 March 1906. Baring Mss (B) PF 180.

49. 30 March 1909. Baring Mss (B) COF 05. 5. 11.

50. Revelstoke to Noetzlin, 27 Oct. 1902. Baring Mss (B). Banque de Paris et des Pays Bas. Uncatalogued.

51. Revelstoke to Thors., 27 Nov. 1903. Baring Mss (B). Banque de Paris et des Pays Bas. Uncatalogued.

52. Revelstoke to Hottinguer, 1 Feb. 1904. Baring Mss (B) PF 281.

53. Revelstoke to Hugo Baring, 17 Feb. 1904. Baring Mss (B) PF 5.

54. Deutsche Bank to Barings, 4 Feb. 1904. Baring Mss (B) PF 281.

55. Noetzlin to Revelstoke, 16 Feb. 1904. Baring Mss (B) PF 281.

56. Hugo Baring to Revelstoke, 30 Sept. 1904. Baring Mss (B) PF 5.

57. Farrer to J. W. Sterling, 5 Oct. 1905. Baring Mss (B) DEP 33/9.

58. Herbert Gibson to Madelaine Place, 5 March 1895. Gibson papers. Estancia Tres Cerros. Argentina.

59. Ferns, *Britain and Argentine*, op. cit., pp. 483–4.

60. 30 June 1898. Baring Mss (B). Letter Books.

61. Tornquist to Barings, 24 March 1902. Baring Mss (B). Private Letters.

62. Windham Baring to Revelstoke, 12 Oct. 1906. Baring Mss (B) PF 181.

63. Farrer to Windham Baring, 20 Aug. 1908. Baring Mss (B) PF 184.

64. Farrer to R. Winsor, 17 March 1914. Baring Mss (B) DEP 33/15.

65. Reade to Barings, 11 Sept. 1902. Baring Mss (B). Private Letters.

66. Balfour to Revelstoke, 22 Feb. 1902. Baring Mss (B) DEP 201. 2.

67. Farrer to Clanwilliam, 6 Feb. 1904. Baring Mss (B) DEP 33/7.

68. Farrer to Hugo Baring, 26 March 1907. Baring Mss (B). Correspondence with Baring, Magoun.

69. Burk, *Morgan Grenfell*, op. cit.

70. Carosso, *The Morgans*, op. cit., pp. 408–11.

71. Cit. John Douglas Forbes. *J. P. Morgan Jr* (Charlottesville, 1981), p. 64.

72. Windham Baring to G. A. Schwenke, 29 Jan. 1909. Baring Mss (B) PF 185.

73. Windham Baring to Farrer, 1 Dec. 1905 and 4 July 1906. Baring Mss (B) PF 180.

74. Windham Baring to Farrer, 4 Jan. 1906. Baring Mss (B) PF 180.

75. Farrer to Windham Baring, 30 Jan. 1906. Baring Mss (B) PF 180.

76. Mildmay to Windham Baring,

20 July 1906. Baring Mss (B) PF 181.

77. Carosso, *The Morgans*, op. cit., p. 844.

78. Mildmay to Windham Baring, 17 June 1908. Baring Mss (B) PF 184.

79. Farrer to William Benedict, 23 Jan 1913. Baring Mss (B). Correspondence with Baring, Magoun.

80. Mildmay to Windham Baring, 8 June 1911. Baring Mss (B) PF 187.

81. Revelstoke to Farrer, 20 June 1911. Baring Mss (B). Private Letters.

82. Mildmay to Windham Baring, 16 June 1911. Baring Mss (B) PF 187.

83. *Evening Times* (4 Sept. 1911).

84. Windham Baring to Mildmay, 18 June 1911. Baring Mss (B) PF 187.

85. Farrer to Shaw-Stewart, 26 March 1914. Baring Mss (B) DEP 33/15.

86. Barings to Hottinguers, 12 April 1897. Baring Mss (B). Letter Books.

87. Revelstoke to Cassel, 21 Feb. and 7 March 1905. Baring Mss (B). Lord Revelstoke's Private Letters.

88. Platt, *Finance, Trade and British Foreign Policy*, op. cit., p. 193.

89. Revelstoke to Farrer, 7 April 1914. Baring Mss (B) PF 255.

90. Revelstoke to W. Koch, 1 and 29 Sept. 1913. Baring Mss (B) COF 05. 7. 4.

91. Record of conversation between Revelstoke and S. S. Kahn, 4 Dec. 1913. Baring Mss (B) PF 224.

92. Barings to Messrs Walsh Hall, 14 July 1898. Baring Mss (B). Letter Books.

93. Barings to Banque de Paris, 9 Oct. 1902. Baring Mss (B). Banque de Paris et Pays Bas. Uncatalogued.

94. Baring Mss (B) Japanese Papers. COF 05. 1. 3.

95. Revelstoke to Noetzlin, 19 Feb. 1904. Baring Mss (B). Banque de Paris et Pays Bas. Uncatalogued.

96. Lansdowne to Revelstoke, 22 Feb. 1904. Baring Mss (B) PF 303.

97. Noetzlin to Revelstoke, 20 Feb. 1904. Baring Mss (B) PF 303.

98. 8 March 1904. Baring Mss (B) PF 303.

99. Farrer to J. Sterling, 2 Nov. 1904. Baring Mss (B) DEP 33/8.

100. Farrer to R. Winsor, 17 May 1904. Baring Mss (B). Private Letters.

101. Farrer to Revelstoke, 1 Sept. 1905. Baring Mss (B) DEP 33/9.

102. Hardinge to Revelstoke, 10 Oct. 1905. Baring Mss (B) HC10. 66.

103. Revelstoke to Barings, 21 Oct. 1905. Baring Mss (B) PF 206.

104. Revelstoke to Farrer, 25 Oct. 1905. Baring Mss (B) HC10. 66.

105. Revelstoke to Barings, 25 Oct. 1905. Baring Mss (B) PF 206.

106. *Memoirs of James Whishaw*, ed. Maxwell S. Leigh (London, 1935), p. 126.

107. 7 Nov. 1905. Baring Mss (B) PF 6.

108. Asquith to Revelstoke, 7 April 1906. Baring Mss (B) COF 05. 1. 7.

109. 18 April 1906. RAL. XI. 130A/0.

110. 20 Nov. 1906.

111. Correspondence in Baring Mss (B) PF 207.

112. Revelstoke to A. Fischel, 28 April 1906. Baring Mss (B) PF 207.

113. Mildmay to Windham Baring, 19 April 1906. Baring Mss (B) PF 180.

114. Farrer to Windham Baring, 19 Jan. 1906. Baring Mss (B). Windham Baring Correspondence.

115. Windham Baring to Mildmay, 27 July 1906. Baring Mss (B) PF 181.

116. Mildmay to Windham Baring, 5 Sept. 1906. Baring Mss (B) PF 181.
117. Farrer to Winsor, 21 July 1906. Baring Mss (B) DEF 33/10.
118. 15 Jan. 1909. RAL. XI. 130A/3.
119. Revelstoke to A. Turrettini, 18 Jan. 1909. Baring Mss (B). Banque de Paris et des Pays Bas. Uncatalogued.
120. Revelstoke to L. Davidoff, 1 Feb. 1909. Baring Mss (B) PF 209.
121. *Memoirs of James Whishaw*, op. cit., p. 161.
122. Lansdowne to Revelstoke, 21 Feb. 1903. Baring Mss (B) PF 272.
123. Dr Gwinner (Deutsche Bank) to Revelstoke, 18 March 1903. Baring Mss (B) PF 272.
124. Rothschild to Revelstoke, 7 April 1903. Baring Mss (B) PF 272.
125. Revelstoke to Cromer, 9 April 1903. Baring Mss (B) PF 272.
126. Revelstoke to Cromer, 1 May 1903. Baring Mss (B) PF 272.
127. *Memoirs of Sir Almeric Fitzroy*, op. cit., vol. I, p. 128.
128. Hamilton Diary, 21 April 1903. BM Add Mss 48680.
129. Cromer to Revelstoke, 7 May 1903. Baring Mss (B) PF 272.
130. Napier to Barings, 7 June 1912. Baring Mss (B) PF 161.
131. 16 July 1912, *Hansard* (Commons). 61. 190; and 15 July 1912, *Hansard* (Lords). 12. 454–71.
132. Revelstoke to Turrettini, 24 July 1912. Baring Mss (B) PF 162.
133. 15 July 1912, *Hansard* (Lords). 12. 471–9.
134. Revelstoke to Foreign Office, 9 Dec. 1912. Baring Mss (B) PF 162.
135. Foreign Office to Revelstoke, 4 Feb. 1913. Baring Mss (B) PF 162.
136. Benac to Errington, 15 June 1913. Baring Mss (B) PF 163.
137. Errington to Raindre, 25 Nov. 1914. Baring Mss (B) PF 164.

CHAPTER 17 (pp. 320–32)

1. Barings to E. B. Lockhart, 28 July 1914. Baring Mss (B) PF 804.
2. Farrer to Winsor. 7 Aug. 1914. Baring Mss (B) PF 804.
3. 5 Aug. 1914.
4. Shaw-Stewart to Ronald Knox, 21 Aug. 1914. Knox, *Shaw-Stewart*, op. cit., p. 101.
5. Mildmay to Lockhart, 7 Aug. 1914. Baring Mss (B) COF 05. 6. 3.
6. Public Trustee Office. Registration Order G. Return of 17 Oct. 1916. Farrer to Sterling, 1 Sept. 1914. Baring Mss (B) DEP 33/16.
7. Farrer to Sterling, 7 Oct. 1914. Baring Mss (B) DEP 33/16.
8. Farrer to Windham Baring, 11 June 1915. Baring Mss (B) DEP 33/16.
9. Benckendorff to Revelstoke, 10 March 1916. Baring Mss (B) COF 05. 9. 3.
10. Farrer to Sterling, 3 April 1918. Baring Mss (B) DEP 33/19.
11. Revelstoke to Lt Col. Cooper, 25 Sept. 1917. Baring Mss (B). Private Letters.
12. Revelstoke to Dr Beauchamp, 25 April 1918. Baring Mss (B). Private Letters.
13. Farrer to Winsor, 11 July 1917. Baring Mss (B) DEP 33/18.
14. Mildmay to Leng, 15 Jan. 1916. Baring Mss (B) PF 201.
15. Farrer to Sterling, Feb. 1916. Baring Mss (B) DEP 33.
16. Barings to Hopes, 10 Feb. 1916. Baring Mss (B) PF 24.
17. Farrer to Winsor, 13 Jan. 1917. Baring Mss (B) DEP 33/17.
18. Windham Baring to Leng, 12 May 1915. Baring Mss (B) PF 199.

19. Farrer to Leng, 12 May 1915. Baring Mss (B) PF 199.
20. Farrer to Leng, 25 May 1915. Baring Mss (B) PF 196.
21. Mildmay to Leng, 13 June 1916. Baring Mss (B) PF 201.
22. Farrer to Sterling, 6 Jan. 1915. Baring Mss (B) DEP 33/16.
23. Revelstoke to Stamfordham, 29 July 1916. Baring Mss (B). Private Letters.
24. Farrer to Sterling, 27 April 1917. Baring Mss (B) DEP 33/17.
25. Mildmay to Leng, 7 Dec. 1916. Baring Mss (B) PF 201.
26. Farrer to Winsor, 17 Nov. 1917. Baring Mss (B) DEP 33.
27. Farrer to Edward Tuck, 19 Oct. 1916. Baring Mss (B) DEP 33/17.
28. Baring Mss (B). Foreign Trade and Finance. Return of March 1916.
29. Barings to Kidder Peabody, 22 Oct. 1914. Baring Mss (B) PF 172.
30. Farrer to Winsor, 23 Oct. 1914. Baring Mss (B) PF 172.
31. Burk, *Morgan Grenfell*, op. cit.
32. Cecil Baring to Winsor, 2 July 1915. Baring Mss (B) PF 172.
33. Barings to Kidder Peabody, 19 Nov. 1915. Baring Mss (B) PF 172.
34. Farrer to Cecil Coward, 18 Feb. 1916. Baring Mss (B) COF 05. 7. 9.
35. Farrer to Sterling, 22 Oct. 1914. Baring Mss (B) DEP 33/16.
36. Farrer to Winsor, 4 July 1918 and to Sterling, 15 June 1918. DEP 33.
37. P. 325.
38. 19 Feb. 1917. Baring Mss (B) DPP 2.
39. Revelstoke to Louis Dorizon, 20 March 1917. Baring Mss (B). Private Letters.
40. 22 March 1917, Baring Mss (B). Russian Accounts 1914–35 f63.
41. 24 April 1917. Baring Mss (B). Russian Accounts 1914–35 ff67–8.
42. Farrer to Sterling, 16 Nov. 1917. Baring Mss (B) DEP 33/18.
43. Baring Mss (B). Russian Accounts 1914–35. f72.
44. Farrer to Austen Chamberlain, 14 March 1918. Baring Mss (B) DEP 33/19.

CHAPTER 18 (pp.333–58)

1. Thomas Jones, *Whitehall Diary*, ed. Keith Middlemass (London, 1969), vol. I, p. 90.
2. Oral information from Lord Ashburton.
3. Oral information from Sir Mark Baring.
4. Windham Baring to Leng, 18 Dec. 1918. Baring Mss (B) PF 204.
5. Farrer to Leng, 29 Dec. 1922. Baring Mss (B) PF 355A.
6. Farrer to J. N. Hill, 26 April 1919. Baring Mss (B) DEP 33.
7. 'R.F.S.K.' *Arthur Villiers. A private memoir*, op. cit.
8. Cecil Baring (3rd Lord Revelstoke) to Lord Stamfordham, 21 May 1929. Baring Mss (B). Uncatalogued.
9. Windham Baring to Mildmay, 4 March 1921. Baring Mss (B) COF 05. 10. 10.
10. Cecil Baring to Stamfordham, 21 May 1929, op. cit.
11. Obituary in *The Times* (20 Nov. 1962).
12. Farrer to Winsor, 23 May 1922. Baring Mss (B) DEP 33.
13. Revelstoke to Peacock, 3 March 1921. Baring Mss (B). Uncatalogued.
14. Farrer to Mildmay, 8 Nov. 1923. Baring Mss (B) DEP 33/22.
15. Cecil Baring to Stamfordham, 21 May 1929, op. cit.
16. 5 March 1929. Baring Mss (B) DPP 2. 4. 4.
17. Frank Ledwith, *Ships that Go Bump in the Night* (London, 1974), p. 63.

18. Mildmay to Leng, 11 Dec. 1918. Baring Mss (B) PF 204.
19. Farrer to Winsor, 17 Nov. 1922. Baring Mss (B) DEP 33/21.
20. Revelstoke to Charles Addis, 1 Feb. 1924. Baring Mss (B). Private Letters.
21. Mildmay to Leng, 23 Jan. 1924. Baring Mss (B) PF 376.
22. Mildmay to Meynell, 15 May 1926. Baring Mss (B) PF 385.
23. Tod to Villiers, 11 June 1926. Baring Mss (B) PF 265.
24. Farrer to ter Meulen, 10 Oct. 1918. Baring Mss (B) DEP 33.
25. 7 Dec. 1918. Baring Mss (B) COF 05. 12. 4.
26. Farrer to Winsor, 4 Aug. 1925. Baring Mss (B) DEP 33/23.
27. Farrer to Winsor, 22 July 1924. Baring Mss (B) DEP 33/22.
28. Revelstoke to Winsor, 19 Nov. 1920. Baring Mss (B) PF 338 Pt I.
29. Vincent Carosso, *The Kidder Peabody Story*, op. cit., pp. 58–9.
30. Windham Baring to Tod, 7 Oct. 1919. Baring Mss (B) PF 260.
31. Farrer to Tod, 13 Feb. 1920. Baring Mss (B) PF 260.
32. Windham Baring to Tod, 27 Jan. 1921. Baring Mss (B) PF 262.
33. Farrer to Tod, 6 April 1920, Baring Mss (B) PF 261.
34. Meredith G. Glassco, 'An Unedited Manuscript of the History of Brascan Ltd'. Copy in Baring Mss (B) DEP 70. Chapter X.
35. Revelstoke to Peacock, 3 Sept. 1926. Baring Mss (B) PF 278.
36. Peacock to E. R. Wood, 28 Jan. 1927. Baring Mss (B) PF 278.
37. Farrer to Winsor, 28 Jan. 1919. Baring Mss (B) DEP 33.
38. R. S. Sayers, *The Bank of England 1891–1944* (Cambridge, 1976), pp. 316–17.
39. Norman to Glyn West, 31 Jan. 1924. Baring Mss (B) PF 38.
40. Farrer to Peacock, 24 Aug. 1924. Baring Mss (B) PF 38.
41. W. J. Reader, *Bowater. A History* (Cambridge, 1981), p. 52.
42. Peacock to Farrer, 16 Feb. 1926. Baring Mss (B) PF 43.
43. Peacock to Taylor, 10 June 1926. Baring Mss (B) PF 46.
44. Peacock to Taylor, 10 June 1926. Baring Mss (B) PF 406.
45. 16 Feb. 1929.
46. *Evening News* (19 Feb. 1929).
47. Memorandum of 3 July 1931. Baring Mss (B) PF 430.
48. Peacock to F. Pick, 3 March 1927. Baring Mss (B) PF 309.
49. E. B. Baring to Tod, 30 May 1928. Baring Mss (B) PF 309.
50. E. B. Baring to Meynell, 30 May 1928. Baring Mss (B) PF 425.
51. Revelstoke to Lansdowne, 13 May 1927. Baring Mss (B) PF 331.
52. Villiers to A. M. Hesse, 17 June 1927. Baring Mss (B) COF 05. 15. 11.
53. Farrer to Peacock, 14 June 1927. Baring Mss (B) PF 422.
54. 8 Aug. 1928. Baring Mss (B) PF 534.
55. Aug. 1927. Baring Mss (B) COF 05. 15. 12.
56. Peacock to Revelstoke, 11 May 1925, Baring Mss (B) PF 39
57. Revelstoke to Peacock, 28 April 1925. Baring Mss (B). Private Letters.
58. Farrer to Lord Eversley, 28 June 1921. Baring Mss (B) DEP 33.
59. Memo of 14 Dec. 1927. Baring Mss (B) PF 366.
60. 16 Jan. 1919. Baring Mss (B). Private Letters.
61. John Swire and Sons to Barings, 24 June 1919. Baring Mss (B) PF 241.
62. Farrer to ter Meulen, 5 Aug. 1919. Baring Mss (B) PF 241.
63. Farrer to Revelstoke, 7 April 1920. Baring Mss (B) PF 241.
64. Farrer to Revelstoke, 8 April 1920. Baring Mss (B) PF 244.

65. Farrer to ter Meulen, 15 Oct. 1923. Baring Mss (B) DEP 33.
66. Windham Baring to Meynell, 17 Sept. 1919. Baring Mss (B) PF 358A.
67. Farrer to Leng, 6 May 1921. Baring Mss (B) PF 356A.
68. Farrer to Revelstoke, 26 Aug. 1921. Baring Mss (B) DEP 33/21.
69. Mildmay to Leng, 22 June 1923. Baring Mss (B) PF 375. Pt I.
70. E. B. Baring to Meynell, 4 May 1925. Baring Mss (B) PF 384.
71. Mildmay to Leng, 24 Oct. 1924. Baring Mss (B) PF 386.
72. Revelstoke to Peacock, 27 April 1925. Baring Mss (B). Private Letters.
73. Mildmay to Meynell, 7 Nov. 1929. Baring Mss (B) PF 426.
74. E. B. Baring to Barings, 12 Dec. 1929. Baring Mss (B) PF 426.
75. Whittlesey and Wilson, *Essays in Money and Banking*, op. cit., p. 54.
76. Farrer to J. S. Morgan, 18 Nov. 1923. Baring Mss (B) DEP 33/22.
77. Feb–March 1927. Baring Mss (B) COF 05. 15. 6.
78. Farrer to Winsor, 15 Dec. 1921. Baring Mss (B) PF 229.
79. Farrer to Winsor, 21 Feb. 1922. Baring Mss (B) PF 230.
80. Farrer to Winsor, 4 April 1922. Baring Mss (B) DEP 33/21.
81. Farrer to Spencer-Smith, 9 March 1922. Baring Mss (B) PF 230.
82. Clerk to Revelstoke, 9 April 1922. Baring Mss (B) PF 231.
83. Farrer to Pospisil, 22 Dec. 1922. Baring Mss (B) PF 232.
84. Farrer to ter Meulen, 15 June 1923. Baring Mss (B) DEP 33.
85. 15 May 1924. RAF. 132. AQ. 5621.
86. 2 July 1924. Baring Mss (B) PF 237.
87. Peacock to Revelstoke, 20 Feb. 1926. Baring Mss (B) PF 226. Pt I.
88. Mildmay to E. B. Baring, 28 Aug. 1928. Baring Mss (B) PF 336.
89. Revelstoke to Peacock, 31 March 1926. Baring Mss (B) PF 155.
90. Farrer to Cecil Baring, 20 Feb. 1924. Baring Mss (B) DEP 33.
91. F.O. to Barings, 31 May 1919. Baring Mss (B) PF 452.
92. Revelstoke to Routkowsky, 19 Oct. 1920. Baring Mss (B) PF 452.
93. Villiers to Lorraine, 30 June 1925. Baring Mss (B) COF 05. 14. 2.
94. Villiers to Lorraine, 15 April 1926. Baring Mss (B) COF 05. 14. 2.
95. Revelstoke to Hugo Baring, 10 May 1928. Baring Mss (B). Private Letters.
96. Farrer to Winsor, 1 Dec. 1927. Baring Mss (B) DEP 33/23.
97. Revelstoke to Peacock, 16 March 1929. Baring Mss (B) DPP 2. 4. 4.
98. Revelstoke diary, 15 Feb. 1929. Baring Mss (B) DPP 2. 4. 4.
99. Revelstoke diary, 22 Feb. 1929. Baring Mss (B) DPP 2. 4. 4.
100. Revelstoke diary, 14 Feb. 1929. Baring Mss (B) DPP 2. 4. 4.
101. Revelstoke diary, 25 Feb. 1929. Baring Mss (B) DPP 2. 4. 4.
102. Pollen, *I Remember, I Remember*, op. cit., p. 220.
103. 21 May 1929. Baring Mss (B). Uncatalogued.
104. 21 May 1929. Baring Mss (B). Uncatalogued.
105. 22 May 1929. Baring Mss (B). Uncatalogued.

INDEX

A comma rather than a semi-colon between entries denotes that both entries are covered by the previous sub-heading.